Trailing Clouds of Glory

Trailing Clouds of Glory

Zachary Taylor's Mexican War Campaign and His Emerging Civil War Leaders

Felice Flanery Lewis

THE UNIVERSITY OF ALABAMA PRESS
Tuscaloosa

The University of Alabama Press
Tuscaloosa, Alabama 35487-0380
uapress.ua.edu

Hardcover edition published 2010.
Paperback edition published 2016.
eBook edition published 2010.

Typeface: Caslon

Manufactured in the United States of America
Cover image: *Battle of Monterey*, Currier print; Library of Congress
Cover design: Todd Lape/Lape Designs

∞

The paper on which this book is printed meets the minimum requirements of American National Standard for Information Science–Permanence of Paper for Printed Library Materials, ANSI Z39.48-1984.

Paperback ISBN: 978-0-8173-5869-3

A previous edition of this book has been catalogued by the Library of Congress as follows:
Library of Congress Cataloging-in-Publication Data
Lewis, Felice Flanery.
Trailing clouds of glory : Zachary Taylor's Mexican War campaign and his emerging Civil War leaders / Felice Flanery Lewis.
p. cm.
Includes bibliographical references and index.
ISBN 978-0-8173-1678-5 (cloth : alk. paper) — ISBN 978-0-8173-8332-9 (electronic)
1. Taylor, Zachary, 1784–1850—Military leadership. 2. Mexican War, 1846–1848—Campaigns. 3. United States. Army—History—Mexican War, 1846–1848 4. Generals—United States—Biography. 5. United States. Army—Biography. 6. United States—History—Civil War, 1861–1865—Biography. I. Title.
E405.1.L49 2010
973.6'3092—dc22

2009030307

For Fran, Lowell, Suzanne, and Galen

Our birth is but a sleep and a forgetting:
The Soul that rises with us, our life's Star,
        Hath had elsewhere its setting
                And cometh from afar:
        Not in entire forgetfulness,
        And not in utter nakedness,
But trailing clouds of glory do we come
        From God, who is our home.
—William Wordsworth, "Ode: Intimations of Immortality
  from Recollections of Early Childhood"

Red and yellow, black and white,
They are precious in His sight.
—Old song

Contents

Maps

Acknowledgments

Two computer experts converted my rough drafts of this manuscript into readable form: initially Patricia Caffrey of Brooklyn, New York, and in recent years Amy Tabor of Glen Head, New York. Without their assistance, this volume could not have been completed. I shall always be grateful for their patience and friendship.

The first readers of earlier versions of this work were U.S. Army colonels, now retired, whom my husband (a U.S. Army chaplain, retired) and I had known on various posts. One has predeceased us, unfortunately: retired Col. Maurice M. "J.R." Bloom Jr. J.R. was a lead navigator in a bomber squadron in World War II. When his plane was shot down, he was held as a prisoner of war for nearly a year. My husband and I were fortunate to have had him and his wife, Charlotte, as neighbors in Germany. After retirement, they settled in Albuquerque, New Mexico, and J.R. became an authority on artifacts and indigenous peoples of that region. His critique of my account of Stephen Kearny's campaign was particularly helpful along those lines.

Another early reader was Joseph Beasley of Chapel Hill, North Carolina. When we first knew Joe and his wife, Ann, at Fort Belvoir, Virginia, he too was a U.S. Army chaplain. Later, he became a history instructor and tenured professor at the U.S. Military Academy, West Point, New York. Following retirement there he has continued to teach and has earned a Ph.D. in history from the University of North Carolina, Chapel Hill.

My third reader, Donald C. Bowman, is a West Point graduate (1957). We became acquainted through a mutual friend, retired Col. Ralph Puckett, another West Pointer and the recipient of five Purple Hearts. Don retired as a lieutenant colonel in 1977 following a distinguished career in the army, including a combat tour in Vietnam with the First Cavalry Division, for which service he was awarded the Purple Heart and several other combat medals. Now a writer of articles on military history, and a certified public accountant,

Don has been kind enough to provide detailed comments on two versions of this manuscript, and I am deeply indebted to him. No one has been of greater assistance than Don.

I am also exceedingly grateful to two anonymous reviewers chosen by The University of Alabama Press. The extensive remarks of those scholars guided me in reshaping my argument, as well as in countless other ways. To the staff at The University of Alabama Press I particularly extend my sincerest thanks for their encouragement and support.

Among the innumerable friends who have strengthened this effort in direct ways is Bill Bartlett of Houston, Texas. Bill sent me maps of the lower Rio Grande and eastern Mexico that are now falling apart from hourly use. And Marco and Sharon Swados generously took time out from their busy days to educate me on the subject of literary agents.

The librarians of all of the institutions mentioned herein were unfailingly helpful, none more so than those of the U.S. Military Academy, especially Alan C. Aimone, Special Collections chief, who went above and beyond the call of duty in aiding my search for letters, diaries, and papers of Mexican War veterans. Also, colleagues at Long Island University, Brooklyn, New York, secured copies of pertinent published articles for me through interlibrary loans, and were most lenient in allowing me to retain that library's books for extensive periods. In addition, I want to thank everyone associated with the National Archives and the Library of Congress, where so much relevant material was discovered during my many visits to their prodigious collections.

Most fervently of all, I thank my family. My husband, Francis R. Lewis (retired colonel and U.S. Army chaplain), uncomplainingly accompanied me on every research trip. He doubled the effectiveness of those searches by photocopying thousands of pages of documents for later study. And our son, whose Ph.D. dissertation in anthropology was published by the University of Chicago Press (J. Lowell Lewis, *Ring of Liberation,* 1992), has been supportive in too many ways to list. Their encouragement never ceased over the thirty years this book has been a work in progress.

Of course, for any mistakes herein, I alone am responsible.

Glen Cove, New York
2009

Preface

The war with Mexico became a vital turning point for the United States, a before-and-after marker. Before, America's destiny was not manifest—Great Britain and the United States jointly controlled the Oregon Territory and could not agree on a division of their interests, while Mexico maintained nominal dominion over California and an immense swath of the southwest trailing back from the Pacific coast through New Mexico to the borders of Texas. Afterward, though disruptive, worrisome problems remained, the United States had ballooned so enormously in territory and concomitant resources that the dreams of almost every resident (except those considered by law to be slaves, of course) seemed within reach. And during the first ten months of that confrontation with Mexico, the dominant military figure in America was Zachary Taylor.

Taylor's place in American history was changed as dramatically by the United States–Mexican War as was the future of his nation. When hostilities commenced in the spring of 1846, Old Zach (as Taylor has long been termed by historians) was a sixty-one-year-old, backwoods, regular army colonel with the honorary title of brevet brigadier general. By the spring of 1847, having led the forces that won the war's first four major battles, he was a regular army major general on the way to becoming, in another two years, the twelfth president of the United States. It was obviously the acclaim he received during his Mexican War campaign that engendered his amazing rise to the highest office in the land. He would don the mantle of president—as had George Washington, Andrew Jackson, and William Henry Harrison before him—"trailing clouds of glory" from having been a victorious general. More significantly for his nation's future, his success in triumphing over adversaries on the battlefields at Palo Alto, Resaca de la Palma, Monterrey, and Buena Vista gave the American government close to a year to remedy its initial lack of preparedness for war—to raise new regular army and volunteer regiments, and to plan and initiate engagements in other sectors of Mexico. Yet leading modern historians have recently written disparagingly of Taylor and his campaign, evidently relying on the questionable opinions of certain of their predecessors.

For most of his life Taylor's attention had centered primarily around three areas of concern: his family, his slave-worked plantations and other substantial investments, and mundane army matters. His involvement in the war with Mexico appears to have been largely happenstance in the beginning. The series of events that started him on his Mexican odyssey commenced in 1844. In April of that year President John Tyler gave Taylor charge of a small force of about one thousand regular army infantrymen and dragoons being assembled at Fort Jesup, in western Louisiana. The closeness of those troops to the eastern border of Texas was intended as proof that Texans could call on American armed forces for protection while negotiations were in progress for the annexation of the Lone Star Republic to the United States. Old Zach may have been selected to implement the Tyler administration's strategy chiefly because, as commander of a section of the army's Western Division, his headquarters were in Arkansas, conveniently near the planned area of concentration in Louisiana, and he was known to be familiar with the Texas border region. He had not been outstanding during his army career of nearly forty years except on two occasions: at age twenty-seven, as a captain in command of Fort Harrison, in Indiana Territory (near present-day Terre Haute), during a potentially overwhelming Indian raid; and at age fifty-three, in 1837, as a colonel in charge of the forces that defeated Seminoles in the swamps of Lake Okeechobee, Florida. At the same time, he had been in hot water just once, and then not with the regular army hierarchy—Missouri volunteers who fought under him in Florida complained vociferously of having been slighted in his reports.[1] Now, in 1844, he was headed for responsibilities far exceeding any he had yet known, which would be closely critiqued at almost every point. He seems to have been sustained by a self-reliant, normally imperturbable disposition. While under enemy fire in Mexico, for instance, he would sit calmly on Old Whitey, one leg around a pommel, issuing orders to unit commanders.

Another extraordinary aspect of Taylor's campaign was that gradually joining the military contingents he would lead, commencing with the formation of his "army of observation" in 1844, would be several hundred men who would later fight in the Civil War, at least 173 of whom would become general officers with Confederate or Union forces.[2] While much has been written about the Civil War service of many of those men, very little attention has been paid to their experiences while they were serving under Taylor. Recent histories of the Mexican War and a recent Taylor biography include mention of less than one-third of them, and make no reference to some who would be among the most prominent such as Daniel Harvey Hill.[3] Furthermore, biographical studies of Mexican War veterans tend to focus almost exclusively on the highlights of a subject's individual history, omitting for the most part his specific duties during that period as well as his contacts with officers who would engage in the next war. In contrast, from a close reading of official documents and accounts of participants, fresh data about the Mexican War careers of numerous Civil War leaders are disclosed herein, and erroneous statements in other sources are corrected. In addition, impressions of General Taylor recorded in diaries, letters, and memoirs provide glimpses of Old Zach as he appeared to his subordinates, most of whom found little to criticize.

For several reasons, this account of Taylor's campaign is told to a large extent through references to the activities and thoughts of men who would be prominent in the next war, and their brother officers. In a very real sense, what was true of one was more or less true of everyone in the same circumstances, including enlisted personnel, and the experiences of each add density to a portrayal of life in Taylor's army. Though the officers enjoyed more privileges and luxuries than did men of lower ranks, all of Old Zach's troops slept in leaky tents much of the time and suffered when the weather was inclement or illness was rampant. Also, as will be seen, even second lieutenants often had occasion to observe and interact with General Taylor, and documents written by men who were in his Army of Occupation, in published form or in libraries and archives, are a rich source of eyewitnesses' comments about Taylor and his campaign. Moreover, Mexican War veterans who participated in America's Civil War were members of a unique assemblage—northerners, southerners, and westerners who, after engaging in the last major battles fought by servicemen of the United States prior to 1861, aligned themselves with opposing armies fifteen years later. As such, their opinions, predilections, and concerns during the Mexican War period provide insight into the attitudes of Americans nationwide in an era when intimations of the next war were looming, attitudes that still haunt us to a considerable extent today.

One widely accepted generalization about those men needs some refinement, however: that the Mexican War was a training ground for Civil War generals.[4] The Confederate and Union general officers who were Mexican War veterans were, typically, men already well schooled in military skills by the mid-1840s. Certainly that was true of the future generals in Taylor's forces: more than one hundred were graduates of the United States Military Academy at West Point, New York; moreover, even in volunteer units most of the senior officers were either West Pointers or veterans of earlier conflicts, or in one way or another had been recipients of prior military instruction. Since scarcely any of them appear to have left us their thoughts about lessons learned in Mexico, usually scholars can only make educated guesses concerning ways in which the military education of those men was furthered during the 1846–48 war.

To do so, it is necessary to keep in mind how widely their service records in Mexico differed with respect to exposure to combat and other matters, such as opportunities to observe the conduct of commanders and comrades. For instance, as shown below, less than a third of Taylor's future generals took part in his initial battles, fought in the spring of 1846 near the mouth of the Rio Grande, across the river from the Mexican city of Matamoros. Among the younger men with him at that time were infantry lieutenants Ulysses S. Grant, James Longstreet, Edmund Kirby Smith, Napoleon Dana, Earl Van Dorn, and Don Carlos Buell; artillery officers Braxton Bragg, George Thomas, John F. Reynolds, and Samuel French; dragoon officers (acting as cavalry) William J. Hardee and Alfred Pleasonton; and topographical engineers George G. Meade and Thomas J. Wood. Before the next major battle in September at Monterrey (or Monterey, as the name of the Mexican city was spelled by Americans of that day), artillerists Daniel Harvey Hill and John Sedgwick were with Taylor's army, as were Colonel Albert Sidney Johnston of the Regiment of Texas Rifle Volunteers, Colonel Jefferson Davis of the First Regiment of Mississippi Rifles, and a flood of other volunteers. But by that time close to half of the future generals who were with Taylor in May were no longer in his Army of Occupation, having been sent north as recruiters or assigned to various other duty stations. As for George McClellan, Thomas J. Jackson (the future "Stonewall"), Cadmus Wilcox, and Dabney Maury, members of the 1846 graduating class of the United States Military Academy, they did not reach the war zone until after the Battle of Monterrey. Similarly, not until late September did thirty-nine-year-old Captain Robert E. Lee arrive at San Antonio to join a column of troops heading into the interior of Mexico under the direct command of Brigadier General John E. Wool, who was in turn subject to General Taylor's orders. Then, just after Christmas, General Winfield Scott arrived at the mouth of the Rio Grande and began commandeering thousands of Taylor's Army of Occupation veterans in preparation for an advance on Mexico City. Two months later Zachary Taylor and most of the troops remaining with him, including Braxton Bragg, George Thomas, John Reynolds, Samuel French, and Jefferson Davis, would fight their final Mexican War battle at Buena Vista, virtually ending the first phase of the conflict.[5] In fact, one of the notable aspects of the Mexican War is the diversity of its veterans' records of service.

Certainly the Mexican War was a training ground to some extent for all of its American participants, some eight hundred of whom would serve in Confederate or Union forces. Not since 1812 had the United States fought as powerful an adversary; and in undertaking their government's first major invasion of another country, General Taylor and his troops were subjected to repeated reminders of the critical importance of transport and supply arrangements, especially when in a hostile environment. Noteworthy too is that Ulysses Grant, in his memoirs, stated that he had benefited during his Mexican War tour of duty by what he learned of the character of men who subsequently became his Civil War opponents. Since the same was presumably true of many other Mexican War veterans, their relationships with one another while in General Taylor's army is a significant aspect of his campaign. At the same time, being in the Mexican War taught none of them "what it was to lose a battle or order a retreat," as has been noted with respect to Lee.[6]

Apparently no personal animosities extant during the Mexican War had a direct, significant effect on Civil War events. There is evidence, however, of the survival of friendships, for instance Daniel Harvey Hill's efforts to console John Reynolds when Reynolds was captured in 1862 by Hill's men. And the memory of another friendship is said to have played a role in the last stage of the Civil War: when Lee, preparing to ride to Appomattox, was hesitant about surrendering, "worried that Grant might demand harsh terms," Longstreet is reported to have assured him that the Union general "would be fair."[7] Other than a few such incidents, and face-offs of opposing commanders who had served together under General Taylor (for example at Fort Donelson), Mexican War experiences seem to have had general rather than specific application in the Civil War. That is scarcely surprising, for not only did the two wars differ widely in almost every respect, but the vast majority of Mexican War veterans who fought in the Civil War held much higher ranks than they had during the earlier war, and thus had quite different responsibilities during the later conflagration than previously. Although Grant asserted he had been taught "many practical lessons" in Mexico, he neither specified what those lessons were nor explained whether they were advantageous thereafter, except in the one way mentioned above—the insight he gained regarding men who became adversaries a few years later.[8] In fact, even that advantage was limited, for during the Mexican War not all of the future Confederate and Union generals were associated with one another. For instance, neither George Thomas, John F. Reynolds, nor Thomas W. Sherman had an opportunity to become acquainted with Lee at that time. Similarly, many men who would fight on the same side in 1861 were never together during the earlier war; neither Jefferson Davis, Braxton Bragg, nor Samuel French served with Lee in Mexico.

Nevertheless, service with Taylor's Army of Occupation was clearly an important stage in the lives of his subordinates, particularly those for whom the Mexican War became a springboard toward prominence in the next war. They too, like Zachary Taylor, benefited from the aura of success that adhered to them as veterans of the earlier confrontation. No doubt many a regular army officer rejoiced when war was declared in 1846, as did graduating Academy cadet George McClellan, viewing it as an opportunity to gain both glory and advancement. But although West Pointers, schooled to honor military heroics, were probably the most eager to participate in Taylor's campaign, generally speaking each of Old Zach's officers, of every description and political persuasion, hoped for combat duty. When Ulysses Grant remarked that fighting was "no longer a pleasure" following the Monterrey battle, he appears to have been speaking mainly for himself; and even for him, as for numerous other Mexican War veterans, the memory of gratifying exploits would never be forgotten. Altogether, it was an exhilarating war for most of Taylor's regular army officers, southerners and northerners alike, as well as for a surprising number of volunteers. That could explain in part why so many Mexican War veterans rushed to join the side of their preference in 1861.[9]

Not all of Taylor's young officers admired him. Brevet Captain Roswell S. Ripley, a West Pointer (1843) and an artillerist during the Monterrey battle who would rise to the rank of Confederate brigadier general, wrote disparagingly of Old Zach in an 1849 history of the war. Lieutenant Daniel Harvey Hill was clearly offended by Taylor's habitually casual dress: he commented in his diary that during a drill of his regiment at Camargo the general rode along their lines in his "undress frock and though looking very much an old farmer, presented altogether a more martial air than I have ever known him to present before." One bitter critic was nineteen-year-old Lieutenant Lew (Lewis) Wallace of the First Indiana regiment, a future Union major general and author of *Ben Hur.*[10] And, as mentioned previously, more than a century and a half later Old Zach still has detractors among scholars.[11] Yet it is evident, from comments then and later by subordinates who served directly under Taylor, that nearly all of his young officers respected him and approved his actions.

Whether his example affected their conduct in the next war is less clear. His dedication to preservation of the Union, which did not become widely known until he became president, obviously was not shared by most southern veterans of the Army of Occupation, although reportedly Braxton Bragg, a confirmed Democrat, supported Taylor's candidacy for the office of president in 1848 in the mistaken belief that his election would decrease sectional antipathy.[12] Another West Pointer who was with Old Zach at Buena Vista, and who fought in the Civil War as a Union brigadier general, Henry W. Benham, declared in 1871 that of all the army officers he had known, Ulysses Grant and George Thomas most resembled Taylor, whom he described as "unambitious but to do right, an honest, reliable, well-judging soldier." Similarly Dabney Maury, likewise a West Pointer, wrote after his service as a Confederate major general, in describing Stonewall Jackson: "General Zachary Taylor, a simple and unpretending gentleman, may have been Jackson's model; for he had more of the silent, rapid, impetuous methods, which Jackson practiced later on, than any American general save [Nathan Bedford] Forrest."[13] At any rate, to most of his men Taylor was "Old Rough and Ready"—not a "spit and polish" commander but accessible, usually amiable, fearless, aggressive, tough yet compassionate, a justifiably inspiring soldier's soldier.

Grant, going further than most of Taylor's admirers, would declare that the general's Buena Vista victory "was probably very important to the success of General Scott at Cerro Gordo and in his entire campaign from Vera Cruz," in that Santa Anna's army was thereby reduced in numbers and demoralized.[14] Certainly, as Grant suggested, Old Zach contributed significantly to the outcome of the war with Mexico. Indeed, for the most part it was his veterans who were the backbone of General Scott's forces at Veracruz and Cerro Gordo. Taylor also was responsible to a considerable extent for the largely peaceful relationship between his forces and the people of northern Mexico, a conciliatory stance followed later by Generals Wool, Kearny, and Scott. Taylor frequently reminded his troops that any abuse of Mexican civilians was forbidden; and, with the exception of unforgiving Texans, most of them obeyed those orders. In fact, quite a few of his young officers, Grant and Hill in particular, expressed sympathy for the Mexican people; and even after vicious battles one finds praise in the letters and reports of Taylor's subordinates for the valor of their adversaries. As for Old Zach, he was merely following War Department instructions in assuring villagers that their property and religious customs would be respected, yet he emphasized and enforced that policy diligently throughout his campaign, and undoubtedly believed it was not only a proper course of action in this instance but that it would hasten agreement to a peace treaty.

Unlike George McClellan and probably many of the ambitious, eager junior officers in the Army of Occupation, Taylor had hoped war could be avoided. Once hostilities commenced, he frequently expressed his longing for the war to end before another battle was fought. He was not lacking in ambition, yet as was true of Grant, Ethan Allen Hitchcock, and others, he regretted the existence of "ambitious views of conquest . . . at the expense of a weak power."[15] Still, neither disagreement with President Polk's decisions nor loss of respect for General Winfield Scott caused Zachary Taylor to reduce his painstaking efforts to do all in his power to help the United States win the war.

Trailing Clouds of Glory

1
Taylor's Corps of Observation

Preparations for a possible military resolution of the numerous long-standing differences between the United States and Mexico began in the spring of 1844, when annexation of the Republic of Texas to its neighbor to the northeast appeared likely, and Mexico had vowed that it would regard such an arrangement as a declaration of war. The initial components of the army that Brevet Brigadier General Zachary Taylor would lead to the Rio Grande—eight companies each of the Third and Fourth U.S. Infantry regiments, and seven companies of the Second U.S. Dragoons—were brought together in the vicinity of Fort Jesup, Louisiana, near the Sabine River border between the United States and the Republic of Texas, immediately after a treaty providing for the annexation of Texas by the United States was signed by Secretary of State John C. Calhoun on April 12, 1844. The men in the seven companies of dragoons, whose regiment had until recently been dismounted for about a year and termed "riflemen," were already quartered at Jesup. The Third and Fourth Infantry companies had for some time been stationed at Jefferson Barracks, about ten miles south of St. Louis, Missouri. On April 11, 1844, the day before the annexation treaty was signed, orders were issued directing members of the Third Infantry who were at Jefferson Barracks to "proceed by water, without delay, to Natchitoches, and thence to Fort Jesup." A similar order went out to the Fourth Infantry commander on April 22.[1]

President John Tyler, in a message addressed to the U.S. Senate the following month, defended these hasty dispositions as well as the Navy Department order directing the Home Squadron to act as a "fleet of observation" in the Gulf of Mexico. A Virginian who, like most southerners, longed to see the Republic of Texas annexed to the United States, he reminded the senators of Mexico's threat to regard such a measure as an act of war, and maintained that because the annexation treaty only needed Senate approval to become effective, the United States could justifiably employ military means to repel any invasion of Texas by hostile forces that might occur before the Senate considered the issue.[2]

Accusations that Tyler was determined to add Texas to the constellation of southern slaveholding states, even to the point of inviting a war, were probably inevitable, Tyler being a lifelong Jeffersonian Democrat who had deserted to the states'-rights wing of the Whig party just in time to be elected vice president on the William Henry Harrison ticket, and to succeed to the presidency when Harrison died, a month after his inauguration, in 1841. But whatever Tyler's reasons for wanting to add Texas to the other twenty-seven states then in the Union, it would be the next president of the United States—another southerner, James Knox Polk of Tennessee—who would transform General Taylor's newly created "corps of observation" in western Louisiana into an "army of occupation," at an isolated Texas hamlet overlooking the Gulf of Mexico called Corpus Christi.[3]

The senior officer at Fort Jesup in early 1844 was Colonel David E. Twiggs from Georgia, who had entered the army as a captain in 1812, and had commanded the Second Dragoons since the regiment's formation in 1836. Now fifty-four years old, with a mane of white hair but a robust physique, Twiggs was a harsh, profane disciplinarian who was nevertheless admired by his officers for demanding that their regiment be superbly equipped and trained, although he was said to be "arbitrary and capricious at times."[4] Among the men with Twiggs at Jesup were several who, like their colonel, would hold high-ranking Confederate commands in the Civil War: Major Thomas Fauntleroy, First Lieutenants William J. Hardee and Henry H. Sibley, and Second Lieutenant William Steele. On the Union side in the next war would be Brevet Second Lieutenant Rufus Ingalls, a graduate of the West Point class of 1843, and Captain Lawrence Pike Graham. But in the spring of 1844 they were all of one mind, jubilant over having been rescued from their inglorious year as mere "riflemen" and restored to the dragoon branch of the army. They had been told that they would be remounted as soon as Congress appropriated the funds.[5]

At that time the Third and Fourth U.S. Infantry regiments each had two companies in Indian Territory just west of the Missouri border, the Third's at Fort Leavenworth, the Fourth's at Fort Scott. The other eight companies of each regiment as well as their regimental commanders had been in reserve at Jefferson Barracks, employed as a "school of instruction and practice" for recruits.[6] Commanding the Third Infantry in the absence of the regiment's colonel, who was too frail for active service, was Lieutenant Colonel Ethan Allen Hitchcock. A feisty, eccentric, scholarly West Point graduate (1817) from Vermont, the grandson of Revolutionary War hero Ethan Allen, he had been on friendly terms with Zachary Taylor since 1819 when Lieutenant Colonel Taylor, then in charge of the Eighth Infantry, had selected the twenty-one-year-old Lieutenant Hitchcock to be his regimental adjutant. Thereafter Hitchcock had enjoyed two tours of duty at West Point, as assistant professor of tactics (1824–27) and as commandant of cadets (1829–33). While at the Academy he had met the Marquis de Lafayette, dined with Washington Irving, called on ex-president John Adams, discussed Academy matters with President John Quincy Adams, and protested the interference of President Andrew Jackson in disciplinary actions at the Point. In 1836, while serving on the western border of Louisiana with Brevet Major General Edmund P. Gaines, Captain Hitchcock was entrusted with the delivery of Sam Houston's historic note informing President Jackson that the Texans had defeated Mexican president Antonio López de Santa Anna at San Jacinto. Decades later, following his service during America's war with Mexico, the happily retired Hitchcock, after rejecting what he understood to be President Lincoln's offer to appoint him commander of the Army of the Potomac, would rejoin the Union ranks as a major general of volunteers in the War Department.[7]

On April 20, 1844, Lieutenant Colonel Hitchcock learned that he and the Third Infantry's companies at Jefferson Barracks were to leave at once for Fort Jesup. He immediately noted in his diary a suspicion that those "unexpected" War Department orders were intended to further the plans of those who, unlike himself, wanted the Lone Star Republic to become part of the United States, a development that Hitchcock feared would eventually lead to secession by the southern states: "Rumors are rife of the annexation of Texas, and this may be a movement towards making a military occupancy of the country beyond the Sabine." With remarkable prescience he added, "I may make the first move into Texas with the colors of the United States, but I am convinced I shall not make the last." A week later he and his officers—among whom were four future Civil War generals, Second Lieutenants Don Carlos Buell, Thomas Jordan, Israel B. Richardson, and George Sykes—had sold unneeded paraphernalia, paid farewell courtesy calls, and boarded a steamboat for their journey down the Mississippi. Two smaller steamers took them up the shallow Red River to Grand Ecore, Louisiana, near Natchitoches. They disembarked on May 6 and were gradually transported by wagon teams some twenty-five miles southwestward along a narrow wooded trail to Fort Jesup.[8]

The dragoons at Jesup were comfortably billeted with their families in white-painted, porticoed buildings facing the rectangular parade ground. Although the post was not a proper "fort," as Hitchcock remarked in his diary, it did have a theater, gymnasium, school, and well-supplied sutler's store. The Third Infantry contingent of General Taylor's army erected their tents adjacent to the post in an area Hitchcock named Camp Wilkins, for President Tyler's secretary of war.[9]

The Third Infantry companies were scarcely out of sight of St. Louis when the Fourth Infantry's officers learned that they were to follow immediately in Hitchcock's wake. Among those accompanying the regiment's commander, Colonel Josiah H. Vose, downriver on May 7 were three who would have leading roles in the next war: Captain Robert C. Buchanan, First Lieutenant Benjamin Alvord, and Brevet Second Lieutenant James Longstreet. The Fourth Infantry companies landed at Grand Ecore on May 13 and camped nearby, but toward the end of the month Colonel Vose decided to station his troops on a high, pine-covered ridge about three miles from both Natchitoches and Grand Ecore which became known as Camp Salubrity.[10] Colonel Vose, who was from Massachusetts, had entered the army as a captain in 1812, as had Colonel Twiggs, and like Taylor and Hitchcock had served in the Eighth Infantry in 1820. Also, having been in charge of Fort Jesup in 1834 as a lieutenant colonel in the Third Infantry, he too was quite familiar with western Louisiana. Praised in 1844 as a "highly respectable officer & eminently moral man" by a fellow regimental commander, Vose was also popular with his subalterns. Ulysses Grant wrote of him the following year, "There are but few Commanding officers as indulgent about giving young officers leaves of absence as the one I am serving under. (Col. Vose)." However, Vose, almost sixty in June of 1844, was growing increasingly feeble, and the Fourth Infantry was commanded much of the time by Longstreet's future father-in-law, Lieutenant Colonel John Garland.[11]

The linchpin of the army being assembled on the Republic of Texas's eastern border, General Zachary Taylor was commanding the Second Military Department and living at Camp Belknap, a mile from Fort Smith, Arkansas, when he was ordered on April 23, 1844, to proceed immediately to Fort Jesup and there take charge of the First Military Department. Four days later a confidential dispatch, sent to Jesup by Adjutant General Roger Jones, informed Taylor that upon his arrival at Natchitoches he was to consider himself to be the commander not merely of a military department but also of a corps of observation, consisting in the first instance of the dragoons in garrison at Jesup together with the companies of the Third and Fourth Infantry regiments recently ordered there; that those troops were to be held in readiness for service at any moment; and that he would continue to receive instructions directly from Washington (despite the fact that his immediate superior was Brevet Major General Edmund P. Gaines, commander of the Western Division).[12]

Taylor was a Virginian, born November 24, 1784, the third son of wealthy, socially prominent parents. When Zachary was an infant the family and their slaves moved westward, to a plantation near the village of Louisville, soon to be a leading Ohio River port in the new state of Kentucky. Zachary, with little formal education, accepted a commission dated May 3, 1808, as a first lieutenant in the Seventh U.S. Infantry, having been recommended by Kentucky congressmen. (The older brother whom he emulated, William, a second lieutenant in the U.S. Regiment of Artillerists, was killed by Indians at Fort Pickering, Tennessee, on May 30, 1808.) Whether Zachary or a member of his family sought his commission is unknown. Also unknown is exactly when Zachary initially reported for duty, but he first served as a recruiter in Kentucky. By 1810 he had been promoted to the rank of captain, and two years later he was awarded the first honorary brevet ever conferred upon an officer of the nation's armed services. The brevet, usually a promotion in title and uniform insignia only, was presented at the direction of his second cousin President James Madison, after Zachary, with the aid of a mere handful of troops and civilians, repelled a seven-hour Indian attack on Fort Harrison in Indiana Territory. Thereafter he seldom had occasion to fight, although during the Black Hawk War of 1832 he was for a short period second in command to General Henry Atkinson. That interval in Taylor's career is of historical interest chiefly because Lieutenant Jefferson Davis was Taylor's adjutant, Lieutenant Albert Sidney Johnston was Atkinson's adjutant, and in the Illinois militia under General Atkinson and Colonel Taylor for eighty days was a twenty-three-year-old storekeeper, Abraham Lincoln. In 1837 Taylor received another honorary promotion, to brevet brigadier general, a reward for his having successfully led a brigade of regulars and volunteers against several hundred Seminoles and Mikasukis at Lake Okeechobee, Florida, in the only major battle of the Second Seminole War.[13]

As has often been suggested, General Taylor's craggy, weathered features and habitually casual dress made him look more like a farmer than a general, and in fact for decades he had owned plantations in Kentucky and along the Louisiana-Mississippi border north of Baton Rouge, all worked by slave labor. The income from his investments had enabled him to provide a comfortable life for his wife, Margaret, and their children, regardless of the lack of amenities on the isolated western posts where they had usually lived. Still, to Taylor's troops he was "Old Zach" or "Old Rough and Ready," remarkable chiefly for his unpretentious, plain-spoken, kindly demeanor.[14]

Why Old Rough and Ready was chosen for the sensitive corps of observation command, and upon whose recommendation, is unclear. According to the secretary of war, William Wilkins, he himself was the individual responsible for the transfer of the Third and Fourth Infantry companies to Fort Jesup, though the order for the Third Infantry's movement was issued by Adjutant General Jones, and the subsequent one for the Fourth Infantry by an assistant adjutant general, in each instance with the notation "By command of Major General Scott." Evidently Winfield Scott, despite being the general-in-chief of the army, had merely a secondary role, at best, in the deliberations that led to the creation of the corps of observation. Indeed, in his memoirs Scott, in referring to the advance a year later of Taylor's corps to Corpus Christi, Texas, mentioned his "concurrence" to the selection of Old Zach as field commander in Texas. Moreover, Scott was mistaken in implying that in 1844 he had purposely assigned Captain W. W. S. Bliss, a brilliant West Pointer, to General Taylor's staff in order to supplement the latter's questionable ability to lead the corps of observation, for Bliss had been transferred to Taylor's staff in 1842, long before Old Zach was being considered for any extraordinary assignment. But whatever occurred during those 1844 deliberations, it is obvious from the adjutant general's letter to Taylor of April 27 that President Tyler intended all initiatives regarding the annexation issue to emanate from him or at his behest. It was not anticipated that General Taylor and his small force of regular army troops would have an active role in influencing future developments. All President Tyler wanted at that point was the presence near Texas's eastern border of a reliable and reassuring symbol of America's military strength, and the availability of that resource in case of need.[15]

On June 17, 1844, General Taylor reached Fort Jesup. Waiting for him was the lengthy, confidential communication of April 27 from Adjutant General Jones which emphasized that Taylor's assignment was to command not only the Western Division's First Department but also a "*corps of observation*" which was to be "held in readiness for service at any moment." In addition Taylor was told, "You will take prompt measures . . . to put yourself in communication with the President of Texas, in order to inform him of your present position and force, and to learn and to transmit to this office (all confidentially) whether any and what external dangers may threaten that Government or its people."[16] In accordance with those instructions, Taylor immediately prepared a message informing Sam Houston, president of the Lone Star Republic, that there were "about a thousand effective men" at Fort Jesup, composed of seven companies of dragoons and sixteen of infantry. To deliver this dispatch Taylor chose Captain Lloyd J. Beall of the Second Dragoons, whose Civil War experience would be as commandant of the Confederate Marine Corps. Taylor mentioned the dragoon captain in his letter to Sam Houston of June 17: "Capt. Beall has instructions to await your convenience before returning to these Head Quarters and will bear any communication you may think proper to make for the information of my Government." But by the time Beall returned the next month President Tyler could no longer claim that the imminence of annexation gave the United States the right to protect Texas from invasion, for on June 8 the United States Senate had rejected the annexation treaty.[17]

Toward the end of July a brevet second lieutenant of the Fourth Infantry, Ulysses S. Grant, wrote from Camp Salubrity to Julia Dent, whose home was near Jefferson Barracks and to whom he had recently become secretly engaged. (The brevet second lieutenant designation for West Point graduates meant they would not become second lieutenants until an opening occurred at that level in their branch of service and they were next in line for promotion, based on their standing at graduation.) Grant told Julia: "In my mind I am constantly turning over plans to get back to Missouri, and until today there has [*sic*] been strong grounds for hoping that the whole of the 4th Regiment would be ordered back there; but that hope is blasted now. Orders have arrive [*sic*] from Washington City that no troops on the frontier will be removed." The genesis of this development, he informed her, was that Mexico was preparing for the "re-conquering of Texas," and Taylor's troops were to remain in Louisiana in order "to preserve neutrality between the United States and the belligerent parties," which was evidently the accepted explanation among his peers.[18]

Grant had been assigned to the Fourth Infantry the previous summer, following his graduation from the United States Military Academy. Although not required to report to his regiment until the end of September, as was usual for Academy graduates, he had checked in at Jefferson Barracks early, on the fifth of that month. For someone who had not been keen on an army career when he entered West Point, and whose preference at graduation was to join the dragoons rather than the infantry, such alacrity was surprising. But Grant had always welcomed opportunities to travel, which in his youth had consisted chiefly of acting as a teamster for people moving away from Georgetown, Ohio, where his parents then lived, and of visiting relatives in Kentucky. Thus the Jefferson Barracks posting, reached by a trip down the Ohio River and up the Mississippi to St. Louis, the bustling gateway to the western plains, had its compensations. Better yet, having brought his own horse with him to Missouri he was able to ride frequently over to White Haven, the nearby plantation home of Frederick Dent, his roommate during their senior year at the Military Academy and a friend who would remain a bulwark for decades.[19]

Accompanying Grant on his first trip to White Haven was a Fourth Infantry comrade, Brevet Second Lieutenant James Longstreet, a distant relative of the Dents who had been at Jefferson Barracks since graduating from West Point a year earlier, and who had been invited to drop by White Haven while Fred was home on leave. If Fred was there when Longstreet and Grant arrived, he must have been in the process of packing, for he was due to report to the Sixth Infantry at Fort Towson, in Indian Territory near the northeastern border of Texas, by the end of the month. Longstreet's recollection was that he and Grant met Fred's seventeen-year-old sister, Julia, as well as other members of the Dent family during that first visit, although Grant dated his courtship of his future wife as having commenced the following February, when she returned to White Haven after spending the winter with relatives in St. Louis.[20]

During Grant's eight months at Jefferson Barracks he and the other officers in his regiment were permitted to leave the compound by Colonel Vose (commander of both the Fourth Infantry and the post) whenever they had free time. Grant, taking advantage of Vose's leniency, had begun spending many of his off-duty hours at White Haven even before he became Julia's shadow, chatting with her hospitable mother and with the Dent children then living at home—two brothers older than Julia, and two younger sisters—as well as with their married brother and his wife. Julia's family resembled Grant's own in numbers, he being the eldest of six children. In other respects their families differed markedly, the head of the Dent household being a wealthy, ardent Jacksonian Democrat whose 925-acre plantation was farmed by slaves, whereas Grant's father was a largely self-educated, outspoken Whig whose prosperity derived principally from his business of tanning hides.[21]

Julia's father, like many southern landowners addressed customarily by the unearned title of "colonel," did not look with favor on Grant's attentions to his eldest daughter. No doubt he realized this suitor did not agree with the credo of southern Democrats, however circumspectly Grant may have dealt with controversial topics. And it was undeniable that a brevet second lieutenant without an independent income was scarcely an outstanding catch for a young woman accustomed to a privileged lifestyle. Nevertheless, by February of 1844, Grant and Julia and various members of their coterie, which included two of his classmates at the post, Bob Hazlitt and Charles Jarvis, were spending many companionable hours together, riding around the Dent plantation, visiting the homes of acquaintances, and attending revival meetings and military balls. Julia's dexterity on horseback no doubt particularly appealed to Grant, who had always been happiest in the saddle. But toward the end of April their halcyon spring abruptly ended. The Third Infantry companies packed up, marched out of Jefferson Barracks, boarded ship, and started downriver, headed for western Louisiana, taking along Lieutenant Charles Jarvis; and a day or so later Grant, unaware that orders had just arrived for his regiment to follow the Third to Louisiana, boarded a steamer for a visit with his family in Bethel, Ohio, where his father was currently engaged in a wholesale leather business. There he learned, via a letter from his Fourth Infantry classmate Bob Hazlitt, that their companies were in the process of moving to Louisiana, which caused Julia Dent's suitor to realize suddenly that he was "exceedingly anxious to get back to Jefferson Barracks."[22]

At the age of twenty-two, of average height, very slender, with wavy brown hair, blue eyes, and pleasant, regular features, Grant was altogether "as pretty as a doll" in the eyes of Julia's little sister Emmy, but financially his prospects were meager. His intention was to obtain a position as a college professor eventually, and in the near future to be detailed as an assistant professor of mathematics at the Academy, which, though his standing at graduation was only twenty-one in a class of thirty-nine, an instructor had indicated was a possibility. Even so, rapid advancement in rank was unlikely as long as the nation was at peace, since officers seldom left the army voluntarily unless offered better positions, there being no provision for retirement with pay.[23] But such inauspicious considerations did not deter Grant once he realized how eager he was to marry Julia. At times easygoing to a fault, cantering through life with a slack hand on the reins, content to let fate dictate his course, in this instance he demonstrated his latent streak of resolve. Upon reaching Jefferson Barracks—nearly deserted since the departure of Vose, Hitchcock, and their infantry units—he persuaded Lieutenant Richard Stoddert Ewell, the dragoon officer then commanding the post, to extend his leave until he was issued a new set of orders.[24]

Ewell, an astute and genial bachelor who was already balding at age twenty-seven, spoke with a lisp, and had a face that fell away from protruding eyes and a beaky nose, had been a senior at West Point during Grant's plebe year. His company of First U.S. Dragoons was stationed on the Great Plains, at Fort Scott, but Ewell had been detailed to St. Louis on recruiting duty; and Stephen Watts Kearny, his colonel and also at that time commander of the Western Division's Third Department with headquarters in St. Louis, had given Lieutenant Ewell charge of the huge Jefferson Barracks complex, now occupied chiefly by the wives and children of the transferred infantrymen.[25] Having assumed command of the post only a week earlier, Ewell was unlikely to have heard about Grant's courting of Julia Dent, although the dragoon lieutenant tended to keep up with army romances. For instance, in writing his brother Ben that summer, he implied that Colonel John Garland's two "devilish pretty" daughters were the only women at Jefferson Barracks attractive enough to lure him into wedlock, adding, "Fortunately one of them is to be married in September to Lieut. [George] Deas of the 5th Inf, and the other to Brevet 2nd [James] Longstreet as soon as she is old enough."[26] As for Grant's request for an extension of his leave, Ewell, whether knowingly or not, obligingly aided and abetted the tactics of Julia's suitor by arranging for fresh instructions to be issued from the Third Military Department. Inasmuch as orders directing Grant to join his regiment in Louisiana, dated May 21, did not arrive at Jefferson Barracks promptly, he gained the leeway he needed to accomplish his mission the next day, or nearly so since Julia would consent only to a secret engagement of indefinite length. The ecstatically happy Grant never forgot the critical part Ewell played in his life. Long after the young dragoon's service as a Confederate general, Grant saluted Ewell as "a man much esteemed, and deservedly so, in the old army," and "a gallant and efficient officer in two wars."[27]

When Grant reached Camp Salubrity, Louisiana, on June 3, after a "pleasant" journey down the Mississippi, a day's sightseeing in New Orleans, and an enlightening introduction to the swampy "Red River country," he found his regiment's officers quartered in tiny, thin linen tents through which the rain ran "in streams." His bed consisted of planks laid atop sticks, head to foot, driven into a floor of pine needles. Though the pine-wooded ridge on which Salubrity was located was high enough to discourage attacks by mosquitoes, myriads of ticks and redbugs were everywhere.[28]

As the months passed, General Taylor took no extraordinary steps to prepare himself or the men under his immediate command for intervention in Texas. Like his regimental commanders, he already knew the border region well, having as a lieutenant colonel supervised the construction of "Cantonment Jesup" in 1822, named by Taylor for his friend General Thomas S. Jesup; and recently in his capacity as head of the Western Division's Second Military Department he had visited Fort Towson and Fort Washita, both in Indian Territory just above the Texas border. He also knew that his regimental commanders were experienced regular army veterans, which may have been why he seldom concerned himself, apparently, with routine affairs, scarcely paying any more attention to his troops on the Texas border than to those garrisoned elsewhere in his extensive geographical command. Moreover, he probably assumed, after the defeat of the annexation treaty, that his corps of observation would not be sent to Texas in the foreseeable future if at all. He was aware, however, that the situation south of the Sabine River border was still extremely volatile, for when Sam Houston's secretary of war wrote Taylor on July 30 he enclosed a proclamation by a Mexican general, Adrian Woll, announcing that a truce with the Texans was no longer in effect. Taylor, in forwarding both documents to Adjutant General Jones, enclosed also his August 8 reply to Houston, a warning that except for the purpose of preserving the neutrality of the United States he did not feel authorized to move the troops under his command without further instructions from Washington.[29]

Taylor's three regimental commanders—Hitchcock, Twiggs, and Vose—often corresponded directly with the adjutant general and occasionally with other senior government officials, including President Tyler. Hitchcock, for instance, had been embroiled for months in a dispute with General Winfield Scott over an incident involving a lieutenant in the Third Infantry who was destined to be a major general of Union volunteers by 1862, Don Carlos Buell. The hot-tempered Buell, who in his student days at the Point had been confined to quarters for hitting a waiter, had recently been court-martialed for striking a soldier with a sword. His acquittal, following a claim of self-defense, so displeased General Scott that he ordered the court to explain why it had not found Buell guilty. Hitchcock, at the behest of members of the court-martial panel, wrote a protest citing the Articles of War as not authorizing such an order. Other angry exchanges followed until President Tyler decided the proceedings against Buell should cease. Hitchcock, long a critic of Scott, fired a final salvo in the Buell controversy from Camp Wilkins, Louisiana, on June 20,

1844, writing President Tyler that a legal extract furnished by the late U.S. secretary of state Abel P. Upshur had been so garbled as to be misleading if not fraudulent, and expressing surprise that this "should have escaped the notice of the Major-General commanding the army."[30]

In other respects Hitchcock was relatively sanguine at the moment. Twiggs, on the other hand, sent indignant missives to the adjutant general about something or other repeatedly throughout the summer and fall of 1844, several of them on behalf of Grant's friend and classmate Lieutenant Rufus Ingalls. Twiggs contended that all officers who, like Ingalls, had been assigned to his regiment while it was dismounted should receive from the government, without charge, a copy of *Cavalry Tactics.* A more consequential dispute arose over the fact that his men were not receiving the relatively high rate of pay accorded dragoons by law, the rationale for this presumably being to offset the cost of maintaining their mounts. The paymaster general insisted that the Second Dragoons would not be entitled to increased pay until they were actually remounted. That argument dragged on for months, as did the regiment's related problem of obtaining the horses and equipment needed by its seven companies at Fort Jesup and the three stationed at Fort Washita.[31]

Even without their mounts the dragoons, as they paraded at Jesup in their distinctive uniforms (blue enhanced by gold braid on fatigue jackets, yellow stripes on pantaloons, and yellow bands on flat forage caps), must have intrigued Ulysses Grant when he visited Fort Jesup, as he did at least once before the end of July. Not only had he selected that branch of service as his first choice when he graduated from the Academy, he had unsuccessfully applied for a dragoon appointment in November of 1843. Luckier were Rufus Ingalls and three other members of Grant's West Point class who, assigned to Twiggs's command as riflemen, were miraculously transformed into dragoons in the spring of 1844 by governmental decree.[32] Ingalls, a lively card-playing gambler, would recall that Grant amused friends at the fort by trotting in from Camp Salubrity on a small pony, a mount contrasting ludicrously with the big brutes Grant customarily rode in daredevil displays of horsemanship at the Point.[33] To Ingalls, the dragoons at Jesup were "splendid fellows" who enjoyed "high old times" when Twiggs wasn't around. As for Grant, he got along well with all of the Fourth Infantry officers except Captain Robert Buchanan. At Jefferson Barracks, Buchanan had censured Grant once too often for being late to evening mess. The sensitive young lieutenant had retorted sharply, and the rupture had not healed.[34]

On July 18 Grant was transferred to another company in his regiment, from one commanded by Lieutenant Benjamin Alvord, a future Union brigadier, to Captain Charles H. Larnard's Company A. Inasmuch as Larnard was on leave, and one of his lieutenants was serving as the regiment's adjutant, the only officers with A were Grant and Lieutenant Robert M. Cochran. That was still the situation in August of 1844 when, in response to orders from Taylor, their company was chosen to repair bridges and ruts on a portion of the road leading from Grand Ecore to Fort Jesup. And when the company's four sergeants, three corporals, twenty-eight privates, and one fifer, shouldering heavy knapsacks, slogged from Salubrity through a pouring rain on August 13 to an unsheltered campsite some five miles distant, Grant marched with them (though not weighed down by a knapsack). From Camp Necessity, as their base of operations on the Old Texas Road was called, he wrote Julia at the end of August: "The first night we had to lay our wet beds on the still damper ground and to make out the best we could—Musketoes and Wood ticks by the hundred pestered us—On the whole I spent a few miserable nights and not much better days at the begining [*sic*] of my first experience at campaigning, but now I find it much better—We will probably be through and return to Camp Salubrity in ten more days."[35] As he predicted, Company A returned to Salubrity on September 10, just as Old Zach was completing a review of all of his corps of observation troops. In making his first comprehensive report on conditions in the corps, Taylor mentioned that the Grand Ecore road had been repaired.[36] He disliked using troops for such purposes, but since infantry officers were often required to oversee construction projects, as Taylor himself had been on numerous occasions, Grant's "first experience at campaigning" was a potentially useful lesson.[37]

Until October no new orders were issued affecting the corps of observation as a whole, but there were a number pertaining to personnel matters. Lieutenant James Longstreet and his future father-in-law, Lieutenant Colonel John Garland, were granted leaves of absence, probably to enable them to attend the wedding of Garland's daughter Elizabeth to Lieutenant George Deas. On September 5 Longstreet's classmate Richard Herron Anderson reached Fort Jesup, having been transferred from the First Dragoons upon being promoted from brevet to full second lieutenant. A few days later, Lieutenant Israel Bush Richardson of Vermont (Third Infantry) obtained a leave of several months. At the end of September, Captain Lloyd J. Beall was dropped from the roster of the Second Dragoons due to his appointment as a major in the Pay Department. And on October 10 Brevet Second Lieutenant Alexander Hays of Pennsylvania finally joined the Fourth Infantry after overstaying his customary three-month leave following graduation from the Point earlier that year.[38]

The arrival of Lieutenant Hays at Camp Salubrity coincided with the receipt by General Taylor of a confidential communication from the War Department which indicated his troops might be ordered into Texas at any moment. He was told to prepare "the great part of the forces" under his command for any movement stipulated by the American chargé d'affaires in Texas, Andrew

Jackson Donelson, "in order to restrain any hostile incursions on the part of the border Indians, as required by the provisions of existing treaties."[39] When General Taylor showed Ethan Allen Hitchcock that confidential letter, the colonel was incensed. To Hitchcock these instructions were proof that President Tyler intended to embroil the country in a war with Mexico in order to expand the number, and thus the power, of the southern states, and thereby facilitate secession. General Taylor tended to agree, but orders were orders. Hitchcock noted in his diary on October 15 that preparations for a march were proceeding, although he was "hutting" his regiment in case it remained at Camp Wilkins all winter. Evidently Colonel Vose followed suit, since Grant wrote Julia somewhat later: "You ought to be here a short time to see how we all live in our winter houses. They are built by puting [*sic*] posts in the ground as if for a fence and nailing up the outside with shingles. . . . The chimneys are of mud and sticks and generally are completed by puting a barrel or two on top to make them high enough." Grant had assumed command of Company A in late October, when the only other officer on active duty with his company, Lieutenant Cochran, was placed in arrest. At Jefferson Barracks, Grant had been in charge of a company for about a month. This time he would have a four-month course in the responsibilities of a captain in a field situation. Official records document some of his administrative preoccupations, such as transmitting ordnance and clothing reports, and signing muster rolls.[40]

News of the election of James Knox Polk, the Democratic candidate for the office of president of the United States who had boldly advocated the annexation of Texas during his political campaign, reached Fort Jesup in late November. Hitchcock's reaction was, as might have been expected: "I look upon this as a step towards the annexation of Texas first, and then, in due time, the separation of the Union." Although Grant's views were similar, he was enjoying life too much to brood very long over political developments. On the first of December he blithely wrote Bob Hazlitt, his closest Fourth Infantry friend who had been absent on sick leave for two months, that there was talk of going to "Corpus [Christi] or San Antonio," adding, "There were five days' races at Natchitoches. I was there every day and bet low, generally lost. Jarvis and a number from Jessup [*sic*] were there. Jarvis was pretty high and tried to be smart all the time. . . . The game of brag is kept up as lively as ever. I continued to play some after you left and won considerable, but for some time back I have not played and probably will never play again—no resolution, though." Intoxication, which doubtless accounted for Charles Jarvis's being "high" on the occasions mentioned by Grant, had long been a problem for army commanders, and overindulgence in alcohol by men of all ranks would be an extremely serious problem in Taylor's army.[41] As for Grant, his intimation that he was cutting down on gambling probably had something to do with his engagement—

perhaps an intention to start saving a bit, or a desire not to appear dissolute in Julia's eyes. On the other hand, he may have been feeling a twinge of guilt, well knowing that gambling and drinking were prohibited at West Point, and that throughout much of society they were regarded as character flaws.

The war clouds were too intermittent and hazy that winter to affect the lives of Taylor's officers to any great extent. They attended parties given by planters on the Red River "coast" and visited friends in other regiments. On New Year's Day, Hitchcock rode, played operatic selections on his flute, read one of the philosophical treatises that were his passion, and counted his books, finding that they numbered 761 not including over 60 bound volumes of music, sheet music enough for 20 more volumes, magazines, pamphlets, and tracts. His officers paid social calls, attended a horse race, and watched a gander-pulling, that "barbarous amusement," as Hitchcock aptly called it, of trying to pull off the head of a greased goose while riding swiftly past it as it hung upside down on a tall pole. General Taylor, who had departed on December 27 to inspect troops elsewhere in Louisiana, probably celebrated New Year's in Baton Rouge, where his wife and their youngest daughter were residing.[42]

In mid-January, Colonel Twiggs learned the immensely welcome news that as of the first of the year his men were to receive the dragoon rates of pay even though they were not yet mounted. That campaign having been won (although he continued to argue that the increase in pay should be made retroactive to the regiment's official date of return to dragoon status the previous April), Twiggs concentrated on securing the promised horses as well as related accoutrements. He wrote the adjutant general on January 13 prophesizing dire consequences if Lieutenant William Steele and the other dragoons he had sent to Missouri to obtain horses should be forced to march from the mouth of the Ohio River northward some 150 miles to Jefferson Barracks due to there being ice on the Mississippi River, as he had heard. Fortunately the dragoon detachment led by Steele (a twenty-five-year-old New Yorker who would command Confederate troops) had already reached Jefferson Barracks without difficulty. Two months later Twiggs reported to the adjutant general that 143 horses had arrived from Missouri in charge of "citizens," but that there was "not a Halter, Saddle, Bridle, Currycomb, or brush at the post."[43]

President Tyler had essentially achieved his annexation goal before leaving office on March 4. By February 28 the Senate and House of Representatives had adopted a joint resolution containing terms under which Congress was willing to admit Texas into the Union, and on March 1 President Tyler signed the document. With regard to slavery, permitted in the Republic of Texas, the resolution was mute except for one proviso: with the consent of Texas, several states could be formed out of its territory, but slavery would be prohibited in any new state formed north of the Missouri Compromise line. To secure approval of the resolution by a majority of the Senate, a passage was added which authorized the president to decide whether the conditions stipulated in the joint resolution should be offered to Texas or whether, alternatively, a new treaty should be negotiated. Senator Thomas Hart Benton of Missouri, an influential Democrat, was adamantly insistent on the treaty course of action, as were many congressmen of both parties. Benton's adherents apparently assumed that the decision would be Polk's, and that he would have a new treaty prepared, but they underestimated President Tyler. On his last day in office, after consulting Polk, Tyler arranged for the terms set forth in the congressional resolution to be submitted to Texas.[44]

President Polk and his cabinet adopted Tyler's policy, making the next question whether Texas would accept the terms offered by the United States. Although Texans had previously sought annexation, they now seemed on the verge of rejecting the Tyler-Polk initiative at the urging of Great Britain. Sam Houston's successor in 1844, President Anson Jones, liked the English plan, which was that Mexico should sanction Texas's independence and then the Lone Star Republic, with her southwestern border secure, should reject annexation and act as a buffer between the United States and Mexico.[45]

While the Texans were debating the annexation issue, General Taylor's army for the most part waited in limbo, but exiting from it were Grant's friends Longstreet and Ingalls, both having been transferred by an order dated March 31 following their promotion to the rank of second lieutenant. Longstreet reported to the Eighth Infantry at Fort Marion, Florida, on the edge of St. Augustine, where he was sick for more than a month; Ingalls, joining the First Dragoons at their Fort Leavenworth headquarters, must have felt like an orphan, for all of the regiment's companies were absent, widely scattered at western camps and forts.[46]

Grant was also turning his back on Louisiana that spring, though only temporarily. He had finally received a leave of absence, and on the first of April was off to see Julia. His one nagging worry was that her father had not yet consented to their union, a concern that accompanied him back to Salubrity in early May. With uncharacteristic temerity Grant had found a moment to ask Julia's father, who was on the verge of departing for Washington on family business, for permission to marry her. He understood the answer to be equivocal—her father would respond by mail. After that brief interval in Missouri, Grant waited anxiously for "Colonel" Dent's promised answer, hearing nothing except hints from Julia that their engagement had still not been approved by her parents. In other ways his courtship by mail continued much as before. "I shall always look back to my short visit . . . as the most pleasant part of my life," he wrote her on May 6, the day he rejoined his regiment. In his absence, Grant realized, Taylor's troops had begun to sense that a move of some sort was not far off. "The officers are all collected in little parties discussing the affairs of the nation," he informed her. "Annexation of Texas, war with Mexico, occupation of Orregon [*sic*] and difficulties with England are the general topics. Some of them expect and seem to contemplate with a great deal of pleasure some difficulty where they may be able to gain laurels and *advance a little in rank*."[47] With James Knox Polk having donned the mantle of the presidency on March 4, it was only to be expected that the government would already be adopting measures designed to accomplish the basic goals that had defined the "Young Hickory" campaign, not the least of which was the annexation of Texas.

While Grant was on leave in Missouri the corps of observation had additional units attached to it—the two companies of the Third Infantry that had been stationed at Fort Leavenworth. They reported to Camp Wilkins for duty on April 24. With these reinforcements were Lieutenants Bushrod Johnson and William T. H. Brooks. The Fourth Infantry's two companies at Fort Scott were left in place until August.[48] By late April Colonel Twiggs had received 260 complete sets of horse equipment in addition to the 143 horses purchased in Missouri, but he let the adjutant general know that no horses had been delivered to his three companies at Fort Washita, nor any items of equipment. In May he wrote that it was impossible to enlist farriers in New Orleans and requested seven to be sent from the general recruiting service. On June 12 he complained to the adjutant general that although 260 sets of equipage had been delivered, 425 sets were required. Within another two days he listed in detail what his troops at Jesup needed: "2 saddles, 2 Bridles, 2 Valises, 2 carbine sockets & straps, 2 holsters, 172 nose bags, 172 pairs of spurs & straps, 172 curry combs, 172 Horse brushes, 172 Mane combs and 157 horses."[49]

General Taylor, who took leave again in May, knew by June that in all probability it would not be long before at least some of his troops at Jesup and Salubrity would be ordered to Texas. President Anson Jones of Texas had called a special session of the republic's congress, and had arranged for a national convention to meet on July 4 at Austin to consider the annexation issue. In anticipation of a favorable outcome with both of these bodies, President Polk's secretary of war, William Marcy, had written General Taylor on May 28: "So soon as the Texas Congress shall have given its consent to annexation, and a convention shall assemble and accept the terms offered in the resolution of Congress, Texas will then be regarded by the executive government here so far a part of the United States as to be entitled, from this government, to defense and protection from a foreign invasion and Indian incursions. The troops under your command will be placed and kept in readiness to perform that duty." Taylor had already asked to be provided with enough medical supplies and surgical instruments to stock five or six posts in Texas, and now, after dispatching a copy of his latest instructions to Anson Jones, he took a hand in preparing the dragoons for a possible overland march. On June 18 he wrote the adjutant general that "150 horses are yet wanted to complete the mounting of the 2nd Dragoons"; that more than 80 mules would be needed and none had been received; and that he had ordered the immediate return from Jefferson Barracks of the detachment of Second Dragoons which had been sent from Jesup in December to facilitate the purchase and delivery of horses.[50]

The officers at Jesup and Salubrity could of course read the signs that something was about to happen, although they evidently did not suspect that all of the troops assembled between the Red and Sabine rivers would be posted to Texas. Grant wrote Julia toward the middle of June: "The Texan Congress has already met and it is thought will soon accede to our terms of Annexation and then in we go without delay, that is, some of the troops from these parts will. The 4th [Infantry] is hardly considered as one bound for Texas unless in case of difficulty with Mexico."[51] Finally, late on the evening of June 29, General Taylor received a message from Washington telling him the Texas convention would probably agree on July 4 to annexation, and that he should move the troops under his immediate command to some American port of his choosing preparatory to executing the rest of his orders—to occupy a healthful position on or near the Rio Grande best suited to repel invasion as soon as he heard the Texas convention had accepted the annexation terms. The next morning General Taylor put the Third and Fourth Infantry regiments under orders for transport to New Orleans. The Second Dragoons were to ride across the Texas border and rendezvous with the infantry at the miniscule Corpus Christi trading post, located on the Gulf of Mexico at the mouth of the Nueces River.[52]

The eight companies of the Fourth Infantry led the way this time, embarking at Grand Ecore on July 3 and landing at New Orleans Barracks, a few miles below the city, two days later. As the Fourth Infantry started down the Red River, the rest of the men in Taylor's army were engaging in ceremonies marking the death of Andrew Jackson, news of whose demise on the evening of June 8 had just been received. The flag was flown at half-staff, guns were fired every half hour, the troops were assembled to hear the official announcement, and the officers were ordered to wear crepe on their left arms and on their swords for six months. Then on July 7 the Third Infantry troops marched out of Jesup at reveille. They boarded two steamboats at Grand Ecore the next day, arrived in New Orleans two days later, and were quartered in the Lower Cotton Press.[53]

General Taylor remained at Jesup until July 9, making arrangements for the dragoons' march and issuing orders for the care of troops who were too sick to accompany their regiments as well as for the public property at the post. He had decided, consonant with advice from Texas, that he would probably initially station his forces close to the mouth of the Nueces River, at or near the Corpus Christi settlement, which happened to be located on the river's southern bank. Mexico having never recognized the independence of Texas, no boundary had been established between those nations, but for a variety of reasons possession of the largely unoccupied region from the Nueces River south to the Rio Grande was particularly in dispute. It would be suggested later that Taylor, by concentrating his army below the mouth of the Nueces, on the beach fronting Corpus Christi, was deliberately making a statement in support of the Texas claim that the Lone Star Republic's southernmost boundary was not the Nueces but the Rio Grande. However, judging by his correspondence with officials in Texas and with the adjutant general, Old Zach based that decision solely on military considerations. The secretary of war of Texas had written Taylor on June 27 that his congress, upon unanimously adopting the American annexation resolution, had voted in favor of inviting "occupation by the United States with such troops as may be necessary" for the defense of Texas; that Austin, San Antonio de Bexar (as the settlement was then called), and Corpus Christi required protection; and that vessels drawing eight feet could "enter the bay of Corpus Christi, and approach within twelve miles of the Village." In an accompanying letter from the American chargé Andrew Jackson Donelson, Taylor was told: "Corpus Christi is said to be as healthy as Pensacola, a convenient place for supplies, and is the most western point now occupied by Texas." In forwarding those messages to Adjutant General Jones on July 8, Taylor summed up his tentative plan of action: Based on the recommendation of both the U.S. chargé and the president of Texas, "unless otherwise ordered" he would concentrate his force "at or near Corpus Christi until the disposition of Mexico" became known, which would keep "all the Corps" close enough together to cooperate in case of "any emergency." Later, if relations with Mexico were "pacific," part of the force could "then be extended towards San Antonio." Leaving Twiggs in command at Jesup with instructions to wait for word of the action anticipated by the Austin popular convention before starting his troopers on their journey through northeastern Texas, Taylor departed for New Orleans on July 9. He thought the dragoons had made remarkable progress in training the horses they had already received, and that other horses were near at hand and would probably arrive in time to accompany Twiggs's column, which was to include at least fifty mule-drawn wagons.[54]

The Fourth Infantry cadre, billeted at New Orleans Barracks, did not at first know their exact destination. Grant wrote Julia: "Our orders are for the Western borders of Texas but how far up the Rio Grand [*sic*] is hard to tell." He did not think he would be in Texas very long. "I am perfectly rejoiced at the idea of going there myself," he told Julia, "for the reason that in the course of five or six months I expect to be promoted and there are seven chances out of eight that I will not be promoted in the 4th [Infantry] so that at the end of that time I shall hope to be back to the U.States unless of course there should be active service there to detain me and to take many others there." His "seven chances out of eight" remark, a reference to there being eight infantry regiments in the nation's regular armed forces at that time, indicates that in early July he believed only one regiment would be sent to Texas, and did not think that "active service" against Mexico was likely.[55] He had also decided that soldiering was "a very pleasant occupation generally," perhaps influenced by his being in charge of Company A. Not only had he supervised preparations for the shipment of his men to New Orleans, but the move downriver had landed his regiment in the lap of luxury, however briefly. As another officer on his way to Texas that September wrote of New Orleans Barracks, "This is by far the most beautiful [post] I have ever seen. The quarters are fine and airy, completely protected from the sun by beautiful tropical shade trees, with extensive yards and gardens about them." Grant's comments were similar: "From what I have seen N. Orleans Barracks is the most pleasant place I have ever been stationed at. . . . The place is much more handsomely fixed than Jeff. Bks." That the yellow fever scourge caused summers in New Orleans to be known as the "sickly season" evidently did not alarm him.[56]

Grant relinquished command of Company A to its captain, Charles H. Larnard, on July 8. A week later the Fourth Infantry lost its beloved colonel. Vose had been drilling the regiment, something Grant had never seen before. The old gentleman left the field before the troops were dismissed, walked a few yards, suffered a seizure as he reached the porch of his quarters, and died. Grant would write admiringly of the first regimental commander under whom he served that Vose was "not a man to discover infirmity in the presence of danger," that he was "a most estimable man, of exemplary habits, and by no means the author of his disease."[57] Unfortunately, with respect to "exemplary habits" Grant would fall short of Vose's example.

The following evening Grant had a comic opera experience. Returning from the city around midnight after informing the newspapers of plans for the colonel's funeral, he saw a couple who seemed to be eloping, and thought he recognized them. Knowing the woman to be married, he galloped to the barracks, confirmed his suspicions, and was ordered to apprehend the absconding pair. With the help of city watchmen he arrested the man and, as he described the denouement to Julia, "brought the *lady* back behind me on my horse to her husband, who she had left asleep and ignorant [*sic*] of her absence."[58]

The day Colonel Vose died, July 15, Zachary Taylor reached New Orleans. Four days later Company E of the Third Artillery regiment, commanded by West Point graduate (1937) Lieutenant Braxton Bragg of North Carolina, arrived at New Orleans Barracks by water from Fort Moultrie, South Carolina, to strengthen Old Zach's army. The battery's other first lieutenant, George H. Thomas of Virginia (West Point, 1840), was with Bragg, as was Brevet Second Lieutenant Daniel Harvey Hill of South Carolina (West Point, 1842). Another of Bragg's officers, Second Lieutenant John F. Reynolds (West Point, 1841), who had been on leave in his home state of Pennsylvania, rejoined Company E that same day. (Their captain, John Addison Thomas of Tennessee, had for some time been assigned to duty at West Point).[59]

John Reynolds, twenty-five years old, the only northerner in that remarkable quartet of future generals, was a rugged, amiable, witty, six-foot bachelor who enjoyed army life—especially the opportunities it offered for hunting, fishing, and horseback riding—but whose heart was in the environs of Lancaster, Pennsylvania, where his widowed father, several of his eight surviving siblings, and other members of the prominent Reynolds clan resided, and where John would be buried after the battle of Gettysburg. His friend George Thomas, also a six-footer, was a very private, laconic person noted for always being cool and collected, never demonstrative. In Florida in 1841 Thomas was promoted to brevet first lieutenant for assisting in the capture of a band of some fifty belligerent Seminoles, and within three years he had attained the rank of full-fledged first lieutenant. More sociable was the newest member of the battery, twenty-four-year-old Daniel Harvey Hill, usually called Harvey by friends. While he tried to keep his slender frame rigidly erect, in his youth he had developed a painful, chronic spinal problem from which he would never recover; however, as the last of his parents' eleven children Harvey had nevertheless helped on the family farm following the death of his father when he was four. It was a devoutly Presbyterian home, and Harvey guided his life by the precepts of that faith, his flinty blue eyes alert to the failings of associates. When it came to someone like his classmate George Sykes of Maryland, a man of "honor, courage and frankness" who would become a Union major general of volunteers, Hill was generous in his praise, but when he thought army affairs were not being conducted properly he wrote castigating articles which, if they had borne his name when published, could have resulted in his being cashiered.

One of the men that Hill, Reynolds, and Thomas respected most, at least in 1845, was the acting commander of their battery, Lieutenant Braxton Bragg, who would become far more celebrated during the war with Mexico than his subalterns. Fifth in his class of fifty at West Point, Bragg was appointed upon graduation as a second lieutenant in the Third Artillery, and within a year had risen to the rank of first lieutenant. However, that was seven years ago. By 1845 his caustic, irascible personality had made him a controversial figure in army circles. Recently he had engaged in a bitter quarrel with the acting commander of his regiment, Lieutenant Colonel William Gates, over housing assignments at Fort Moultrie. Bragg's appearance—his tall, thin frame dominated by piercing dark eyes under bushy brows—was as daunting as his temper. Still, many artillery officers were devoted to him, and his brilliance, tenacity, and dedication to his profession during the Mexican War were undeniable. He was twenty-eight that summer of 1845. At age thirty he would be a national hero, with more than a little bit of help from General Taylor.[60]

Bragg must have been surprised to find Old Zach and the Third and Fourth Infantry companies in New Orleans. When his orders of June 18 were issued, the War Department was under the impression Taylor would depart for Texas from some port near the mouth of the Sabine River; thus Bragg's instructions read: "A battery of two pieces [cannon] and two howitzers, fully equipped for service, (with horses,) and supplied with its necessary ammunition, has been ordered to New Orleans Barracks for your company. You will take charge of it immediately on your arrival at the barracks, and then proceed as expeditiously as possible to join the brigade ordered to the Gulf of Mexico near the mouth of the Sabine, under the command of Brig. General Taylor, to whom you will report."[61] Taylor, on the other hand, had been informed that a Third Artillery company at Fort Moultrie had been ordered to pick up a field battery at New Orleans and thereafter join him, though neither the company nor its commander was specified. In that document the adjutant general, as in Bragg's orders, described the ordnance to be provided at New Orleans as "a field battery of two pieces and two howitzers, equipped for service with horses," adding that the procurement of such horses "as may be required for the company" was being left to Taylor, to avoid delay.[62] The wording of those two documents laid the foundation for Bragg's forthcoming celebrity. By signifying that his company was to receive two light field guns and two howitzers to be drawn by horses, the War Department appeared to have approved it for service as a "light" field battery, the type of relatively rare artillery unit whose dramatic mobility and effectiveness would elicit fulsome praise in both official and newspaper reports during Taylor's campaign; but a few months later the adjutant general took issue with that perception of the company's status when a question arose over whether it was entitled to additional allowances, ruling that Company E could not be "legally regarded" as "Light artillery" inasmuch as an 1821 law provided that "*one* company of each [Artillery] Regiment" should be so designated and equipped, and for the Third Artillery the company thus designated was C (Brevet Major Samuel Ringgold's). Fortunately for Bragg and his officers, Company E, which began training as light artillery on the beach below Corpus Christi as soon as field guns and horses were available, was allowed to continue functioning in that capacity by General Taylor despite the adjutant general's decree that E was a "foot artillery" unit.[63]

When Bragg's company landed at New Orleans on July 19 he probably learned immediately that Taylor was there and promptly contacted him, while Thomas, Reynolds, and Hill, each of whom had a classmate or two in the infantry companies in Taylor's command, no doubt looked up acquaintances. Most of the senior infantry officers were presumably occupied seeking needed supplies from the quartermaster, ordnance, and commissary departments, but Bragg could do little along those lines since the ordnance he had been promised was nowhere to be found. Ethan Allen Hitchcock would claim, once they were on the beach at Corpus Christi, that he had been the only commanding officer sufficiently farsighted in accumulating supplies from government depots during their New Orleans hiatus: "No horse can be shod, no bridle rein mended, no tent-pole made or repaired, no rope had, but from me."[64]

General Taylor, after hearing from Andrew Jackson Donelson that the Texas popular convention had unanimously consented to the U.S. Congress's annexation resolution, left New Orleans aboard the steamer *Alabama* on July 23. With him, in addition to members of his staff, were Hitchcock and eight companies of the Third Infantry among whom were future generals Don Carlos Buell and Israel Richardson. (Thomas Jordan, whose Third Infantry company was on the *Alabama,* was on leave.) The next day the sailing vessels *Suviah* and *Queen Victoria* followed, escorted by the U.S. sloop of war *St. Mary's.* On the *Suviah* were Ulysses Grant and the other officers and men of the Fourth Infantry's Companies A, G, H, and K; on the *Queen Victoria* were Bragg, Thomas, Reynolds, Hill, and their artillerymen, together with the Fourth Infantry Companies B, E, F, and I, whose ranks included Alexander Hays and a sick Robert Buchanan. Bringing up the rear on July 26 was the steamer *Monmouth,* which stopped at Galveston before proceeding on to Corpus Christi. On the *Monmouth* were the Third Infantry's other two companies—B, to which George Sykes belonged, and I, to which Bushrod Johnson and William T. H. Brooks were assigned. Those were the units, consisting of about 850 troops altogether, with which General Taylor initially formed his line of defense at Corpus Christi.[65]

2
Taylor's Army of Occupation at Corpus Christi

Exactly where General Taylor's camp would be established had not been decided when the *Alabama* dropped anchor near Aransas Pass, a few miles north of Corpus Christi Bay, on the evening of July 25. The next day Hitchcock began landing Third Infantry companies on St. Joseph's Island, one of a necklace of long, narrow sandy formations hugging the concave bend of the Texas mainland all the way from Galveston to the mouth of the Rio Grande. Taylor, in writing the adjutant general two days later, mentioned he was awaiting the report of a boat expedition before selecting a location.[1]

Before the main body of the troops on board the *Alabama* disembarked, Hitchcock sent Lieutenant Daniel T. Chandler ashore to plant a small United States flag on St. Joseph's Island. Hitchcock believed that Chandler was the bearer of "the first stars and stripes ever raised in Texas by authority," having no way of knowing that Twiggs and his column of Second Dragoons had finally begun their southwestward trek on July 25 and may have borne the flag onto Texas soil before Chandler reached the island's verge.[2] Until early August, when the *Suviah* and the *Queen Victoria* arrived, the Army of Occupation, as Taylor's command was now termed, consisted in effect solely of the eight companies of the Third Infantry that camped initially on St. Joseph's Island, a total of about 350 soldiers. They were landed in a manner that became standard operating procedure for the several thousand troops whose transports would anchor near Aransas Pass within the next three months. The soldiers, along with the servants of officers and the "camp women" (as laundresses and wives of enlisted men were often called), were lowered at sea from deep-draft vessels to smaller ships, and when close to St. Joseph's Island they waded ashore, some of the soldiers carrying women on their backs. By July 28 the tents of Hitchcock's regiment stretched three miles along the island's sandhills. The troops found fresh water, caught an abundance of fish, and shot ducks and deer at will.[3]

General Taylor's chief impediment for several weeks was the difficulty of moving companies and supplies some twenty-five miles down Aransas Bay and Corpus Christi Bay to the mainland beach finally chosen by him for the army's camp, on the southern bank of the Nueces River. The problem became all too clear when Taylor and Hitchcock, with two companies of the Third Infantry, attempted to reach Corpus Christi from St. Joseph's Island aboard a steamer on July 29. About five miles down the bay it ran aground in the shallow passage. Other than a few infantrymen who managed to reach the mainland on a raft, for two days and nights Old Zach and the troops with him were held captive by the shoals. At last Taylor ordered his quartermaster to hire local fishing boats hovering near the spectacle. Hitchcock and his cadre were safely transferred to those vessels, and in that manner a contingent of the Third Infantry finally reached the selected site. Taylor, returning to Aransas Pass, waited until the middle of August before moving his headquarters to the "Camp near Corpus Christi."[4]

The *Suviah* and the *Queen Victoria* dropped anchor at Aransas Pass on the second of August. Within another two days the *Monmouth* was offshore. All of the newly arrived infantrymen and artillerymen, other than a few detained on St. Joseph's Island to assist the quartermaster in establishing a depot there, were shipped gradually, in small detachments, to the Corpus Christi base. Company A of the Fourth Infantry, to which Grant was still assigned, disembarked at St. Joseph's Island on August 3 and reached the encampment on the beach below Corpus Christi six days later. However, Grant's career nearly ended at Aransas Pass. Having had occasion to reboard the *Suviah,* still several miles out at sea, he encountered a disturbance which the captain of the ship insisted constituted a mutiny. Although Grant suspected that the incident was blown out of proportion by the captain, he dutifully put the accused, unresisting sailors in irons and then attempted to lower himself, unaided, off the ship to the "lighter" steamer alongside. Mistaking the way the pulleys worked, he fell twenty-five feet headlong into the ocean. According to Grant, when he was drawn up from the bay in a bucket, unhurt, onlookers laughed instead of sympathizing, and he "rather enjoyed the joke" himself.[5]

For almost two weeks after August 15, the day on which Taylor moved his headquarters to the burgeoning camp adjacent to Corpus Christi, the total number of officers on duty with units assigned to the Army of Occupation was less than forty-five, the rest being for the most part on leave, or on detached service, or en route to Aransas Pass. Under those circumstances Taylor probably kept a closer eye than usual on the company-grade officers in his command. At any rate, while the approach to the Corpus Christi harbor was being deepened by soldiers, the general was particularly impressed by Ulysses Grant on one occasion, or so Lieutenant Lafayette McLaws, a future Confederate major general, recalled having been told by the general himself: "Lieut. Grant was in charge of a party of men detailed to clear the way for the advance of boats laden with troops from Aransas Bay to Corpus Christi by removing the oyster beds and other obstructions. Failing either by words or signs to make those under him understand him, Lieut. Grant jumped into the water, which was up to his waist, and worked with his men." That caused Old Zach, happening by, to wish he "had more officers like Grant, who would stand ready to set a personal example when needed."[6]

A few Texas troops called Rangers were stationed on the upper edge of the ranch that hosted the Corpus Christi trading post, on a rise covered with mesquite and thickets of prickly chaparral overlooking the expanding line of army tents south of the bay into which the Nueces River emptied. Between the Rangers and General Taylor there was apparently little collaboration at that time, perhaps because Texas would not be annexed formally until the Congress of the United States admitted it to statehood in December. The person upon whom Taylor principally depended for information and assistance was "Colonel" Henry L. Kinney, the proprietor of the trading post around which, by fall, twenty or thirty thatch-roofed buildings were grouped. Until entrepreneurs began arriving in the wake of the army, most of the inhabitants of the Corpus Christi hamlet, many of them friendly Mexicans, were evidently associated with Kinney in some manner. A lieutenant wrote that Kinney "was forced to keep a regular company of men, at his expense to defend his 'ranch.'" Hitchcock said of Kinney, "He lives by smuggling goods across the line,"[7] meaning the ephemeral border between Mexico and Texas.

The smuggling operations obviously fascinated Taylor's officers. Hitchcock noted toward the end of August: "Some Mexican traders have come from the Rio Grande, to sell their goods and buy tobacco, etc. They bring their money in silver bars, moulded in sand, each embracing $50 to $60, of pure silver. Exchanged by weight." Ulysses Grant reported in his memoirs that smuggling was profitable largely because tobacco, a government monopoly in Mexico, was both extremely expensive there and constantly smoked in the form of hand-rolled cigarettes by everyone, male and female, "above the age of ten years, and many much younger." Lieutenant George Gordon Meade of the Corps of Topographical Engineers wrote his wife in October, a month after joining Taylor at Corpus Christi: "The Mexicans from the frontier, who come in great numbers to trade, bring with them the most exquisite fabrics, which they call blankets, all made by hand by the females, and of the most beautiful patterns and colors. I have been tempted to get a couple for you, as they would make beautiful piano or table covers; but their cost, varying from ten to fifty dollars, according to the workmanship and variety of colors, has prevented me."[8]

In August Taylor borrowed some old cannon from Kinney after receiving New Orleans newspapers with articles proclaiming, erroneously as it turned out, that Mexico was preparing to issue a declaration of war. That rumor was supported by information from the Rio Grande provided by Kinney's favorite spy, Chapita, a Mexican "in the prime of life" with "muscles like whipcords" (who would, months later, accompany the American dragoons involved in the ambush marking the war's commencement). Chapita had heard that a Mexican general was moving toward Matamoros, on the western shore of the Rio Grande about 150 miles south of Corpus Christi, with 1,500 troops, a third of them cavalry. Taylor had as yet no cavalry with him, no artillery of consequence (Bragg's battery not having received its equipment), and only a few hundred infantrymen with which to counter a Mexican assault. That situation did not change until the seven companies of the Second Dragoons arrived.[9]

Colonel Twiggs had ridden out of Fort Jesup on July 25 accompanied by the dragoon companies stationed there and a fifty-wagon train with provisions for forty-five days. Before leaving he had notified both General Winfield Scott and Adjutant General Jones of his intention to proceed to San Antonio by easy marches of not more than twenty miles a day. While acknowledging that General Taylor had told him to proceed directly to Corpus Christi, he explained he had decided, based on information he had received from Polk's representative in Texas, Andrew Jackson Donelson, to go to San Antonio and there await further orders unless instructed otherwise while en route. Twiggs, a Democrat, probably reasoned he could not go wrong by following the advice of Donelson, a devoted supporter of the president. Nevertheless, he carefully justified his course of action in his letter to Scott by pointing out that San Antonio was centrally located and its protection of paramount importance.[10]

A sketch of the dragoons' route drawn by one of the regiment's officers, Lieutenant George Stevens, shows that they first marched from Fort Jesup past the village of Many, Louisiana, crossed the Sabine River into Texas the next day, and reached Nacogdoches four days later. On the second of August they forded the Angelina River, and the following day the Neches River, camping at Crockett on August 4. They crossed the Trinity River at Robins's Ferry on the fifth, after which they rode through Bedias and arrived at Washington-on-the-Brazos by August 8. Three days later they passed through Rutersville, and by the twelfth of the month were on the right bank of the Colorado River. They rested there, not resuming their march until the sixteenth. Whether Twiggs received fresh instructions during that interval is unclear, but instead of proceeding to San Antonio he and his dragoons turned southward, following the Lavaca River for some distance, swinging westward through Victoria, crossing the Guadalupe River, and on the twentieth the San Antonio River at Goliad, the village that would forever be associated with the execution of more than three hundred Texas prisoners by the Mexicans in 1836. They reached the Aransas River in two days, and were nearing San Patricio, a deserted site on the northern bank of the Nueces River about thirty miles from Corpus Christi, when they made camp on the twenty-third.[11]

General Taylor, having been informed that the dragoons had almost reached San Patricio, started toward that former settlement on August 23 to meet Twiggs, expecting to cover the distance in a single day. The fact that Old Zach and his escort were led astray by their guide and forced to sleep in the open that night illustrates how little was known about the unpopulated sectors of the territory claimed by Texas. Taylor finally found the dragoons a mile or so below San Patricio on the twenty-fourth. They were rushing to his defense, having mistaken that morning's violent thunderstorm over Corpus Christi for artillery fire.[12]

Leaving the reassured Twiggs to bring up his wagons before commencing the last leg of his monthlong trek, Taylor returned to Corpus Christi. He had originally planned to station the dragoons at San Patricio, and indeed had also at some point contemplated moving his headquarters there. In hindsight, that could have been advantageous. Although the various units would apparently have had no convenient open area in which to drill, as they had on the beach below Corpus Christi, there would have been a good source of potable water, wood for fires, and presumably less access to drinking and gambling establishments. Also, critics would have had no reason to claim that Taylor, by establishing his base south of the Nueces River, long deemed by many to be the lawful boundary between Mexico and the Republic of Texas, was making a political statement. Perhaps the deciding factor was that, as Hitchcock pointed out, a location so far inland from the army's supply depot on St. Joseph's Island could conceivably have allowed a hostile force to cut the Americans off from access to that vital lifeline. However, if Taylor was thinking of basing all or a portion of his army at San Patricio when he rode up the Nueces, he had abandoned that thought before concluding his rendezvous with Twiggs, for on the twenty-seventh the dragoons were erecting their tents on the beach below Corpus Christi, after being greeted on the village's outskirts by Old Zach, Hitchcock, and several members of the general's staff. Hitchcock learned that Twiggs had not been well on the long march; that there had been four deaths along the way, three from natural causes, one resulting from an accident; and that around three dozen men had deserted. One horse had drowned, but the others were in excellent condition except for sore backs occasioned by the new saddles.[13]

Twiggs and Hitchcock probably exchanged condolences; Hitchcock had suffered from diarrhea almost constantly since landing at Corpus Christi. Later, volunteer units that joined Taylor would be decimated by countless health problems, usually attributed to poor sanitation practices; but the regular army officers and men likewise experienced painful and debilitating spells of illnesses, albeit generally less virulent than those of the volunteers. At Corpus Christi the chief causes were reportedly inadequate tents, scarce firewood, and brackish drinking water. (The water that Taylor's troops were forced to drink most of the time was obtained by capturing it in barrel-enclosed holes dug in the sand surrounding their campgrounds.) A surgeon with Taylor's army at Corpus Christi, Dr. John B. Porter, also included variable temperature in his list of causes, adding that attention given to privies was "necessarily bad" in a "whole army of diarrhea-patients, with camp followers." Taylor has been accused by one eminent twentieth-century historian of being "slow to recognize that the conditions under which the army found itself were detrimental to health and discipline." Yet Dr. Porter wrote, "Each regimental hospital had two or three large hospital tents, and when those were too much crowded, or particularly severe and long-continued cases occurred, patients were transferred to the general hospital, which was a long framed building in the village of Corpus Christi." He added that the hospital tents had stoves in winter, and he cited information provided by Captain Bliss which revealed that headquarters collected daily reports on health conditions among the troops. Hitchcock thought his illness was caused in part by his "disgust at the state of things" at Corpus Christi, together with "the haste and ignorance displayed" in moving Taylor's army to Texas.[14]

By the end of August the Army of Occupation's forces included two companies of Louisiana volunteer artillery. The Louisianians, who had signed up for a three-month tour of duty, had been sent by General Edmund Gaines on his own authority. When they disembarked the regular army officers, many of whom thought volunteers as a class were hopelessly unruly, no doubt welcomed their guns and horses more than they did the artillerymen. However, those volunteers were probably not much more undisciplined than some of the regulars, if at all. Hitchcock wrote in October: "It is noteworthy that since the arrival of the 2nd Dragoons there have been several disgraceful brawls and quarrels, to say nothing of drunken frolics. The dragoons have made themselves a public scandal. One captain has resigned to avoid trial, and two others have had a dirty brawl. Two others still are on trial for fighting over a low woman."[15]

From August through October, scarcely a day passed without the landing of reinforcements. At the end of August, eight companies of the Seventh U.S. Infantry joined the Army of Occupation, bringing among other officers seven future Civil War generals: Captains Theophilus H. Holmes and Gabriel J. Rains; Lieutenants Richard C. Gatlin, Gabriel R. Paul, Napoleon J. T. Dana, and Earl Van Dorn; and Brevet Second Lieutenant Franklin Gardner, a classmate and friend of Ulysses Grant. In September, five companies of the Fifth U.S. Infantry added their manpower to General Taylor's army, and more came from Detroit in October. In the latter group were two future Confederate leaders, Lieutenants Carter L. Stevenson and Daniel Ruggles, as well as a New Yorker who would lose a leg fighting for the Union, Lieutenant John C. Robinson. The September crop of reinforcements also included eight companies of the Eighth U.S. Infantry, drawn from their Florida posts. With those troops was their regimental commander, Brevet Brigadier General William J. Worth, whose officers at Corpus Christi that autumn included Captain William R. Montgomery of New Jersey, Lieutenant Robert P. Maclay of Pennsylvania, and Lieutenant James Longstreet, born in South Carolina but reared in Georgia and appointed to West Point from Alabama.[16]

Longstreet had rejoined his Eighth Infantry company at Corpus Christi on September 27 from detached service at Apalachicola Arsenal, where he had been participating in a court-martial. Having been with Worth's regiment less than five months, he probably felt more comfortable with the officers whom he had known at Jefferson Barracks and Camp Salubrity than with Eighth Infantry associates. At least what he recalled most vividly about his months at Corpus Christi was that he and two of his Fourth Infantry friends, Ulysses Grant and Theodoric Porter, were members of an enterprising group that built a theater at their own expense and took part in nightly performances of comedies and farces, brashly attempting both male and female roles. Longstreet was twenty-four, tall (six feet two inches), well proportioned, and altogether quite attractive, having dark brown hair, deep-set blue eyes, a high forehead, and prominent cheekbones. In those days he was as easygoing as was his friend Grant. At West Point, where his standing at graduation was only fifty-four in a class of fifty-six, his favorite studies had been football (noncompetitive at the time), sword exercises, and horseback riding. Decades later he would tell a reporter that in Louisiana and Texas he and Grant had "frequently engaged in the game of brag and five-cent ante and similar diversions," and that Grant was too honest to suspect others of cheating.[17]

Fate was not kind to many of the soldiers camping near the mouth of the Nueces that fall. In August a private in Grant's company drowned in Corpus Christi Bay while on boat service. During the thunderstorm that sounded like artillery fire on August 24, one of Braxton Bragg's slaves was killed and another stunned when the metal pole in the center of their tent was struck by lightning. (In his diary Hitchcock, though a Vermonter, evidenced sympathy for Bragg's loss but none for the unfortunate slaves; and a New York surgeon serving with the army appears to have been equally unmoved by the incident. Their casualness doubtless reflected the paucity of objections to the habitual employment of slaves as servants in army circles.) Then, on September 12, the boiler of the steamer *Dayton* exploded, killing or fatally wounding ten soldiers, including two Fourth Infantry lieutenants, Thaddeus Higgins and Benjamin A. Berry.

The death of Higgins, who had recently married the daughter of a Fourth Infantry captain, particularly shocked Grant.[18]

The *Dayton* tragedy occurred on the day that Second Lieutenant George Gordon Meade, of the Corps of Topographical Engineers, arrived at St. Joseph's Island from New Orleans. Meade, a West Pointer who would have an active reconnaissance role throughout much of Taylor's campaign but no significant command experience, would years later lead thousands of Union troops during the crucial Gettysburg battle. At Corpus Christi in the autumn of 1845 he was nearing his thirtieth birthday. Waiting in Philadelphia for Meade's return were his wife, Margaretta, the daughter of a prominent Whig congressman, and three small children. His father had been a prosperous shipping magnate in Cadiz, Spain, when George was born there, the ninth child of his American parents, but disputes with that nation's government over financial matters caused his father to be imprisoned in Spain. Although the Meade family was eventually reunited in Philadelphia, when George was twelve his father died without having retrieved any of the fortune he had lent Spain. His widow, left with several children to support, applied for George's admission to West Point. He had previously attended a private military academy, but evidently he had little desire for an army career. Certainly it did not take him long to discard his uniform. Just over a year after graduating from the Military Academy in 1835 (with a ranking of nineteen in a class of fifty-six), he resigned his appointment as an artillery second lieutenant to accept a position as a civilian surveyor for the Bureau of Topographical Engineers, which by 1838 had been removed from the Corps of Engineers and established as a separate army department termed the Corps of Topographical Engineers. Only after a new law provided that just members of that corps would be allowed to conduct the type of government boundary and harbor surveys that had been providing Meade with employment did he, in 1842, reenter the army as a "topog," as the corps' officers frequently referred to themselves.

Lieutenant Meade was a tall, thin, bespectacled, "delicate-looking" man. His wide-set eyes were framed by a high forehead and an aureole of sandy, wavy hair. When he went ashore at Corpus Christi from St. Joseph's Island on the morning of September 15, accompanied by two other topographical engineers assigned to Taylor's command, Captain Thomas J. Cram and Brevet Second Lieutenant Thomas J. Wood, Meade was delighted to find that many old friends had preceded him there. One of the first mentioned in his letters to Margaretta was Captain George A. McCall, a Pennsylvanian whose Fourth Infantry company had until recently been stationed at Fort Scott. McCall had reached Corpus Christi only a few days before Meade, having fallen ill on his way to Texas. Another close friend, Captain George D. Ramsay of the Ordnance Department who arrived in October, arranged for his tent to be erected next to Meade's, and they spent many of their leisure hours together.[19]

Meade was pleased to hear that the army's commander was rumored to be a "staunch Whig." As a member of Taylor's staff, the young topographical engineer had frequent contact with the general. He found Taylor to be "a plain, sensible old gentleman, who laughs very much at the excitement in the Northern States on account of his position, and thinks there is not the remotest probability of there being any war." While delighted at being invited to join the general's mess, Meade occasionally succumbed to depression. He thought his endeavors since graduating from West Point had been "a waste of energy and time." The former classmates who outranked him at Corpus Christi—four of whom were first lieutenants and one a captain—served as reminders of how much his resignation in 1836 had cost him in terms of advancement in the army.[20] Yet Meade did not brood about his relatively low status as a junior second lieutenant if he was in good health and engaged in what he regarded as important duties; and less than two weeks after reaching Corpus Christi he and his fellow topographical engineers, Cram and Wood, were ordered to reconnoiter the Nueces River as far north as San Patricio. Traveling in five Mackinaw boats with an escort of thirty troops and two infantry officers, they left on September 19 and reached the site of the deserted settlement in four days. While rowing upriver they had become lost amid bayous and lakes until, on the third day, Meade located the Nueces's main channel. After their return from the otherwise uneventful expedition, Meade was happily engaged for a while in constructing maps of the river's course.[21]

Meanwhile, for a month the Army of Occupation had only one artillery unit, Lieutenant Braxton Bragg's field battery, which, lacking its own cannon, experimented with old pieces borrowed from Colonel Kinney. Bragg, admired by nearly everyone in his role as the senior officer on duty with Company E, Third Artillery, probably benefited from being Taylor's sole artillery commander during those days. As time passed it became evident that the demanding, opinionated young officer, after years of alienating his superiors, had won Old Zach's unqualified respect. Bragg's battery lost its unique position in the Army of Occupation toward the end of August with the arrival of the battalion of Louisiana artillery volunteers raised by General Gaines, and the Second Artillery regiment's field battery. In the Second Artillery unit, commanded by Bragg's close friend Lieutenant James Duncan of New York, was Ulysses Grant's classmate Brevet Second Lieutenant John J. Peck, likewise from New York. Duncan's company, after a month on St. Joseph's Island, joined the army's camp at Corpus Christi in October, as did other artillery newcomers. Among the latter were the cadre of the Third Artillery light field battery C, commanded by Major Samuel Ringgold, of which Lieutenant Samuel French, a New Jerseyan who would fight for the Confederacy, was a member. In addition, helping to bring Taylor's army to around four thousand troops were a number of artillerists acting as infantry who would be prominent in the next war: Lieutenants John B. Magruder, Abner Doubleday, and Seth Williams (First Artillery); Captain Charles F. Smith, and Lieutenants Arnold Elzey and William Hays (Second Artillery); and in the Fourth Artillery companies, Lieutenants John P. McCown, John C. Pemberton, Robert S. Garnett, Mansfield Lovell, and Joseph J. Reynolds.[22]

Also reporting to Corpus Christi for duty that fall were several members of the West Point class of 1845 who would serve as general officers during the Civil War, one being John P. Hatch, a brevet second lieutenant assigned to the Third Infantry. Hatch, a New Yorker, liked almost everything about his assignment to Hitchcock's regiment. He wrote to his sister Eliza that his outfit was one of the best behaved, with no drinking or gambling and, unlike the dragoons, no untidy long hair or bushy mustaches. The army's camp, to him, was a pretty sight, extending more than a mile along the shore, close to the water. The officers in his regiment, most of whom ate together in a thatched mess house, had a variety of game and fish, albeit eaten on tin plates and with iron tableware. Among the many friends he found there was a fellow New Yorker, the dragoon lieutenant William Steele, who would become a Confederate brigadier general. As for his impression of General Taylor, that too was glowing. The young West Pointer was pleased that Old Zach seemed sensible and plain, like a good old farmer. To illustrate how busy he was, Hatch recounted importantly that he had been on guard duty twice and had served on a court-martial board.[23]

Appointment to some type of court was almost as routine as participation in drills and parades. Month after month officers were detailed to serve on court-martial panels.[24] Most of the men on trial were privates accused of drunkenness on duty, sleeping on post, being absent without leave, insubordinate conduct, unsoldierlike conduct, mutinous conduct, disobedience of orders, neglect of duty, or desertion. A guilty verdict for sleeping on post would typically result in the soldier being sentenced to forfeiture of pay and confinement at hard labor with a ball and chain attached to his leg for six months. If found guilty of desertion the punishment was apt to be fifty lashes laid on the offender's bare back with a rawhide whip. General Taylor, however, frequently reduced or remitted the sentences handed down by the courts.

The officers at Corpus Christi also served on various kinds of investigative boards, for example ones looking into matters such as the condition of certain provisions (George Sykes); stolen firearms (Robert Buchanan); the condition of camp tents (John Reynolds); clothing damaged or unfit for use (Abner

Doubleday); and medical supplies (William T. H. Brooks).[25] But it was the drilling of troops, of course, that preoccupied nearly everyone. George Meade complained: "A camp where there is no active service is a dull and stupid place, nothing but drill and parades, and your ears are filled all day with drumming and fifeing." John Hatch observed that the regiments that had not been together for some time particularly needed drill practice. After Braxton Bragg's artillery battery obtained fifty horses left behind by the departing Louisiana volunteers in early November, John Reynolds wrote his sisters that he had been "much employed" in teaching horsemanship "to 20 or 30 stupid Germans, Irishmen, etc." in his battery. Dr. Porter recalled, "In good weather, the drills were uninterrupted."[26]

General Taylor, for his part, was trying to learn more about the region he was expected to defend. Apparently he had received almost no guidance from Washington concerning the geographical features of Texas before reaching its shores, and not much thereafter. Hitchcock fumed in August, "The government has actually no information of the coast, harbors, bars, etc., and as little of the interior." Later that month a map of Texas sent from the quartermaster general's office was scorned by Hitchcock because someone had "*added to it* a distinct boundary mark to the Rio Grande." General Taylor must have been less than satisfied also, for in October his assistant adjutant general and acting chief of staff, Captain William Bliss, wrote the War Department requesting additional maps of the area. While waiting for a response, on November 7 Taylor ordered Lieutenant Earl Van Dorn to assist Captain John Sanders of the Corps of Engineers in reconnoitering the "lower route" to Matamoros, Mexico, as far as the Little Colorado. They were to be escorted by two companies of dragoons and provisioned for fifteen days. The same order authorized Lieutenant Meade (due to the illness of his superior, Captain Cram) to lead an exploration of the Laguna Madre, the channel leading southward to Point Isabel, a few miles east of Matamoros. Apparently Taylor had already decided he would camp opposite Matamoros, the largest town on the lower Rio Grande, about sixty miles above the river's mouth, if ordered to advance southward. In preparation for such a move, he had earlier organized his infantry regiments and artillery companies into brigades. Lieutenant Napoleon Dana explained the components of each group in writing his adored young wife, Sue, on October 17. In the First Brigade were the Eighth Infantry and the companies of artillery serving as infantry; in the Second Brigade, the Fifth and Seventh Infantry; in the Third Brigade, the Third and Fourth Infantry. Elevated to the command of these units were the Eighth Infantry's General Brevet Brigadier William J. Worth (First Brigade); the Fifth Infantry's Lieutenant Colonel James S. McIntosh (Second Brigade); and the Fourth Infantry's Colonel William Whistler, the late Colonel Vose's successor (Third Brigade).

The Second Dragoons remained a separate command, as did the artillery companies serving with batteries.[27]

By November Taylor was sending paymasters and supply trains northward to the three companies of Second Dragoons that had been summoned from Camp Washita to provide protection for San Antonio and Austin. Each trip by paymasters gave officers at Corpus Christi an opportunity, if they could get leave, to explore regions north of Corpus Christi; and when special orders were issued on November 28 directing that an escort of dragoons was to be ready shortly to march with a paymaster to San Antonio and Austin, thirty-day leaves of absence to visit the interior were approved for Ulysses Grant and Mansfield Lovell, and the following day for Christopher Augur and Lafayette McLaws.[28] On Grant's orders his affiliation was indicated as Seventh Infantry rather than Fourth. His promotion to the rank of full second lieutenant, official notice of which he had finally received a week earlier, had taken him out of the Fourth Infantry but only to another outfit on the beach at Corpus Christi—the Seventh Infantry company commanded by Captain Theophilus Holmes—and not, as he had so long hoped, any nearer to Julia. That being the case, he had promptly written the adjutant general asking to be transferred back to his former regiment; and his classmate Frank Gardner, whose recent promotion had sent him from the Seventh to the Fourth Infantry, requested that he and Grant be exchanged for one another. Having gained the consenting endorsements of their regimental commanders and of General Taylor, they were waiting to hear from Washington when Grant went north with the paymaster's party.[29]

Clearly, Grant's trip was for him an exhilarating adventure. On January 2, immediately after his return, he hastened to tell Julia about it: "From San Antonio I went across to Austin, the seat of Government. The whole of the country is the most beautiful that I ever have seen, and no doubt will be filled up very rapidly now that the people feel a confidance [*sic*] in being protected. San Antonio has the appearance of being a very old town. . . . The whole place has been built for defence. . . . The town is compact, the houses all one story high only, the walls very thick, the roofs flat and covered with dirt to the depth of two or three feet."[30] From Austin, Grant and two friends—his classmate Christopher Augur and a Fourth Artillery lieutenant, Calvin Benjamin—started back to camp ahead of the paymaster's train to insure that they would not overstay their leave. The territory through which they passed was replete with deer, antelope, and wild turkeys, but was for the most part uninhabited. Augur, who like Grant and Frank Gardner had been promoted to the rank of full-fledged second lieutenant that fall, had joined the Fourth Infantry at Corpus Christi in November from his previous posting at Fort Ontario, New York. Perhaps because he was not yet acclimated, or because he and his companions had usually been forced to sleep in the open without shelter, Augur became seriously ill before he, Grant, and Benjamin reached Goliad. With difficulty, since Augur's horse had given out as well, the three young lieutenants managed to reach the cabin of the only man residing in that shrunken, historic settlement, a Louisianian who had lived near Fort Jesup and knew many of Taylor's officers. When, after two days, Augur was still not able to travel, Grant and Benjamin left him in the care of the friendly homesteader and his female slave, knowing the paymaster's wagon train and escort would soon pass that way on their return to headquarters. That episode, which ended fortuitously with Augur returning to duty on January 4, was memorable also because Grant suddenly realized while at Goliad that he was not cut out to be a hunter, although hunting was one of the chief recreational activities of General Taylor's officers. Having accompanied Benjamin to a nearby creek in search of prey, Grant startled a flock of twenty or thirty wild turkeys from the timber and watched them fly overhead without so much as raising his shotgun.[31]

When he reached Corpus Christi around the first of January, Grant learned that his request to be transferred back into the Fourth Infantry had been approved in Washington and had resulted in his being assigned to Captain George McCall's Company C. Because McCall had until recently been stationed at Fort Scott for some three years, he and Grant were not well acquainted. McCall was forty-three and an 1822 West Point graduate from Pennsylvania. During the Seminole War, while attached as aide-de-camp to General Gaines, he had served with Twiggs and Hitchcock. He was a zestful, extremely well-educated sportsman whose letters to relatives and friends dating from his introduction to army life are dotted with French, Spanish, and Latin expressions and classical references, and reveal an unflagging curiosity about flora, fauna, and cultural oddities. As a Union brigadier general during the Civil War, he would have the dubious distinction of being captured by Longstreet's men and of discouraging, by his aloof manner, any acknowledgment by Longstreet of their association while serving with General Taylor. Grant, in his memoirs, politely distanced himself from McCall: "In the old army he was esteemed very highly as a soldier and gentleman. Our relations were always most pleasant."[32]

The New Year's Day celebrations of the Army of Occupation at Corpus Christi were much like those of the previous year at Fort Jesup. Hitchcock, after noting that the weather was "[m]ild and balmy," prophesied before celebrations commenced: "The day will go as other days—drinking, horse-racing, gambling, theatrical amusements. A ball is advertised for this evening in Corpus Christi." George Meade, seemingly somewhat chagrinned at having spent "a rather stupid" New Year's Day, wrote his wife that evening: "In the morning I was engaged making official complimentary visits to the 'big-bugs' of the camp, all of whom had egg-nogg [*sic*] and cake for their visitors; then we had a race, gotten up by the officers for their amusement; and then I dined with a party who endeavored to be as merry as they could be under the circumstances; and, in the evening, I accompanied them to the theatre."[33]

Meade, born on December 31, 1815, had just celebrated his thirtieth birthday. He had by this time despaired of returning to his wife and children before summer. From various sources the men had been led to believe that Mexico had agreed to negotiate the boundary dispute, but they assumed from President Polk's annual message to Congress and from the secretary of war's report, which had reached them on December 22, that they would not be recalled from Texas before negotiations were concluded. At Christmas, Meade had sent his wife a remarkably cheerful report: "I have been quite well now, over a week, the weather has cleared up, and I have been riding every day. In addition to which I have had my tent made more comfortable, by lining inside, and have a rough chimney-place constructed, in which I have a little fire that I sit by to read and write." On January 10 he was once more depressed, fearing border negotiations would be delayed by political upheaval in Mexico, where it appeared that General Mariano Paredes y Arrillaga was about to overthrow President José Joaquin de Herrera. On January 21, Meade cheered up again when he learned that he was to take part in another marine expedition, this one under Captain Joseph K. F. Mansfield of the Corps of Engineers. They were ordered to go up the coast past Matagorda Island to Port Lavaca in search of a good location for a supply depot for the inland posts.[34]

By the turn of the year there were other developments as well. Texas had been formally admitted to the Union on December 29, becoming the nation's twenty-eighth state. Harvey Hill was no longer with Taylor's army, his promotion to second lieutenant in October having sent him to a Fourth Artillery company garrisoned at Fort Monroe, Virginia. Sam French, whose standing was fourteen in general merit in his 1843 West Point graduating class but who had not yet been promoted to the rank of full second lieutenant, received orders permitting him to accompany a wagon train to San Antonio. French reached that village in time to witness the serious wounding of Lafayette McLaws by a fellow officer's careless, pointless shot at a tree.[35]

At Corpus Christi, there was now a weekly newspaper, and in addition to the "Union Theatre," erected earlier, the hamlet had acquired an "Army Theatre" where worship services were occasionally held. Surgeon Nathan S. Jarvis wrote of having twice heard "the Rev. Mr. Eaton" of Galveston preach there, without indicating the minister's denomination, or under whose auspices such services were held, or the size or composition of the congregations. At the Kinney ranch there were occasional Catholic services. Later, Catholic and Protestant chaplains accompanied some of Taylor's volunteer units. In letters and diaries of the era, enlisted men and officers alike, regardless of their religious affiliation, wrote of their own reliance on a higher power. However, though they described Mexican cathedrals and the many ways in which all Mexicans exhibited their strict adherence to Catholic rituals,[36] most of Taylor's soldiers appear to have been unconcerned about religious orientation issues; and only a few American Catholics, such as the deserters who served in Mexico's famed San Patricio battalion, are known to have fought alongside Mexican combatants. Once the war commenced, two Catholic priests were assigned as adjuncts to Taylor's army (though not as army chaplains), at the request of President Polk, to assure Catholic clergy in Mexico that their "religion and church property would be secure" and thereby, hopefully, to prevent the "active hostility" of the Mexican clergy.[37]

During February, interspersed with routine orders, General Taylor issued numerous directives in preparation for a march southward, for on the third of that month Old Zach had received instructions from Secretary of War William L. Marcy dated January 13 to move his forces closer to the lower Rio Grande as soon as it could be "conveniently done." While assuming Taylor would concentrate his army at Point Isabel or some other location near Matamoros, Marcy said the general was to use his "better knowledge" in determining "the post or posts" to be occupied. With regard to initiating an offensive drive, he said: "It is not designed in our present relations with Mexico that you should treat her as an enemy, but should she assume that character by a declaration of war or any open act of hostility towards us you will not act merely on the defensive if your relative means enable you to do otherwise." In conclusion he informed Taylor: "Texas is now fully incorporated into our union of States—and you are hereby authorized by the President to make a requisition upon the Executive of that state for such of its militia force as may be needed to repel invasion or to secure the country against apprehended invasion."[38]

3
Encounters with "the enemy"
Corpus Christi to the Rio Grande

Evidently the advance from the mouth of the Nueces River toward the Rio Grande, which began on March 8, was ordered by President Polk with little thought that it might be perceived by Mexican officials as the last straw, an unendurable affront to their country's honor. True, Secretary of War Marcy's fateful letter to General Taylor containing that order (dated January 13, but received by the general on February 3) was sent immediately after Polk learned that the Herrera regime had refused to receive John Slidell, recently appointed as America's minister to Mexico in the belief that Herrera had agreed to enter negotiations with the United States. That setback, together with the fact that Slidell was nevertheless still waiting in Jalapa for further instructions from Washington, caused the movement of the American army southward to be viewed by some as proof that Polk intended to achieve his expansionist goals by provoking a war unless Mexico capitulated to his demands. Certainly that was the opinion of Lieutenant Colonel Ethan Allen Hitchcock. Yet a close reading of Polk's diary indicates that he may not have regarded the stationing of American forces in the region below the Nueces River (historically never considered part of Texas, and occupied by Mexican facilities and farms on both sides of the Rio Grande) as a particularly significant change in the status quo. Neither at the time nor for three months thereafter did he mention in his voluminous reflections anything about Taylor's army having been ordered to establish a "post" or "posts" close to the river. Apparently the Rio Grande boundary was a nonnegotiable issue to Polk, and military penetration into the territory between that river and the Nueces, which the Lone Star Republic had claimed was part of Texas, was to Polk no more than a natural next step following annexation. When he thought of Mexico at all it seems to have been in the context of his plan to persuade that country, for a substantial payment, to cede New Mexico and certain ports in upper California to the United States, and to

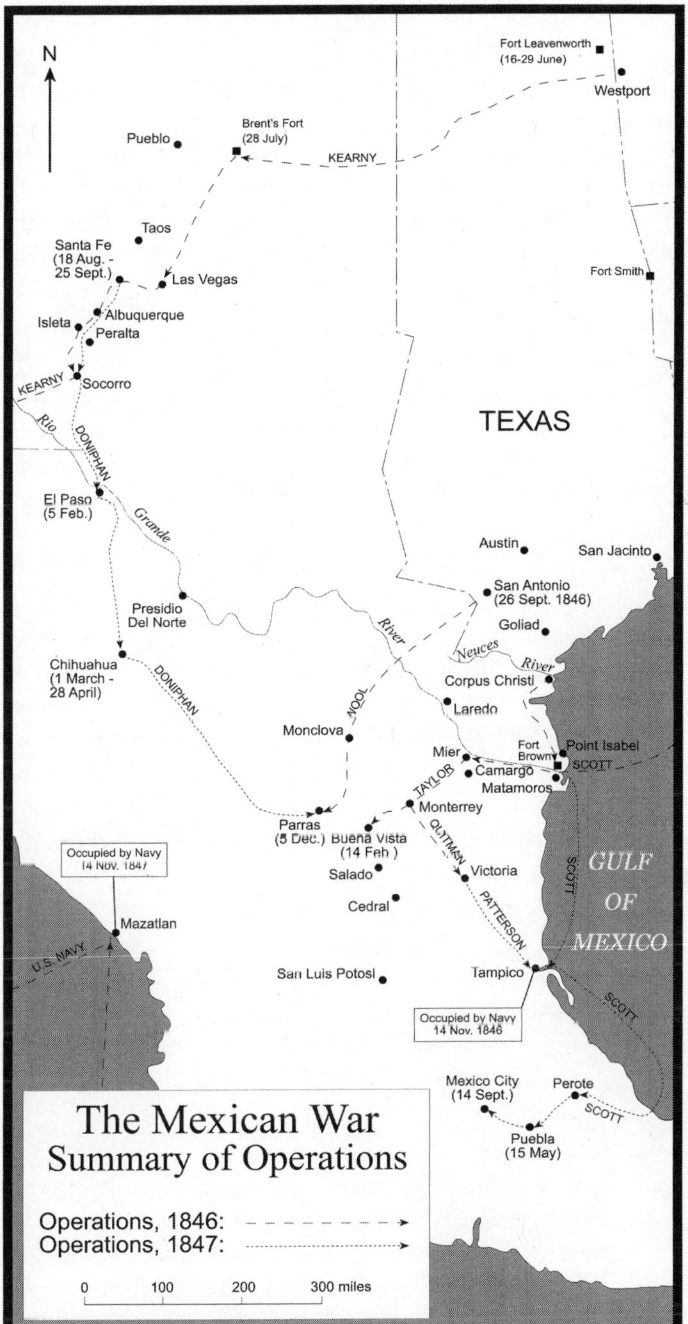

1. The Mexican War (Eastern Theater), 1846–47

agree that the Rio Grande would be the permanent boundary between the two nations as far north as "Passo" (El Paso, Mexico).[1]

On February 6, three days after receiving Marcy's directive of January 13, General Taylor alerted his troops to the imminence of the long-anticipated advance: "The several Regiments and Battalions of the Army will be prepared for a field movement at short notice. The responsible Commanders will take measures to dispose of all baggage beyond the allowance for campaign, and to hold their commands in all respects ready for the field. The horses of the Artillery will be shod all around." That same day Taylor ordered Captain Ebenezer S. Sibley of the First U.S. Artillery, an assistant quartermaster, to investigate the current condition of the inland road leading southwestward to the region opposite Matamoros, Old Zach's earlier reconnoitering parties having been turned back by inclement weather. Since Taylor was also considering an approach to Matamoros via Padre Island (the narrow hundred-mile-long sandbar that marked off the Laguna Madre from the curving Texas shoreline and led to Brazos Santiago Pass and Point Isabel), he dispatched a dragoon detachment led by Captain William J. Hardee, which was accompanied by a topographical engineer, Lieutenant Jacob Edmund Blake, to examine that route.[2]

Captain Hardee, a tall, lean Georgian descended from wealthy planters and destined to become a Confederate lieutenant general, had thus far enjoyed a remarkable army career. His standing at graduation from the Point in 1838, though only average (twenty-six in a class of forty-five), was sufficient to gain him an assignment as a second lieutenant in the Second Dragoons. Within eighteen months he had attained the rank of first lieutenant, and a year later he and two other officers were sent to the Royal Cavalry School at Saumur, France, for a year's instruction in tactics. Once Hardee rejoined his regiment, he and the dragoons under his tutelage were soon performing impeccably on horseback; and in 1844, a month before his twenty-ninth birthday, he became the first member of his West Point class to reach the lineal rank of captain. Happily married with two infant daughters, his prospects in early 1846 could scarcely have been better, but his conduct during the ambush that commenced the war between Mexico and the United States would temporarily cast a pall over his reputation.[3]

Hardee, Blake, and their party crossed a shallow ford of the Laguna Madre to reach the head of Padre Island, where they found a hut which appeared to be the domicile of three or four people. Farther down the beach they came across several skeletons, two lying on the hatch of a wrecked boat, others marking the site of a skirmish that Hardee and Blake concluded had been between Mexicans and a band of Indians. While the Americans were examining the southernmost part of Padre Island, a Mexican revenue official at Point Isabel contacted Hardee through an emissary who rowed across from the mainland.

A meeting with the revenue agent was arranged, and Hardee informed him that American troops would be coming into the region but would not molest the residents and would trade with them as friends. The Mexican official seemed delighted with Hardee's assurances, a response that the young dragoon officer probably accepted at face value since most of the Mexicans with whom the Americans had been in contact thus far had likewise appeared friendly. Indeed, Taylor had recently received messages suggesting that Brigadier General Antonio Canales, an influential political figure in northeastern Mexico, would be willing to cooperate with the Americans under certain circumstances.[4]

Lieutenant Blake, also a West Pointer (1833), collected topographical data about the coastal terrain from the head of Padre Island to the mouth of the Rio Grande, including the Point Isabel harbor region, which Taylor intended to occupy and utilize as a supply base. The village at Point Isabel, called Frontón, was twenty-seven miles from Matamoros, Blake would report. Situated on a small bluff not more than twenty-five feet high, it overlooked the Laguna Madre and faced Brazos Santiago Pass. The hamlet consisted of a dozen or so "rude habitations" for about fifty Mexican mercantile officers and dockworkers. There were no troops or visible means of defense of any kind, nor evidence of any in the vicinity. Cargoes were frequently landed just below Padre Island, at Brazos Island, the water there being deep enough for anchorage near its shore. Ships drawing seven to eight feet could enter the bay but were usually guided over the bar by a resident pilot who charged for his services. An American schooner was glimpsed standing off the town, taking in a cargo of hides and wool. Blake also pointed out several drawbacks to approaching Matamoros by way of Padre Island. Loaded wagons might have difficulty crossing the marshy shoals between Corpus Christi and the island. Grass along the route was too sparse to feed large numbers of horses and oxen. And at the low, exposed foot of the island there was neither a ford to Point Isabel nor deepwater anchorage.[5]

Shortly after receiving Blake's and Sibley's reports, Taylor elected to follow the inland track that linked up with a road connecting Point Isabel to a Matamoros ferry crossing; and on March 4, in preparation for the army's advance, a train of one hundred men and sixty wagons hauling forage and rations lumbered southward to establish a forward depot about forty miles below Corpus Christi. The army's order of march provided that the different corps should start seriatim, a day apart over a period of four days. In the vanguard on Sunday, March 8, were 23 officers and 378 men, consisting of the dragoons (serving as cavalry) under Colonel Twiggs, together with Major Samuel Ringgold's Third Artillery mobile "flying" field battery, to which Lieutenant Sam French was assigned. The dragoon officers accompanying Twiggs included Alfred Pleasonton (a recent arrival) but not Richard Herron Anderson, who had been given a health leave. Lieutenant George Meade, ordered to ride with the cavalry for the duration of the march and to keep both a journal and a sketch of the route for use at headquarters, was also in the lead contingent, as was Captain Abraham C. Myers, an assistant quartermaster.[6]

The First Brigade, commanded by General Worth, joined the column on March 9. It was composed principally of the Eighth Infantry, which at the time included James Longstreet, Henry M. Judah, Robert P. Maclay, and William R. Montgomery; Captain James Duncan's Second Artillery light battery, in which were John J. Peck and William Hays (the latter a transfer from another company); and a battalion of artillery companies acting as infantry, among whose officers were John B. Magruder and Seth Williams (First Artillery), Charles F. Smith and Arnold Elzey (Second Artillery), and John P. McCown, Joseph J. Reynolds, and Robert S. Garnett (Fourth Artillery). Also with the First Brigade was Joseph K. F. Mansfield of the Corps of Engineers, who was put in charge of the column's entrenching tools and would soon have the job of designing the American fort opposite Matamoros.[7]

The Second Brigade, consisting of the Fifth and Seventh U.S. Infantry regiments, Lieutenant Colonel James J. McIntosh commanding, left the camp near Corpus Christi the next day. With the Fifth Infantry were Edmund Kirby Smith (a relatively new arrival following his graduation from the Point in 1845), Carter L. Stevenson, Randolph B. Marcy, Daniel Ruggles, Thomas G. Pitcher (also from the West Point class of 1845), and John C. Robinson. With the Seventh Infantry were Theophilus Holmes, Earl Van Dorn, Franklin Gardner, Gabriel Rains, Richard Gatlin, Lewis H. Little, and Joseph H. Potter.[8] Lieutenant Napoleon Dana, who had been with the Seventh Infantry at Corpus Christi, was on leave due to the illness of his young wife, Sue, but would rejoin the regiment in April.

On the morning of March 11, the Third Brigade, commanded by Colonel William Whistler, brought up the rear. In it were the Third and Fourth U.S. Infantry regiments and Braxton Bragg's battery, Company E of the Third Artillery. Bragg's company included, as before, George Thomas and John Reynolds. With the Third Infantry were Ethan Allen Hitchcock, Don Carlos Buell, William T. H. Brooks, Israel Richardson, and two graduates of West Point the previous summer, John P. Hatch and Barnard Bee. With the Fourth Infantry were Ulysses Grant, Christopher Augur, George McCall, Robert Buchanan, and Benjamin Alvord.[9]

General Taylor's plan called for a few of his troops to be transported to Point Isabel by sea. In the first such flotilla, scheduled to arrive about the time Taylor expected to reach there, were troops belonging chiefly to a Fourth Artillery company under Major John Munroe to which John Pemberton and Mansfield Lovell were assigned. They embarked at St. Joseph's Island for Point

Isabel on March 23 accompanied by engineer, ordnance, and quartermaster personnel as well as several large siege guns, surplus ammunition, subsistence and medical supplies, and excess baggage. One of the officers with Munroe was George Meade's friend Captain George D. Ramsay. Convoying the transports were the revenue cutter *Woodbury* and the United States brig *Porpoise.*[10] The men who were too sick to travel were ferried to the army's hospital on St. Joseph's Island. Major John Erving (Second Artillery) was appointed to command the remnant of the regular troops still in the Corpus Christi area. Ulysses Grant's classmate Bob Hazlitt, now a second lieutenant in the Third Infantry, and another officer in Hazlitt's regiment, Lieutenant Thomas Jordan of Virginia, were among the subalterns ordered to continue on duty at Corpus Christi for the time being. Jordan, who would become a Confederate brigadier, was detailed to take care of the camp women with children who chose not to travel with the overland expedition. In charge of the cadre protecting the hospital and depot on St. Joseph's Island was Captain Giles Porter, commander of Company A, First Artillery, under whom Lieutenant Abner Doubleday of New York was serving. A contingent of Texan volunteers camping in the vicinity retained their position pending further orders. Otherwise, as Bob Hazlitt would dramatically announce in writing a friend, the village was almost lifeless.[11]

General Taylor left Corpus Christi a few hours after the Third Brigade on the eleventh, intending to pass gradually to the head of his army. Ulysses Grant, riding in the Third Brigade, was astride a wild mustang. He was fortunate to be astride a horse at all. Recently his servant, a youth named Gregorio whom Grant and Hazlitt had hired while in Louisiana, had allowed the three mounts Grant had bought in Texas to run away. Convinced that the loss was an accident, Grant was not greatly disturbed. He believed that an infantry officer should tramp along with his men, which was what he had planned to do. But Grant's captain, George McCall, who had his blooded horse Champion with him, and also owned another fine animal which his servant would ride, did not like to think that his lieutenant would be forced to walk. McCall solved the problem by purchasing for Grant a five-dollar unbroken mustang. The incident came to the attention of Taylor's acting chief of staff, William Bliss, who dismissively said he understood Grant had lost "five or six dollars' worth of horses." That comment was to the horse-proud Grant nothing less than slander. His three mounts had cost him nearly twenty dollars![12]

Dispersed among the columns of troops were more than three hundred wagons. Each company had its own baggage wagon, the load for each limited to 1,500 pounds of baggage and 200 of oats. There were also wagons containing ammunition, one for each of the four columns, and others hauling subsistence and supplies, pulled by teams of mules or in some instances by oxen. Traveling in one of the ox-drawn wagons among boxes of ammunition was Lieutenant Colonel Hitchcock, who had been quite sick again for several days before the Third Brigade marched. Although an intimate friend of General Taylor for more than twenty-five years, Hitchcock had suspected earlier that the general was more eager to advance southward from Corpus Christi than was appropriate for someone supposedly opposed to war with Mexico, that Old Zach was perhaps "instigated by ambition" and desirous of "an additional brevet." Yet Taylor, having been authorized by Secretary Marcy the previous October to move near the Rio Grande, had waited for a direct order to do so, evidently concluding that an intrusion by his army below the Nueces would doubtless precipitate resistance from Mexican armed forces, a development he had been hoping could be avoided.[13]

Persons not legitimately attached to the army had been warned they would not be permitted to accompany the troops, but many noncombatants traveled with the train—guides, teamsters, slaves and other personal servants, and laundresses. One of the latter, Mrs. Sarah Bourdett, the rugged, hardworking wife of an enlisted man, was immortalized by Braxton Bragg in a newspaper article praising her unflagging devotion to "her boys." Some female camp followers who were less admirable may have tagged along as well, judging from certain remarks by Hitchcock.[14] Apparently almost all of the men were glad to be on the move. Grant wrote Julia that "fight or no fight evry [*sic*] one rejoises [*sic*] at the idea of leaving Corpus Christi." His view of the army's prospects was less positive. "From accounts recieved [*sic*] here I think the chances of a fight on our first arrival on the Rio Grand [*sic*] are about equal to the chances for peace, and if we are attacked in the present reduced state of the troops here the consequences may be much against us." By the "reduced state of the troops" he evidently meant that the regiments were not up to strength due to illnesses, desertion, expiration of enlistments, resignations, and a dearth of new recruits. As for himself, he no longer considered resigning. "In my previous letters I have spoken a great deal of resigning but of course I could not think of such a thing now just at a time when it is probable that the services of evry [*sic*] officer will be called into requisition; but I do not think that I will stand another year of idleness in camp." Although he had become "contented with an army life" he was determined, honor permitting, to do whatever was necessary to enable him to marry Julia.[15]

In the lead column, with Ringgold's mobile artillery battery, was Lieutenant Sam French, who would become a Confederate major general despite having been born and reared in southwestern New Jersey. He dismissed that incongruity in his autobiography, pointing out that at the time of his birth in 1818 New Jersey had not yet abolished slavery; that when the state did so two years later the measure applied only to the unborn; and that as late as 1850 there were still 236 slaves in the state. He might have added that following his 1843 graduation from West Point he became accustomed to being stationed in slaveholding states, first in North Carolina and then, after a year in Washington during which he drew illustrations for a horse artillery manual, in Maryland at Fort McHenry. Moreover, his fellow officers for the most part seem to have been indifferent to the fact that many of the servants at army posts and camps were slaves. Certainly some of the most popular and highly regarded officers were attended by slaves, as was true of Randolph Ridgely of Maryland, a lieutenant in French's battery.[16] With the utmost good humor French recalled, toward the end of the nineteenth century, his association at West Point and during the Mexican War with Grant and other Civil War opponents. He recalled that on the march to the Rio Grande, he was armed with a brace of old pistols belonging to his classmate Grant. Eager to use them, he fired both pistols, without effect, into an old bull that pickets had separated from a herd of wild cattle. He finally managed to wound the animal with his shotgun, but the maddened target charged and injured nearby horses until a dragoon killed it with a shot to the forehead. To French, this one-sided contest provided delightful recreation, with "a dozen picadors and a matador" performing "daring deeds" in a mock amphitheater. Unfortunately for those who enjoyed such sport, the fusillade caused so many troops to rush forward toward the disturbance that General Taylor, upon learning of it, forbade all firing thereafter on the march unless, in French's words, "necessitated by the presence of the enemy."[17]

General Taylor first referred to Mexican soldiers as "the enemy," at least in his written orders, when his army was approaching the Arroyo Colorado, about thirty miles from Matamoros. Having learned that the dragoons had seen five or six Mexicans setting fire to the prairie on March 14, and that the next day a face-to-face threat of resistance had been delivered by a detachment of Mexican militia to a party of U.S. dragoons serving as an advance guard, Taylor let his army know on the sixteenth that "the enemy" was reported in his front, told the cavalry and the First Brigade to slow their march in order to permit the rear brigades to close up, and issued an order of battle. Until that time there was no particular reason to think that war was imminent. In fact, as Taylor was preparing to leave Corpus Christi a ship had brought a reassuring message from Commodore David Conner, aboard the *Falmouth* off Veracruz: John Slidell was still at Jalapa, and Conner thought that Slidell would yet be received by the Mexican government.[18] As for Taylor's men, they were by and large supremely confident that they had nothing to fear, and were finding the march a welcome diversion. Grant, by now sporting a reddish beard two or three inches long, marveled at the "immense herd of wild horses" he saw, so numerous that the band extended to the western horizon. His captain, George McCall, happily "chased the wild horse and antelope, and killed the wild bull and the wild boar." On one such foray he and Colonel Garland were charged by a "large bull." Garland took the first shot, missed, and McCall, pursuing the animal, needed four shots to kill him. McCall wrote his brother: "I took his tongue and the meat from one side; but left some six or seven hundred pounds of beef for the wolves and vultures. His tail, which I took as a trophy and placed on my horse's head, I gave to Captain Bragg, whom I happened to meet as I entered the camp, and with it a good steak."[19]

In the Second Brigade Captain Ephraim Kirby Smith, the older brother of Lieutenant Edmund Kirby Smith, was impressed by the beauty of the uninhabited country through which they had initially passed: "After marching about eight miles the Nueces was seen on our right, winding through the prairie like a blue ribbon carelessly thrown on a green robe. The prairie was covered with flowers such as bloom at the North during the summer." Less idyllic was their second night out. The Fifth Infantry's camp was full of "varmints," Captain Smith wrote his wife: "From one hole a rabbit, a rat, a rattle snake, and a tarantula were dislodged, these animals, incredible as it may appear, living in common in the same den. I killed with my sword immediately in rear of my tent, a huge rattler nearly six feet in length." By the evening of the thirteenth, when General Taylor and his staff passed them, Smith's regiment was just beyond the army's temporary depot, on "a beautiful ground with good wood and water," but soon a cruelly hot, sandy desert wasteland tested their endurance. They were all suffering from blistered lips and feet when they heard from General Taylor on the sixteenth that the enemy was in their front and that the rear brigades were to "push on with as much dispatch as possible and join the advance of the army."[20]

Two days ahead of the Second Brigade, Sam French was sheltering himself from the merciless sun under an "immense sombrero," despite frequent warnings from fellow officers that he would be put in arrest if General Taylor saw him out of uniform. That moment came ten days or so after the march commenced. As French told the story, "The army concentrated near the Arroyo Colorado, where the general commanding overtook us. I went over to call on him the next morning, and found him in front of his tent sitting on a camp stool eating breakfast. His table was the lid of the mess chest. His nose was white from the peeling off of the skin, and his lips raw." As French came up, Old Zach said, "Good morning, lieutenant, good morning; sensible man to wear a hat."[21]

It was on March 18 that General Taylor camped with his cavalry and the First Brigade about a dozen miles north of the Arroyo Colorado, a sluggish saltwater lagoon approximately one hundred yards wide and four or five feet deep beneath precipitous banks. That evening he wrote Adjutant General Jones that the Second Brigade was about seven miles to his rear and the Third

Brigade about nineteen miles distant; that within the last two days his advance guard had met small parties of armed Mexicans who had avoided the Americans and were doubtless thrown out to get information about the army; that all of the corps were in fine condition and spirits; and that he would concentrate his men upon reaching the Little Colorado.[22] Not until the following afternoon, when Taylor and the leading units had halted within three miles of the arroyo, were there signs that a Mexican army might be hiding in the thick undergrowth on the far side of the ravine. A party of Taylor's men, sent ahead to examine the crossing, reported that they had seen rancheros (irregular Mexican horsemen) on the opposite bank who signaled that the Americans would be considered to have committed a hostile act and would be treated as enemies if they attempted to ford the lagoon. Taylor, with no way of judging how large a force he would encounter on the other side of the arroyo, immediately issued fresh orders. The cavalry and First Brigade were to march the next morning at six o'clock. One wagon of engineer tools was to move with the light battery of that brigade. All other wagons were to remain in the rear of those two columns, under guard. Captain Mansfield and Lieutenant Jeremiah Scarritt (Corps of Engineers), accompanied by a dragoon escort, were to point out where the artillery batteries should be placed to enable their cannon to fire across the ravine. Once the batteries were in position, the army was to be led down into the shoulder-deep water by four infantry companies from the First Brigade, followed initially by a squadron of dragoons and then by the rest of the brigade's infantry and the remaining cavalry. The artillery companies were to cross as soon as was practicable.[23]

Daylight brought further Mexican threats. While Taylor's men were positioning themselves for the descent into the lagoon, the rancheros reappeared. Mansfield, whom Taylor sent to communicate with them, reported that those he saw claimed to have positive orders to commence shooting if the Americans attempted to pass the river. Another group of Mexicans forded the channel to speak with Taylor, gave him a proclamation recently issued at Matamoros by General Francisco Mejía, and repeated earlier assertions that a crossing by the Americans would be regarded as a declaration of war and would result in armed resistance, to which Old Zach replied that his army would cross immediately and that any Mexican troops remaining on the opposite bank would be fired on by his artillery. Meanwhile the Second Brigade, after overtaking staff officers and camp followers hurrying to the rear for safety, formed on Taylor's right.[24]

While Old Zach could have waited a day for his Third Brigade to come up, he evidently never considered pausing longer than was necessary to plan which units should be the first to surge down the arroyo's steep banks. He was in a poor position to provoke a battle—in the open, more than one hundred miles from the nearest Texas settlement, with nowhere to retreat except back into the desert his men had just crossed, and with supply wagons and civilians in his rear. However, he had reason to assume, in light of the frequent reports of Kinney's spy Chapita, as well as Captain Blake's recent observations at Point Isabel, that no Mexican regular army units of any size were in the area. Moreover, he was doubtless convinced that no large force could possibly be hidden in the scraggly chaparral on the lagoon's opposite bank, and even so he had been ordered to advance. Also, to appear intimidated could have encouraged his opponents to carry out their threats and might have demoralized his own men. At any rate no fight ensued, as Captain Ephraim Kirby Smith, watching the confrontation with Twiggs's Second Brigade from the channel's edge, would write his wife: "The movement was begun at half-past ten, by four companies . . . under the command of Captain C.F. Smith. . . . As they struck the margin, General Worth rushed to the head of the column to lead the charge. . . . When they were half way over and not a shot fired the disappointment of the men was shown from right to left in muttered curses. A squadron of Dragoons followed immediately . . . and the entire army marched over rapidly, reaching the opposite bank in thirty minutes from the order to move. . . . A few Mexicans were seen retreating, and the great battle of Arroyo Colorado was terminated."[25]

The Third Brigade troops missed most of the March 20 excitement, having been a few miles in the rear. They forded the lagoon the next day in the wake of the supply trains of the other regiments. Forty years later Grant recalled in particular the procedure employed to control the wagons as their mule teams descended and ascended the fifteen-foot-high banks of the deep channel. A complicated system of attaching ropes to both a wagon's tongue and its back axle enabled the soldiers to control a wagon while the mules pulled it into the ravine and then dragged it up the opposite side. That Grant, after so many years and battles, should have vividly remembered details of that caliber illustrates how closely he observed all aspects of life in the Army of Occupation.[26]

The unhesitating plunge into the arroyo by Captain Charles Ferguson Smith, General Worth, and the men they led, was the highlight of the march toward Matamoros. Smith, born in Pennsylvania in 1807, was well known to most of the young West Pointers, having returned to the Academy a few years after his graduation in 1825 to teach infantry tactics, and then also having served as commandant of cadets from 1838 to 1842. By 1862 he would be a Union major general of volunteers, but would die of an infection contracted prior to the Battle of Shiloh. Ulysses Grant would say of him, "His personal courage was unquestioned, his judgment and professional acquirements were unsurpassed, and he had the confidence of those he commanded as well as of those over him." The admiration occasioned by Smith's fearless charge across the Little Colorado was fully deserved, for as Captain Ephraim K. Smith explained to his wife,

Mexican horsemen and troops had been "showing themselves at many points on the bank as if parts of a strong body deployed in order of battle," and bugle calls had been suggesting that the Mexicans were indeed ready, willing, and able to carry out their threats. One of the lieutenants who participated in that charge, "Prince John" Magruder, would, while defending Richmond, Virginia, stage a charade like that of the Mexicans at the Arroyo Colorado, deliberately parading Confederate troops back and forth within sight of Union forces to convey the impression that they numbered far more than was actually the case.[27] Whether Magruder recalled having witnessed such a ruse at the Arroyo Colorado is unknown, but the ploy would prove invaluable in 1862.

After most of the American troops were concentrated south of the lagoon, General Taylor delayed another day, waiting for a slow-moving ox train with its guard of sixty men to reach the army's camp. Meanwhile, to be better prepared to meet an attack, he directed that both Bragg's and Ringgold's horse artillery batteries were to be reinforced temporarily with soldiers from the Second and Third brigades, notwithstanding the War Department's earlier declaration that Bragg's company was not officially "light artillery." Another of General Taylor's orders of March 22 provided for skirmishers to be thrown forward the next day in advance of the "pioneers" who were to clear the trail of debris; in addition, he directed that a party of dragoons and the topographical engineer attached to the cavalry—meaning George Meade, apparently—were to stay a mile ahead of the foremost column of troops and to send back intelligence, at least hourly, concerning the enemy and any obstruction encountered.[28] At sunrise on the twenty-third the marchers commenced the last leg of their journey, moving in four parallel columns trailed by 320 wagons, and by nightfall, without further incident, they were camped "near San Juan, Texas." That evening Taylor's orders mentioned Meade by name: "The routes to be opened and the points at which the banks of a creek are to be cut down will be indicated by Lt. Meade, who will make a reconnaissance through the timber under an escort of a Subaltern and fifteen men of Dragoons. Lt. Meade and the Commander of the escort will report at Head Quarters at 6 o'clock."[29]

The next morning the Americans came to a road that led on the southeast to Point Isabel, some ten miles away, and on the southwest to a ferry crossing leading to Matamoros, about eighteen miles distant. When that intersection was reached, General Taylor called a two-hour halt while he arranged for a small detachment of troops and a train of empty wagons to accompany him to Point Isabel, where at any moment the men and materiel coming by sea from Corpus Christi were due to arrive. Although Taylor had been informed that no sizeable Mexican force was currently in that area, he wanted to be sure that there was no interference with the establishment of a depot at Point Isabel. Taking with him the seven companies of dragoons and Ringgold's light artillery battery, Taylor hastened toward the gulf port. General Worth was told to lead the rest of the army westward toward the Rio Grande until a suitable campsite was located and then to wait, keeping the road under observation, for Taylor's return.[30]

Colonel Twiggs, despite being given the honorific role of riding with General Taylor to Point Isabel, must have been galled by Worth's prestigious assignment. Twiggs and Worth each regarded himself as rightfully being the second in command to Taylor, and each had supporters among the other officers. In terms of lineal rank Twiggs was senior to Worth, the former having become a colonel in 1836 and the latter in 1838, but Worth had been awarded the title of brevet brigadier general in 1842 in recognition of his service against Indian tribes in Florida. Taylor, although only a brevet brigadier general himself, was not directly affected by the controversy. Regardless of which view prevailed, he was senior to both men in length of appointment, and his current assignment placed him beyond their wrangling. However, since the previous autumn, the dispute between Worth and Twiggs over the significance of brevets had been causing a great deal of acrimonious debate among the officers. Although the issue had long been troublesome to army officers, it was of immediate concern to those serving with Taylor in Texas, for obviously illness or injury could force Old Rough and Ready to yield command abruptly, and in perilous circumstances. After waiting tensely for a definitive ruling on the matter from the War Department, the Corpus Christi garrison had received a circular around the first of December in which General Winfield Scott upheld brevet rank as being determinative of seniority, as he had long argued. Within a few days a lengthy, scathing rebuttal citing a contrary ruling by President Andrew Jackson had been drafted by Hitchcock, signed by more than 150 officers of all ranks at Corpus Christi, and mailed to the Senate. Then on February 24 General Taylor, in preparing for the march southward, stirred the pot again by ordering Colonel Twiggs, "the senior officer," to present all of the troops for review by the commanding general, either forgetting Scott's contrary ruling, or anticipating that Scott's view would not be upheld by President Polk. What Worth said when he saw Taylor's announcement concerning Twiggs is unrecorded, but the grand review was cancelled, the putative reason for the change in plans being "the unfavorable state of the weather." A month later, when Taylor along with Twiggs, the dragoons, Ringgold's artillery battery, and a long train of empty wagons turned toward Point Isabel, Old Zach's troops were unaware that President Polk had decided to reaffirm President Jackson's order of 1829 "giving command to lineal over brevet officers."[31]

Taylor's detour, to insure that his heavy guns and supplies were safe and would be properly stored at Point Isabel, was interrupted. First, he was overtaken by a deputation from Matamoros, riding in two carriages and bearing a white flag. When Taylor refused to talk with them until he found water for his men and horses, the Mexican party halted but sent a messenger after the Americans with a written protest against the army's intrusion, signed by the prefect of the Northern Tamaulipas district. Taylor accepted the document on the outskirts of Point Isabel. However, noticing that some structures in the village of Frontón were on fire, he told the messenger he would respond to the prefect when he reached the Rio Grande. Although only three or four empty buildings were destroyed before the dragoons extinguished the flames, Taylor was incensed when he heard that General Mejía had instructed the port captain to set the fire before leaving the area. To Taylor that was an unwarranted, flagrantly hostile act. He was convinced that the Mexican general knew Taylor had directed his troops to scrupulously respect "the rights of all persons who may be found in the peaceable pursuit of their respective avocations, residing on both banks of the Rio Grande," an order that had not only been published in the *Corpus Christi Gazette* but had been translated into Spanish and carried to Matamoros and other Mexican settlements on the river.[32]

Offshore on March 24, waiting for a signal from Taylor, were the officers and men who had just arrived by sea from St. Joseph's Island. As they disembarked the next day, hampered by weather so stormy that the *Monmouth* ran aground, they commenced marking off perimeters for a depot. There was no armed resistance from the handful of Mexican civilians still in the area, but Taylor sent for a company of the First Artillery which was still on St. Joseph's Island to reinforce the Point Isabel cadre. That order brought Lieutenant Abner Doubleday, a West Pointer and future Union major general of volunteers, to Point Isabel the following month.[33] Command of the Point Isabel compound was given to Major John Munroe. Captain John Sanders of the Corps of Engineers was charged with "the establishment and construction of such defensive works as may be deemed necessary for the protection of the depot." Captain George Ramsay was directed to "take full measures to land the ordnance stores and secure them properly."[34]

By noon on March 27 General Taylor and his army were for the most part back together again at Worth's campsite. The following day, a Saturday, while President Polk was placidly presuming that President Herrera's successor, General Mariano Paredes y Arrillaga, would agree to a treaty settling the boundary dispute if offered "a half a million or a million dollars" immediately, plus additional millions once a treaty was ratified, Taylor's troops advanced to the Rio Grande. Since Taylor had been told that there were several thousand Mexican soldiers in Matamoros and more reputedly expected, why did he choose to divide his army, leaving Captain John Munroe in charge of the tiny Point Isabel segment while he accompanied the bulk of his troops to fields directly facing Matamoros's fortifications? The War Department had left the location of Taylor's troops in the lower Rio Grande region up to him. Why did he not concentrate his entire army at Point Isabel, one of the places suggested as a base of operations by the War Department, where there would have been no face-to-face confrontation with regular Mexican government forces, where there was no need to travel back and forth across nearly thirty potentially dangerous miles to keep his forces opposite Matamoros supplied, and where backup by the U.S. Navy would predictably have been available if needed? Perhaps he thought it was poor policy to surround the little Mexican village of Frontón with the tents of close to four thousand American soldiers, inasmuch as he had promised not to interfere with persons "in the peaceable pursuit" of their personal interests "on both banks of the Rio Grande." But whatever his reasoning, his plan appears to have evolved fully the previous fall, judging from the attention he gave to information about routes to both Matamoros and Point Isabel. He must have concluded that camping opposite Matamoros would best demonstrate the American government's position with respect to the region from the Nueces River to the Rio Grande. Evidently Taylor and his closest high-ranking confidant, Ethan Allen Hitchcock, each wanted to avoid war with Mexico but differed in the means they believed would achieve that end—Hitchcock desirous of avoiding a confrontation in the hope that a peaceful compromise could be reached, Taylor certain that a display of military strength would convince Mexican leaders of the inadvisability of their starting a war. That Taylor thought a show of force would cause Mexico to seek a peaceful settlement is clear from one of his reports to Adjutant General Jones.[35] To him, that goal must have justified a base opposite Matamoros even though it necessitated taking the risk of putting twenty-seven miles between his supply depot and most of his army. Moreover, there was no better way to illustrate how unswerving were the Polk administration's views regarding the boundary issue. At any rate, while war with Mexico may have already become inevitable, Taylor was now making decisions that would have far-reaching consequences, and could have been responsible for persuading Mexican leaders that they had no option other than to endeavor to force the withdrawal of Taylor's army from the lower Rio Grande.

The Americans started forward in four columns around daybreak on March 28 as if on parade, at first over a prairie of tall grass, then in single file along a narrow stretch of road choked by thick chaparral, and finally through a beautiful mesquite grove which opened onto a few cultivated fields and thatched houses. In the lead were the dragoons and Worth's First Brigade; following were McIntosh's and Whistler's brigades, and more than three hundred heavily loaded wagons. Their progress did not go uncontested. Two dragoons were captured, and a young bugler had his horse taken from him. Whether the Mexican harassers were regular or irregular cavalry or brigands was apparently never determined, even after the dragoons were returned, at Taylor's request, by General Mejía. Otherwise, there was little to mark that fateful day. The Americans could not see the Rio Grande until they entered the area across from Matamoros which became their campsite—ploughed fields in a cul-de-sac bordered on three sides by a huge western-protruding bend in the Rio Grande, guarded on its eastern flank by a large lake. Observing from across the way were groups of Mexican soldiers and civilians. The midmorning scene, as described by a Third Infantry captain, was eerily casual: "The several brigades were ordered to stack their arms on their respective grounds and the Officers and men were permitted to go to the river for water and to have a view of the town and people of Matamoras" [*sic*]. A flagstaff was devised, General Taylor ordered the "Stars and Stripes" to be raised, and a band "struck up our National air."[36]

4
The Ambush
"Hostilities may now be considered as commenced"

During the afternoon of March 28, while the American troops were pitching their tents along the verge of the Rio Grande, General Taylor directed General Worth to convey to the Mexican soldiers within hearing distance on the opposite shore, through an interpreter, that Worth wanted to speak with General Mejía. With the only boats in the vicinity moored on the Matamoros side of the channel, the American delegation—Worth and five of his lieutenants, one of whom was John Bankhead Magruder—were unable to cross the river until they were picked up by a Mexican craft and crew. To Mejía, protocol required that his second in command, General Rómulo Díaz de La Vega, should be the one to receive any dispatches Worth proffered. La Vega met Worth with "great suavity and grace" at the water's edge, but the Americans were not allowed to enter the city, where foreign flags over consulates demonstrated that Matamoros was an important, long-established center of commerce. Above and below the city there were ferry landings. A small fort guarded the upper crossing.[1]

Worth's remarks were translated into French by a First U.S. Artillery lieutenant, Minor Knowlton, and then into Spanish by one of La Vega's officers. In that manner Worth and La Vega conversed for quite a while with, as General Taylor would tell Adjutant General Jones, "no satisfactory result." Worth refused to release the dispatch Taylor had addressed to Mejía, having been told to deliver it in person. Instead, he read aloud Taylor's message—in substance, that Old Zach had been ordered to take peaceable possession of the region up to the Rio Grande and hoped that the American troop movement would not occasion a hostile reaction. La Vega's response echoed the position previously asserted by representatives of the Mexican government, that the American advance was an act of war. Thereafter Worth delivered to one of the Mexicans present Taylor's reply to the protest of the prefect of the Northern Tamaulipas district, as had been promised at Point Isabel, and asked to see the American consul stationed at Matamoros. La Vega, while refusing that request, informed Worth that the consul was not under arrest. At last, after Worth warned that any armed body of men found east of the river would be treated as enemies, the Americans were ferried back to their camp by their Mexican hosts.[2]

It is not clear when or why General Taylor decided a huge earthen fort should be built opposite Matamoros. Doubtless Taylor had realized at the Arroyo Colorado, if not earlier, that his army's advance into the region below the Nueces—historically part of Mexico's province of Tamaulipas, and never a settled part of Texas—might provoke the armed countermeasures threatened by Mexican authorities. Although he does not appear to have been apprehensive while at Point Isabel, perhaps because Hardee and Blake had seen no Mexican troops there, on the evening before his march to the Rio Grande he spoke with Hitchcock about the possibility of their being ambushed the following morning as they approached the river, proof that his uneasiness was increasing. But it was not until after General La Vega's hostile accusations during the meeting with General Worth on March 28 that Taylor took further defensive measures. He issued a special order the next day directing his senior engineer, Captain Joseph K. F. Mansfield, and an assistant, Lieutenant Jeremiah M. Scarritt, to select "a defensive position for a permanent Camp," and for the placement of batteries "to command the town of Matamoros." The order also provided that wagons escorted by three companies of dragoons were to proceed to Point Isabel and bring back, at once if practicable, four eighteen-pound guns and a suitable supply of ammunition. In advising the adjutant general of his army's arrival at their camp opposite Matamoros, and the steps being taken to construct "defensive works," he reiterated his request for recruits and told of the hostile attitude of the Mexicans.

Old Zach made no mention of a fieldwork fort in his March 29 orders, and would not do so for the next several days. However, it became evident that the camp was indeed intended to be "permanent" when, on the first of April, he directed his brigade commanders to supply Captain Mansfield with fatigue parties daily, for as long as their services were needed. The soldiers were to procure "entrenchment materials" for the battery sites the engineers selected. At the same time, in a general order he reminded officers of all grades of "the necessity of observing proper courtesy and dignity" in their contacts with inhabitants "on either bank of the river" in order to convey America's "conciliatory" intentions. On April 6, the eighteen-pounders having arrived, the general arranged for those weapons to be mounted in the just-completed breastwork overlooking Matamoros and to be serviced by a Second Artillery company to which Lieutenant Arnold Elzey belonged. The two-sided breastwork had "a deep ditch on the outside and a magazine . . . inside under ground," the latter covered with timber, fascines (bound bundles of wooden sticks), and earth.[3]

Ever since Old Zach had spoken with Hitchcock about the possibility of an ambush as they approached the Rio Grande, he had constantly been wary of a sudden attack on his troops. While he had assured Hitchcock that he did not believe the enemy would "attack Point Isabel or the train," he had immediately thereafter, Hitchcock noted, sent "three companies of dragoons down to defend Point Isabel." Taylor had also arranged for the Seventh Infantry to escort the wagon train through the chaparral-hedged section of the route to his supply depot, and ordered a company of dragoons to investigate whether Mexican forces had, as reported, crossed the river. But although he strengthened his camp's defenses each day, he kept his concerns largely to himself, judging from the insouciance of his officers. For the most part certain there would be no war, they initially wrote chiefly about their new surroundings. Of Matamoros, Grant told Julia: "The city from this side of the river bears a very imposing appearance and no doubt contains from four to five thousand inhabitants." The Rio Grande, he said, was "a small muddy stream of probably 150 to 200 yards in width and navigabl[e] for only small sized steamers." George Meade informed Margaretta that "[t]he summer weather has commenced, clear days and nights, with steady sea-breezes. The ground on which we are encamped is a ploughed field, and is not so good for walking as the shell bank of Corpus Christi, but we have [an] abundance of wood at hand, and a fine river of running water at our feet."

However, being so close to a Mexican city had its drawbacks for officers whose servants were slaves: several slaves disappeared, presumably having escaped across the river. Also, a few enlisted men deserted, some of whom were believed to have been shot by pickets as they attempted to reach the opposite shore. But desertion was not a new problem, as shown by the three dozen dragoons who vanished somewhere in eastern Texas during Twiggs's march from Fort Jesup. Enlisted personnel were frequently immigrants—principally Irish or German—for whom service in the army at seven dollars or so a month must have had little appeal except as a means of temporary succor.[4]

The Americans labored incessantly after construction of a field fort began. By the seventh of April every man available for fatigue duty in each brigade was employed on successive days in building the fort and related artillery fortifications, working under their own officers but as directed by Captain Mansfield.[5] Although Taylor relied on Mansfield to a remarkable extent, the two were not personally close at that time. Brilliant enough to have ranked second highest in his West Point class of 1822, Mansfield was a married, prickly, forty-three-year-old Connecticut Yankee with three young children at home in Middletown. In his relations with fellow officers he may not have been as dictatorial as he was in letters to his wife, but he was coldly critical of many of them. While he found General Taylor good-hearted and honorable, he did not trust

Worth or General Winfield Scott. But Mansfield—who as a Union brigadier general would die of wounds received at Antietam—would prove himself to be indisputably effective under Taylor as an engineer, and exceptionally brave under fire.[6]

As the fatigue parties, laboring under the frown of Mexican guns some two hundred yards across the Rio Grande, began to erect the bastioned fort and other defensive works, Taylor's officers weighed each day's developments for their portents. At times, such as when Mexican women were glimpsed laughing and waving as they swam unclad near American troops bathing in the same channel, an armed conflict seemed almost unimaginable. Even when word was received that Major General Pedro de Ampudia was bringing three thousand troops from Monterrey to reinforce the estimated two thousand Mexican soldiers already in Matamoros, the Americans tended to believe there would be a peaceful resolution to the territorial dispute. Occasionally the firing of American pickets at deserters caused everyone in Taylor's camp to think that hostilities had commenced, but according to Captain George McCall, writing on April 14, the general impression among his fellow officers was that the Mexicans would not go so far as to start a war, and the same opinion was expressed in letters written up to the twenty-fifth of that month by George Meade, Joseph J. Reynolds, Napoleon Dana, and Ulysses Grant. General Taylor, however, was less sanguine. He had warned Adjutant General Jones on April 6 that the attitude of Mexican forces in the area was "still hostile." Yet even though officials in Matamoros continued to send threatening messages to Taylor, as late as April 14 the Third Brigade commissary was still being permitted to sell subsistence stores to Mexicans living nearby.[7]

If there had not been such a pervasive air of confidence in the American camp that the Mexicans would scarcely be so foolhardy as to attack, perhaps the resolution of the brevet rank issue would have been greeted with more circumspection by General Worth. By April 2 the Americans on the Rio Grande had learned that President Polk concurred with Colonel Twiggs's contention that brevet rank should not determine seniority, a point of view that had been exhaustively justified in the document prepared by Hitchcock and forwarded to the Senate in December. The War Department order upholding lineal seniority caused Hitchcock to be hailed as the hero of the hour, as he noted ecstatically in his diary: "The President of the United States has decided the brevet question on the basis of General Jackson's decision of 1829, and in accordance with our numerously signed memorial. The order was brought to me and I read it aloud to all the officers, who knowing that I wrote it [the document presenting Twiggs's argument], gathered rapidly around to rejoice and congratulate me." Brevet Brigadier General Worth immediately informed General Taylor that he was tendering his resignation to the secretary of war, and asked to be given a leave of absence as soon as he could be spared. Taylor, having decided that Worth could be spared at once, announced on April 8 that henceforth the commander of the First Brigade would be Brevet Lieutenant Colonel William G. Belknap of New York, second in seniority to Worth in the Eighth Infantry. Hitchcock, and apparently Taylor as well, thought Worth's defiant response to President Polk's order was inexcusable. "I cannot help asking myself," Hitchcock remarked in his diary, "what would have been thought of the patriotism of a revolutionary officer who had abandoned his post in the presence of the enemy on an alleged grievance which, in the opinion of almost everybody, is without proper or defensible foundation." But Lieutenant Benjamin Alvord, writing to an absent Fourth Infantry friend, indicated that in his opinion Worth's departure greatly weakened Taylor's command.[8]

Five more officers submitted their resignations within the next week, evidently emboldened by Worth's example although without his excuse since none of them had been the recipient of a brevet. During that period as well Hitchcock finally accepted health leave and departed for New Orleans at the urging of Taylor, Twiggs, several doctors, and various Third Infantry subordinates. Meanwhile a few other officers, having landed at Point Isabel following leaves of absence, were trickling into Taylor's "Camp near Matamoros, Texas," as he invariably termed the fort until he formally named it Fort Brown. Arriving on April 14 were Lafayette McLaws, Napoleon Dana, and Alexander Hays. McLaws had been in San Antonio since the previous December, recovering from his wounding by a careless colleague. His friend Dana, like McLaws a member of the Seventh Infantry regiment, had been given leave in November, as soon as he was informed that his beloved young wife, Sue (Susan), residing at Jefferson Barracks with their newborn daughter, was extremely ill. She had recovered enough by the following March to accompany him to New Orleans, where he and some recruits in his care had boarded ship for Point Isabel. Alexander Hays, a Fourth Infantry brevet second lieutenant who would die as a Union brigadier in the Wilderness battle of 1864, had been on sick leave since December.[9]

McLaws, Dana, Hays, and Dana's party of recruits had left Point Isabel at 2 a.m. on April 13, traveling with a three-mile-long supply train of 240 wagons and a squadron of dragoons. The previous evening, Easter Sunday, they had been roused from their beds in response to orders just received from General Taylor. The wagons were to be set in motion immediately. The urgency, the men were told, was due to a message from Major General Pedro de Ampudia, now commanding at Matamoros, who had warned General Taylor on the twelfth that if the American army was not withdrawn beyond the Nueces River within twenty-four hours the Mexican government would consider its presence as a declaration of war. Taylor's prompt call for provisions to be rushed from his depot to the fort demonstrated, of course, that he had no intention of withdrawing from the Rio Grande. Fortunately for the Americans, the wagon train rolled along unchallenged and had camped within ten miles or so of the fort by 4 p.m. on the thirteenth. It was joined shortly by the Fourth Infantry, one company of dragoons, and Ringgold's artillery battery, units to which Ulysses Grant, Robert Buchanan, Christopher Augur, Benjamin Alvord, George McCall, and Sam French belonged. Taylor, with Ampudia's fresh threat in mind, and having been told by spies that the Mexican army in Matamoros now numbered around six thousand men, had decided that a larger than usual detachment should be detailed to escort the expected train through the potentially hazardous stretch of thickets near the fort. As it happened, after an "uncomfortable night" in the open, according to McCall, the only hostile force encountered before the wagons pulled into Taylor's camp the next morning was a chilling, remorseless rain. "I am quite sleepy, having been under arms all last night," McCall explained to a correspondent on the fourteenth. Mentioning that his regiment and Ringgold's battery had been ordered to intercept the supply train, he added, "We met it at the distance of ten miles, but the cattle were unable to proceed during the night, and we were compelled to lie on our arms on the prairie, without wood for fires, except such flimsy brush as we could collect in the dark, and without tents or blankets." They arrived caked with mud and "pretty well wet," Dana wrote Sue.[10]

After General Taylor answered General Ampudia's ultimatum, saying in effect that withdrawal was out of the question so long as his government decreed otherwise, he authorized the raising of two companies of Texas mounted men in order to "relieve the regular cavalry of a portion of their duties," as he explained to Adjutant General Jones. In addition Taylor redeployed his immediate command, moving the First Brigade upriver a few hundred yards athwart the road to Point Isabel, and the Second Brigade to the far side of the large pond adjacent to the campsite of the dragoons. Located between those troops, directly across from Matamoros in roughly descending order from the river, were Braxton Bragg's battery, the earthen fort with its artillery embrasures and batteries, the Third Brigade, and the tents of Taylor and his staff, all concentrated in the cul-de-sac formed by the surrounding convex curve in the river, with the aforementioned deep pond behind them.[11]

As the Second Brigade was assuming its new position next to the dragoon campsite, Taylor increased the command of Colonel Twiggs to include that brigade's regiments (the Fifth and Seventh Infantry), and subsequently termed those troops, together with the seven companies of dragoons, the "Right Wing" of the Army of Occupation. There was also a change in the leadership of the Third Brigade due to Colonel Whistler's having been placed in arrest on a charge of neglect of duty and intoxication. Whistler, who would shortly be released from arrest and allowed to depart on leave pending a court-martial trial, was succeeded as commander of the Third Brigade by Lieutenant Colonel John Garland.[12]

Adding to the turbulent state of affairs during the Easter season was the fact that Colonel Trueman Cross, an assistant quartermaster general with thirty-two years of distinguished army service who had been an outstanding member of Taylor's staff during his Seminole campaign, had gone riding alone on April 10 and failed to return. His absence that evening at tattoo caused Old Zach to have minute guns fired, hoping to help Cross find his way back to camp, and detachments of dragoons were sent out to look for him. A captain in charge of one of the search parties, believing he had traced the colonel to the upper ferry, concluded that he had been captured and was being held in Matamoros. Taylor, who informed Adjutant General Jones that he feared Cross had been murdered by "Banditti," dispatched an inquiry about him to General Ampudia on April 15. The latter's response, delivered the following day by four richly uniformed Mexican officers, disclaimed any knowledge of what had happened to Cross. Unconvinced and still hopeful, the Americans continued to scout the area, spurred on by the presence of one of the colonel's sons who had been acting as his father's clerk, but Cross's fate remained a mystery for almost two weeks after his disappearance.[13]

Following receipt of Ampudia's ultimatum, Taylor also asked that the commanders of two ships standing off Brazos de Santiago Island, the U.S. brig *Lawrence* and the U.S. schooner *Flirt,* be asked to help enforce a blockade of the Rio Grande. His request was conveyed initially through Major Munroe at Point Isabel, who thereupon authorized a naval officer, Lieutenant Francis B. Renshaw, to hire a cutter to run Taylor's blockade message out to the two American naval vessels. While aboard the cutter on April 17 Renshaw warned off two privately owned schooners, both bringing flour from New Orleans to Matamoros. Subsequently the U.S. naval commanders contacted by Renshaw sent Taylor letters assuring him of their willingness to cooperate with the Army of Occupation but mentioning several reasons why their assistance might be limited, for example that they were low on supplies and would have to depart shortly to restock, and that high tides would occasionally make entry into the mouth of the river hazardous or impossible.[14]

Until Taylor requested the blockade of the Rio Grande on April 14, for the purpose of depriving Mexico of much-needed goods such as flour, everything he had done was in accordance with his instructions from the War Department. In contrast, the blockade carried the aggressive American occupation of the lower Rio Grande region a significant step further than the orders Taylor had received. In fact, Secretary of War Marcy had earlier directed Taylor not to interfere with shipping on the Rio Grande. Yet, surprisingly scant attention has been paid by historians to the potentially decisive provocativeness of Taylor's unauthorized blockade. True, relations between the United States and its southern neighbor had recently worsened—John Slidell, having concluded there was no chance of his being received by Mexican authorities, had written President Polk that he was returning to Washington—but Old Zach apparently did not hear of that development until a week after the blockade commenced. General Taylor himself would admit that the blockade was an "act of war," in responding later in the month to General Ampudia's protest of April 22, but would defend it by contending that, in light of all that had occurred since his army had left Corpus Christi, it was the "least offensive act of war" of the many he would have been justified in undertaking. Though Taylor no doubt thought he was merely reinforcing the Polk administration's effort to persuade Mexican leaders, through a show of strength, to agree to negotiations that would settle their nations' differences peacefully, in actuality he had initiated a course of action that could have been responsible for starting a war. However, the die was already cast. Major General Mariano Paredes y Arrillaga, who had succeeded Herrera in January as president of Mexico, had decided as early as April 4 that General Mariano Arista, upon relieving General Ampudia in Matamoros, should lead the forces concentrated there in an attack on the Army of Occupation.[15]

For the most part, in mid-April life went on much as before in Taylor's army. The dragoons were constantly busy searching the countryside and escorting wagon trains to and from Point Isabel. Infantry officers spent much of their time supervising fatigue parties, and regularly took turns standing guard. On April 17 Napoleon Dana wrote his wife: "I am senior officer of the guard today. The guard is sixty men, and we are on the edge of the river with a Mexican picket guard directly opposite us within half [a] musket shot. . . . Our guard house is one quite primitive. It is pretty nearly as good as your father's stable. . . . It is open nearly all round but still is the most comfortable place I have lived in since I have landed in Texas. The men are sitting, lying, and standing all around me." On the nineteenth Lieutenant Joseph J. Reynolds informed his brother William that he had read his letter while on guard at night, between visits to his sentinels. Similarly, George McCall closed a letter on the twenty-third by saying: "I am on duty to-night (Officer of the Day), and as it is past two o'clock, it is nearly time for me to visit guards and pickets; I will therefore bid you good night."[16]

Antipathy toward the Mexicans increased on April 21, the day Colonel Cross's remains were found three or four miles from camp, stripped completely of all clothes and personal effects. The Americans concluded that he had deliberately been murdered, in all probability by a party of rancheros. Napoleon Dana, who participated in the Cross funeral ceremony three days later, described the impressive burial cortege: an escort of 350 infantrymen, 100 cavalry, and a band, all commanded by Colonel Twiggs and followed by other senior officers; "the hearse, which was a gun carriage," bearing Colonel Cross's remains, "rolled in the Star Spangled Banner"; Colonel Cross's son, "on foot and dressed in black"; the colonel's horse, with "boots and spurs in the stirrups, turned heel foremost"; then "all the officers . . . who were not on duty, closed in rear by General Taylor and his staff." Dana concluded: "We laid the colonel's remains at the foot of the flagstaff. The service was read and we fired three volleys, which . . . told the Mexicans that our powder was plenty dry enough."[17]

Dana's remark about their powder being dry was a reference to another tragedy that had recently occurred, one that must have been especially regretted by Ulysses Grant—the death of Lieutenant Theodoric Porter of the Fourth Infantry. Porter was killed on the eighteenth while leading a dozen or so troops on a search for bandits rumored to have been responsible for Colonel Cross's disappearance. As the story was told by survivors of the incident, Porter's party had initially succeeded in scattering a small group of Mexicans and capturing their horses. Then, following a heavy rain, Porter and his men had unexpectedly encountered a band of around a hundred more Mexicans who commenced shooting at them. The guns of Porter's troops, exposed during the downpour, failed to fire, and he alone was able to get off a few shots, killing one assailant and wounding two before he and a private fell, dead or dying. Not until the rest of his party began straggling back into camp, a few at a time, did Taylor hear of the skirmish. Thereafter, detachments of troops looked in vain for the bodies of the two victims.[18]

While Theodoric Porter, son of the late Commodore David Porter, was "loved by all" according to George Meade, he and his wife and their little son had been particularly close to Ulysses Grant and Julia Dent. In an effort to keep their engagement a secret, Ulysses and Julia had enclosed their letters to one another in those exchanged by Porter and his wife. Grant, however, usually tended to report the death of a friend in the starkest of terms, both then and later. In this instance he told Julia merely: "Col. Cross has been killed by the Mexicans. . . . Lt. Porter with twelve men were attacked by a large number of Mexicans and Mr. Porter and one man was killed the rest escaped."[19] From other letters it is evident Grant was a deeply sensitive, emotional man, yet in writing to Julia he chose, for whatever reason, not to dwell on any distress he felt at the loss of officers with whom he had been closely associated in Taylor's army.

Despite the deaths of Cross and Porter, most of Taylor's officers seem to have remained confident that war was unlikely. They likewise appear to have shrugged off the news received on April 19 that John Slidell, President Polk's minister plenipotentiary to Mexico, had finally acknowledged the failure of his mission, as previously mentioned, and was returning to the United States. Nevertheless, General Taylor kept his troops hard at work on the six-bastioned earthen field fort and took additional defensive measures as well. He ordered that troops sent out to gather fuel were to clear the chaparral-obscured sector of the Point Isabel road to the width of ten feet on each side, and arranged for Captain Samuel Walker's company of Texas Rangers to be mustered into his army. As detachments of recruits arrived, the general immediately assigned them to understrength units.[20]

It was Tuesday evening April 21 that Colonel Cross's skeletal remains were recovered and brought into camp. The following morning, April 22, General Ampudia, who had the day before ordered all Americans to leave Matamoros for Victoria within twenty-four hours, sent across the river yet another angry, ominous message, this one prompted by Taylor's blockade of the Rio Grande. Ampudia mistakenly thought that the two schooners that had been prevented from entering the mouth of the Rio Grande, and that were loaded with flour for his army, had been captured by American naval forces; he indicated that there would be serious consequences if the ships were not released. Taylor, who was aware that two schooners bearing flour for Matamoros had been turned away, sent Ampudia a scathing reply, as mentioned below, one that was cheered by Meade, Dana, and others, and indeed appears to have been applauded by the entire command. His answer consisted chiefly of a litany of the hostile words and acts encountered by his army since early March, and of his own contrasting efforts, as he saw it, to maintain peaceable relations pending some resolution at a higher level of the dispute over Texas. In addition, he chided the Mexican general for the rude tone of his letter, defended the blockade as being an exceedingly mild and reasonable reaction to Ampudia's threats, and in a variety of ways conveyed his determination to meet force with force if necessary. At the same time, he offered to raise the blockade if Ampudia would agree to a truce until their governments settled the boundary issue or war was declared.[21]

Meade believed that General Taylor's salvo would bring the Mexicans "to their senses." As for his own condition, on April 23 he informed his wife: "I am in fine health and spirits, enjoying myself as well as I can away from you and the dear children. . . . My time is principally occupied in drawing, and all my spare moments I am on my horse's back, galloping about within the line of our camp. I find the more I exercise the better I am."[22] On April 24, however, the situation changed. General Mariano Arista, who had just taken command of the forces in and around Matamoros, informed General Taylor that he regarded hostilities as having commenced. Although the Americans were unaware that the previous day President Paredes had proclaimed his nation would conduct a defensive war against the United States, Arista's announcement coincided with reports that Mexican troops were crossing the Rio Grande in large numbers both below and above the American camp, leading Taylor to send out dragoons that evening to reconnoiter. A detachment of dragoons that rode south some twenty-five miles returned the next day without seeing any Mexican troops. A squadron of sixty-two that went upriver under the command of Captain Seth B. Thornton of F company, Second Dragoons, who was supported by Captain William Hardee of C company and their lieutenants, George T. Mason and Elias K. Kane, likewise had discovered no conclusive sign of an imminent attack when they halted for the night. Yet the next morning, upon entering a chaparral-fenced ranch bordering the river, about twenty miles above Taylor's camp, they were ambushed and overwhelmed by a contingent of some 1,500 Mexican cavalry and infantry regulars.[23]

It was Captain Thornton's guide, Chapita, who first brought word to General Taylor that a skirmish had occurred. As was later confirmed by survivors, Chapita had refused to go more than a few miles further upstream with the squadron on the morning of the twenty-fifth, having become convinced by people questioned along the way that a large Mexican force had indeed crossed the Rio Grande in that vicinity. Upon hearing volleys of musket fire, Chapita had hidden, abandoning his horse, and thereafter had seen two mounted Mexicans searching the area, but he could tell the Americans at the fort nothing more when he managed, after nightfall, to return to Taylor's camp.[24] Chapita's tale was at first considered questionable, no doubt because there had been so many false alarms and scarcely anyone thought the Mexican authorities would deliberately commence an all-out war with the United States. However, Taylor and his troops became increasingly anxious as hour after hour passed without the squadron's return. At last, around noon on the twenty-sixth, a wounded Company C private was brought into camp on a cart with a note from his captor, Brigadier General Anastasio Torrejón, and Zachary Taylor learned that Thornton's command had been defeated in an encounter with Torrejón's troops. The sketchy information gleaned from those sources was at once passed on by Taylor to Adjutant General Jones: "I regret to report that a party of Dragoons sent out by me on the 24th inst. to watch the course of the river above on this bank became engaged with a very large force of the enemy, and after a short affair in which some sixteen were killed and wounded, appear to have been surrounded and compelled to surrender. Not one of the party has returned, except a wounded man sent in this morning by the Mexican Commander, so that I cannot report with any confidence the particulars of the engagement or the fate of the officers except that Capt. Hardee was known to be a prisoner and unhurt." Moreover, despite his incomplete knowledge of the incident's details at that point, Taylor proceeded without hesitation to declare that the United States was at war: "Hostilities may now be considered as commenced, and I have this day deemed it necessary to call upon the Government of Texas for four regiments of volunteers—two to be mounted and two to serve as foot. As some delay must occur in collecting these troops, I have also desired the Governor of Louisiana to send out four regiments of Infantry as soon as practicable."[25]

General Taylor was evidently confident that the attack on the dragoons would, together with America's numerous other grievances against Mexico, cause a formal declaration of war to be enacted, which proved to be the case. Taylor's missive of April 26 reached Washington on the evening of May 9, a Saturday. Posthaste, around 6 p.m., Adjutant General Jones personally took it to the president. An hour and a half later Polk met with six members of his cabinet, and with their unanimous agreement he immediately began drafting a message to Congress which, in its final form, accused Mexico of shedding "American blood upon American soil." Over the weekend copies of his message were prepared for delivery on Monday to both houses of Congress, as were copies of Taylor's report of April 26 and related State and War Department documents. Meanwhile certain influential Democrats, having been apprised of the situation, began composing a bill along the lines desired by Polk, a declaration that war existed, which included measures providing for an appropriation of ten million dollars and the induction of fifty thousand volunteers. On Monday it won overwhelming approval in the House of Representatives, the vote being 174 to 14 with 20 abstentions. The next day, despite objections by a number of Whigs and some Democrats, the bill passed by the House was adopted by the Senate, with a few "immaterial" amendments, by a vote of 40 to 2 with 3 abstentions, and the House then consented to the amendments. The following day the measure was signed into law by Polk.[26]

On the Rio Grande during the last days of April, General Taylor responded to the ambush by tightening his rules regarding the dissemination of watchwords and countersigns. He also required his officers and men to sleep, Lieutenant Dana wrote, "with armor on, boots, swords, belts and all," and told them to keep their horses harnessed and saddled day and night. Of primary concern, of course, was completion of the fort. Although alternate battalions of each brigade had been laboring at the job in six-hour shifts, dawn to dusk, since the middle of the month, on the twenty-ninth more stringent orders were issued: "The great importance of bringing the field work into a state of defense renders it necessary for the Commanding General to call upon the Commanders of Battalions and Company Officers to use all their exertions to forward the work. Every man will be sent out with the working battalion that is not detained by other indispensable duty, and the Battalion Commanders will themselves superintend their Commands and cause all to do their duty." Also, the usual end-of-the-month muster of the troops was to be "so regulated as not to interfere" with work on the fort.[27] Taylor's focus had narrowed. Diplomatic matters were no longer a consideration. Now there was a war to win.

Old Zach's men soon realized that their general, believing a large Mexican force was massing in his rear for an attack on Point Isabel, was planning to march the bulk of his army in that direction as soon as the fort opposite Matamoros was defensible. But although everyone assumed a major clash was near, the officers appear to have been thinking less about what lay ahead than about the conduct of the two dragoon captains involved in the devastating ambush. On the twenty-seventh, Captain Hardee's written account of the skirmish sparked heated controversy in Taylor's camp within moments after his captors sent that document across from Matamoros, along with another wounded Company C private. As Hardee described the events that preceded the attack, Thornton ignored information gathered on the twenty-fourth that pointed to a Mexican army having forded the Rio Grande some miles above the American fort. Hardee, in the rear of the dragoon column, was "the last to enter" the enclosure where the attack occurred, a field containing buildings, bordered on three sides by a high chaparral fence and on the west by the river. He contended that the entire dragoon detachment had filed through the field's gateway "without any guard being placed in front, without any sentinel at the back, or without any other precautions being taken to prevent surprise." Hardee gave Thornton full credit for leading a charge toward the opening through which his men had entered once "a cry of alarm" rang out, but Mexican infantrymen "had stationed themselves in the field on the right of the passage way and the cavalry lined the exterior fence." With the enemy shooting at them from every direction, and the dragoons in a "state of disorder," Hardee had turned his horse toward the river and told the men nearby to follow him, which a number of them did. Finding they could neither ford the river nor establish a line of defense—the bank of the river being too boggy, and the vastly outnumbered dragoons having lost most of their sabers, pistols, and carbines—Hardee finally surrendered to General Torrejón upon being assured that he and the remnant of the command with him, about twenty-five altogether, would be granted the consideration required "by the rules of civilized warfare." Hardee added that he, Lieutenant Kane, and forty-five members of the detachment, four of them wounded, were being held as prisoners of war in Matamoros. He did not know what had happened to Thornton or Mason or the rest of the detachment. Not until the next morning did General Taylor find out, through a note scribbled by Thornton, that the squadron's commander was also imprisoned in Matamoros. Apparently Lieutenant Mason, a close friend of the artillerist John B. Magruder, was among the Americans killed (eleven altogether).[28]

Thornton reported he was captured after his horse fell on him, leaving him unable to rise at first. He did not criticize Hardee for surrendering; rather, he declared that the officers and men "both individually and collectively behaved in the most gallant manner." This did not, however, assuage Hardee's detractors, particularly an influential captain in his regiment, Charles A. May, whom Hardee, acting as his own attorney, questioned during a hearing by a court of inquiry convened at Hardee's request a month later. Colonel Twiggs, while testifying during the inquiry proceedings that he himself had "made no imputations against" Hardee, at that time repeated a number of negative remarks he had heard, and gave no indication of having discouraged them.[29] Fortunately for Hardee, after seven days of hearings he was completely vindicated by the court, on which sat the highly respected Captain Charles F. Smith and two Fifth Infantry officers, and which heard the testimony of Thornton, Kane, and eleven of the other survivors. Yet there is evidence that Hardee was still considered a pariah by Twiggs—and no doubt by Captain May and others—in late July.[30]

Thornton's actions of April 25 were subsequently scrutinized in a court-martial proceeding. He was charged with "Neglect of Duty" and "Disobedience of Orders," in that he omitted "the necessary and customary precautions to secure his command against surprise, and did suffer it to be ambuscaded [*sic*], and entirely cut off, by a large force of the Mexican army." Assisting in his defense were Lieutenant Braxton Bragg and a Third Infantry captain. The court found Thornton not guilty of either charge, reasoning that he had taken customary precautions until "the troops entered the field," and that although he "omitted thereafter" to put his command "in order of battle," the ambush was not "a consequence of any want of precaution, nor even of the condition of the troops when attacked." The matter was at long last formally settled in August by an order issued by Adjutant General Jones. Announcing that President Polk had approved the court's proceedings, Jones directed that Thornton be "released from arrest, and restored to duty."[31]

For General Taylor, during the waning days of April the main problem posed by the defeat of Thornton's squadron was how to offset the loss—by death, wounding, or capture—of two companies of his already overtaxed dragoons. He resolved that problem partially on the twenty-eighth by instructing Captain McCall to lead a detachment of seventy-five troops drawn from the First and Third brigades to ascertain whether a Mexican force was near the American camp. Old Zach obviously had a great deal of confidence in McCall, who was not only a West Pointer but one who had served reliably in the Fourth Infantry for nearly a quarter of a century, and who was a close friend of both the general's acting chief of staff, Captain Bliss, and of Lieutenant Colonel Hitchcock. McCall's party, which included Lieutenant John Porter McCown of the Fourth Artillery and two other officers, began searching along both sides of the Point Isabel road that evening. The next night they returned, bringing with them three captured rancheros for interrogation. Their grueling twenty-four-hour examination of thickets, prairies, ravines, and ponds had convinced McCall that no enemy troops were or had recently been within seven miles of Taylor's camp.[32]

McCall's report, supplemented by a map of the terrain his detachment had covered, reinforced Taylor's belief that the Mexican troops encountered upriver by Thornton's squadron, and others rumored to be preparing to ford the Rio Grande below the American camp, were not mustering for an assault on the fort but instead were planning to attack his Point Isabel supply depot. He therefore continued to rush preparations for leaving a portion of his army in the fort while taking the rest, along with a wagon train, to Point Isabel. In special orders dated April 29 he assigned a Seventh Infantry lieutenant to duty as "Quarter Master and commissary with the command to be left in the Fort," and added: "All the Wagons not otherwise indispensably employed will be engaged under the direction of the Quarter Master's Department hauling fuel to the fort." He also told a Third Infantry captain that the army would march on May 3 to fight the enemy wherever he might be found, and that the units left behind to defend the fort would be the Seventh Infantry and the artillery batteries commanded by Braxton Bragg and Allen Lowd.[33] In order to maintain his position opposite Matamoros he would obviously need to insure that both the fort and his supply depot could withstand an attack, and that there was no impediment to their being accessible to one another.

Anticipation of a major encounter with Mexican forces increased on the thirtieth, when Taylor learned that a party of Mexican cavalry had attacked the nearby camp of Captain Samuel Walker's company of Texas Rangers in their commander's absence, leaving five men killed and five missing.[34] Seemingly as a result of that incident, Taylor moved up the date of his scheduled march to Point Isabel to the afternoon of May 1. Still unfinished was one face of the fort, through which passed "the sally port and drawbridge." Among the men left behind to garrison the fort were fifteen future Civil War general officers—in addition to Bragg, his lieutenants George Thomas and John Reynolds; Arnold Elzey, a lieutenant in Lowd's Second Artillery company; Joseph Mansfield, designer of the fieldwork; and a host of Seventh Infantry officers: Captains Richard Gatlin, Theophilus Holmes, Gabriel Paul, and Gabriel Rains; and Lieutenants Lewis Little, Napoleon Dana, Franklin Gardner, Lafayette McLaws, Joseph Potter, and Earl Van Dorn. In charge of the fort's defenders, who numbered about five hundred, was the Seventh Infantry's acting commander, Major Jacob Brown. In his care also were the army's sick, and its public stores and excess baggage.[35]

Dana considered it an honor for his regiment to be selected to defend the fort. Although on guard duty May 1, he took time out to assure Sue that he was in no immediate danger. The only way he could be certain of getting a letter to her was by sending it with the departing column, for there had been no mail service between the camp and Point Isabel for several days, and it was assumed there would be none until the army returned. "Today everything is bustle and business," he told her, "and I have scarcely time or opportunity to close this." His regiment was moving into the fort while he was writing.[36]

General Taylor's order of march called for Captain McCall to start at noon, leading an irregular detachment of light troops consisting primarily of the men with whom he had conducted his recent reconnaissance, together with a small Fifth Infantry contingent. By 2 p.m. all of the units were in motion, with wagons distributed between the different corps: under Colonel Twiggs, one company of dragoons, the Fifth Infantry, Ringgold's battery, the Fourth Infantry, the Third Infantry, followed by two more companies of dragoons; under Lieutenant Colonel Belknap, the Eighth Infantry, Duncan's battery, the Artillery Battalion ("red leg" artillery companies serving as infantry), and a squadron of dragoons as rear guard. Taylor's order concluded with instructions for the deployment of his troops if they were attacked on the chaparral-edged section of road near their fort, but the Americans discovered no sign of the enemy as they hastened eastward with their wagons. Around midnight, after the 2,200 troops with Taylor had covered about half the distance to Point Isabel, they slept on the prairie, Brevet Major Philip N. Barbour (Third Infantry) wrote his wife, "without fire, water, or blankets," and by noon on May 2, tired and hungry, they reached their destination.[37]

At the nearly deserted American fort opposite Matamoros, as yet unnamed (and never officially called "Fort Texas," as it has often been termed by historians), Second Lieutenant Napoleon Jackson Tecumseh Dana, a West Point graduate in 1842, son of a deceased West Point graduate, grandson of a Revolutionary War veteran, ardent husband of Sue, devoted father of their infant daughter, Mary, and just turned twenty-four years of age on April 15, was supremely confident that General Taylor would defeat any hostile force he met. "The enemy will not hold out long," he predicted in his hasty note to Sue of May 1. "The army will return in a very few days and will bring mails with them and then I shall hear from my darling."[38] Evidently neither he nor anyone else anticipated that Arista's first move would be to open a blistering artillery attack on the fort, as he did at reveille on Sunday, the third of May.

5
Palo Alto, Resaca de la Palma, and Fort Brown

From inside the American fort opposite Matamoros on May 4 Napoleon Dana described for Sue the previous day's artillery exchange across the Rio Grande: "[W]e had just commenced washing, etc., before going to work when the batteries of the enemy opened, and their shot and shells began to whistle over our heads in rapid succession. . . . We were all at our arms in a moment and the artillerists at their guns, and soon our big guns began to pay them back in their own coin and with interest. . . . In the first eight shots we silenced their nearest battery." After some six hours of incessant firing, the fort's defenders were ordered by their commander, Major Jacob Brown, to save their remaining ammunition (about half) for emergencies. Only one man, a Seventh Infantry sergeant, had been killed or severely wounded that day.[1]

At Point Isabel, General Taylor and his troops presumed that the fort was under attack when they heard the rumble of distant artillery fire at daylight on the third. Ulysses Grant, who like Dana had celebrated his twenty-fourth birthday a few days earlier, at once wrote Julia that the army was going to start back to the fort at one o'clock that afternoon and would probably have "an engagement." It was understood, he said, that "several thousand" Mexicans were camped nearby. Another officer wrote that there was "great excitement" in the army at the prospect of a battle, but Grant's reaction was pragmatic. "Dont [*sic*] fear for me My Dear Julia for this is only the active part of our business. It is just what we come [*sic*] here for and the sooner it begins the sooner it will end and probably be the means of seeing my Dear Julia soon." Many years later Grant would declare that the sound of hostile guns made him feel sorry he had enlisted, but clearly in 1846 he chiefly viewed the war through the prism of its effect on his all-consuming desire to marry Julia.[2]

Grant was not the only officer who was under the impression that the 2,200 troops Taylor had brought with him to the coast were scheduled to start their return to the fort within hours after the firing commenced—Captain Ephraim

Kirby Smith wrote his wife from Point Isabel on May 3, "We are to march from here at one o'clock today to the rescue, as we suppose, of our little command before Matamoras [*sic*]." However, since there is no record of a formal order to that effect, Taylor must have decided very quickly that he would postpone his departure for a day or two at least. On the third he informed the adjutant general that he intended to remain at Point Isabel "if not necessarily called back to the river, until the arrival of some ordnance supplies and perhaps recruits from New Orleans." It was of course a risky decision. Nevertheless, as far as is known, he did not discuss alternative courses of action with any of his high-ranking subordinates, four of whom were no longer with his army—Worth, Whistler, Hitchcock, and the murdered Colonel Cross. Taylor seems never to have been particularly close to Colonel Twiggs, or to most of his other senior officers. In this instance he might have asked the opinion of Captain Samuel Walker, whose Texas Rangers had been scouting the Point Isabel–Matamoros route.[3]

Whether or not consulted, on May 3 Captain Walker was sent with a party of his Rangers to investigate conditions at the fort. Accompanied by a detachment of dragoons, they set out that afternoon. Within six or seven miles of the river, at the edge of the chaparral in which Mexican forces were believed to be hiding, the dragoons bivouacked for the night while the Texans drifted into the dense thickets. The next morning, Walker's men having failed to reappear, the dragoons galloped back to Point Isabel. Their approach in a cloud of dust caused Taylor's nervous soldiers at the depot to prepare for battle, confident that the approaching horsemen were the enemy.[4] The dragoons, as they returned, had seen about seventy Mexican cavalrymen at a distance, and signs that a large party of enemy troops had recently come up from the direction of Burrita, a village on the river's southern bank near its mouth. Of course the dragoons could tell General Taylor nothing about the Rio Grande artillery battle, now in its second day, but Old Zach's reliance on Sam Walker proved justified. Walker had arrived at the fort the previous night, Dana wrote Sue, and had killed five Mexican "videttes" while passing through the enemy forces surrounding the American fieldwork. The following morning Walker had been unable to find a way to avoid the Mexican lines. He would be going through that evening, he informed Dana, who hoped the Texan would take the letter he was writing with him.[5]

As planned, Walker managed to slip past the Mexican soldiers after dark on May 4, and before sunrise the next morning reached Point Isabel with the welcome news that the fort and its garrison had suffered little damage from the intermittent but occasionally heavy shelling of the last two days. Moreover, a letter from the fort's commander which Walker delivered contained a number of reassuring comments. Major Brown reported that the unfinished "curtain and gateway" were nearly completed. Initially, all of the fort's guns had answered those on the opposite shore. Later, after the enemy's nearest guns were silenced, Brown had ordered his six-pounders (Bragg's battery) to cease firing and to be positioned to repel any assault from the rear, having found that those guns were largely ineffective against the enemy's remaining batteries, and wishing to husband his "men" and "means." The Mexicans had then concentrated on Captain Lowd's battery (the eighteen-pounders) but had done little harm.[6]

General Taylor, having been assured that thus far the fort had withstood a blistering, unceasing bombardment with light damage, continued to place greater emphasis on thorough preparation for the seemingly certain hostilities that lay ahead than on haste. On May 5 his men were ordered to work on the port's entrenchments in alternating half-day shifts, from 6:30 a.m. to 6 p.m. The following day the recruits that had just arrived were assigned to units garrisoning the depot, and officers and men recently brought from St. Joseph's Island were told to rejoin their companies without delay. Old Zach also authorized the hiring of up to one hundred laborers to assist in completing the depot's defenses. Three days earlier, perhaps in anticipation that he would soon be sending wounded men to the port, he had transferred two medical officers to Point Isabel, one being his daughter Ann's husband, Dr. Robert Crooke Wood.[7]

Meanwhile the garrison of the American fieldwork opposite Matamoros, occasionally menaced by sharpshooters and by a howitzer that the fort's artillerymen had been unable to silence, waited confidently for Taylor to come to their relief. At tattoo on May 3, Dana and his company had crept out of the fort very quietly to bury the only soldier in the fort's garrison thus far killed, Sergeant Weigart, on the bank of the river. On the night of the fifth, Dana went with a sortie party under Captain Mansfield to destroy some sheds and other buildings that had been used to shelter enemy attackers surrounding the American fort. The next morning a howitzer shell "took off the leg of Major Brown below the knee," Dana wrote Sue. That afternoon General Arista sent four officers to the fort under a white flag with a letter demanding the garrison's surrender. Captain Edgar Hawkins, who had succeeded the fatally wounded Major Brown as the fort's commander, declined to comply after convening a council of officers, all of whom agreed that Arista's summons was ridiculous. But according to Dana, on May 7 the bombardment was "still hotter and the shells were thrown better" than previously. "A shell fell at the feet of Corporal Van Voorhies, another rolled over a man's back and another between a man's legs whilst he was eating dinner, and although they all burst, they hurt no one. A shot went through Capt Hawkins' tent just over his head when he was eating breakfast . . . a shell and a grapeshot through mine, a shell through

[Daniel] Whiting's, [Washington] Seawell's, and so forth. . . . Fifteen of our horses were killed."[8]

The Mexicans did not attempt to storm the earthwork, although several hundred rancheros approached it on at least two occasions, firing their muskets harmlessly. They were answered by "rifles on the parapet," Dana wrote, but for the most part the Americans continued to husband their ammunition, merely throwing "a few eighteen-pound shot" whenever they sighted human targets. On the fifth day of the siege the garrison suffered more casualties—one man's arm and another's leg were broken. Major Brown, whose shattered leg had been amputated, was feverish. The only safe place to put him, Dana explained, was "in a magazine where it was so hot he could scarcely breathe." At long last, on the afternoon of the eighth the fort's garrison heard cannonading to the east, lasting from about three o'clock until sundown, which told them that "the general was on the move and had met the enemy."[9]

The main body of the American army, with some three hundred wagon-loads of provisions and ammunition, had commenced its return march along the Point Isabel–Matamoros road on May 7 at 3 p.m. The order for the movement, issued by Brevet Captain William Bliss, the assistant adjutant general who served as Taylor's chief of staff, stated in part: "It is known that the enemy has recently occupied the route in force—if still in position, the General will give him battle. . . . He wishes to enjoin upon the battalions of Infantry that their main dependence must be in the bayonet." That reference to reliance on the bayonet has led to an assumption by historians that Taylor had long anticipated that at some point a bayonet charge would be required in order to force a passage through Mexican ranks. Yet whether there would be a fight that day was anyone's guess: Captain Walker had reported just before the march began that he had seen no Mexicans when he scouted the route that morning, and Captain Ephraim Kirby Smith wrote his wife on the seventh, "This afternoon we start back with the wagon train, but it is thought doubtful whether the enemy [will] oppose our march."[10]

As the column was preparing to depart, George Meade wrote of his concern that the "large train of provisions and ammunition" they would be taking with them would impede their movements. He did not suggest, however, as certain critics would later, that Taylor should not have caused his troops to be hampered by the need to protect a long, slow-moving supply train. Indeed, Meade seemed to agree with Taylor's assumption that the fort was probably in desperate need of ammunition, a reasonable apprehension since the Americans at Point Isabel had been hearing cannonading for five days.[11] Moreover, Taylor could not have known on May 7 that there would be a battle before his column reached the fort, much less that all contending Mexican forces would retreat across the river, and it would have been pointless to have relieved the fort without the means to defend it. More of everything would have been required shortly to enable them to maintain their position opposite Matamoros; and small detachments could not have continued to serve as escorts for several hundred wagons loaded with vital ordnance and provisions, as they had previously, if hostile Mexican forces remained nearby.

That they would be greatly outnumbered if the Mexicans elected to make a stand was assumed, since spies had assured the Americans that General Arista's command was at least six thousand strong; yet on May 7 all of the men preparing to march with Taylor, regardless of rank, seem to have been "in the best of spirits," as Meade wrote Margaretta. Indeed, the officers were anxious to have their regular army regiments give the Mexicans "a sound thrashing" before the arrival of any of the volunteer units requested by Taylor. Doubtless there were some, as Ulysses Grant said of himself years later, who reacted more soberly to the thunderous distant cannonade, but scarcely anyone appears to have feared defeat, however outnumbered they might be.[12]

Their boundless confidence was not tested on May 7. Without hindrance the American column covered about seven miles before halting for the night on the open prairie. Equally uneventful was the next day's march until, shortly after noon, the advance guard sighted Mexican cavalrymen blocking the road some two or three miles ahead. The moments that followed would become legendary: there being a large pond at hand, Taylor ordered his men to take turns filling their canteens and watering their horses while the wagon train was brought up and parked.[13]

Evidently neither Taylor nor the troops with him gave much thought to how important it was for them to win this first battle of the war. In a sense, the Army of Occupation was in a better position than at the Arroyo Colorado. The men and heavy artillery pieces transported by sea from Corpus Christi to Point Isabel were available to strengthen the units with Taylor, and other troops were due to arrive shortly. Moreover, the fortified American depot at Point Isabel could be resorted to if retreat became necessary. On the other hand, of course, the bulk of Taylor's army was separated by many miles from the five hundred troops and civilians in the fort opposite Matamoros. The entire Seventh Infantry, as well as Bragg's and Lowd's artillery companies, would inevitably have become prisoners of the Mexicans, along with the already captured dragoons, unless the units with Taylor were able to rescue them. Even more important in the long run, perhaps, would have been the psychological result of an American loss. Mexican authorities, emboldened, would naturally have been even more determined to fight rather than to negotiate differences.

At first, while the Americans were refilling their canteens at the so-called Palo Alto water hole, they could not see the Mexican forces distinctly, perceiving them as a long, dark smudge stretching across the horizon. Then, moving toward that ominous shadow, "in perfect parade order, . . . without beat of drum," in McCall's words, and "with the measured step of a drill-day," they approached within about a mile of Arista's army. Riding ahead, dangerously close to the Mexican lines in an effort to locate their artillery, was topographical engineer Lieutenant Jacob Blake.[14] In an hour most of Taylor's column was deployed for battle. Captain Walker and a squadron of dragoons took the lead initially, about two hundred yards in front of the line of infantry and artillery. Another squadron of dragoons was positioned in the rear with the wagon train. Colonel Twiggs commanded the dragoons and the rest of the right wing of the army, which consisted of, from the right to the center of the line, the Fifth Infantry, among whose officers were Edmund Kirby Smith, Carter Stevenson, Randolph Marcy, Daniel Ruggles, Thomas Pitcher, and John Robinson; the Third Artillery's Company C light battery of three six-pounders and one howitzer under Brevet Major Samuel Ringgold, to which Sam French belonged; the Third Infantry, assigned to which were Buell, Hatch, Bushrod Johnson, Israel Richardson, Barnard Bee, Thomas Jordan, and William T. H. Brooks; two eighteen-pound iron cannon drawn by oxen in the center of the road under the direction of William Churchill (Third Artillery) who was assisted by Thomas J. Wood (topographical engineer); and near them, to their left, the Fourth Infantry, with Ulysses Grant, George McCall, Robert Buchanan, Christopher Augur, Benjamin Alvord, and Alexander Hays. A party of Texas Rangers was on the far right flank. The left wing, commanded by Lieutenant Colonel Belknap, consisted of, from left to right, the Eighth Infantry with Longstreet, Robert Maclay, Henry Judah, and William R. Montgomery (in formation as reserve); Captain James Duncan's Second Artillery Company A light battery of two six-pounders and two howitzers to which were assigned John J. Peck and William Hays; and the Artillery Battalion (foot artillery) under Lieutenant Colonel Thomas Childs, whose members included "Prince John" Magruder and Seth Williams (First Artillery), Charles F. Smith (Second Artillery), and John McCown, John Pemberton, and Robert Garnett (Fourth Artillery). In one or another of the dragoon squadrons were Lawrence Pike Graham, William Steele, and Alfred Pleasonton. George Meade, being a member of Taylor's staff, was with the general's party. Very few of the men in Old Zach's marching column had previously engaged in combat.[15]

It soon became evident that General Arista's troops, as they waited in line of battle across the Matamoros road and on the Palo Alto plain, vastly outnumbered those in the approaching American force. McCall noted that the Mexican "right and left extremes were nearly the length of our whole line beyond either flank of our little army." After the battle he wrote: "The Mexicans were drawn up in two lines, as we have since learned, with a strong reserve. The first line consisted of twelve hundred cavalry, of whom eight hundred were lancers. The second line was of infantry, with eleven pieces of artillery distributed in the intervals between battalions; their entire force, as since ascertained, was something over six thousand, while ours was under two thousand three hundred."[16]

The lines of Arista's army, forming a front a mile or more long, were essentially one—a left and a right sector, each extending well beyond the flanks of the American line approaching them around 2 p.m. As would later be established, the Mexican right wing contained a body of cavalry under General Luis Noriega, a four-pounder cannon, a company of sappers, light infantry, and brigades of infantry commanded by Brigadier Generals José Maria García and Rómulo Díaz de La Vega, the infantry units separated by artillery batteries (two eight-pounders, five four-pounders). On their left, beyond a space of about four hundred feet and somewhat forward, were regiments of cavalry and two small guns under General Torrejón, whose command held the Matamoros road. Further leftward were irregular cavalry under General Canales, which did not join the fight. Ampudia's brigade, arriving just before the battle commenced, was deployed between Torrejón and the infantry. Reputedly, these various Mexican commands differed widely with respect to their training, equipment, and leadership. The estimate by American participants that the forces they faced on May 8 numbered six thousand would be revised sharply downward by historians, but there seems to be little doubt that Arista's army numbered more than twice as many as Taylor's 1,700 effectives, the rest of his marching column of 2,228 having been posted as guards for the wagon train.[17]

In retrospect, General Taylor's dispositions on May 8 proved fortuitous. They were simple—his two divisions were stretched across the road, McIntosh's on the left, Twiggs's extending rightward, beyond the ox-drawn iron eighteen-pounder siege guns occupying the road. However, it was the placement of the two American light artillery companies, Duncan's on the line's left flank and Ringgold's on the right, together with that of Churchill's siege cannon in the center, that enabled Taylor's artillery to command the whole of Arista's army. Indeed, even the wagon train contributed to the strength of Taylor's position, anchoring as it did the American troops to its forefront and providing an incentive for them to remain concentrated in a tight phalanx whose firepower protected the entire column.

Mexican artillery opened the battle around 2:30 or 3 p.m. The Americans halted within half a mile of Arista's lines, and the guns of Duncan, Churchill, and Ringgold responded, scouring the grassy prairie and creating temporary gaps in the facing Mexican regiments. As Ulysses Grant indicated in his memoirs, neither army had an advantage when it came to small-arms fire, but the Mexican field artillery at Palo Alto was apparently more limited in its capa-

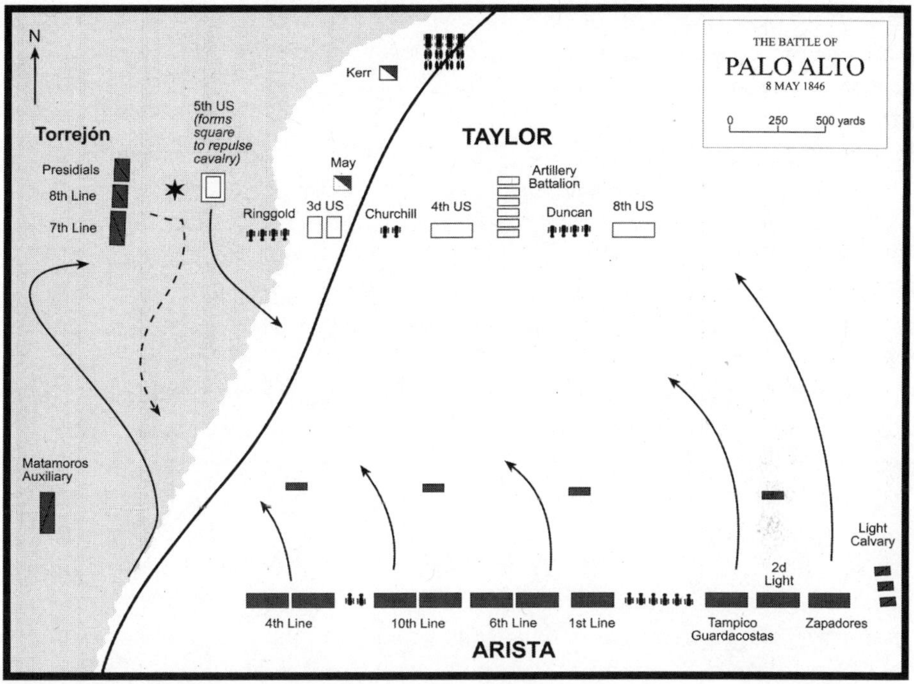

2. Palo Alto, May 8, 1846

bility: "The infantry under General Taylor was armed with flint-lock muskets, and paper cartridges with powder, buck-shot and ball. At the distance of a few hundred yards a man might fire at you all day without your finding it out. . . . The Mexicans were armed about as we were so far as their infantry was concerned, but their artillery only fired solid shot." In contrast, Duncan's and Ringgold's batteries were equipped not only with six-pounder brass cannon but with twelve-pounder howitzers employing ammunition that fragmented after firing, such as canister and grape.[18] Grant may have been correct in asserting that during the Palo Alto battle the Mexican artillery fired only solid shot, but other officers mentioned the enemy's having employed grape and canister at Resaca de la Palma.

Still, though Taylor's artillery was far more effective than Arista's, men on both sides were being wounded and killed. Grant's friend Sam French, serving with Ringgold's light artillery battery, would long remember his first encounter with death in battle: "My rank assigned me to the duty of sitting on my horse to look at the fight and watch the caissons. Presently a small shell came along and struck the driver of the lead horses. The shell entered his body after carrying away the pommel of his saddle, and exploded the moment it left his body, as fragments of it wounded his horse in the hip, split the lip and tongue, and knocked out some teeth of a second horse and broke the jaw of Lieut. [Randolph] Ridgely's blooded mare." According to French, he immediately dismounted, took command of the howitzer on his right, and proceeded to help load, aim, and discharge it. One reason Arista's casualties far exceeded those of Taylor's troops, French intimated, was that "[t]hey turned their guns on our batteries; we fired at their infantry as instructed." He did not say which American officer issued that order. Somewhat later, French also helped the Fifth Infantry repulse the chief Mexican charge of the afternoon. He and Lieutenant Ridgely, with two pieces of Ringgold's battery, were rushed to the right flank after about an hour of cannonading, when hundreds of Mexican cavalrymen undertook an encircling movement threatening the wagon train: Torrejón's lancers and the two small guns he commanded began swerving leftward, around Taylor's right wing, toward the three hundred wagons parked near the Palo Alto pond. The Americans, unaware of the extent to which Torrejón's approaching cavalry and guns were hampered by marshy ground, credited his repulse mainly to Taylor's forces. Brigade commander Lieutenant Colonel James McIntosh described the incident in his report to Taylor's chief of staff, Captain Bliss. His regiment, in obedience to orders, had moved "to the right and rear" covering the wagon train, and had formed a square. With the aid of Captain Walker's Texans, the Fifth Infantry had repulsed several charges by some "*one thousand*" of the enemy's cavalry when suddenly the Mexican lancers were reinforced by "two guns of horse artillery." Then, McIntosh recalled, Ridgely's battery galloped up. "He opened his fire so promptly and with such effect that the *enemy's artillery* was completely routed, and retreated precipitately under the protection of their cavalry, without discharging a gun." McIntosh commended both French and Ridgely for their "gallant bearing," and also the conduct of Captain Walker and his small command of Texas Rangers. Among the Fifth Infantry officers whom McIntosh specifically praised were Brevet Second Lieutenants Edmund Kirby Smith and Thomas Pitcher, and First Lieutenants Carter L. Stevenson, Randolph B. Marcy, and Daniel Ruggles. A report by Colonel Twiggs likewise mentioned the part played by French and Ridgely, as well as the Third Infantry's supporting role in the action.[19]

As Torrejón's cavalry retreated, leaving behind men and horses "pitched in every direction," McCall asserted, one of Duncan's guns on the American left flank set the tall prairie grass on fire. A breeze swirled a curtain of smoke across the whole battlefield, hiding the two armies from one another. For an hour or more during that interlude, with the artillery on both sides largely silent, General Taylor "rode along the line chatting with the officers, and those of different regiments visited each other," McCall wrote. To him the interval was memorable for the personal pain it presaged. "Major Ringgold rode up to our regiment, and I talked with him for half an hour. Alas! When I next saw him a few hours afterwards, he was mortally wounded."[20]

Meanwhile, both the Mexican and American lines tilted about thirty-five degrees toward one another on their right flanks, the American right pushing ahead southwestward into the area held at first by Torrejón, and the Mexican right more northeastward, toward Duncan's battery and the Eighth Infantry, on the left of Taylor's lines. The American change of position followed the firing of two of Ringgold's guns into Torrejón's retreating cavalry, forcing the latter to seek safety further back on Arista's left than formerly, and permitting Taylor's eighteen-pounders to move forward almost to the chaparral-edged sector of the Matamoros road that was originally occupied by Torrejón's lancers. Then, as the smoke began to clear, Taylor ordered the Third and Fifth infantry regiments to cover both the wagon train and the army's right flank, and sent the Fourth Infantry forward. The advance of the Fourth in "double column" was, McCall said, "something like groping in the dark," and ended tragically for Captain John Page and an enlisted man. "We at length found the enemy at some distance to *their* left of their former position; they had filed off during the burning of the prairie. . . . A flank movement of our column was ordered, and at that time a cannonshot carried off the lower jaw of an old companion of mine, Captain Page. . . . As I passed him, poor fellow, he presented a shocking sight. The next instant the head of the soldier on the right of the division was carried away, and his brains were dashed into the faces of those around me." McCall's second lieutenant, Ulysses Grant, also described the havoc wrought by the missile that fatally wounded Page. "Although the balls were whizzing thick and fast about me," he wrote Julia, "I did not feel a sensation of fear until nearly the close of the firing a ball struck close by me killing one man instantly, it nocked [*sic*] Capt. Page's under Jaw entirely off and broke in the roof of his mouth, and nocked Lt. [Henry D.] Wallen and one Sergeant down besides, but they were not much hurt."[21]

Arista's change of position was evidently undertaken in preparation for an attack by Noriega's cavalry, with the assistance of some of Torrejón's lancers and supported by the several Mexican infantry regiments facing Taylor's left. Noriega's charge came within three hundred yards of the Eighth Infantry's lines and Duncan's cannon before being repulsed by those units and a squadron of the Second Dragoons under Captain Croghan Ker that had been guarding the supply train. Colonel Belknap said it was Duncan who discovered that the entire Mexican right wing was moving toward the parked American wagons. With Belknap's permission, Duncan's battery "dropped back to the left flank in full view of the enemy, and engaged him within point blank range of his small guns," throwing the whole Mexican right "into the utmost confusion." Another segment of Belknap's command, the Artillery Battalion, was at the same time engaged in fighting off a Mexican effort to take Lieutenant William Churchill's eighteen-pounders.[22]

Although the artillery battle raged until dark, the opposing armies "never came to close quarters" after Taylor's right wing advanced, McCall declared. He described the final positioning of the combatants: "Both armies may be said to have slept on the field of battle;—we had advanced and they had retired a little; but our right was not a half mile from their right, and we could distinctly hear the cries of the wounded during the stillness of the night." Grant added in his letter to Julia of May 11: "When it become to [*sic*] dark to see the enemy we encamped upon the field of battle and expected to conclude the fight the next morning. Morning come [*sic*] and we found that the enemy had retreated under cover of night. So ended the battle of the 8th of May. . . . It was a terrible sight to go over the ground the next day and see the amont [*sic*] of life that had been destroyed. The ground was litterally [*sic*] strewed with the bodies of dead men and horses."

In a brief report to the adjutant general on the morning of May 9 from his "Camp near Palo Alto," Old Zach estimated that about one hundred of Arista's troops had been killed, while American casualties were "comparatively trifling—4 men killed—three officers and 39 men wounded, several of the latter mortally." (Historians have varied slightly in their findings; one respected source states Mexican losses were 92 killed, 116 wounded, 26 missing; American, 9 killed, 44 wounded, 2 missing.) Taylor, rather than claiming to have won the battle, said merely that his men had "dislodged" the Mexican army from its position and had then "encamped upon the field." Their success, he explained, was mainly due to the column's artillery units, "the arm chiefly engaged," and to "the excellent manner in which it was manouvered [*sic*] & served." George Meade, one of the general's several staff members employed in carrying Old Zach's instructions to his subordinates on the battlefield, believed that if Taylor had not been encumbered with the supply train he could have completely routed Arista's army when it began to withdraw at the close of the day. But conditions were not propitious for an attack by the Americans. Taylor's troops were still badly outnumbered, especially from the standpoint of cavalry, which made their flanks extremely vulnerable on the Palo Alto plain. Moreover, with darkness descending the situation was unclear, and even though Arista's troops seemed to be retreating in disorder, their movements were obscured by chaparral west of the battlefield.[23]

At daybreak on May 9, Taylor's scouts glimpsed Mexican infantrymen withdrawing into the dense thickets beyond which lay the American fieldwork, but could not determine for several hours whether the enemy's troops were recrossing the Rio Grande or were reassembling in strength somewhere up ahead, still blocking the road to the besieged fort. While work parties buried the dead of both armies, Taylor's medical officers tried to ease the suffering of the wounded, including Mexican soldiers left behind on the battlefield. Old Zach, after holding a council of war, ordered his supply train to be "strongly parked at its position"; left with it Churchill's two eighteen-pounders as well as two twelve-pounders which had not seen action the previous day; assigned most of the Artillery Battalion and a squadron of dragoons to guard the train; arranged for the wounded to be escorted back to Point Isabel by a dragoon squadron under Lieutenant William Steele; and moved the rest of his army forward a bit, to the edge of the chaparral obscuring the next seven miles of his line of march. The fact that the American artillery had been able to fend off Arista's army did not embolden Twiggs and several of the other senior officers. They argued that the army should wait for reinforcements before risking another such encounter. Taylor, in contrast, paused barely long enough to let them have their say before going ahead with preparations to lead his army forward, or so a Third Infantry captain heard: "General Taylor called a council of war upon the presentation of Col. Twiggs that the commanders of corps generally were in favor of intrenching our camp where it was and awaiting reinforcements. It leaked out after the council broke up that 7 out of 10 were in favor of this suggestion of inaction. Col. McIntosh, Capt. [Lewis N.] Morris [Third Infantry] and Duncan to their praises be it spoken were in favor of fighting again. The General sided with them. His mind was doubtless made up beforehand."[24] Why Taylor called a council of war is unclear—perhaps as a courtesy to Twiggs, or to discuss whether the slow-moving, long wagon train and ox-drawn eighteen-pounders should accompany the marching column into the chaparral-enclosed stretch of road ahead. There was good reason to keep pressing forward, as Twiggs and the others should have realized. The number of recruits that could have been obtained from Point Isabel within a day or so would not have been significant enough to warrant a delay, for any holdup would have allowed Arista to obtain additional reinforcements as well.

Another occurrence that morning had particular import for George Meade. He became once again the senior topographical engineer on Taylor's staff with the fatal wounding of Lieutenant Jacob Blake, struck down by the discharge of his own pistol when, as he was sitting down to eat, it slipped from his belt. Meade wrote of "poor Blake" that he, "having gallantly borne himself through the conflict yesterday, unfortunately shot himself accidentally today, . . . and it is feared the wound is mortal."[25]

Around two o'clock that afternoon, still without knowing whether Arista's army was regrouping in the woods bordering the road, Taylor resumed his march toward the fort. In the lead was a hodgepodge of mounted troops commanded by Grant's captain, George McCall. Having been ordered to "feel the enemy and ascertain his position," McCall first sent Sam Walker and a handful of his Texas Rangers to scout ahead on the road, then told Charles F. Smith to take four light companies of First Brigade men, among whom were James Longstreet and John Pemberton, through the thickets on the right while McCall, Lieutenant John McCown, and the rest of the advance combed the chaparral on the left. A detachment of dragoons led by Lieutenant Alfred Pleasonton rode behind McCall's mixed columns of infantry. For more than two miles McCall's party "followed the trail of the enemy." After being fired on a few times "from a masked battery" near a ravine, by what the Americans believed to be the rear guard of the retiring Mexican army, McCall summoned Smith to join him and was on the verge of mounting an attack when he learned that a large body of enemy troops had been sighted on the left, and lancers on the road. Convinced that Arista's entire force was nearby, McCall dispatched three dragoons to inform General Taylor of his discovery.[26]

Of the manner in which the American troops were then deployed, Taylor wrote the adjutant general: "Ridgely's battery and the advance under Capt. McCall were at once thrown forward on the road and into the chaparral on either side, while the 5th Infantry and one wing of the 4th, was thrown to the forest on the left, and the 3d and other corps were deployed as skirmishers to cover the battery and engage the Mexican infantry." McCall's command and the infantry regiments having spread out into the road's wooded borders, the Third Artillery battery that had been commanded by the late Major Ringgold and was now led by his successor, Lieutenant Randolph Ridgely, became the army's spearhead. Ridgely's brevet second lieutenant, Sam French, implied in his autobiography that Taylor had expected too much of them: "Here then was the singular tactics of a battery of horse artillery all alone, leaving the entire army behind, moving down the road through the woods without any support whatever."[27] Writing fifty-five years after the incident, French obviously failed to take into account that an American unit of some type was needed to cover the road, and that no other was better equipped to locate and at the same time counter the hidden Mexican batteries. As for support, none would be necessary until obstacles to their progress were encountered, and Captain Charles May's dragoon squadron was waiting in reserve on the eastern edge of the woods. At any rate Ridgely dashed ahead with his guns, guided by Captain Sam Walker. They had advanced about half a mile, according to French, when cannonballs began crashing around them through the trees from "unseen batteries in front." Although there was no longer any doubt that the road was indeed blocked by Mexican forces, Ridgely did not halt his command until they were facing several of Arista's cannon, situated on both banks of an old riverbed which the Americans understood was called Resaca de la Palma. Even then Ridgely's artillerymen could not see all of Arista's lines, for the *resaca* curved irregularly as it crossed the road, roughly west to east, and Mexican contingents were covering each side of the narrow corridor along which the battery had clattered. In the meantime French had been dispatched twice to ask Taylor, a short distance behind the advance units, for reinforcements. Evidently after the first request Old Zach had sent for May's squadron, which had not yet shown up when French returned a second time to speak with Taylor and Bliss, for the general reputedly swore, saying, "I can't get him up!" Minutes later, May and his dragoons finally reached Ridgely's position. It was as Captain May prepared to charge that Lieutenant Randolph Ridgely became the hero of the day, shouting to May to wait while Ridgely drew the enemy's fire. That gesture assumed mythic proportions in the retelling, certainly so in the minds of Sam French, James Longstreet, and other memorializers of the incident.[28]

May's dragoons were unable to retain possession of the batteries they attacked, but they scattered the Mexican gunners and surrounded a consolation prize—Brigadier General Rómulo Díaz de La Vega. General Taylor was present when May galloped back to the American position east of the *resaca* bearing La Vega's sword. The dragoon captain, triumphantly announcing the capture of the Mexican general, presented the sword to Old Zach who, French recalled, "looked at it a moment and returned it to May." Longstreet, who was nearby when La Vega was trapped by May's dragoons, sent infantrymen to take charge of the prisoner.[29] Earlier, Longstreet had stumbled across the body of a young Mexican woman in the chaparral. "She had ceased to breathe, but blood heat was still in her body, and her expression life-like. A profusion of black hair covered her shoulders and person, the only covering to her waist."[30] She was perhaps one of the women Arista allegedly brought onto the battlefield to strip fallen Americans.

Joining the widening, increasingly disorganized struggle to overwhelm Arista's eight or nine artillery pieces were McCall's contingent and elements of the Third, Fourth, and Fifth infantry together with the regiment that had been held in reserve, the Eighth. Because the battle was fought principally amid dense woods enveloping the gullies of the old Rio Grande bed which spanned the route to the fort, it inevitably ended up as a ragged, disjointed affair, a kaleidoscope of haphazard actions, with groups of infantrymen being led by whatever officers happened to be at hand. Robert Buchanan, for example, supported by Lieutenants Hays and Wood and three companies of the Fourth Infantry, seized an artillery piece on the Mexican left which was thereafter protected by a Third Infantry captain against attempts to retake it. Some of the Fifth Infantry's officers and men, among them Edmund Kirby Smith, with the assistance of troops in McCall's command, stormed sectors of the Mexican line in hand-to-hand combat, capturing five of the enemy's largest guns.[31] Unlike at Palo Alto, Taylor's admonition to rely on the bayonet, issued as his army was

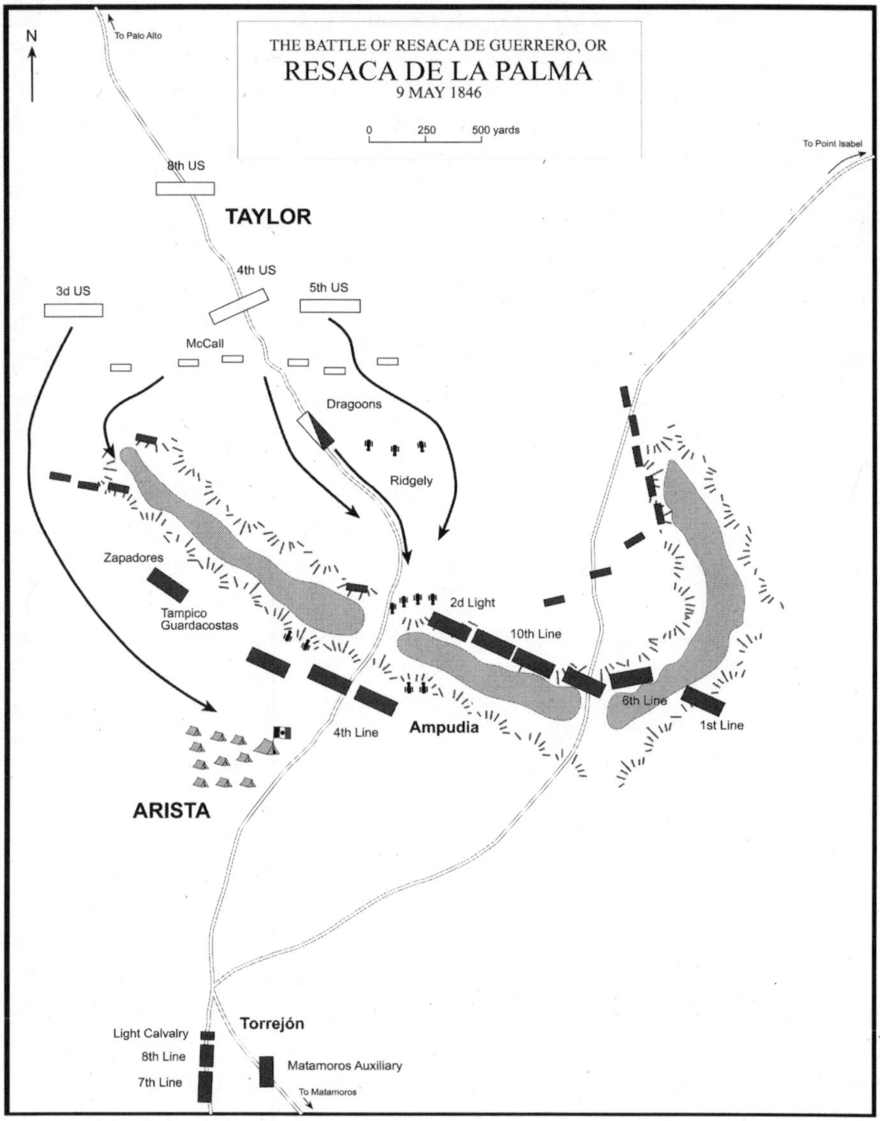

3. Resaca de la Palma, May 9, 1846

about to leave Point Isabel on May 7, was pertinent at Resaca de la Palma. The Americans, as well as their counterparts, suffered considerably from such thrusts. One of the most severely wounded officers, Lieutenant Colonel McIntosh, received three nearly fatal bayonet wounds. Also among the twelve officers wounded were future generals Robert Maclay and William R. Montgomery.[32]

Although for the Americans the most dramatic incident of the battle was the dragoon charge against Mexican artillery pieces along the banks of the *resaca,* Taylor's enlisted men and the lieutenants and captains who commanded them were just as responsible, if not more so, for the victory of May 9. That is evident from their having captured eight cannon as well as one hundred or more Mexican soldiers, including fourteen officers. One of the many company-grade infantry officers leading men through chaparral toward unseen foes that afternoon was Lieutenant Ulysses Grant who, with Captain McCall in charge of the advance contingent, was acting commander of the Fourth Infantry's Company C. In his usual self-deprecatory manner he would tell of suddenly realizing, after capturing "a Mexican colonel, who had been wounded, and a few men," that the ground "had been charged over before." Nevertheless, his account demonstrates, as do others, that many of Taylor's young infantry officers were very much on their own as they met Mexican forces in the dense woods. Old Zach implicitly recognized their significant contribution in his report of that evening, saying: "A heavy fire of artillery and musketry was kept up for some time until finally the enemy's batteries were carried in succession by a squadron of Dragoons and the regiments of Infantry that were on the ground. . . . The affair of today may be regarded as a proper supplement to the cannonade of yesterday, and the two taken together exhibit the coolness and gallantry of our officers and men." In his more detailed report he would remark that the American victory was doubtless due to "the superior quality of our officers and men."[33]

Once the Mexican army lost its protective artillery shield, it quickly disintegrated. Taylor's Fourth Infantry troops occupied Arista's headquarters camp, acquiring his official correspondence, personal baggage, and hundreds of other trophies such as the drum used as a table by Grant in writing Julia on the eleventh. Ridgely's light artillery gunners, delayed by the loss of horses and drivers, finally followed pell-mell on the heels of Duncan's battery, Captain Croghan Ker's dragoons, the Third Infantry, and the artillery companies that had been guarding the baggage train, all the way to the Rio Grande. At the river there was pandemonium. Napoleon Dana recalled that he and others in the fort "saw retreating columns of the enemy hurrying from the field of action towards the upper ferry. . . . Horse and foot had thrown away their arms and fled like the wind, trying to strike the river at the nearest points, where they would plunge in to swim over. Many were drowned."[34] Taylor had no opportunity to instruct the Seventh Infantry troops in the fort to cooperate in capturing or harassing Arista's fleeing thousands, which in any case would seem to have been inadvisable in light of the disparity in numbers.

Old Zach, having received assurances from eyewitnesses that the Mexican army had "recrossed the river," and that the fieldwork had "sustained itself handsomely," remained that evening near the Resaca de la Palma battlefield with the bulk of his army. At 10 p.m., from his "Camp 3 miles from Matamoros," he dictated a brief summary of the afternoon's events. The enemy's loss was "most severe," he informed the adjutant general. After naming the American officers killed and a number who were wounded on the ninth, Taylor reverted to the casualties caused by the bombardment of the fieldwork, mentioning in particular the loss of the fort's "heroic and indomitable" commander Major Jacob Brown, who had died that day. In his subsequent, more detailed report, Old Zach would say of the 2,222 troops in his marching force on May 9 that no more than 1,700 were engaged with the enemy, whereas Arista's army, which had been reinforced overnight, probably numbered six thousand men. American casualties consisted of three officers killed and twelve wounded, thirty-six men killed and seventy-one wounded. Mexican troops buried by Taylor's men in the days following the battle numbered over two hundred. Arista is said to have reported 154 killed, 205 wounded, and 156 missing.[35]

As it happened, the same day the battle of Resaca de la Palma was fought President Polk received Taylor's letter announcing the April 25 Mexican attack on the American dragoon patrol. Of course, General Taylor would not hear for some time that by May 13 the U.S. Congress had declared that the nation was at war with Mexico, but months ago he had been told by Secretary of War Marcy that he need not act merely on the defensive if Mexico engaged in "any open act of hostility" toward the United States. Yet until May 18 Taylor did not attempt to follow Arista across the Rio Grande. His failure to undertake an offensive campaign immediately, he would explain to the adjutant general, was due to his having "very limited means for crossing rivers." That was his own fault, critics would insist. He could have had pontoons built rather than hoping, as he had, that the War Department would respond to his repeated requests for them. But throughout most of April the American regiments opposite Matamoros had been rushing to complete the fieldwork fort, and Taylor could scarcely have anticipated that within a fortnight of the April 25 ambush he would be in a position to cross the Rio Grande.[36]

The troops who camped with General Taylor at Resaca de la Palma from the ninth to the eleventh spent most of their time burying the dead of both armies, rounding up prisoners, and inventorying captured articles—cannon, small arms, ammunition, entrenching tools, provisions, kettles, water casks, personal baggage, band instruments, drums, wagons, oxcarts, horses, saddles, mules, and silver coins. The carnage of May 9 was far worse than that of May 8. A Third Infantry captain commented, "It is exceedingly painful for me to dwell upon the horrors of that day—dead bodies of men and horses were piled up on each other exhibiting every expression of torture the most vivid imagination could picture, and so horribly mangled and torn, in many cases by cannon shot, that it was sickening to behold them." Ulysses Grant wrote, "After the battle the woods was strued [*sic*] with the dead. Waggons [*sic*] have been engaged drawing the bodies to bury. How many waggon loads have already come in and how many are still left would be hard to guess. I saw 3 large waggon loads at one time myself." But shocking as the loss of life was, the officers exuded pride over the momentousness of their accomplishment. Grant told Julia, "I think you will find that history will count the victory just achieved one of the greatest on record." Meade wrote his wife, "It will make you happy I know to hear of so brilliant an affair, and of your good husband having had a share in it." Lieutenant Edmund Kirby Smith rejoiced not only that the battle of the ninth was "a victory without equal in our history," but that it was "fought without the aid of militia."[37] Neither Grant, Meade, nor Edmund Kirby Smith would receive a brevet for having contributed to the American army's defeat of Arista's forces, though each would on other occasions; however, ten of the fifty-three future generals who fought in those battles or defended Taylor's besieged fort would be rewarded with a brevet promotion in rank.[38]

Another satisfying aspect of their triumph was that an exchange of prisoners brought back the dragoons who were captured when Thornton's squadron was attacked, although their return was marred, as mentioned previously, by the immediate arrest of Thornton, charged with neglect of duty and having disobeyed orders. And while Hardee, who resumed command of his company on the eleventh, escaped formal censure, certain of his fellow officers remained adamantly insistent that he acted improperly during the ambush.[39]

Following the battles of May 8 and 9, there appears to have been remarkably little animus on the part of either the American or the Mexican combatants, at least insofar as the officers were concerned. On May 12 General Taylor informed the adjutant general, in mentioning an exchange of prisoners, that the Americans that had been held as prisoners in Matamoros had been treated "with great kindness by the Mexican officers." General La Vega, after being captured at Resaca de la Palma, commented graciously on how well Taylor's army had fought. And George Meade, whose wife and family all spoke Spanish fluently, invited General La Vega to visit the Meade residence in Philadelphia if the Mexican general happened to be in that city. Writing of having extended the invitation, Meade said, "You will find him a most gentlemanly man and will be pleased, I am sure, with him."[40]

General Taylor, after congratulating his army, gave command of the troops in the immediate vicinity of the fieldwork to Twiggs, and returned to Point Isabel. There he consulted with Commodore David Conner, who had reached Brazos Santiago Pass on May 8 aboard his flagship *Cumberland,* accompanied by several other vessels, and had sent some five hundred seamen and marines ashore to assist the defenders of the depot. In addition to conferring with

Conner about "a combined move up the river," Taylor issued orders naming the Point Isabel installation "Fort Polk" in honor of the president, commended army and navy personnel and civilians for their help in fortifying the facility, and arranged for General La Vega and other captured officers who had refused parole to be escorted to New Orleans. The latter action, he explained to the adjutant general, was due to his not being "conversant with the usages of war in such cases." Selected to escort those prisoners was one of Grant's classmates, Lieutenant Joseph J. Reynolds.[41]

Volunteers from New Orleans and Mobile arrived before Taylor left Point Isabel, as did Lieutenant Colonel Henry Wilson with four companies of the First Infantry whose officers included three future Civil War generals: Brevet Major John J. Abercrombie and Second Lieutenants Schuyler Hamilton and Joseph B. Plummer. On May 14 Colonel Wilson was ordered to proceed with his battalion, together with other newly landed reinforcements from New Orleans and Mobile, to Burrita, the Mexican village on the Rio Grande's southern bank below Matamoros, and to "effect a junction with the naval force operating up the river." This maneuver was intended as a diversionary tactic, Taylor said later. His plan was for Wilson's 440 men, upon being joined by navy ships, to appear to threaten an assault on Matamoros from the south by seizing Burrita, while the main body of the American army crossed the river above Matamoros. However, Commodore Conner decided before Wilson's command reached the rendezvous point that the tides near the river's mouth made cooperation by the navy inadvisable, and so informed Taylor. Moreover, Conner warned against allowing the worm-eaten steamer *Neva,* which was transporting Wilson's supplies, to enter the choppy waters at the channel's mouth. But the *Neva,* though delayed by high winds, navigated the bar safely, and by 4 p.m. on May 17 Wilson occupied Burrita without resistance, his men being the first of Taylor's army to cross the Rio Grande.[42]

Taylor, who meanwhile had returned to his fort opposite Matamoros, was ill on the fourteenth. On the sixteenth a contingent of reinforcements reached the fort—a company of Alabama volunteers, and four more First U.S. Artillery companies which included Lieutenants William H. French, Joseph A. Haskin, Irvin McDowell, James B. Ricketts, and John N. Brannan. They had left Point Isabel on the fourteenth, escorting a train of two hundred wagons. Among the supplies transported may have been the heavy mortars for which Taylor had been waiting before moving against Matamoros, for by the seventeenth he was ready to cross the river. A few boats had been acquired, some taken from the opposite shore at night, some built. Remaining behind as garrison for the fieldwork would be the Seventh Infantry and Lowd's battery. Most of the other troops under Taylor's immediate command, including Bragg's battery, were ordered to be ready by 1 p.m. to march upriver to the site chosen for crossing. Given charge once again of the two eighteen-pound guns that had roared from the center of the American line at Palo Alto were Lieutenant William Churchill and his topographical engineer assistant, Lieutenant Thomas Wood. In another order dated May 17, Taylor named the fieldwork "Fort Brown" in memory of "the gallant commander who nobly fell in its defense," Major Jacob Brown.[43]

As the Americans were preparing to assemble at the crossing point selected by Meade, two or three miles above Fort Brown, Arista sent over a proposal for an armistice. Taylor rejected it, saying he did not have the authority to stop the war now that it had commenced. However, he offered to let Arista withdraw his troops from Matamoros without interference providing the Mexican general would agree to do so before the next day, and would also stipulate that he would not remove any public property. At sundown, having heard nothing more from Arista, Taylor left Fort Brown and joined his men at their upriver campsite.[44]

6
Occupation of Matamoros, Reynosa, Camargo, and Mier

Early on the morning of May 18, the main body of the Army of Occupation began crossing the Rio Grande. With Churchill's eighteen-pound cannon together with the field artillery batteries commanded by Bragg and Ridgely providing cover, "the light companies of all the [infantry] battalions were first thrown over, followed by the volunteer and regular cavalry."[1] The few boats Taylor had accumulated—some cut loose from their moorings by American soldiers who swam to the Matamoros side of the river at night, others hastily constructed at Fort Brown—turned out to be superfluous. As Old Zach later reported, "Arista had abandoned the town with all his troops the evening before, leaving only the sick and wounded."[2] After a group of Matamoros officials met with Taylor and formally surrendered the city, the rest of the general's column crossed at the upper ferry, welcomed by the American flag that some of the occupying troops had already raised over Fort Paredes. By the evening of May 18 Taylor, having elected to camp with his regiments on the outskirts of the city, had established his headquarters in a tent directly opposite Fort Brown. During the crossing a dragoon officer had drowned, Lieutenant George Stevens, a member of Grant's class at West Point whose demise was deeply lamented. It was Stevens who had meticulously mapped the route traveled by the seven companies of dragoons from Fort Jesup to Corpus Christi. A dragoon sergeant also drowned.[3]

The troops who had crossed the river with Taylor, housed in thin, leaky linen tents, took turns patrolling the town's streets, searching every inch of it under the direction of Colonel Twiggs, whom General Taylor appointed military governor of Matamoros. They discovered pieces of artillery, several caches of small arms and ammunition, and in the hospitals some three hundred of the enemy's wounded. They also found quantities of tobacco and cigars, which Old Zach confiscated and divided among his men, believing those articles to be government-owned property.[4] Meade was ordered to "make a survey of the city of Matamoros and the adjacent country to a distance of one and a half miles," assisted by a party of men from the First Brigade.[5]

Arista's army, estimated by the Americans to have shrunk to no more than four thousand men, was retreating in the direction of Monterrey and was no longer considered a threat. Taylor's cavalry, led by John Garland, had pursued Arista for sixty miles or so before returning to Matamoros on the twenty-second. They had captured "a small rear party, after a trifling skirmish"[6] during which a Mexican man and woman were killed and two of Garland's men were slightly wounded. "The scarcity of water and condition of his horses made it useless to proceed farther," Taylor informed the adjutant general.[7]

For weeks thereafter, the daily routine of the main body of General Taylor's army was much as it had been at Corpus Christi. Although many of the officers and men occasionally had duties that took them into Matamoros, or were able to visit its taverns, billiard parlors, and other attractions when off duty, they were generally kept busy with mundane military pursuits. On the twenty-first Taylor directed that the army's laundresses were to be brought to Matamoros without delay, as well as the baggage of the units stationed there.[8] The next day he decreed the assemblance of a court-martial at Fort Brown to try four officers.[9] The Seventh Infantry, Napoleon Dana's regiment, was relieved of garrisoning Fort Brown, and its commander was told to "encamp for the present at some good position near the Fort." Replacing that regiment in or adjacent to the fort were, in addition to Captain Lowd's battery, two companies of the First U.S. Artillery under Captain George Nauman.[10] The court of inquiry requested by Captain William Hardee, in an effort to defend his actions during the April 25 ambush, was convened on May 25, engaging many of Taylor's officers and various other individuals, such as the publisher of a Matamoros English-language newspaper, in the still-virulent controversy over the incident.[11]

Men who had described Mexican products and mores in great detail while at Corpus Christi tended to devote only a few lines to their impressions of Matamoros and its citizens in their letters and journals. Meade, characterizing it as "a town constructed of brick and stone houses," observed: "It is built in the Spanish fashion—low houses with flat roofs—but has evidently been on the decline for many years, as a majority of the houses are decayed and falling to pieces. It is almost entirely abandoned by the better part of the community." Captain William S. Henry referred briefly to having visited the city prison, the "Hall of Justice," and the "unfinished Cathedral." Captain Phil Barbour wrote that Matamoros was "laid off in squares"; of the houses he said, "The few windows they have are without glass and protected by iron railings in front." Ulysses Grant focused on cultural differences: "The Mexican house is low with a flat or thatched roof, with a dirt or brick floor, with but little fur-nature [*sic*] and in many cases the fire in the middle of the house as if it was a wig-wamb [*sic*]. The majority of the inhabitants are Indians." Napoleon Dana, having crossed the river from Fort Brown one morning, declared Matamoros a "mean, dirty-looking place." On the other hand, Captain Ephraim Kirby Smith liked its ambience: "The town is much like St. Augustine, only with larger, wider streets and finer public buildings." Lieutenant Bushrod Johnson and Captain Barbour, returning to their Third Infantry camp from an afternoon stroll through Matamoros, "got permission from a Mexican gentleman to walk through his garden," which contained "many pretty flowers and a great quantity of shrubbery and fruit trees." The officers emerged with a "beautiful bouquet." And George McCall, describing a dinner sponsored by the army's right wing in honor of a visiting delegation from Louisiana, commented that it "was given in town at *Arista's Headquarters,* a fine large mansion."[12]

During the latter part of May numerous personnel changes occurred. Carter L. Stevenson received a two-month leave "for health reasons." Robert P. Maclay, wounded in the battle of Resaca de la Palma, was granted sixty days' leave. On the twenty-eighth Taylor announced that Brevet Brigadier General Worth, having withdrawn his resignation and returned to the Army of Occupation "of his own volition," would "resume the command of the 1st Brigade." The next day Lieutenant Joseph Hooker of Massachusetts, a member of one of the newly arrived First U.S. Artillery companies, was detailed as "chief commissary" to the brigade of Louisiana volunteers commanded by Persifor F. Smith.[13] But by far the biggest change in personnel was effected by daily landings of hundreds of volunteers at Brazos Island and Point Isabel. As early as May 19 Taylor had begun worrying about being inundated with many more volunteers than the eight regiments he had requested in April from the governors of Louisiana and Texas.[14] The problem was that large numbers of volunteers could not be usefully employed until the Army of Occupation acquired the steamboats and wagons needed to begin a planned upriver offensive. In the meantime the volunteers would be largely idle but would of course require supplies and oversight. Although Old Zach was not yet aware that the Polk administration was in the process of calling up twenty thousand of the fifty thousand volunteers authorized by Congress in its declaration of war, he knew and regretted that General Gaines had, on his own initiative, asked the governors of several states to provide reinforcements for the Army of Occupation.[15]

Another complicating factor was that whereas the volunteers raised by Congress were required to enlist either for twelve months or for the duration of the war, most of the volunteers sent in response to the appeals of Taylor and Gaines had enlisted for no more than three or six months. Taylor informed the adjutant general on July 1 that the number of volunteers enrolled for less than twelve months was approximately eight thousand.[16] Nearly all of those men would be discharged by the end of August, inasmuch as few of them wanted to reenlist for twelve months and the unclear legal status of the six-month enlistees caused Taylor to release them prematurely. As a result, arrangements were required for a constant stream of departing volunteers during the summer of 1846.[17] Meanwhile, throughout that period, twelve-month volunteers from a variety of states were landing at Brazos Santiago Island—so many, in fact, that during Taylor's next battle, at Monterrey, he would have volunteers from Kentucky, Ohio, Tennessee, Mississippi, Maryland, the District of Columbia, Louisiana, and Texas serving directly under him, not to mention contingents from other states huddled in camps at intervals up and down the Rio Grande. His regular army troops would never again be able to brag of having won a battle without the help of volunteers.

For a time the majority of the volunteers, generally living apart in their own camps, had little contact with regular army troops, but George Meade, who until the end of May was constantly surveying Matamoros and its environs, complained: "The volunteers continue to pour in, and I regret to say I do not see it with much satisfaction. They are perfectly ignorant of discipline, and most restive under restraint. They are in consequence a most disorderly mass, who will give us, I fear, more trouble than the enemy. Already are our guard-houses filled daily with drunken officers and men, who go to the town, get drunk and commit outrages on the citizens."[18] Ulysses Grant, likewise incensed at the way in which certain of the troops treated the populace, told Julia: "Some of the volunteers and about all the Texans seem to think it perfectly right to impose upon the people of a conquered City to any extent, and even to murder them where the act can be covered by the dark." General Taylor confessed, in acknowledging that Texas volunteers had indeed committed reprehensible acts, as alleged by his son-in-law Dr. Wood: "I have not the power to remedy it or apply the corrective, I fear they are a lawless set." A week later, again referring to remarks by Dr. Wood about the Texans, Taylor wrote, "I expect if they could be made subordinate they would be the best, at any rate as good as any volunteer corps in service; but I fear they are & will continue too licentious to do much good."[19] As he apparently foresaw, the Texans, unforgiving of the brutal treatment many of their countrymen had received from Mexican generals in the recent past, would prove unmatchable in battle but frequently could not be deterred by their officers from taking out their wrath on Mexican civilians also. They often appeared unable or unwilling to differentiate between vicious Mexican leaders and the nation's populace who, as a whole, evidenced no antagonism toward the invaders as long as the treatment they received from Americans was not abusive, their religious or social customs were not affected, and they were recompensed for items supplied.

A substantial personnel change occurred within the ranks of the regular army men by the first week of June. Adjutant General Jones had informed Taylor on May 12 that the army needed more officers to serve as recruiters, due to a recently enacted law increasing to one hundred the number of privates permissible in army companies. Toward that end, Taylor was to break up a stipulated number of companies in each of his regiments, retaining only their privates to bolster remaining units, and their lieutenants if required to fill vacancies. Among the officers transferred out of the Army of Occupation as a consequence were: Third Infantry, Thomas Jordan and Barnard E. Bee; Fourth Infantry, Alexander Hays; Fifth Infantry, Daniel Ruggles and Randolph B. Marcy; Seventh Infantry, Gabriel J. Rains; Eighth Infantry, William R. Montgomery; and Second Dragoons, Richard H. Anderson and Henry H. Sibley.[20]

An exception was made with respect to Ringgold's and Duncan's artillery companies—the adjutant general said they were not to be broken up.[21] Why he excluded those batteries but not Bragg's is unclear. Perhaps the distinction arose merely because Bragg's company was not, as were Duncan's and Ringgold's, officially regarded as "light artillery." Yet, since Duncan's and Ringgold's were the only companies singled out as sacrosanct, the failure to treat Bragg's battery similarly seems to indicate that someone in Washington wanted to emphasize that the three batteries did not have equal standing as far as the government was concerned. In any case, if General Taylor had found Bragg to be exasperatingly disputatious, as had other senior army officers previously, he could have used the directive of May 12 as an opportunity to rid himself of the young artillery lieutenant. Instead, Bragg's was not among the three artillery companies Old Zach decided to disband. In fact, although Bragg had as yet demonstrated little unusual ability as a commander, except perhaps in the drilling of his troops, Taylor continuously insured that the Third Artillery's Company E was provided with the horses, equipment, and manpower needed for it to function as mobile light artillery, despite the War Department's designation of the battery as "foot artillery."

On June 4 General Taylor, though having received no instructions from Washington concerning future operations by his army since his battles of May 8 and 9, took the first step toward transporting most of his troops upriver to Reynosa and Camargo, and thence inland to Monterrey, to which location Arista's army had reportedly retreated. Reynosa (often spelled "Reinosa" by the Americans) was about sixty miles by land above Matamoros; Camargo was another sixty miles or so further north, on the San Juan River near its juncture with the meandering Rio Grande. Apparently Taylor was certain that President Polk would want him to continue such offensive movements until the Mexican government sought to end the war. On May 21 he had suggested to the adjutant general a plan for seizing Monterrey: "Could we establish and keep up by water a depot at Camargo, operations might be carried on in the valley of the San Juan toward Monterey. . . . I shall lose no time in ascertaining the practicality of the river for steamboats, and shall occupy Reinosa and such other points as a boat may be able to reach." On June 3 he again described the Monterrey campaign he was preparing to mount, emphasizing that a "large depot" would have to be established at Camargo but he did not yet have the required means of transportation.[22] However, he suddenly decided to wait no longer when a group of Mexican citizens from Reynosa asked for protection from Indian marauders. On June 4 he directed that Lieutenant Colonel Henry Wilson's First U.S. Infantry battalion was to march from Matamoros to Reynosa, accompanied by a section of Bragg's battery (led by Bragg's second in command, Lieutenant George H. Thomas), and a company of mounted Texas volunteers.[23]

Earlier, Wilson and his infantrymen, after occupying Burrita, had trudged up the river's southwestern bank to Matamoros, arriving on May 24 together with 1,500 Louisianians under militia Brigadier General Persifor Smith, and had camped across the Rio Grande at Fort Brown. Upon receipt of the order to proceed to Reynosa, Wilson's battalion recrossed to Matamoros, and on the morning of June 6, along with Lieutenant George Thomas, commanding the selected section of Bragg's battery, and a company of mounted Texans, followed the river northward. Thus among the first of Taylor's future generals to advance toward Camargo were George Thomas and three First Infantry officers: Brevet Major John J. Abercrombie, and Lieutenants Schuyler Hamilton and Joseph B. Plummer.[24]

When Wilson's column reached Reynosa at noon on June 10, they were received in a "most friendly" fashion by "the authorities of the town." The chief official of the village, called the *alcalde,* who offered "to supply every thing" that the village afforded "for the comfort & convenience" of the Americans, was obviously much more afraid of Comanches than of the Army of Occupation. That evening the *alcalde* asked for permission to send out "an armed party of rancheros" to chase off the Indians. Wilson denied the request in order to guard against the proposed force being "misapplied."[25]

A fortnight later George Meade ascended the Rio Grande as far as Reynosa aboard a "clean and comfortable" steamboat. He had been ordered to examine the river route, he wrote his wife upon his return toward the end of June, and went on to describe the countryside as glimpsed from his steamer, the village itself, and his impression of Reynosa's occupants: "We found the river perfectly navigable all the way to Reinosa, and cultivated for nearly the whole distance, one hundred and eighty miles by water. . . . In Reinosa I was much disappointed. It is a small place, not having at present over six hundred inhabitants, and containing evidences of magnificent designs most meagerly executed. The town is laid out in squares upon a hill." Of the people he said, "They appeared to be more affably disposed towards us than the population of Matamoras [*sic*], and the few who called themselves of the better order invited us to their houses and were exceedingly civil."[26]

Descriptions of Reynosa abound in the letters of Lieutenant John Sedgwick, whose Second U.S. Artillery company formed part of the hamlet's garrison by early August (and who would die in battle while serving as a highly respected Union major general of volunteers). On August 8 Sedgwick wrote his father: "This town, of more than two thousand inhabitants, is held by three hundred soldiers. Everything goes on as usual. . . . Our camp is thronged with country people with milk, eggs, etc., to sell. They say our soldiers treat them much better than their own, that we pay for everything, while they take everything they want without it." A week later he provided his sister with a more detailed picture of Reynosa and its inhabitants: "In the center is a large square, the streets coming in at the angles. On the sides facing the plaza are the public buildings, stores, and the aristocratic residences. The troops are quartered in the public buildings and some private ones hired for the purpose; the officers in tents on the square. . . . Every morning at sunrise the [Cathedral] bell rings for prayers, and . . . the same in the evening. . . . The women all bathe everyday; they go down to the river about four o'clock with a large earthen vessel . . . take a bath, and bring back their water for the next day."[27]

The movement of troops to Reynosa had just commenced when General Taylor heard he was to be superseded by Major General Winfield Scott. Taylor received a letter from Scott explaining that the latter had been given command of the army's forces in the war zone but that for the time being Scott wanted Taylor to carry on as he thought best. This news did not disturb Taylor, who had been expecting it and indeed thought Scott should be offered the field command. But before the end of June communications from Washington revealed a change in plans. Taylor was informed that he himself had been selected to conduct the army's campaign in northeastern Mexico, and that he had been promoted to the rank of major general by brevet.[28]

By then it was common knowledge that President Polk had decided Scott should not be allowed to lead the army's troops in Mexico. Polk had somewhat reluctantly offered that role to Scott during the afternoon of May 13, after signing the declaration of war. In his diary Polk remarked, "Though I did not consider him in all respects suited to such an important command, yet being commander in chief of the army, his position entitled him to it if he desired it."[29] Whatever Polk's reasons for questioning Scott's suitability—one being no doubt that the general was known to be a Whig with presidential aspirations—it would seem that Scott's service record should have trumped any perceived personal shortcomings, his more than thirty years as a general being as impressive as his physical appearance. Scott's background was in several respects similar to Zachary Taylor's, both having been born in Virginia in 1786 to wealthy parents, and both having been appointed as army officers in 1808. Scott, however, was far better educated: he had briefly attended the College of William and Mary and thereafter had studied law with prominent attorneys in Virginia and South Carolina before enlisting as an artillery captain. Moreover, at the age of twenty-seven already a brigadier general, and at twenty-eight a brevet major general in recognition of his performance in the War of 1812, he had continued to earn accolades throughout his career until, in 1841, he had been promoted to the lineal rank of major general and appointed commander in chief of the army. In appearance he was equally outstanding, being several inches over six feet tall and inclined to corpulence as well as sartorial splendor. Ulysses Grant remembered being awed by Scott while the former was a cadet at West Point: "With his commanding figure, his quite colossal size and showy uniform, I thought him the finest specimen of manhood my eyes had ever beheld, and the most to be envied."[30]

President Polk and Secretary of War Marcy had conferred harmoniously with Scott for a day or so after May 13. As recorded by Polk, they agreed to "call out immediately for service 20,000 volunteers" and to "apportion this force among the States of Texas, Arkansas, Illinois, Missouri, Ohio, Indiana, Kentucky, Tennessee, Alabama, Mississippi, & Georgia." There was also assent to Polk's opinion that "the first movement should be to march a competent force into the Northern Provinces and seize and hold them until peace was made." Yet after a meeting with Scott and Marcy of more than three hours on the evening of May 14, Polk noted: "Gen'l Scott did not impress me favourably as a military man. He has had experience in his profession, but I thought was rather scientific and visionary in his views. I did not think that so many as 20,000 volunteers besides the regular army was necessary, but I did not express this opinion, not being willing to take the responsibility of any failure of the campaign by refusing to grant to Gen'l Scott all he asked."[31] The president's opinion of Scott further deteriorated five days later, due to his having ascertained that the general might not "take command" on the Rio Grande "until about the 1st of September." In discussing the matter with Marcy and secretary of the navy George Bancroft, Polk insisted that Scott must "proceed very soon to his post"; otherwise, he would be replaced. Marcy responded, according to Polk, that Scott "was embarrassing him by his schemes" and "was constantly talking and not acting." On the twenty-first the situation went from bad to worse. The president was shown two letters Scott had written, one to a senator in February and one just received by Marcy, which together caused Polk to conclude that the general was bitterly hostile to his administration and could not be trusted to carry out orders. In the Marcy letter, as quoted by Polk in his diary, Scott explained why he did not intend to leave at once for the seat of the war by saying, "I do not desire to place myself in the most perilous of positions, a fire upon my rear from Washington and the fire in front from the Mexicans."[32]

President Polk decided immediately that he would appoint someone else to lead the Army of Occupation if he could find "another suitable commanding officer." The problem was that Major General Scott, the army's highest ranking officer, could scarcely be passed over except by someone of the same or superior standing. Polk was hoping for the passage of a bill then before the Senate which would authorize the appointment of two more major generals and four additional brigadier generals. When he heard rumors that Scott, Brigadier General John Ellis Wool, and Adjutant General Jones, "all whigs & violent partisans," were "using their influence with members of Congress to prevent the passage of the Bill," Polk became still more determined to find a way to give direction of the army's campaign on the Rio Grande to almost anyone other than Scott, although preferably to a Democrat. Evidently no consideration was given to promoting Zachary Taylor until intelligence of his victories on May 8 and 9 reached Washington on the evening of Saturday, May 23. The following Monday, without official reports of the battles yet in hand, Polk directed the secretary of war to inform Scott at once that he was excused from command of the army in Mexico, and that he was ordered to remain on duty in Washington. That evening Taylor's reports describing the battles were delivered, and the next day Polk "sent a message to the Senate" nominating Taylor "a Major-General by brevet, for his gallant victories over the Mexican forces." The president was unmoved by a letter from Scott in which the general in effect disclaimed any intention of criticizing Polk.[33] Taylor, as of May 28 designated a brevet major general, was appointed to the rank of lineal major general on June 29, Congress having passed a bill creating one such opening,[34] but of course Major General Scott was still Old Zach's superior.

Polk also spent many hours deciding whom he would like to appoint as officers for the newly established regular army Regiment of Mounted Riflemen, authorized by a bill he signed into law on May 19. To serve as the colonel of the regiment he chose Persifor F. Smith, who as a Louisiana militia general had just joined Taylor in Mexico; and for the position of lieutenant colonel he designated topographical engineer John Charles Frémont, a brevet captain, son-in-law of the influential Democratic senator Thomas H. Benton. (Frémont had been awarded the honorary rank of brevet captain in 1844 for expeditions to the Rocky Mountains and the Pacific Coast.) On May 21, after conferring with the secretary of war and other members of his cabinet, Polk wrote: "We agreed that a portion of the officers should be Whigs. As I had determined to appoint Persifor F. Smith (Democrat) Colonel, and Capt. Fremont (politics unknown) Lieut. Col. we determined to select a Whig for Major."[35] Polk's choices for captains and lieutenants in the regiment offended Ulysses Grant, George Meade, John Reynolds, and apparently most of their regular army comrades, not necessarily because of their political affiliations but because the president appointed civilians almost exclusively, albeit for the most part men with a modicum of military training, rather than giving regular army officers the opportunity for advancement that the new positions potentially represented. That, the West Pointers believed, proved how little regard the president had for the regular army.[36]

Polk and Secretary of War Marcy also launched two new incursions into Mexico. It was agreed that Brigadier General John Ellis Wool "should be forthwith ordered to proceed west & assist in organizing the Volunteers & march with them to the Del Norte [Rio Grande]." It had not yet been decided whether Wool should "proceed to the lower Rio Grande or go in a separate command to the Upper Provinces." His orders would "follow him." Of greater interest to Polk, judging from his diary, was his resolve that the commander of the First U.S. Dragoons, Colonel Stephen Watts Kearny, whose headquarters were currently at Fort Leavenworth, should organize an expedition of regulars and mounted Missouri volunteers to move against Santa Fe and then, weather permitting, take half of his force to California before the onset of winter. Polk's rationale for sending an army contingent to California was explained to his cabinet members on May 30: "I stated that if the war should be protracted for any considerable time, it would in my judgment be very important that the U.S. should hold military possession of California at the time peace was made, and I declared my purpose to be to acquire for the U.S. California, New Mexico, and perhaps some others of the Northern Provinces of Mexico whenever a peace was made." In these views the Cabinet concurred.[37] However, Polk was still thinking in terms of remunerating Mexico for any territory that nation relinquished, as he indicated on July 26: "I told Col. Benton that if Congress would pass an appropriation of two millions of dollars, such as was passed in 1803 to enable Mr. Jefferson to purchase Louisiana, or in 1806 to enable him to purchase the Floridas, I had but little doubt that by paying that sum in hand at the signature of a Treaty we might procure California and such boundary as we wished."[38]

Sandwiched between arrangements for prosecuting the war was a treaty settling the Oregon boundary dispute with Great Britain. Although Polk had long maintained that the status of relations with Mexico would have no bearing on his negotiations with Britain, and vice versa, in the summer of 1846 he did in fact retreat from his original position on the Oregon issue.[39]

General Taylor was not overjoyed to learn, toward the end of June, that he rather than Scott would have the responsibility for prosecuting the war in Mexico. That volunteers were "arriving at Brazos Santiago [Island] in thousands" made him uneasy, for there were not enough steamboats or wagons available to move his rapidly growing army upriver.[40] One encouraging development, however, was that Taylor had previously served with and greatly admired several of the volunteer officers. That was particularly true of Persifor Smith and Albert Sidney Johnston.[41] Johnston, who in 1861 would become the Confederacy's second ranking general, had reached Point Isabel on June 6 as a civilian but was shortly elected by a Regiment of Texas Rifle Volunteers as their colonel. Born and reared in Kentucky, he had stood eighth highest in the West Point graduating class of 1826 and, while serving successively with the Second and Sixth U.S. Infantry regiments, had impressed many of his fellow officers, particularly those who, like Zachary Taylor, had witnessed his performance as aide-de-camp to General Henry Atkinson during the Black Hawk War. Yet in 1834 Johnston, bowing to the pleas of his wife, Henrietta, who had contracted tuberculosis, relinquished his promising army career, intending to farm. Following Henrietta's death two years later he left his two surviving children with her mother in Louisville, rode across the Sabine River into the newborn Republic of Texas, introduced himself to Sam Houston, and within a month was appointed adjutant general of the infant nation's army with the rank of colonel. Having made Texas's cause his own, he was rewarded with other prestigious appointments until he decided in 1840, for unspecified reasons, to resign his position as the Lone Star Republic's secretary of war. When war broke out between Mexico and the United States, Johnston and his beautiful young second wife and their year-old son were visiting friends in Galveston, Texas. Though he was forty-three years old and had held no public office in his adopted Texas homeland for six years, Johnston immediately answered Texas governor James Pinckney Henderson's call for volunteers. From Point Isabel on July 10 he wrote a friend that his regiment was composed of "ten companies, numbering 650 fine riflemen, ready and anxious to take the field." (In a group of people Johnston happened across while riding from Galveston to Point Isabel was "George Wilkins Kendall, of the New Orleans *Daily Picayune.*")[42]

Throughout July, while volunteers continued to pour into the staging areas around Point Isabel, there were changes in the regular ranks as well. When three artillery companies were broken up on July 7, pursuant to instructions from the adjutant general's office, Lieutenant "Prince John" Magruder was one of the officers assigned to the recruiting service.[43] Within the next week, Lieutenant Bushrod Johnson and Captain A. C. Myers were given leaves of absence. On the fifteenth Lieutenant Christopher Augur was transferred to duty as a recruiter,[44] and by the end of the month the same was true of Lieutenant Benjamin Alvord.[45] As of the seventeenth, Lieutenants John Hatch and Daniel M. Frost were reassigned to the new Regiment of Mounted Riflemen.[46]

The next day Henry Judah was relieved of service with the Eighth Infantry and directed to report to the commander of the Fourth Infantry, having been promoted to the rank of second lieutenant in the latter regiment.[47] Meanwhile, landing with the Fourth U.S. Artillery companies that reinforced the Army of Occupation in July were Lieutenants Daniel Harvey Hill, Fitz-John Porter, and John W. Phelps.[48]

A trial that month of the Fourth Infantry's colonel, William Whistler, must have been particularly distressing for Ulysses Grant and all the rest of the regiment's cadre. Whistler, who had been accused the previous April of being too inebriated to take command of the regiment during a sudden call to arms, was charged with disobedience of orders, drunkenness on duty, and conduct prejudicial to good order and military discipline. Having found him guilty on all counts, the court sentenced him to be cashiered, though a recommendation that he be allowed to resign was appended. Captain Charles F. Smith served as the judge advocate for the court, and Brevet Major John J. Abercrombie was a member of the panel. Three months later, however, President Polk overturned the court's findings and ordered Whistler to be returned to duty.[49]

July was memorable for the advance of most of General Taylor's regular army troops, by water or by land or a combination of both, to Camargo. Although Henry Wilson's First Infantry had been camped at Reynosa since June 10, as well as George Thomas's section of Bragg's battery, Taylor summoned the Seventh Infantry from Fort Brown to take possession of Camargo. On July 8 three companies of the Seventh Infantry, commanded by Captain Theophilus Holmes, paused at Reynosa after a "tedious passage of three days" aboard a steamer. Three other Seventh Infantry companies, led by Captain Dixon S. Miles, who was then commanding the regiment, marched upriver from Matamoros on the evening of the sixth. The men with Miles, one of whom was the topographical engineer Thomas Wood, after struggling through miles of flooded prairie and heat so oppressive that a corporal died of sunstroke, were picked up by the steamer *Enterprise,* reaching Reynosa on the night of the twelfth.[50] Theophilus Holmes and the three companies he commanded left Reynosa on the thirteenth, marching overland toward Camargo with George Thomas's artillery detachment and Ben McCulloch's mounted company of Texas volunteers. Dixon Miles, leaving Reynosa the same day, boarded a faster steamboat, the *Brownsville,* with his Companies E and F, leaving D to follow on the *Enterprise.* Captain Miles was hesitant about occupying Camargo with only two companies, due to information that not only was General Antonio Canales in the vicinity but that nearby were some two hundred rancheros led by a popular Mexican colonel. Nevertheless, the *Enterprise* having failed to catch up with the *Brownsville,* Miles led his two hundred or so men into the town on July 14. Although the village's *alcalde* "was kind in granting all demands," and no challenge by Mexican forces occurred, Miles was relieved when Holmes's column joined him the next morning, a day earlier than expected. The *Enterprise* did not reach Camargo until 8 p.m. on the fifteenth, having had to stop twice to replenish its supply of wood to fuel its boilers.[51]

Holmes, in a written report to the Seventh Infantry's adjutant, pointed out that he had marched his column mainly at night, a practice he thought the climate necessitated. He enclosed a description by Earl Van Dorn of each leg of the route they traversed. Napoleon Dana, temporarily commanding his company (due to the higher-ranking First Lieutenant Lewis Little being sick and their captain, Holmes, otherwise occupied), wrote detailed accounts for Sue along the way, telling her proudly about being the only officer who had accompanied his men on foot the entire distance.[52]

Camargo, reported Dixon Miles, was "dreadfully dilapidated and injured" from a recent torrential flood, and the people were "in great distress." He estimated the population as numbering five thousand, adding: "There are no accommodations for dwellings except those wanted for store houses and none whatever for the common necessaries of life, the inhabitants being reduced to the greatest want and poverty by the late flood—it is also the hottest place I ever was in, and I fear will be sickly." The orders he issued, which were also translated into Spanish, echoed in part those that Taylor had issued before the war began: "The Commanding Officer directs that all under his command shall strictly observe the utmost propriety and decorum towards the inhabitants of this town, violating no privileges or personal rights respecting the religion, and municipal regulations, and paying promptly for all articles or necessaries obtained from the people." Continuing, he directed: "The 7th Infy will furnish the guard of the plaza. Capt McCulloughs [*sic*] company will furnish the one for the Commissary and Quartermasters store houses—Lieut Thomas will furnish his own guards." Napoleon Dana described the village as it appeared after being occupied by his regiment: "We are now encamped, my dearest wife, in the plaza, or public square of Camargo, K and I companies on one side, C and F on another, and D and E on another, whilst the guardhouse, hospital, adjutant's office, and so forth occupy the fourth. The church is on my side of the square and is by far the prettiest one we have yet seen, although its style of architecture is ancient and odd. It is also the only one we have seen with a finished steeple."[53]

By the middle of July there were finally enough small steamboats on the river to transport most of the rest of General Taylor's regular army troops to Camargo, though only relatively few men at a time. The Fifth Infantry landed at Camargo piecemeal from July 18 to 22. The Eighth Infantry's men followed, reaching Camargo between July 23 and 29. Brevet General Worth, who was under orders to command the American forces in and around Camargo until General Taylor arrived, had established his headquarters there by the twenty-ninth, as had several companies of artillery and two companies of mounted Texans. On the morning of July 29, Worth sent Captain John Vinton and the eighty-four men in his Third Artillery company some twenty-five miles upriver by steamboat to occupy Mier, a village whose residents, fearful of a band of Comanches they believed was nearby, had asked for protection.[54]

Both the Third and Fourth infantry commanders were directed to leave two companies in Matamoros temporarily, to serve as escorts for the Third Brigade's baggage train. The other four companies of each of those regiments were on their way to Camargo by water at the end of the month. With a Third Infantry company on the *Big Hatchee* was George Sykes, who had recently returned from an extended sick leave. Captain Phil Barbour wrote of calling on General Worth immediately after disembarking at Camargo, being shown to his regiment's campsite by Lieutenant Thomas Wood, and dining the next day on "fried peaches" with Lieutenant George Thomas.[55] With the Fourth Infantry companies that ascended the river by water was one of Grant's classmates, Henry M. Judah, newly promoted to that regiment. Grant, however, was in one of the companies directed to march with his brigade's wagon train.[56]

As for the artillerymen, George Thomas's section of Bragg's battery had been the first to reach Camargo, but by the end of the month several other units were on their way. Next was the lead company of the First Artillery regiment, E, to which Abner Doubleday had been transferred in July, though the young New Yorker, stationed at the mouth of the Rio Grande until reassigned, did not catch up with E until August 4. Among other artillery officers who landed at Camargo around the end of July or shortly thereafter was Lieutenant Daniel Harvey Hill, who had commenced a diary when he embarked in June at Fort Monroe, Virginia, for a second tour with the Army of Occupation. He wrote of having spent most of July at Fort Polk before he and his company boarded the *Troy* at the mouth of the Rio Grande on July 31, and of several instances of despicable behavior by volunteers at stops along their journey upriver. At Camargo he recorded being disturbed at night by the "yells and shouts" of members of the "Louisville Legion, Col. [Stephen] Ormsby's Regiment of Volunteers," whom he accused of setting fire to "the Quartermaster's inclosure" and shouting "like maniacs as the fire progressed."[57]

General Taylor's orders of July 30 announced the manner in which various of the volunteer regiments were to proceed to Camargo, some by water and others by land. David Twiggs, now a brigadier general, was told to "remain at Matamoros in command of all the troops in the vicinity" until the last of the volunteer regiments ordered forward by land had departed, after which he was to proceed to Camargo with the dragoons and remaining mobile artillery.[58]

Taylor left Matamoros on the evening of August 4 by steamboat. Delayed by a broken rudder, his craft did not reach the town until the evening of the seventh. He was accompanied by Joseph Mansfield, and no doubt by William Bliss and other members of his staff. George Meade would have liked to go by water also but his topographical corps superior, Captain William G. Williams, who had joined Taylor in July, had elected to march by land to Camargo with the baggage train led by the Third Brigade's commander, John Garland, and Meade felt compelled to do likewise.[59]

Ulysses Grant was once more commanding the men in his company when they, together with another Fourth Infantry company and two companies of the Third Infantry, departed Matamoros with Garland's train on August 5. Grant had been left in charge of his company when George McCall, detailed to muster out volunteer units being shipped back to Louisiana for that purpose, started for New Orleans on July 22.[60] Of the "fatiguing" eight-day march to Camargo, Grant had little to say other than that his troops "suffered considerably from heat and thirst." George Meade, riding with the same train, penned a note to his wife from Reynosa, telling her that after two days of rain they had traveled under a "burning sun, with often a space of sixteen miles without water." The muddy condition of the route nearest the river, Meade said, had forced them to veer inland, lengthening their journey by thirty miles, but for him the physical exercise had proved beneficial.[61] Traveling with Meade and Grant, though in the Third Infantry's contingent, was Grant's friend Robert Hazlitt. Don Carlos Buell, who had been detached from his Third Infantry company for service on Garland's staff as acting assistant adjutant general of the Third Brigade, evidently rode with the baggage train as well. In Garland's wake on August 6 were Braxton Bragg, John Reynolds, and the soldiers belonging to their battery who had not been among those accompanying George Thomas to Reynosa. The artillerymen marching with Bragg reached Camargo on the fourteenth, and a mere three days thereafter the battery's precision and rapidity of movement while drilling would awe a major of the First Regiment of Ohio Volunteers.[62]

Among the last of the regular troops to start upriver were Twiggs and four companies of Second Dragoons. On August 16 their party left Matamoros along with Randolph Ridgely's artillery battery. With them also were Lieutenants William W. Mackall and James G. Martin, the only officers with the newly landed First U.S. Artillery light battery. After reaching Camargo on the twenty-first, Mackall, the company's acting commander, wrote his wife that due to the weather having been extremely hot and water scarce, they had lost nine horses.[63] With the addition of Mackall's battery, Taylor's army now had three authorized "light," mobile, horse-drawn artillery units (those approved for the First, Second, and Third Artillery regiments), plus Bragg's, still considered technically "foot artillery."

Only a relatively few volunteer units traveled by land to Camargo, General Taylor having arranged for most of them to be transported by the shallow-draft steamboats that made two miles an hour against the Rio Grande's current. Among those whose volunteer regiments traveled by water were a number of future Civil War generals: Major Goode Bryan and Lieutenant William H. Forney (Alabama); Colonel Henry R. Jackson and Captain Allison Nelson (Georgia); Captain Speed S. Fry and Lieutenant Edward J. Hobson (Second Kentucky); and Colonel Jefferson Davis, Captain Douglas H. Cooper, and Lieutenants Carnot Posey and Richard Griffith (Mississippi Rifles). Two such volunteer officers were in units divided between the land and water routes: Colonel George Washington Morgan (Second Ohio) and Captain John R. Kenly (Maryland and District of Columbia Battalion). Colonel Albert Sidney Johnston and a portion of his Regiment of Texas Rifle Volunteers boarded ship at Matamoros on August 5, after having been transported from Point Isabel under special orders, and landed at Camargo on the thirteenth.[64]

The tragedy that linked General Taylor and Colonel Jefferson Davis had occurred eleven years earlier. Davis had married Taylor's daughter Sarah Knox against her father's wishes. The wedding, at the home of Taylor relatives in Kentucky without the presence of either of the bride's parents, took place in June of 1835. Three months later, while visiting Davis's sister Anna in Louisiana, the bride and bridegroom both became desperately ill, probably with malaria or yellow fever, and Sarah Knox Taylor Davis (usually called "Knox") could not be saved.[65] Davis had met Knox in 1832, four years after graduating from West Point, while serving as Taylor's adjutant at Fort Crawford, Michigan Territory. Why her father objected to the courtship is unknown—he may have heard that the young lieutenant was a far-from-model cadet while at the Academy, or he may have observed conduct of which he disapproved—but at any rate Old Zach went so far as to forbid Davis from visiting the family's Fort Crawford home. The following year Knox's suitor transferred out of Taylor's First Infantry command, joining the First U.S. Dragoons as a first lieutenant, but he and Knox kept in touch by mail. Before the wedding Davis resigned his army commission, intending to build a home a few miles below Vicksburg on a farm belonging to his eldest brother, Joseph. The residence of their widowed mother was located further south, near Woodville, Mississippi, where the ten Davis children were reared following moves from Georgia and later Kentucky, the birthplace of Jeff, their youngest, in 1808.[66]

For eight years after Knox died, Davis led a reclusive life. With the assistance of slaves he cleared his plantation, Briarfield; planted cotton and other crops; read extensively; and occasionally visited his mother as well as friends farther north. Finally, in 1845, having become active in his state's political affairs, he was elected to a seat in the U.S. Congress as a Democrat. Thus, while General Taylor was advancing toward the Rio Grande in the spring of 1846 Jefferson Davis was in Washington as a first-term member of the House of Representatives, where he rose to speak occasionally in support of President Polk's policies.[67] With Davis in Washington was his second wife, twenty-year-old Varina Howell Davis. She pleaded with her husband not to volunteer when war with Mexico was declared, to no effect. Waiting only until July 4, by which time Davis had been elected in absentia as colonel of the regiment of volunteers being organized in Mississippi, he and Varina returned to Briarfield, where he arranged for his slave James Pemberton to oversee plantation affairs in his absence. By July 17 Davis was in New Orleans, accompanied by one of his brother Joseph's slaves. The ten companies of the First Regiment of Mississippi Rifles-Volunteers were already there, awaiting transport to the war zone, but they had not yet been outfitted with the new Whitney percussion-cap rifles which, at Davis's insistence, President Polk and General Winfield Scott had agreed to secure for the Mississippians in place of the smoothbore, flintlock muskets then in use throughout the army. By July 29 Davis, aboard the *Alabama,* was standing off Brazos Island with three of his companies, the others having preceded him. As he waited for a lighter to land them, he already knew that General Taylor no longer harbored negative feelings toward him, for when they had chanced to meet earlier on a Mississippi River steamboat, Taylor had greeted his former son-in-law cordially. Nevertheless Davis must have been gratified at receiving, a few days after disembarking, a warm note of welcome from Taylor. In it the general expressed "much pleasure" at Davis's safe arrival and explained that he hoped to have the Mississippians "with or near" him at Camargo shortly.[68]

At age thirty-eight, the six-foot Davis still stood rigidly erect. Contributing to his imposing appearance were deep-set, wide-spaced gray eyes beneath a high, broad forehead. He seems to have been firmly in control of his regiment, though there was some dissension in its ranks. By August 21 all of his companies had been outfitted with rifles, as promised. While waiting in their camp near the mouth of the Rio Grande for orders to move forward, Davis drilled them rigorously. He wholeheartedly supported the war effort, and no doubt looked forward to meeting good friends from his earlier regular army service. Apparently Davis believed the war might end in time for him to attend the next session of Congress, for he had not yet given up his seat in the House of Representatives. The letter of resignation he had drafted was being held by his brother Joseph, pending further developments.[69]

Before Davis reached Camargo aboard the *Virginian* on August 31, two brigades of regular army troops were on their way to Monterrey via Cerralvo. Old Rough and Ready had chosen the northern, Mier-Cerralvo route to Monterrey based on reconnaissance reports. Early that month a detachment of the First Regiment of Texas Mounted Volunteers under Colonel John C. Hays had investigated conditions on the lower San Juan River as far as China, some sixty miles west of Camargo, as had Captain Ben McCulloch and his Texan "spy" company. Subsequently an examination of the route north of the San Juan as far as Cerralvo had been conducted by Captain James Duncan, assisted by topographical engineer Thomas Wood and a detachment of Rangers commanded by Captain McCulloch.[70]

Taylor planned to take around six thousand troops with him to Monterrey, divided into two divisions of regular army men and two of volunteers. With respect to the regular army contingent, on August 17 he ordered the three brigades of infantry formed at Corpus Christi to retain their organization and numerical designations as established there, and provided for a fourth brigade of infantry, to consist of the First Infantry battalion commanded by Lieutenant Colonel Henry Wilson together with any Second Infantry troops that showed up in time to join the brigade. About two weeks later he submitted to the adjutant general a somewhat amended and expanded plan. In the First Division of regular troops, commanded by Twiggs, were units of the Third Brigade (the dragoons, Ridgely's and Bragg's mobile artillery batteries, the Third and Fourth infantry regiments, and Captain William Shivors's company of Texas volunteers) as well as the Fourth Brigade (the First Infantry regiment and the Baltimore Battalion of volunteers). In the Second Division of regulars, commanded by Worth, were the First Brigade (Duncan's light artillery company, the Artillery Battalion, and the Eighth Infantry regiment) and the Second Brigade (the Fifth and Seventh infantry regiments, Captain Albert Blanchard's company of Louisiana volunteers, and William Mackall's mobile artillery battery). In addition, one heavy battery of twenty-four-pound howitzers, detached from the First Artillery, was set aside as an independent company.[71]

Most of the volunteers chosen to accompany Taylor were placed in the "Field Division," which was commanded by a major general of volunteers, William Orlando Butler of Kentucky. Butler's division was divided into two brigades, each led by a brigadier general of volunteers, Thomas L. Hamer of Ohio and John A. Quitman, a Mississippian born in New York. In Hamer's brigade were the First Kentucky and First Ohio regiments; in Quitman's, the First Tennessee and the Mississippi Rifles. In addition to Butler's division, Taylor created a "Texas Division" under that state's governor, Major General James Pinckney Henderson. It was composed of the First and Second regiments of Texas Mounted volunteers, led respectively by Colonel John C. Hays and Colonel George T. Wood.[72]

The generals in the Field Division,—Butler, Hamer, and Quitman—were among the eight men, all prominent Democrats, selected from civilian life and appointed by President Polk in late June and early July to lead volunteer forces, as authorized by Congress. The others were the Irish-born Major General Robert Patterson of Pennsylvania, and Brigadier Generals James Shields of Illinois, Joseph Lane of Indiana, Thomas Marshall of Kentucky, and Gideon J. Pillow of Tennessee. Almost all of them had either been engaged in earlier military actions or had for many years participated in the militia of their states. The exception was Pillow, a successful lawyer and plantation owner who was an extremely close friend and enthusiastic supporter of President Polk. Although Pillow had held office in the Tennessee militia, his military experience was chiefly as adjutant general of the state for four years.[73] General Taylor seems to have respected these political appointees as a whole, except for Pillow. Shortly after the Tennessean reached Camargo, Old Zach entertained Pillow at dinner on "ham and bread." Two days later Taylor commented, in writing his son-in-law, Dr. Wood, that the Tennessee lawyer had "much to learn as regards his new profession." Pillow would become one of the most unpopular senior officers in Taylor's army, ridiculed by many for reputedly having had a ditch dug on the wrong side of a breastwork while he was second in command at Camargo. Although he at first found the general "a frank and manly old gentleman," when Pillow was left at Camargo, rather than being allowed to accompany the First Tennessee regiment to Monterrey, be began to criticize Old Zach mercilessly in writing confidentially to President Polk.[74]

Throughout August, General Taylor fumed over supply difficulties. By mid-August the number of steamboats serving the army on the Rio Grande had increased to fourteen, according to Joseph Mansfield, yet Old Zach was far from satisfied. On August 11 Taylor wrote Dr. Wood that there was a "great deficiency of forage, tools & many other articles" which he had requisitioned from the ordnance and quartermaster departments long ago. A week later he complained that the steamboats were "about twice as long in making their trips from the mouth of the river to this place as they should be, & when they get here have very little in them." Moreover, he had still not received the "supply of horse shoes & nails" he had been trying to get for three months, and his brigades could not "possibly move without them" since the road over which they would be marching when they advanced was "covered with sharp rocks or stone." Also, the ordnance department had not furnished the twelve-pound guns "on traveling carriages" that he had requested. On September 3, just before leaving Camargo, he wrote that his forces were "very much in want here of medicines & supplies of various kinds," adding that these particularly needed items had been shipped by the quartermaster "on the slowest boat on the river, whether by accident or design I am unable to say."[75] (His decades of admiration for Brigadier General Thomas S. Jesup, the army's quartermaster general since 1818, had become a casualty of supply difficulties.)

The medicines to which Taylor referred were certainly badly needed: there was an increasing incidence of illness in the ranks of his troops, regulars and volunteers, at Camargo. Dr. John B. Porter, the senior medical officer with Worth's division, noted in a report on the First Brigade that upon reaching Camargo "there was an addition to the sick report, and the cases were more severe than at Matamoros." Indeed, General Taylor himself was "somewhat indisposed" in mid-August, as was Lieutenant Ulysses Grant.[76] But in contrast to the usually rapid recovery of the regular troops, the volunteers were dying by the hundreds, one example being the men of Colonel William B. Campbell's First Regiment of Tennessee Volunteers. Campbell wrote a relative in late August from Camargo that he had landed at Brazos Island around the end of June with "43 officers and 1000 non-commissioned officers and privates," yet currently he could scarcely name 500 who were well enough to march with Taylor's expedition to Monterrey. Although many of the deaths among Campbell's men had resulted from the outbreak of measles while they were earlier stationed at Lomita, near the mouth of the Rio Grande, at Camargo "fever was causing one or two deaths a day." Nearly three hundred of his men were "on the sick list,"[77] a report that was not exceptional. In mid-August almost every volunteer regiment had one-third of its number sick, Meade observed, and in many cases even more. Grant told Julia that exposure had caused "a great deel [*sic*] of sickness, especially among the Volunteers," about "one in five" being "sick all the time." General Taylor feared the "whole country" would soon be "filled with sick volunteers."[78]

His army's extreme health problems, Old Zach asserted, were caused by the climate, the lack of "suitable accommodations," the "great scarcity of medical officers in proportion to the number of raw troops," and the fact that many of the medical officers recently appointed to the volunteer regiments were "entirely without experience as regards their duties in the field." In Taylor's opinion, volunteers "were never intended to invad [*sic*] or carry on war out of the limits of their own country."[79] Meade blamed the volunteers' terrible health conditions on their "utter ignorance of the proper mode of taking care of themselves," yet many if not most of the senior volunteer officers had either been trained at West Point, as had Jefferson Davis and Albert Sidney Johnston, or had previously fought under regular army officers, and thus should have known how to help their men avoid or minimize the consequences of unsanitary conditions in the camps insofar as that was possible. But in addition to poor discipline, the volunteers were as a whole less prepared than the regulars to withstand the inescapable hardships encountered by members of the Army of Occupation, especially at Camargo, where thousands of troops were assembled around a tiny, destitute village, bringing with them measles and typhoid fever and other contagious diseases, and where everyone depended for water solely on the San Juan River, which probably became polluted very quickly.[80]

Evidently General Taylor usually left to regular army physicians the matter of overseeing preventative measures, but he had himself been endeavoring for some time to ease the suffering of ill troops. At Matamoros in late July he had issued orders for as many as two thousand of the sick soldiers on the lower Rio Grande to be cared for in that city while a new hospital was being constructed at Fort Polk. He assured Dr. Wood, who was in charge of army hospital facilities at Point Isabel and Brazos Island, that "neither expense or anything else as far as my authority will go, will be spared to afford ample accommodation to the sick." On August 4 he suggested to Dr. Wood that a medical officer should be permanently stationed on Brazos Island. He also said an assistant surgeon was needed at Fort Polk, and that one should be employed if no army surgeon was available. Shortly thereafter he and his senior medical officer, Dr. Presley H. Craig, signed a contract providing for the engagement of an additional surgeon. At Camargo, still concerned about conditions downriver, Taylor suggested to Dr. Wood that if a medical officer were to be stationed at Brazos Island he "might act as health officer so far as to prohibit any contagious disease from spreading among the troops and laborers there." Furthermore, he wrote, an assistant surgeon was also needed at St. Joseph's Island, where "over 90" were sick. Regarding the situation at Camargo, Old Zach believed the troops that had preceded him there were "in tolerable health." They, of course, had been mainly regular army men. A week or so later, his tone changed dramatically. Of the volunteers, he wrote in part: "I greatly fear many of them will suffer for want of many of the necessaries of life, as well as for medical advice." He hoped the regular army doctors would "do all in their power to alleviate the sufferings" of the volunteers they encountered. On September 3, as he was preparing to leave Camargo for Cerralvo, the next point of concentration on his planned march to Monterrey, he mentioned again that the volunteers had "a very large sick report," adding: "I can but feel very sensibly for them." He had directed that "competent medical aid" should be employed whenever possible. However, during the latter part of August he was primarily occupied with arrangements for the Monterrey campaign. He was still short of requested ordnance and wagons but believed he should delay no longer.[81]

Old Zach's first order sending a portion of the Army of Occupation forward from Camargo, dated August 17, applied among others to Lieutenant Daniel Harvey Hill's artillery company, one of the eight that acted as infantry in the First Brigade's "red-leg" Artillery Battalion (so called due to the red stripe on the trousers of their uniforms). Hill had spent most of his free time during his two weeks in Camargo sightseeing and visiting old regular army friends in other camps. Though a Presbyterian to his toes, on August 9 he recorded in his diary that he "went with some officers to witness mass in the Catholic Church." That same day, at "evening parade," Hill noted, General Taylor reviewed the Artillery Battalion. "He had on his undress frock and though looking very much like an old farmer, presented a more martial air" than Hill had ever observed before. On the sixteenth Harvey again attended a church service, this one conducted by "Mr. [Antony] Rey, the Catholic Chaplain for the Army." The oddness of the occasion impressed him. "The Church was crowded to overflowing with officers & soldiers. I scarcely saw a Mexican. 'Twas a strange sight that of our own Chaplain officiating & our own soldiers worshipping in the Church of the enemy we had come to fight." Hill ridiculed Taylor's order of the seventeenth for the First Brigade to advance: "We do not number more than six hundred effective men & it seems an act of madness to push us forward so near the enemy & so far in advance of the main Army."[82] Hill failed to take into account that the inadequate supply of wagons was the chief factor controlling Taylor's spacing between contingents. Each brigade was forced to await the return of the wagons accompanying the preceding one before moving forward.

7
March to Monterrey

General Taylor's order of August 17 specified that the First Brigade of regulars was to proceed toward Cerralvo on the nineteenth, weather permitting, where another depot was to be established. Two companies of "Texas horse" were to accompany the brigade's train, which due to the scarcity of wagons was to return to Camargo for additional supplies, supervised by quartermasters.[1] Leading the brigade on the sixty-mile march to Cerralvo was the Artillery Battalion, accompanied by twenty wagonloads of rations and about a thousand pack mules carrying baggage and camp equipment. General Worth was with the Artillery Battalion, as were Duncan's battery of four guns, and Lieutenant George Meade. Although Meade regretted somewhat the transfer from Taylor's staff to Worth's, he was glad he would be with the troops leading the advance, "always considered the most honorable position," he explained to Margaretta. Better yet, in Worth's brigade he would be the senior topographical engineer, in contrast to serving under Captain Williams while on Taylor's staff.[2]

The companies of the Artillery Battalion crossed the San Juan on August 18 and camped opposite Camargo in preparation for the march northward to Mier, where the route chosen by General Taylor turned southwestward. They and Duncan's battery started toward Mier around sunset the next day. Lieutenant Daniel Harvey Hill, however, was not among them, he and a fatigue party having been detailed to stay behind overnight, without tents, to help escort a baggage train of pack mules and a few wagons. Hill's party and the Eighth Infantry, the other major contingent of the First Brigade, followed the Artillery Battalion on the twentieth shortly after noon, in heat so oppressive that a "great number of the men fainted and fell by the wayside"; but that evening they were able to bathe in a "beautiful lake." The next day Hill and his party were ordered to rejoin the Artillery Battalion, which by the twenty-second had halted "within a few miles of Mier." Although the battalion waited there a day for the commissary mule train, Hill was denied permission to visit the town. He was told that General Canales and his rancheros were nearby, and that the column might be ordered forward at any moment. After the artillerymen caught up with the Eighth Infantry the following day, the Texas cavalry turned back, leaving "no mounted men" with the First Brigade. As a result, the ever-critical Hill asserted, "[I]t would have been an easy matter for an enterprising enemy to have dashed down on the other bank [of the stream they were following], given us a withering volley, and escaped with impunity." Instead, as they trudged on they battled only heat and dust. James Longstreet, who was still commanding his Eighth Infantry company, reached Cerralvo on August 25, as did the companies of the Artillery Battalion. Their brigade had traveled approximately sixty-five miles from Camargo—nearly halfway to Monterrey—without seeing or hearing "anything of the enemy."[3]

Old Zach, despite being anxious for his troops to reach Monterrey, scheduled the departure of the regular army brigades several days apart. In telling the adjutant general on August 25 that the Second Brigade, "524 strong," was moving out that morning, he explained that "the means of transportation" had been slow in arriving and that "many unavoidable delays" had been encountered. The Second Brigade was directed to halt temporarily at the village of Punta Aguda, about twelve miles short of Cerralvo, while an accompanying train of provisions, guarded by a company of dragoons, was to proceed to Cerralvo and then return to Camargo to pick up more supplies. In charge of the Second Brigade was Persifor Smith, who after joining the Army of Occupation as a general of Louisiana volunteers had since been given an appointment in the regular army, as colonel of the newly created Regiment of Mounted Riflemen. Smith was continuing to serve with Taylor, at the latter's request, while the Regiment of Mounted Riflemen was being organized at Jefferson Barracks.[4]

The Seventh Infantry's progress was described in Napoleon Dana's almost daily scribblings to his young wife, Sue. On the afternoon of the twenty-second, after surrendering nearly all of their personal baggage to the regiment quartermaster, the unit's cadre had turned their backs on Camargo's plaza and encamped on the opposite side of the San Juan in order to be ready to start for Punta Aguda at a moment's notice. Due to the limitation on the number of tents allowed each regiment, Second Lieutenant Dana began sharing one with a more senior Seventh Infantry friend, First Lieutenant Lewis H. Little. Their regiment took up the line of march at 3 a.m. on August 25, reaching their first halting place, halfway to Mier, by 9 that morning. They were delayed there a day, the baggage train having caught up with them so late that everyone, "officers and men," were forced to sleep under the stars "upon the naked ground," without bedding. Dana and Little, stretching out on a horse blanket which

Little happened to have brought along, were bitten by ants all night but otherwise "got a pretty good night's rest," Dana wrote Sue.[5]

To avoid the worst of the heat, their regiment kept roughly to the same schedule each day, the reveille bugles and drums summoning them at 1 a.m. and the day's march ending around midmorning. At Mier, which they reached on the twenty-seventh, Dana assured Sue they did not "fare so badly in the field" as she might imagine. "We get chickens, eggs, mutton, and milk at all our halting places." Of Mier, he said it looked "very pretty" as they approached, and they could tell even at a distance "that it was the nicest town" they had "yet seen in Mexico." He added, "There are some quite nice stone houses here, all nicely whitewashed, two churches, and so forth. The town is built on the summit of a hill of rock, so that its streets are naturally paved. Two little streams meander through the town and empty into a large creek called the Alamo, which runs like a mountain torrent. And indeed we shall before long see real mountain torrents, for we have now left the muddy Rio Grande and tomorrow's march will take us about fifteen miles interior from it." The following morning the regiment turned southwest, ending that day's trek a dozen or so miles short of Punta Aguda, "beside a beautiful torrent, a branch of the Alamo," with water so pure that Dana looked forward to bathing in it and then donning a "clean shirt." He had once again walked with the men in his company, and this time other officers had followed his example. It had been a "very toilsome" march, "all up hill and down hill, with rocky and stony roads," slowed by their wagons getting "jammed in a crossroad" and one breaking down. However, they were treated to their first view of the Sierra Madre mountains. "We can see them forty or fifty miles off, dark and blue, the peaks towering high up towards the skies and extending for many miles from northwest to southeast."[6]

A march of another fourteen miles brought them to the village where they were to await further orders, Punta Aguda. To Dana one of its chief attractions was its proximity to the clear, swift stream in which he had bathed the previous day, and in which he planned to soak regularly while they were camped nearby. Scarcely had they erected their tents when the men were put to work clearing the ground in preparation for the arrival of the Third Brigade.[7] Presumably Albert Blanchard's company of Louisiana volunteers had marched adjacent to the Seventh Infantry, for Dana said of them, "They are a fine company, as well behaved so far and pretty nearly as precise and well disciplined as the regulars."[8]

One element of the Second Brigade, the First Artillery battery currently commanded by Lieutenant William Mackall, did not exit its camp near Camargo until September 6. Mackall, twenty-nine years old, a West Point graduate from Georgetown, D.C., was extremely anxious to hear from his wife, Aminta. She was in Savannah, her hometown, where she had recently borne their first child, a daughter. In his letters to Aminta he frequently mentioned his second lieutenant and good friend James G. Martin, a West Pointer from North Carolina who, like Mackall, would serve as a Confederate brigadier general.[9]

Leaving Camargo on August 31 was the Third Brigade of regulars, a component of recently promoted Brigadier General David Twiggs's First Division, composed primarily of the Third and Fourth infantries and the Second Dragoons, units of the Army of Occupation that had been with General Taylor the longest. The brigade's other contingents were the two mobile artillery companies under Randolph Ridgely and Braxton Bragg, and Captain William R. Shivors's Texas volunteers. The latter were a remnant of Colonel Albert Sidney Johnston's regiment. Many of the men in Johnston's command, among them a company of German-Americans, had refused to reenlist for a longer tour of duty and had been mustered out of service in late August, leaving Johnston footloose until Taylor appointed him to a temporary, quasi-official position on General Butler's staff.[10]

Of the seven companies of Second Dragoons that had served with General Taylor since 1844, only four accompanied him on the march to Cerralvo, two of the other companies having been broken up and one transferred to Baltimore. The officers of the four Monterrey-bound companies included William Hardee, William Steele, Alfred Pleasanton, and Lawrence Pike Graham, but the first three were left at Camargo when their comrades joined Taylor's column on August 26—Hardee was ill, Steele was on duty there as the regiment's acting assistant quartermaster, and Pleasanton was there on detached service, training recruits. (Hardee rejoined his company on September 3.) The dragoon squadrons, initially serving as the rear guard of the Second Brigade as well as the leading unit of the Third Brigade, halted after traveling about seven miles toward Mier and waited at that location, which the Americans called Camp Butler, for the rest of their division to pass.[11]

Bracketed with the dragoon squadrons in Taylor's report to the adjutant general of September 3 was Ridgely's mobile light artillery company, whereas Bragg's battery was shown as being attached to the Third and Fourth Infantry regiments and Shivors's company of Texans. Yet it was Bragg's men who joined the dragoons on the twenty-seventh at Camp Butler, while Ridgely's command remained in Camargo until after the Third Brigade's infantry had crossed the San Juan River. This change would have been inconsequential under other circumstances, inasmuch as Taylor had decided that the dragoons and all of the mobile artillery batteries except Duncan's company, which had accompanied Worth's advance, should serve as the rear guard of Twiggs's division, and that meanwhile they should proceed no further than Camp Butler, where there was good grazing for their horses. Nevertheless, in light of a complication which arose the day after Bragg reached Camp Butler, and which must have been anticipated and a solution devised earlier, it is obvious that Taylor started Bragg for Cerralvo on the twenty-seventh in order to circumvent his being superseded as commander of the Third Artillery's Company E.[12]

The officer who was expecting to assume command of E was a West Pointer from Rhode Island, Captain Thomas W. Sherman. In July of 1846 the War Department, having promoted Sherman to the rank of captain, had sent him to take charge of Braxton Bragg's company, whose former captain (John A. Thomas) had resigned. Sherman was stationed in Florida with another of the Third Artillery's companies when he learned of the promotion and new assignment. He immediately departed for Mexico and, consonant with War Department orders, reported for duty with his company at Camp Butler on August 28. Normally, of course, Captain Sherman would have at once become the commander of E since Bragg was only a brevet captain; but General Taylor, hastening to prevent that potentially disruptive substitution in the leadership of a vital unit in his advancing army, took the unusual step of issuing a special order, dated that same day, detailing Sherman for temporary duty with the quartermaster department, and made sure that Captain Charles May, the dragoon in command at Camp Butler, would be able to produce a copy of the order when Bragg's superior arrived there. Sherman, a member of the Third Artillery since his graduation from the Academy, immediately and repeatedly informed Taylor that he objected to serving even temporarily as a quartermaster.[13] For several weeks, however, his strenuous protests fell on deaf ears. Bragg remained in charge of E throughout September, and Captain Sherman continued to protest.[14]

Taylor's special order of August 28 would have significant consequences for both Sherman and Bragg. Sherman would, as a result, not be among the participants in Taylor's next battle, thereby losing a good chance to gain a brevet, whereas Bragg would emerge from that engagement not only with a second brevet but with much greater acclaim than had followed his battery's largely ineffectual firing during the Fort Brown siege. Eventually Taylor would move Bragg to Company C and reinstate Sherman as commander of E, to the dismay of that company's usually amiable Lieutenant John F. Reynolds, who would assert a year later that "the eccentricities of Capt [*sic*] Sherman are becoming unsupportable."[15]

Another addition to Company E was pending as well. Sam French, who had finally been promoted to the rank of full-fledged second lieutenant, was transferred to E from Ridgely's company. On the Third Artillery roster the reassignment was shown as having taken place in August, but French did not join Bragg's battery until ordered to do so by General Taylor on September 12. In his memoirs French would write of Braxton Bragg and his lieutenants, George Thomas and John Reynolds: "They were all agreeable officers, but even to this day I recall, like a woman, my first loves, Ringgold, Ridgely and [Lieutenant William H.] Shover." A further change in Bragg's company, proposed by the War Department, did not occur: the promotion of John F. Reynolds to the rank of first lieutenant was to have taken him to a Third Artillery company then in Florida, but Taylor decreed otherwise (doubtless at Bragg's request). In the same set of orders in which French was told to join Bragg's company, Taylor said that Reynolds was "for the present" to remain on duty with E.[16]

On August 31, four days after the dragoons and Bragg's battery had marched seven miles along the Mier road and paused at Camp Butler, the Third and Fourth Infantry regiments, the principal units of the Third Brigade, crossed to the northern bank of the San Juan River. The next afternoon they and the provision train they were escorting started toward Mier, covering five miles. The pack mules carrying their baggage did not pull into their camp until after dark, and "great confusion" resulted when the baggage of the two regiments was intermingled while the mules were being unpacked. On September 2, tempers flared again—the brigade was forced to march eleven miles during the hottest part of the day.[17]

Ulysses Grant, recently appointed as the Fourth Infantry's acting quartermaster and commissary, was as usual regretting each and every mile that took him further away from Julia. He had thought while at Fort Brown, before the fighting commenced, that any change of station would necessarily shorten the distance between them, since the Army of Occupation was then in the extreme southwestern corner of the territory claimed by Texas. In his letter of August 14 from Camargo, with Taylor preparing to march two hundred miles or so further southwestward to Monterrey, Grant acknowledged that the current prospect was "very different." Yet he and others—General Taylor included—still believed the war might end at any moment, without further fighting. "Upon the whole," he told Julia, "taking the expression of opinion here the chances are about equal whether there will be another battle or not."[18] He was deeply disturbed over having been assigned, against his wishes, to serve as a staff officer. His protest at being removed "from sharing in the dangers and honors of service with my company," addressed to the Third Brigade's commander, Colonel John Garland, was evidently referred to General Taylor before being rejected, for on August 29 William Bliss wrote Garland: "The Commanding General desires that you will retain Lieut. Grant to his position of Quarter-Master to the 4th Infantry—his service being represented as very useful to Major [George W.] Allen" (the acting commander of the Fourth Infantry).[19]

Although General Taylor remained in Camargo until September 4, most of his regular army troops had started for Monterrey via the Mier-Cerralvo route by the end of August. Also still at Camargo was the Third Artillery's Company C (Ridgely's battery). The regimental roster does not indicate when that company followed the rest of the Third Brigade; probably it accompanied the four companies of the First Infantry which left Camargo on September 2, the last corps of regular infantrymen to join the march. Led by Lieutenant Colonel Henry Wilson, the First Infantry, together with the Maryland and District of Columbia volunteers commanded by Lieutenant Colonel William H. Watson, formed the newly created Fourth Brigade of Twiggs's First Division.[20]

The Fourth Brigade halted for the night at Camp Butler on September 3, its overnight stop there recorded in a letter from John Reynolds to his sister Jane. He also told her that all of the dragoons were there, and all of the artillery except one battery which was with General Worth (meaning Duncan's).[21] However, two First Artillery companies were still stationed near Camargo, one "opposite Camargo" (Captain Lucien Webster's howitzer battery C), and one ten miles from Camargo (K, the horse artillery company of Captain Francis Taylor, commanded at that time by Lieutenant William Mackall). They joined the marching force on consecutive days, C on September 5 and K on the sixth, each apparently starting from its camp near Camargo. Special orders for the two companies were issued by General Taylor on September 9, assigning Webster's "heavy howitzer battery" to Major General Butler's volunteer Field Division, and "[Francis] Taylor's battery" to the Second Brigade of regular troops commanded by Colonel Persifor Smith. Absent from Webster's company was Lieutenant Irvin McDowell, who was on special duty as aide-de-camp to General Wool. Another of the First Artillery companies, E, seems to have been split between Camargo and Cerralvo for a few days, at least with respect to its officers, but it appears to have been reunited for the most part by September 11.[22]

When General Taylor left Camargo on September 4, the men riding with him included, presumably, William Bliss, Joseph K. F. Mansfield, and Robert S. Garnett, the latter a Fourth Artillery lieutenant who had been appointed as an aide to the general.[23] Old Zach had planned to leave on the fifth, or so he had informed the adjutant general, but in writing Dr. Wood from Cerralvo he said he had left on the fourth, without explaining the reason his departure was a day earlier than scheduled. Possibly he decided that further delay was unnecessary after Major General Robert Patterson arrived at Camargo on the fourth. Taylor had issued orders giving Patterson, upon his arrival, command of all the troops that were to remain in Camargo, as well as those in the rear along the Rio Grande, "at Matamoros and other points." Reporting to Patterson at Camargo would be two brigadier generals: Thomas Marshall, with responsibility for the Second Kentucky and Second Ohio regiments as well as any First Kentucky and First Ohio volunteers left behind by "the marching regiments"; and Gideon Pillow, in charge of the Second Tennessee, Georgia, and Alabama regiments, together with any First Tennessee, Baltimore Battalion, and Mississippi volunteers remaining in Camargo.[24] Brigadier General Joseph Lane, who had formerly been colonel of the Second Indiana regiment, was serving in the rear with his state's volunteers.[25]

On September 6, the same day the dragoons and the artillery companies at Camp Butler began their movement toward Mier and Cerralvo, volunteer regiments in the Field Division, commanded by Major General William O. Butler, commenced crossing to the left bank of the San Juan, preparatory to following the Monterrey-bound regulars. The First Kentucky and the First Ohio regiments were in Brigadier General Hamer's First Brigade of Volunteers; the First Tennessee and the Mississippi Rifles were commanded by Brigadier General Quitman (Second Brigade of Volunteers). Officers destined to become Civil War generals in Butler's division included Colonel Jefferson Davis, Captain Douglas H. Cooper, and Lieutenants Carnot Posey and Richard Griffith (Mississippi Rifles); Lieutenant Ferdinand Van Derveer (First Ohio); and Colonel William B. Campbell, Lieutenant Colonel Samuel R. Anderson, and Captain Benjamin F. Cheatham (First Tennessee). Hamer's brigade left the Camargo area on the sixth, Quitman's on the seventh. No doubt riding with Butler, Hamer, and Quitman were the regular army officers Taylor had assigned to them: Major Lorenzo Thomas with Butler, Lieutenant Joseph Hooker with Hamer, and Lieutenant William A. Nichols with Quitman.[26] Also assigned to Butler's division as acting inspector general "for the campaign" was Albert Sidney Johnston. Taylor had especially devised that role for Johnston when the men in his regiment of Texans had been mustered out of service, most of them having, in Taylor's words, "expressed a disinclination to serve another term of three months." Johnston, in contrast, had "expressed a desire to participate in the campaign," Taylor told Adjutant General Jones, and "forage and subsistence" for him had been authorized without his being given rank in the regular army or "assurances of pay."[27]

The Texas Division of volunteers, commanded by Major General James Pinckney Henderson, the state's governor, was not consolidated when the march toward Monterrey began. Earlier, before General Taylor left Matamoros, the Texas Division's First Regiment of Texas Mounted Rifle Volunteers, led by Colonel John C. Hays, had been supplied for a "tour of detached service." Hays and his men had headed toward Monterrey by way of San Fernando, a route not previously examined. By August 27 they were in China, a village on the southern bank of the San Juan River some sixty miles below Camargo, where they received orders to remain for the time being. Civil War generals-to-be on the roster of Hays's regiment (all Confederates) included Captains Thomas Green and Henry E. McCulloch (the latter a younger brother of Captain Ben McCulloch) and Lieutenant Walter P. Lane.[28]

Meanwhile, companies of the Second Regiment of Henderson's division had reached Camargo. Their immediate commander was Colonel George T. Wood, among whose officers was Major William R. Scurry (Confederate brigadier general). General Taylor had arranged for two companies of Wood's regiment to be ready to accompany Worth and his division's First Brigade of regular troops to Cerralvo, and to escort the train of pack mules on its return. A few days later General Taylor assigned the quartermaster of Henderson's division, Major Henry L. Kinney of Corpus Christi fame, to take charge of all teamsters, primarily Mexicans, who had been hired as "conductors of the mule supply train."[29] Two companies of mounted Texans, Ben McCulloch's and Robert A. Gillespie's, were employed under Taylor's "immediate orders as spy companies." To those two company commanders Old Zach gave orders on the first of September to proceed to Cerralvo and report to Worth. But by September 10 Taylor had decided to send the bulk of Henderson's division via China to Marín, about twenty-five miles above Monterrey, where the Texans were to reunite with the main column of regulars and volunteers.[30] Apparently he had no hesitancy about dividing his forces when he thought the situation called for it. In this instance he was obviously attempting to insure that no sizeable enemy force would be in his rear when he arrived at Monterrey.

Just before leaving Camargo, General Taylor told Adjutant General Jones he did not know how many of Governor Henderson's men would "go forward." His uncertainty was doubtless based on the tendency of the Texans to volunteer for no more than three months, though in the past many had, upon being discharged, reenlisted for another three-month period. He estimated that with the Texas Division he would have "a force of 6,000 men" at his disposal for the Monterrey campaign. He had thought it advisable to include volunteers from as many states as possible, and intended to bring more of them forward if the "state of supplies" in the Monterrey-Saltillo area was found sufficient to maintain them.[31]

His decision to take around six thousand troops with him was arbitrary, guided by his limited means of transporting equipment and provisions, for he had little information about the strength of opposition forces he was likely to meet. Nevertheless, he did not seem to anticipate much difficulty in capturing Monterrey. On August 25 he wrote Jones that a "confidential messenger" had brought word that the number of regular Mexican troops in the city was 2,000 to 2,500, and that there were evidently no approaching reinforcements. As General Taylor was preparing to leave Camargo, a message from Worth quoted reports that Santa Anna had "taken the reins of government," and that "2,000 troops of the line" and several pieces of artillery had recently arrived at Monterrey, although no cavalry was there. In forwarding Worth's letter to the adjutant general, together with a proclamation by Ampudia, who was the new general-in-chief at Monterrey, Taylor not only sounded unperturbed but suggested that Ampudia might not attempt to hold the city. Old Zach was expecting to be in Saltillo, sixty miles or so beyond Monterrey and the Sierra Madre peaks west of the city, by the first of October.[32]

Similarly, Taylor's officers appear to have entertained no trepidations, perhaps inspired by Taylor's calmness or the Army of Occupation's success thus far. During the march their letters were filled almost exclusively with descriptions of the beauty of distant mountains, the abundance of crystal-clear streams along the way, the corn and flour purchased by the army that produced delicious "corn bread, hard bread, flour bread, mush, grits, or tortillas." At the same time most of the regular army officers seem to have thought that the war would end shortly, hastening the day they would say farewell to Mexico.[33]

General Taylor reached the leading units of Worth's division at Cerralvo on September 9, accompanied by Twiggs's division. Butler's division of volunteers was expected to arrive during the next day or two. Napoleon Dana told Sue, "Cerralvo is quite a pretty town, with a great many large and fine trees in it. The houses are all of stone, and the church has one of those three-story steeples which puts us in mind of our own churches at home. . . . A mountain torrent winds through the town, crossing the streets at many places and supplying [an] abundance of pure water and delightful bathing." Meade wrote of Cerralvo that it was "in the valley of a mountain stream." Its "pure, cool water" was deemed "a great luxury." The people had received them "most kindly" after they were assured that the Americans would pay "in cash, at fair prices" for everything the residents were asked to provide, such as wood, corn, and flour.[34] The only cloud Meade perceived as darkening their prospects for a successful campaign was intelligence that followers of General Antonio López de Santa Anna were clamoring for his return to power, and had already deposed President Paredes. Until being exiled in 1841 Santa Anna, whom Meade termed the "master-spirit" of Mexico, had held political offices of one kind or another for decades, and had been among the most influential of his country's leaders. Soon Meade would hear that Santa Anna had not only breached the American blockade at Veracruz "with the cognizance of Commodore Connor [*sic*]" but that the two men had secretly conferred together, from which rumor he judged that the famed Mexican leader "was favorable to adjusting the difficulty" between Mexico and the United States. He could not know, of course, that the former dictator's return from Cuba had been facilitated by President Polk, after intermediaries had vouched for Santa Anna's willingness to accept, for the most part, Polk's terms for peace. Meade prophesied, however, that a "long and severely contested war" would result if the Mexican general should decide to "energetically . . . prosecute the war."[35]

Soon after the march to Monterrey began, certain of the officers heard, directly or indirectly, that they had been awarded brevets for their participation in the May conflicts. Meade was not among them, despite having been included in the list of officers recommended by General Taylor for that honor. When his wife raised the subject, Meade replied that he understood Taylor had included his name on the "long list, the one considered too large to send to the Senate," but he was not disappointed at being "passed over," having been "always aware that the nomination of the commanding general was one thing, and the nomination by the 'President' another, the one requiring hard service, the other political influence, the curse of our country." He went on to explain he had "little claim as far as the two battles" were concerned, having simply done his duty, and that staff officers seldom had opportunities "to perform brilliant feats, such as ensure promotion."[36]

Grant, who had fought beside the men of his company at Palo Alto and had led them at Resaca de la Palma, was not mentioned in the official reports and thus could not hope to be awarded a brevet. During the march to Monterrey, his days were spent in fulfilling the many new duties he had acquired upon being appointed acting regimental quartermaster. From Punta Aguda on September 6 he sent Quartermaster General Thomas S. Jesup "a monthly report of Privates of the 4th Infantry employed on extra duty: also a 'Summary Statement' of the moneys received, expended, and remaining on hand for part of August, 1846." Unwelcome as Grant's quartermaster appointment was to him, it gave him insight into the interrelationship between the ability of an army to advance in an enemy's territory and the transportation of its supplies. He would long remember the patience, skill, and forbearance needed when lashing camp equipment to the backs of pack mules: "Sheet-iron kettles, tent-poles and mess chests were inconvenient articles to transport in that way. It took several hours to get ready to start each morning, and by the time we were ready some of the mules first loaded would be tired of standing so long with their loads on their backs. Sometimes one would start to run, bowing his back and kicking up until he scattered his load; others would lie down and try to disarrange their loads by attempting to get on top of them by rolling on them; others with tent-poles for part of their loads would manage to run a tent-pole on one side of a sapling while they would take the other."[37] For Grant, one of the few bright spots on the horizon was his belief that Julia's brother Fred, with whom he had been corresponding, would be reporting for duty with Taylor in the near future. Fred had been with the Sixth Infantry at Fort Towson since the fall of 1843, following their graduation from West Point. In March of 1846 he had finally been promoted to the rank of full second lieutenant and had been transferred to an Army of Occupation regiment, the Fifth Infantry. Thereafter, in letter after letter Grant mentioned to Julia that he expected to see Fred on the Rio Grande. Instead, his classmate was given charge of the Baton Rouge Arsenal. Not until the next spring did their paths cross, at Veracruz.[38]

As Grant commenced the march to Monterrey he could at least rejoice that Brigadier General Thomas L. Hamer would be heading toward that same destination. The former Ohio congressman, who had recommended Grant for admission to the United States Military Academy, had been a friend of Grant's father when Ulysses was a child. However, political differences had caused Jesse Grant and Tom Hamer to deliberately shun one another for several years until Jesse, learning that the Democratic congressman's approval was needed in order for Ulysses to be admitted to West Point, wrote a plea for his assistance. Hamer complied so hastily that he forgot the young man's name at birth was Hiram Ulysses Grant, calling him instead "Ulysses S. Grant," an error that Ulysses sought in vain to change while at the Academy. Before entering West Point he had himself unofficially adopted the name Ulysses Hiram Grant, evidently to avoid having "H.U.G." as his initials. Ulysses would tell Julia that he did not know what the middle initial "S" was supposed to represent, though historians would later assume that Hamer believed Ulysses' middle name was Simpson, his mother's maiden name. At any rate, neither Hamer's error nor differing political affiliations reduced Grant's regard for his benefactor. He would always remember Hamer as "one of the ablest men Ohio had ever produced," and one who might well have been "President of the United States." Hamer thought highly of Lieutenant Grant as well, as he indicated in a letter to a friend after he and Grant had chatted with one another in Mexico. Unfortunately, during the Monterrey campaign Hamer began suffering from dysentery. He would die in December of that year while still a member of Taylor's army.[39]

General Taylor, who remained at Cerralvo until Sunday the thirteenth, informed Dr. Wood that he was detained there "principally to have the horses & mules shod, as it is impossible for either that are worked in harness or under the saddle to get along without, the greater part of the road being over sharp stone at best difficult to travel over." Needing to provide for the defense of his depot at Cerralvo once the army resumed its march, he directed that two companies of the Mississippi regiment should be left there to garrison it. Time was taken as well for a court-martial at the camp of the Second Division. Among those detailed for that duty were Captains Charles F. Smith and Theophilus H. Holmes; one of the supernumeraries named was Lieutenant John W. Phelps of Vermont, a member of Daniel Harvey Hill's company and a future brigadier general of Union volunteers.[40]

It was at Cerralvo that Taylor assigned Mackall's mobile artillery battery to Colonel Persifor Smith's Second Brigade, and Webster's heavy howitzer battery to Major General Butler. In addition, Old Rough and Ready ordered Ben McCulloch's Texans and a squadron of dragoons to cover a "pioneer party" which, together with two topographical engineers, was to precede the main column on September 12 and improve the road, "rendering it practicable" for artillery and wagons. He also divided Gillespie's company of Texas volunteers, giving half to Butler and half to Worth, the men in those detachments to serve as outposts, videttes, and expresses.[41] Upon departing Cerralvo, the general specified the new marching order of his army. Leading off on the thirteenth would be Twiggs's First Division along with General Taylor and his staff, followed on successive days by Worth's Second Division and Butler's Field Division of volunteers. Each division would be followed immediately by its baggage and supply trains, with a "strong rear guard." The ordnance train under Captain George Ramsay was to march between the Second Division's baggage and supply trains. The one-day interval between divisions was to be maintained until they were consolidated at Marín, twenty-five or thirty miles beyond Cerralvo. The troops were to "take 8 days rations" and "40 rounds of ammunition."[42]

The officers assigned to the "pioneer party" included George Meade. He had just returned on September 11 from a reconnaissance of the route from Cerralvo to Marín, escorted by eighty mounted troops. At one point they had come within a mile of a huge group of enemy cavalry. The Americans "drove in their pickets," but being vastly outnumbered they had returned, "unmolested," to Cerralvo. Meade said everyone was in "fine condition and spirits," and the "impression of the majority" was that there would be "no fight."[43] The pioneer detachment, protected by dragoons and Ben McCulloch's Rangers, left Cerralvo on the twelfth at daybreak, as directed. The next day General Taylor and Twiggs's division started for Marín.[44] The troops escorting the detachment of pioneers exchanged fire with the enemy, an incident said by Taylor to have occurred at the small village of Ramos, "a trifling affair" that "took place between McCulloch's Rangers and the enemy's rear guard." A few days later Meade wrote of the episode that the American advance contingent, numbering a "little over two hundred men," were fifteen miles in front of the First Division when they discovered a large party of enemy cavalry and chased them. "[O]ur Texas boys made a rush at them and delivered a fire, by which they tumbled two out of their saddles and got their lances and carbines. The Mexicans returned the fire without effect, and continued retiring. As they appeared to be increasing in force, General Taylor ordered us to halt until the First Division came up, so that we should be just in front of it, and we preserved this order of march up to our arrival at this place, Marin." In contrast, Napoleon Dana credited the dragoons, led by Captain Lawrence Pike Graham, with having driven off the enemy during the skirmish at Ramos, they having been sent out "as a picket in advance." Probably both dragoons and Texans fired at the Mexicans, although General Taylor's account, much like Meade's, mentioned only the latter. Inasmuch as Meade was a close friend of William Bliss, who was in effect Taylor's chief of staff, the young topographical engineer may have influenced Taylor's version of the affair, or vice versa.[45]

Just as the column reached Marín, an incident occurred illustrating that General Taylor, contrary to the claims of some critics, was on quite friendly terms with many volunteer officers. In Old Zach's advance was a captain of the Battalion of Baltimore and District of Columbia Volunteers, John Reese Kenly, a friend of regular army Lieutenant Randolph Ridgely. Kenly had been introduced to General Taylor by Ridgely late in July at Matamoros, following a riot between Baltimore and First Ohio troops (over ownership of a catfish). At that meeting Kenly had liked the general's "simplicity of manner, the total absence of all pretension in dress and address." Now, a month and a half later, on September 15, Kenly was pleased to find that Taylor still remembered him. Old Zach and his staff surprised the young captain by riding up to him suddenly while Kenly and other members of his company were admiring the beautiful valley below Marín, "surrounded by mountains," in which lay Monterrey. The general dismounted, smiled, extended his hand, referred to their Matamoros interview, and asked Kenly if he "had anything to report." Upon being told that no Mexicans had been seen since the company "left camp at daybreak," Taylor directed Kenly to march through the town (pointing to Marín, which appeared deserted), and to "halt on the other side until the column gets up." By that evening Taylor and Twiggs's First Division troops were camped just beyond Marín, on the bank of the San Juan River once again, although the stream was now "knee-deep" and "thirty yards wide." Worth's Second Division caught up with them the next night, and Butler's division brought up the rear on the seventeenth. Taylor, having heard from a messenger that Major General Henderson had been intending to have his command leave China by the fourteenth, was hoping the Texas Division would rendezvous with the main column momentarily. Nevertheless, Old Zach was determined to move on the next day, whether or not the Texans showed up.[46]

Even at Marín, less than twenty-five miles from Monterrey, General Taylor continued to doubt that Ampudia "would attempt to hold" the city. In a letter to the adjutant general on September 17 he mentioned having heard that the enemy was in "considerable force" there but that Ampudia had no more than five thousand men in his command, only three thousand of whom were regular army troops. Taylor had no "authentic intelligence from the interior," although he had received "vague reports" of a movement by Santa Anna toward Monterrey with reinforcements for Ampudia. The enemy had been "continually in sight" from Papagallo to Marín, yet no combat had occurred except for the "trifling affair" at Ramos. A Mexican cavalry force "perhaps 1000 strong" under General Torrejón had been scouring the countryside just ahead of Taylor's column, "driving off the citizens and committing many outrages upon person and property." Lieutenant Dana believed the Mexican soldiers were harassing people in the villages in order "to keep them from trading with us and from seeing how well we treat them."[47]

Meade likewise commented on General Torrejón's abusive treatment of Mexican citizens, as alleged by the few men the Americans found in Marín. After carefully weighing the factors bearing on the possibility of a fight at Monterrey, Meade was now certain there would be no combat, a conclusion with which Dana and others completely agreed. Of the "beautiful country" thereabouts, Meade wrote that it was "magnificent, the air balmy and pure, all the tropical fruits growing and we are just entering a level table-land, which leads to the mountains, twenty-five miles off, but so high we can see them towering away above the clouds, a most magnificent sight." If he were single, he added, he would be tempted to live "in this lovely climate." Dana described the region more fully: "Marin is a very pretty town of three thousand, built entirely of stone. . . . The streets are entirely level and clean." The village, he explained, was "situated just on the brow" of "a very large, level plain" that stretched "to the foot of the mountains." Through that plain, he continued, "meanders the San Juan, and there we are encamped."[48]

At Marín on September 17, with Henderson's division not yet there, Taylor again changed the order of march, his principal provisions for the next day being that the pioneer party was to be broken up and its members returned to their regiments; an advance, consisting of McCulloch's and Gillespie's companies of Texans and a squadron of dragoons, was to march at 5:30 a.m., headquarters and the First Division at 6, followed immediately by that division's baggage and half of the ordnance train; an hour thereafter the Second Division was to start forward, followed by its baggage and the remainder of the ordnance train; and an hour later the Field Division was to take up the line of march, followed by its baggage and the general supply train. The rear guard was to be composed of two companies of regulars, one from the First Division and one from the Second.[49]

Taylor went on to specify how those arrangements were to be amended if Henderson's division arrived in time to join the main column. Fortunately for the Americans, by the eighteenth Major General Henderson's column of Texans had appeared; and at the village of San Fernando, twelve miles southwest of Marín, General Taylor directed that Texans were to "form the advance" the next day, but that two of their companies were to serve as the army's rear guard. The advance was to march at sunrise, followed at one-hour intervals by the divisions of Twiggs, Worth, and Butler, in that order. On the morning of September 19, General Taylor and his staff at last reached the outskirts of the city of Monterrey.[50]

8
Battle of Monterrey

The road the Americans were following from Marín on September 19 descended to the plain on Monterrey's northeast side. When Taylor's advance neared the city, he and his staff were close to the head of his long column, which stretched more than eight miles back to their last campsite. According to George Meade, who was with Old Zach that morning, they were still uncertain whether the commander of the Mexican forces in the city, General Ampudia, intended to defend it. For some time Taylor must have had a mental picture of the overall configuration he now glimpsed, since he had several times mentioned in reports his intention to proceed beyond Monterrey to Saltillo. On its southwestern face the city was encircled by a series of mountainous eminences, part of the vast Sierra Madre range. Emerging from each of the far sides of the city was a tributary of the San Juan, the Santa Catarina River, which ran through a gorge between the city and the mountains. Entering Monterrey on its southwest corner from a narrow pass through the mountains was the Saltillo road. As the Americans pressed forward within a mile of the city, one fortification was clearly visible, the ruins of a cathedral called the Citadel, with embrasures in its bastioned walls for cannon. It was situated about one thousand feet northeast of the city, in fields to the right of the road from Marín. Probably too far away to be individually distinguishable were "several small works" on the eastern side of the city, of which Taylor had previously been informed. On a hill adjacent to the Saltillo road was the famous old stone Bishop's Palace around which fortifications were visible, as well as other structures evidently housing troops and artillery. Thus at first glance it was obvious Ampudia had been preparing for defensive action, an observation confirmed when Mexican cavalry suddenly appeared. Shots were exchanged, and the enemy's artillery opened fire. One ball passed within two feet of George Meade.[1]

Troops miles away in Taylor's rear were startled and excited by the booming of cannon. Lieutenant Daniel Harvey Hill, about halfway back in the column, noted in his diary under the day's date, "Heard hostile guns today for the first time in my life." Major Luther Giddings of the First Ohio volunteers, about ten miles behind the advance, hearing the gunfire and assuming a battle had commenced, rushed forward with his men until they met a dragoon whose horse was covered with mud and foam. From him Giddings learned that "the firing was from one of the Mexican forts upon General Taylor and the Texan troops, who had ventured within range of the enemy's guns."[2]

The general and his advance, retreating a mile or so from the belching Monterrey guns, camped in a grove with "two delicious springs of water" which the Americans thereafter called Walnut Springs or Walnut Grove, and where all of the brigades gradually joined them. That afternoon Old Zach and an escort "went out again" to study the city's defenses "and again received a hot fire." By that time Taylor had formulated a plan of attack: a two-pronged assault, one from the southwest where the Saltillo road left the city and passed through the adjacent mountain heights, and another from the northeast, down the Marín–Walnut Springs road. To ascertain whether his tentative scheme was practical, that afternoon he sent out reconnaissance teams. Captain Mansfield departed with a party at 4 p.m. to see what could be ascertained about fortifications near the Bishop's Palace in the southwestern hills, while Captain William Williams of the Topographical Engineers corps attempted to gather further information about the eastern redoubts.[3]

Old Zach had never previously had occasion to participate in an assault on a town of any consequence, much less to design and lead one. He was handicapped by the failure of the Quartermaster Department to provide him with requested wheeled siege guns, yet to all appearances he entertained not the slightest hesitancy or self-doubt. He did, however, delay adoption of his assault plan until Mansfield confirmed, around 10 p.m., the "practicability of throwing forward a column to the Saltillo road" and thereby, hopefully, cutting the enemy's western "line of communication" through the mountains. Whether or to what extent Taylor had discussed his intentions earlier with subordinates is unclear, but before the day ended he consulted with the commanders of his divisions and brigades, and subsequently "orders were given to Bvt. Brigr. Genl. Worth, Commanding the 2nd Division to march with his command on the 20th—to turn the hill of the Bishop's Palace, to occupy a position on the Saltillo road, and to carry the enemy's detached works in that quarter, where practicable."[4]

Why Worth rather than Twiggs was chosen for what Taylor termed "an operation of essential importance" is an intriguing question, since Twiggs was now a lineal brigadier general and thus clearly senior to Brevet Brigadier General Worth. No doubt that decision was based largely on the manner in which Worth had conducted himself since withdrawing his resignation and returning to duty with the Army of Occupation once war was declared. After once more being given charge of the First Brigade, Worth had begged for his command to be allowed to lead the advance upriver from Matamoros, and promised that Taylor's orders would be carried out "with zeal, energy, and discretion." His plea having been granted, he seems to have performed creditably in Camargo and as commander of the Second Division on the march to Monterrey. Yet he was evidently much the same as formerly in certain respects, for Lieutenant Napoleon Dana, who had known him previously, said of him after an hour's informal chat at Cerralvo: "I believe he does not lack much of being a little cracked. He is very much inclined to make a noise about nothing, and a fuss out of trifles." Somewhat later Daniel Harvey Hill would write that "Gen. Worth after his usual manner had contrived to make a very easy march exceedingly fatiguing." Still, George Meade wrote favorably of him after being assigned to Worth's division at the commencement of the Monterrey march, and Meade's opinion may have reached General Taylor's ears through Captain Bliss.[5]

Then too, Taylor undoubtedly knew that Worth's service record was more diverse and impressive than that of Twiggs. A New Yorker who had enlisted as a private in 1813 at age eighteen, Worth had been commissioned as a first lieutenant within a year, had served with Winfield Scott at the Battle of Chippewa, and had earned the respect and admiration of nearly everyone while he was commandant of cadets at West Point from 1824 to 1828. Being on extremely friendly terms with General Winfield Scott had led to various prestigious assignments, most recently his appointment as colonel of the Eighth Infantry when that regiment was formed in 1838. He had also been successful in all of his endeavors, including his 1840s campaign in Florida against the Seminoles.[6] Twiggs, in contrast, had been outstanding only as a dragoon colonel; and his reluctance, following the Palo Alto battle, for Taylor's army to advance without reinforcements probably marked him permanently in Old Zach's eyes as excessively cautious.

Looked at another way, General Taylor was giving Worth a task that headquarters believed to be less dangerous, from the standpoint of assaults on fortifications, than that facing the troops remaining at Walnut Springs. George Meade said of the engineers' reports of September 19, "It was found the town was most strongly fortified in the direction of Marin, and weak in that of Saltillo." Such proved to be the case, although many of Worth's officers, aware of the strategic importance as well as the extreme steepness of the southwestern heights on which Mexican forts and redoubts were built, thought otherwise. Napoleon Dana, to whom the capture of those fortifications was the toughest challenge Taylor's army would encounter, was proud to be in the division selected for the assignment. Dana explained to Sue, after describing the rugged heights and the defensive structures overlooking the declivity through which ran the Saltillo road and the Santa Catarina River: "On these if they fought at all they would fight hard, for if these were taken, their retreat was cut off. . . . Here, then, we thought must come off the grand struggle. Here was the post of honor and of danger. . . . Who was to do this? . . . Our Division, the second, was a solid mass of regulars except one company of Louisianians; our commander, General Worth, was known to be a desperate man, and we thought it would be us."[7]

As Dana pointed out, Worth's division was composed chiefly of regulars. In his First Brigade, commanded by Lieutenant Colonel Thomas Staniford, was Duncan's battery of mobile light artillery; the Artillery Battalion, under Brevet Colonel Thomas Childs; and the Eighth Infantry regiment, led by Captain Richard B. Screven. In the division's Second Brigade, commanded by Colonel Persifor Smith, was the mobile artillery battery led by Lieutenant William Mackall; the Fifth Infantry, headed by Major Martin Scott; the Seventh Infantry, under Brevet Major Dixon Miles; and Captain Albert Blanchard's company of Louisiana volunteers. Assigned to assist those brigades, in addition to George Meade, were Captain John Sanders of the Corps of Engineers, and the First Regiment of Major General J. Pinckney Henderson's division of Texas Mounted volunteers, led by Colonel John Hays.[8]

Worth's column, starting toward its destination on September 20, wheeled abruptly right from the Marín–Walnut Springs road through cultivated fields, to avoid the Citadel's guns, then turned westward on the Presqueria-Grande road, which connected to the main Saltillo highway. As for the exact time the division left Walnut Springs, accounts differ. Both Taylor and Worth stated that the maneuver began at 2 p.m., but Daniel Harvey Hill noted in his diary that the division marched at 1 p.m., whereas Lieutenant Edmund Bradford's recollection was: "We left Camp about 12 o'clock and marched on the road to Monterey about a mile; we then struck off the road to the right, passing through chapparal [*sic*] and corn fields to the left of the town." Napoleon Dana agreed with Hill: "At one o'clock we all bade our friends goodby and left the camp [Walnut Springs] to commence our movement." George Meade said only that on the morning of the twentieth, after receiving orders to report to Worth, "I immediately repaired to him, found the column ready to move, and in a few minutes marched with it."[9] Of course, the individual units in Worth's command necessarily joined it at varying times.

Monterrey, the capital of the state of Nuevo León, extended about twice as far from east to west as it did from north to south. The Walnut Springs road, which angled down from Marín and San Fernando in the northeast, entered the city toward the center of its northern suburbs, as did a road from Monclova, considerably north of Monterrey. Just to the right of the Walnut Springs

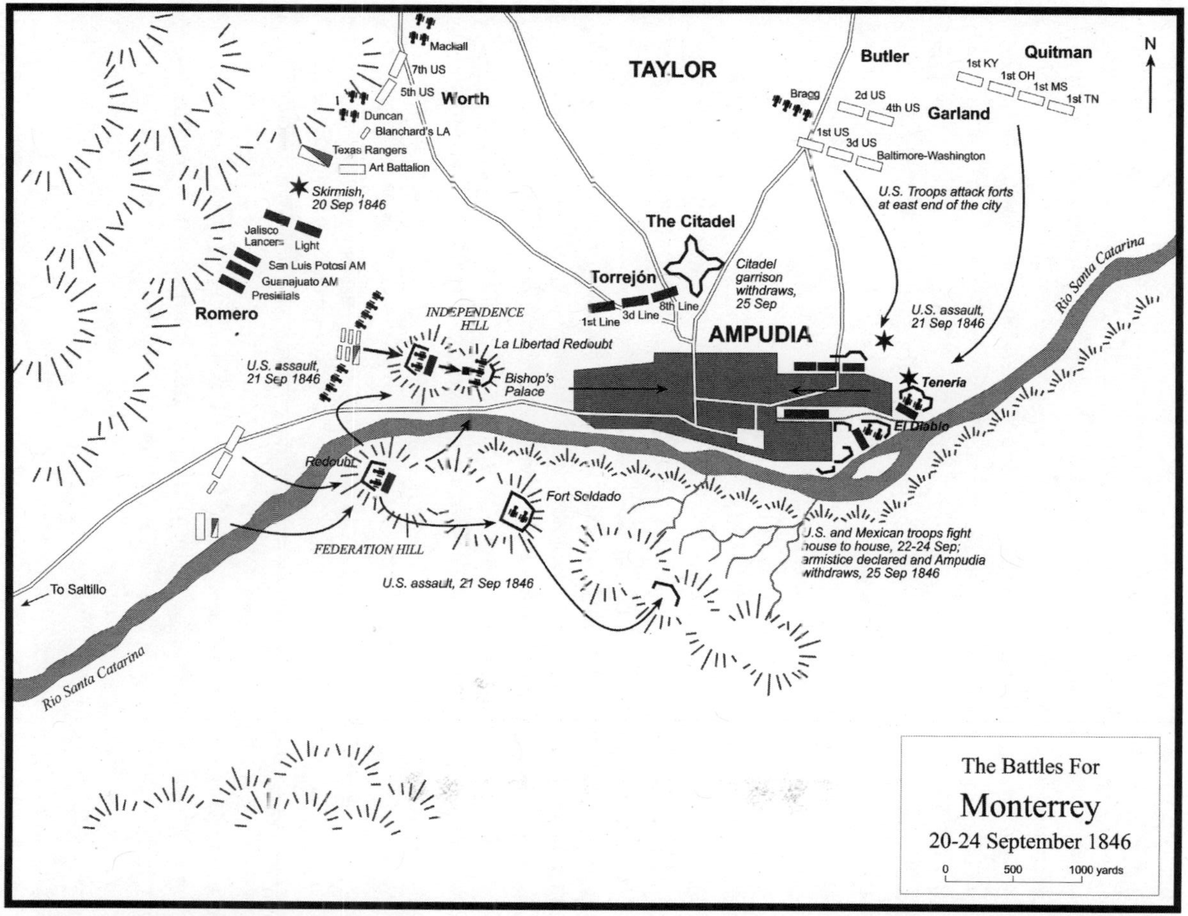

4. Monterrey, September 20–24, 1846

road as it neared Monterrey stood the Citadel, protecting access to the city from that direction. Other than the Citadel, and the fortified southwestern hills toward which Worth's troops were moving, Monterrey's chief defensive works were located on its eastern side. There a small stream, a channel of the San Juan, cut into the center of the city, trickling under the Purisima Bridge; and along this shallow waterway, roughly across from one another, loomed two major forts, La Tenería and El Diablo. South of the bridge and El Diablo (called Fort Diablo by most Americans) were the city's main plaza and cathedral, and into that sector ran a road to Cadereyta, southward. Beyond Monterrey's main plaza flowed the Santa Catarina River which, like the rugged foothills of the Sierra Madre range, enclosed the city on three sides and formed the city's primary natural defense. Dotting the eastern border, and blocking the entrances to streets on which stood El Diablo and La Tenería, huddled several enemy batteries. They extended as far as the northeastern corner of Monterrey, the nearest point to the Walnut Springs camp.[10]

General Taylor would later report that during the afternoon of the twentieth he was informed by some of the officers "reconnoitring [*sic*] the town" that Worth's movement had been discovered by Ampudia's forces, and that the Mexicans were "throwing reinforcements" toward Independence Hill, on which the Bishop's Palace was located. After sending Worth a warning, Taylor ordered Twiggs's and Butler's divisions to be "displayed in front of the town, until dark," hoping to divert the enemy's attention. A Maryland volunteer in Twiggs's division, Captain John R. Kenly (with whom General Taylor had spoken at Marín), wrote of that "Sabbath evening": "We marched out from camp into the plain, and found Butler's volunteer division, Ridgely's and Bragg's batteries of flying artillery, and Webster's regular battery of twenty-four-pound howitzers, ready to move with us. General Taylor and staff were also there. We marched toward the city, halted within a mile of its works, and formed line of battle. . . . Still standing to our arms, night fell upon us, and with it a deluge of rain." The regulars and volunteers stood in sight of the city's houses and churches from late afternoon until after 10 p.m. without firing a shot. During those hours General Taylor arranged for both mortar and howitzer entrenchments to be constructed east of the Walnut Springs road, roughly the same distance from Monterrey as the Citadel. Evidently that had been one purpose of the exercise from the beginning. Overnight those batteries, "two 24 pdr howitzers and a 10 inch mortar," were guarded by the Fourth Infantry.[11]

Meanwhile, at about 6 p.m. Worth had halted his division (numbering around two thousand men) after they had marched "only six miles." They had been delayed by "difficulties of the ground" upon leaving the Walnut Springs road, time having been lost particularly while Captain Sanders made "the route practicable for Artillery." While his column remained on the Presqueria-

Grande road, at a rancho out of range of the enemy's guns, Worth pressed on southward two miles or so to the main Saltillo road on the near side of the Santa Catarina River gorge, accompanied by his staff and "about fifty Texans." Becoming convinced that Mexican forces in large numbers were close, they were returning to their camp when they were fired on by what must have been a small contingent of Ampudia's forces, hidden behind "a fence alongside the road." Worth could have been cut off from the rest of his column if the Mexican defenders had been more numerous, which would of course have been a serious setback for the Americans. As it was, the Texans' prompt responding fire allowed Worth's party to return "quietly back to camp," although at some point they were also "subjected to a plunging fire from the two pieces on the top of Independence Hill," from which they "sustained no damage."[12]

Worth undoubtedly needed much more information about the nearby terrain. Taylor's orders, except for his mention of the Bishop's Palace, were extremely vague, an indication that Mansfield did not obtain a comprehensive picture of the sector's fortifications during his evening survey of the nineteenth. As Worth would discover, in order to control the principal Saltillo route his troops would have to assault the two heights between which ran the road and the Santa Catarina River. The Americans usually called the nearer eminence Independence Hill, and the more distant one Federation Ridge. Each had batteries on its summit and a fort somewhat lower on its slopes. The Bishop's Palace was the fort that dominated Independence Hill; the fort on Federation Ridge was termed El Soldado. The Saltillo road divided near the city, one spur crossing a low point on Federation Ridge and running through a valley on its southwestern side before rejoining the more northerly, primary route, which followed the Santa Catarina through the gorge between the two heights. It was the latter that the Americans considered *the* Saltillo road, since it could best accommodate any reinforcements or supplies that might arrive through the pass leading to Saltillo, although Federation Ridge commanded both branches of the road.[13]

Apparently little more of a specific nature was ascertained from Worth's reconnaissance on the evening of September 20. The Saltillo road sector, in his opinion, constituted both a weak and a strong aspect of the Mexican defensive position, "the weak point, because commanding the only lines of retreat, and of supply, in the direction of *Saltillo,* and controlling that in direction of Presqueria-Grande; the strong point, because of the peculiarly defensive character of the hills and gorges, and of the very careful and skillful manner with which they had been fortified and guarded." He had seen enough to convince him, however, that further advance by his column "would be strenuously resisted." From remarks by Worth and Meade, and from a map that Meade sketched, it seems they surveyed the enemy's positions from the lip of the gorge, with Independence Hill on their left and the western tip of Federation Ridge directly ahead though a short distance southward, across the main Saltillo road and the Santa Catarina River. Being fired on from the summit of Independence Hill had alerted them to some of the works in the vicinity of the Bishop's Palace, but evidently there was no firing from Federation Ridge that evening, and the next day's events indicate that until those batteries came alive the Americans knew little about them.[14]

At 9:30 that evening Worth sent Taylor a note requesting that a diversionary action be undertaken on the eastern front the next day. Worth's troops settled down on the ground in a pouring rain, without tents, forbidden to light fires and forced to rely on whatever was in their knapsacks for supper, despite having had no food since morning. "That was the most cheerless, comfortless, unhappy night I ever spent," Lieutenant Napoleon Dana declared. A Seventh Infantry comrade celebrating his twenty-sixth birthday, the handsome blond, blue-eyed Lieutenant Earl Van Dorn, was probably somewhat more comfortably situated that evening, thanks to his being an aide to Colonel Persifor Smith; and of course the same was doubtless true of George Meade, John Pemberton, and other members of Worth's staff, since the brevet brigadier general had found cover inside a corn shed.[15]

The following morning Worth's division commenced moving southwestward again at 6 a.m., heading straight for the edge of the gorge near which, the previous evening, a large enemy force was believed to have been posted. To "occupy a position on the Saltillo road," as ordered, Worth's troops marched through a narrow valley between Independence Hill on their left and another large foothill jutting out from the mountains on their right. Worth apparently gave no thought to whether he might be outnumbered by enemy forces in that quarter, although he may have reasoned that nearby Mexican units could scarcely be much more numerous than his own inasmuch as Ampudia's troops were presumably scattered throughout the city's various forts, redoubts, and redans. (General Taylor would later estimate that the entire Mexican force defending the city consisted of "at least 7000 troops of the line and from 2000 to 3000 irregulars," whereas his army at Monterrey numbered "425 officers and 6220 men.")[16] Leading Worth's advance at dawn on the twenty-first were "Hays' Texans, supported by the light companies 1st Brigade under Capt C.F. Smith . . . closely followed by Duncan's Light Artillery, and Battalion heads of columns." Although Worth did not explain why he singled out Charles F. Smith for such duty, he had six months earlier witnessed the artillery captain's unhesitating charge across the Arroyo Colorado against a hostile Mexican force of unknown strength. Moreover, while Worth was not with the Army of Occupation at Resaca de la Palma he had doubtless heard that Smith, together with George McCall, had fearlessly and successfully led General Taylor's advance on that occasion.[17]

Smith was equally effective when, "on turning an angle of the mountain, at a Hacienda called *San Jeronimo,*" the Americans "came upon a strong force of Cavalry and Infantry, mostly the former." Of the conflict that "immediately ensued," Worth wrote: "The Texans received the heavy charge of cavalry with their unerring rifles, and usual gallantry; the light companies opened a rapid and well directed fire; Duncan's battery was in action in the minute (promptly supported by a section of Mackalls [*sic*]), delivering its fire over the heads of our men." Holding his Second Brigade in reserve, Worth called up the rest of his First Brigade, and within fifteen minutes "the enemy retired in disorder," leaving on the ground "one hundred killed and wounded," and the Americans in charge of the Saltillo road.[18]

Other accounts add to Worth's description of the Monterrey battle's first direct clash between Ampudia's and Taylor's troops. Daniel Harvey Hill noted in his journal that when the morning's march commenced "two companies of the Artillery Battalion were thrown forward as skirmishers," evidently referring to the artillerymen acting as infantry in Smith's command. Similarly, Meade stated that the Texans were "supported by two companies of infantry, acting as skirmishers."[19] Napoleon Dana, whose regiment was one of the units initially held in reserve, provided Sue a more complete description of that morning's encounter with Mexican forces: The movement of Worth's column had begun at dawn, with "about 100 rangers" riding ahead of the skirmishers and brigades. Within half an hour the Americans were within range of the Mexican artillery on Independence Hill, which commenced firing. "The shot and shells came very near, but all the damage done that time was one soldier of the Fifth Infantry lost his leg, one horse killed and one of the wagons injured." Suddenly, as Worth's advance reached the Saltillo road, a regiment of Mexican lancers emerged from behind a hill and "charged the rangers at a gallop," badly injuring several of the Texans. As the Rangers met the Mexicans head-on and shot lancers from their saddles, they were joined by the First Brigade's light companies under Smith. Soon, pelted by Duncan's guns, the lancers and their supporting infantry companies fled.[20]

Worth's praise for "Lt. Longstreet comdg light Co. 8th" suggests that James Longstreet had a prominent part in the brief confrontation. Worth did not indicate how involved Longstreet was, but the young lieutenant's contribution to the action was at least significant enough to warrant special mention.[21]

As to the number of enemy troops opposing the Americans on the Saltillo road, Meade said two thousand; Lieutenant Charles Hamilton (Fifth Infantry) said Worth's division "encountered a squadron of the enemy's cavalry"; and Lieutenant Edmund Bradford wrote: "The force of the enemy was estimated at 300 cavalry supported by a column of Infantry." Probably Meade was quoting the version adopted by Worth. Whichever was the most accurate, the Americans appear to have been considerably outnumbered, at least from the standpoint of cavalry, yet in their favor were several factors. In the confusion of the sudden skirmish, the Mexicans probably did not realize that they outnumbered the Americans. Moreover, though led by General Manuel Romero, the lancers were doubtless alarmed by the mortal wounding of Lieutenant Colonel Juan N. Nájera. They broke into separate wedges, many retreating toward Saltillo, and that development may have prompted the withdrawal toward Monterrey of the rest, together with their supporting infantry contingents. At that point, with Duncan's guns firing over the heads of his comrades, the Americans had the advantage when it came to artillery: due to the height of Independence Hill, at the base of which the fighting was occurring, Mexican cannoneers near the Bishop's Palace were unable to strike the American troops immediately below, and evidently Worth's men were out of range of the artillery on Federation Ridge.[22]

Both Duncan's and Mackall's batteries had unlimbered on a hill north of the gorge. Duncan's men continued to fire toward the Saltillo road, believing the enemy's forces that at first retired into the city showed signs of "renewing the contest." Mackall's guns, however, aimed at those defending the Bishop's Palace. He and another lieutenant were nearly hit by a Mexican battery which, according to a diagram he sent his wife, was on Federation Ridge.[23]

From Mackall's comments and those of other participants, it seems apparent that the firing from Federation Ridge did not commence until around the time the Americans took possession of the main Saltillo highway. George Meade, for one, wrote that, as Mexican troops dispersed toward the town, "a plunging fire from a piece on the top of Federation Hill was opened on us, obliging us to retire out of range of the shot." Daniel Harvey Hill, after recording that the Mexicans with whom they had been fighting had "fled leaving a goodly number of dead and wounded," wrote: "The enemy had been throwing shells at us for some time from the hill upon which is situated the Bishop's palace, and a heavy fire was now opened upon us from the other hill." That development precipitated an order for the Americans to move "some eight hundred yards farther" on the Saltillo road, out of range of the guns on both hills. Worth did not specify the direction in which he had directed them to move, but Mackall's diagram shows the units on the road marched away from the city, toward the pass that led to Saltillo; and Worth would call Federation, which extended further toward the western mountains than Independence, "the nearest hill" in reporting his noontime plan to silence the guns emitting the "plunging fire" from Federation's summit.[24]

Although Worth mentioned issuing only one order for his column to change its position that morning, the ever-critical Lieutenant Daniel Harvey Hill accused his division commander of "harassing and exhausting the troops by changing position three times" before deciding at noon to assault Federation

Ridge. Hill was scarcely unbiased—he had been entering derogatory comments about Worth in his journal ever since leaving Camargo, including his understanding that Worth had publicly declared his determination to sacrifice himself and the men he commanded, if necessary, "to regain his lost reputation." Yet with respect to Worth's having changed the division's position more than once on the morning of the twenty-first, Hill seems to have been correct. Lieutenant Edmund Bradford (Fourth Artillery) told of his company forming on the road after the skirmish while "Capt [C. F.] Smith & Capt [John B.] Scott [were] sent out with their companies to reconnoitre." Lieutenant Bradford wrote that subsequently the First Brigade "was ordered to march into a corn field in order to have a flank fire on any [enemy] troops which might make a sally from the castle." Continuing, he said, "Whilst we were lying in the field the enemy opened a heavy fire on us from two guns on the 2nd hill. . . . In this position we remained for 1 ½ hours, the balls passing a few feet over our heads; one shower of grape fell in and about my company in every direction, but struck no one. At this time we received an order to march out of the reach of the shot. In doing this we were exposed to full view for half an hour and I assure you they took advantage of us." After noting that during this change of position Captain Henry McKavett (Eighth Infantry) was killed, Bradford described the manner in which they were next deployed, in anticipation of an attack: Duncan's and Mackall's batteries were formed back to back on the road, the latter in rear of the former, with the Artillery Battalion on Duncan's right, "occupying a hedgefence," and the Eighth Infantry and Second Brigade on Mackall's left.[25]

In relating the Second Brigade's movements after the Mexican troops scattered, Napoleon Dana told of corresponding shifts of position. Having "formed in line of battle, with two fronts where the Saltillo road joined the [Presqueria-Grande] road," his brigade's troops stood in that position half an hour, waiting for Mexican forces to counterattack. When "a piece of heavy artillery" opened on them from Federation Ridge, the hill now nearest them, they "drew off a little further, just out of range," but not before Captain McKavett was killed. They then "stacked arms in line of battle" and laid down "to eat and sleep" while remaining "ready to catch the enemy should he come to make his retreat to Saltillo."[26]

If Edmund Bradford was correct, there was further reconnoitering by Captains Smith and Scott before Worth decided how he wanted to proceed. By noon Worth had directed Captain Smith to lead a detachment "to storm the batteries on the crest of the nearest hill, called *Federation,* and after taking that to carry the Fort called *Soldada* [*sic*] on the ridge of the same height, retired about 600 yards." For this movement, Worth reported, Smith's command of "about three hundred effectives" was comprised of four companies of the Artillery Battalion: K, Second Artillery (Smith's); B, Third Artillery (John Vinton's); G, Fourth Artillery (John Thomas's, to which Edmund Bradford belonged); and H, Fourth Artillery (Harvey Brown's, currently led by Lieutenant John W. Phelps, in which was Daniel Harvey Hill). However, Worth seems to have been mistaken about G, Fourth Artillery, for Bradford's comments reveal that his company was not with Smith in this instance. Probably Worth had in mind I, Fourth Artillery, John B. Scott's company, since Scott was praised later in Worth's report as being, like Charles F. Smith, a leader of Artillery Battalion light troops. Designated to act "in cooperation" with Smith were six companies of Colonel Hays's Texas Mounted Rifles regiment, under Major Michael H. Chevalier.[27]

Until then the firing from Federation and Independence heights had struck very few of Worth's men, the Mexican gunners having for the most part shot over the heads of the Americans. Nevertheless, Worth realized "the impracticability of any effective operations against the city until possessed of the exterior Forts and batteries." He particularly emphasized the importance of Federation Ridge, saying that the guns on its summit, together with those abutting Fort Soldado, "effectively guarded the slopes and roads in either valley, and consequently the approaches to the city," but Worth did not explain why he decided to assault those works first rather than the ones on Independence Hill. Federation presented at least one difficulty that Independence did not—Worth's men would have to wade across the Santa Catarina to attack its fortifications—and although Federation was closest to the position then held by the Americans, they would have an extremely precipitous climb to reach its summit. On the other hand, with Federation's guns captured the Americans would have a double lock on all of the southwestern approaches to Monterrey.[28]

According to Napoleon Dana, Charles Smith's storming party took a "circuitous route" to the base of Federation Ridge, probably in an attempt to reach the furthest face of the height and thus be shielded from the guns on Independence Hill. The detachment "started about 12 ½ o'clock p.m." Daniel Harvey Hill, who was with Charles Smith's command, wrote of passing through "several cornfields," crossing the river, and being subjected to "a heavy fire from the enemy's Artillery" before reaching a hedge behind which the detachment "lay concealed about an hour, whilst Capt. Smith was reconnoitering the ground." Worth, who noted that the movement could not be masked, commented on the "plunging fire" from Federation's batteries as well as the enemy's "numerous light troops" that were "seen descending and arranging themselves at favorable points on the slopes." Evidently due to the Mexican defenders' visible preparations for "determined resistance," Worth at once ordered the Seventh Infantry, under Brevet Major Dixon Miles, to support Smith's party.[29] The Seventh Infantry's men, Dana included, had just gotten "out of reach" of Federation's guns and lain down "to eat and sleep" when the regiment was told "to support and cooperate with" Smith's party. Dana had been dozing, after lunching "on hard bread and bologna sausage." Rather than take the same route to Federation Ridge as had Smith and the artillery companies, his regiment "went straight towards the foot of the hill, through high corn." The enemy's cannon shot over their heads until the Americans commenced fording the Santa Catarina, "a very rapid river . . . nearly waist-deep." Then the Mexican infantry "poured in their lead as fast as they could send it." Incredibly, the Seventh Infantry troops succeeded in reaching the foot of Federation Ridge and found cover under rocks at its base without anyone being hit. There they waited, as ordered, for a signal to join Charles Smith's advance up the steep hill.[30]

From Dana's remarks it is clear that his regiment reached the foot of Federation Ridge during the hour's interval before Smith's men commenced their ascent, and that the Seventh Infantry's officers, and probably Worth as well, did not know at that point what was holding up the assault. Daniel Harvey Hill apparently believed that Smith, whom he said "at one time looked upon the escalade as entirely impracticable," had spent that hour in cautiously searching for the best way to climb the ridge. Dana credited the delay to Smith's having seen that "the troops on the hill had been reinforced by a column of 1000 men," adding that Smith had thereupon "sent this word back to General Worth." Dana's explanation fits with Worth's account of his next order: "The appearance of heavy reinforcements on the summit, and the cardinal importance of the operation demanding further support, the 5th under Major [Martin] Scott, and Blanchard's company of Volunteers were immediately detached, accompanied by Brigr. General [Persifor] Smith, who was instructed to take direction in that quarter" (ignoring the fact that Persifor Smith, though formerly a Louisiana brigadier general, was now a colonel in the regular army).[31]

Captain Charles Smith's force had taken the "first object of attack," the summit of Federation Ridge, Worth said, before Persifor Smith led the second attack on the height. Daniel Harvey Hill indicated the same in describing the summit's capture. Under heavy fire, he and the rest of Charles Smith's detachment had struggled up the "almost perpendicular height," and with "the enemy running in all directions" had captured one of the two cannon on its summit. That detachment was advancing against Fort Soldado, the work lower on the hill and closer to the city, when they "perceived Col. [Persifor] Smith's Brigade winding through the gorge for the same purpose."[32]

Meanwhile the Seventh Infantry soldiers had been hugging the rocky base of the ridge "for some time, waiting impatiently to hear of Capt S[mith]," but the stimulus that galvanized them into action turned out to be the arrival of the Fifth Infantry "with 200 Texan rangers on foot with their rifles." Of the reaction in his regiment when those troops "came up," Dana wrote: "We raised a tremendous shout, and up the hill we went with a rush, the Texans ahead like devils." Five companies of Texans, commanded by Colonel John Hays, together with the Fifth and Seventh infantry soldiers and Captain Albert Blanchard's Louisianians, led by Colonel Persifor Smith, assisted Captain Charles Smith's men in chasing the Mexicans from Federation's height toward Fort Soldado. The Americans were bombarded by a nine-pound cannon that Ampudia's artillerymen had rescued from the height while retreating, but to little effect; and Colonel Smith, after occupying the summit and capturing a nine-pounder that the Americans subsequently fired into the ranks of the fleeing enemy, decided he could also capture Soldado. As Lieutenant Dana described that fresh charge, "[w]hen we were on top of the hill we saw right before us and a little lower than we, their second height. There was a stone fort on it and the top of the hill was covered with large tents. . . . Colonel Smith, who was in command, gave the order to charge, and on we rushed again like a torrent on the enemy. . . . They fled like good fellows, scarcely stopping to look behind once, and left in our hands the two heights, two brass nines, and a very large amount of ammunition. . . . We planted our colors on the hills and cheered like real Americans."[33]

Once both heights on Federation Ridge were seized, the Americans utilized the two captured nine-pounders to bombard the Bishop's Palace on Independence Hill, situated a mere six hundred yards across the intervening Santa Catarina gorge. By dusk on the twenty-first, however, a severe thunderstorm enveloped the area and all operations ceased. "The troops had now been thirty six hours without food, and constantly taxed to the utmost physical exertions," Worth reported. "Such as could be permitted, slept with arms in hand, subjected to a pelting storm, and without covering 'till 3 a.m. when they were aroused to carry the hill *Independencia*." As for Worth's casualties on the twenty-first, Meade said they amounted to "about 20 killed and wounded, one captain killed, and two officers wounded." The officers to whom he referred were evidently the slain Captain Henry McKavett and two slightly wounded lieutenants, Nathan B. Rossell (Fifth Infantry) and Joseph H. Potter (Seventh Infantry). Dana, concluding his description of the day's events, wrote: "The sun went down with the guns from the bishop's palace playing on our hills. The Seventh was left to hold the places which had been carried, whilst the remainder of the division returned to General Worth. I was ordered to take a detail and serve the cannon on our hill against the [Bishop's] palace, so I prepared all for the morning's work and spent another most rainy, chilly, and comfortless night."[34]

In comparison with the relatively few casualties suffered by Worth's forces while assaulting Mexican positions bordering the city's southwestern sector on September 21, the troops on the northeastern side of Monterrey were struck down in shocking numbers that day, a total of 394 being killed or wounded. At the time, the officers involved in the fighting appear not to have blamed the casualties on the tactics employed by General Taylor, who personally directed the advance into the city. Later, various nineteenth- and twentieth-century critics would accuse Old Zach of having underestimated the number and resolve of the Mexican defenders, and of having failed to provide for enough siege ordnance, among other charges.[35] In his defense, Taylor clearly believed he had "to attempt something"; that a successful attack on Monterrey "would do more to bring about a peace, than anything else";[36] and that despite his limited means he would be able to "reduce" the city, capture the troops who opposed him there, and "take their artillery & military stores" if they had any. And except for bringing the war to an end he did indeed succeed in reaching all of his goals, though at a dismaying cost.[37]

Taylor must have been anticipating a hard fight once he realized General Ampudia's forces had not left the city. After all, Santa Anna and his generals had undoubtedly known for a month or more that a sizeable American army was on its way to Monterrey, and clearly in the interim the Mexicans had been increasing the town's garrison and strengthening its fortifications. Moreover, Old Rough and Ready must have realized that at some point his regiments might be exposed to crossfire as they moved into the city's northeastern sector, since he had been informed that there were several enemy batteries on Monterrey's eastern face, and he could see for himself that the Citadel loomed all too prominently over the northern suburbs. His placement of howitzer and mortar batteries across the road from the Citadel indicates his awareness of that particular threat. What he did not know was that within the town many streets had been barricaded, and every building was essentially a fort from which muskets could be fired through ground-level apertures in their walls and from parapets on their flat roofs. These aspects of Ampudia's defensive preparations were largely hidden from exterior view by trees, gardens, and walls.[38]

Old Zach was not able to oversee developments from the field, as had been the case at Palo Alto and Resaca de la Palma—the situation was too many-sided. For his first incursion into the city he relied chiefly on Joseph Mansfield and John Garland, an unfortunate team for the job as it turned out. Mansfield, a top-notch staff engineer, had little reconnaissance experience. Garland, a staunch, reliable Fourth Infantry lieutenant colonel (brevet colonel) with thirty-three years in the regular army, had achieved his seniority largely through the death of Colonel Vose and the incompetence of Colonel Whistler. The men Taylor needed were the absent enterprising George McCall and General Worth's superb subordinate Charles Ferguson Smith. The artillerymen with Bragg's battery were ordered to support the infantry units, but their guns could not maneuver in the town's narrow, winding streets. No doubt Colonel Albert

Sidney Johnston could have helped; however, as inspector general of Butler's volunteers he was not in line for field command.

Of the manner in which the troops in the eastern sector were initially deployed, General Taylor wrote the adjutant general: "Early on the morning of the 21st, I received a note from General Worth, written at ½ past 9 o'clock the night before, suggesting what I had already intended, a strong diversion against the center and left of the town, to favor his enterprise against the heights in rear." The regiments at Walnut Springs were directed to select one company each to remain as camp guards. Sent to the far right quarter of the city, out of range of Monterrey's eastern forts and the Citadel, were the Second Dragoons and Colonel Wood's Regiment of Texas Mounted Volunteers, commanded by Major General Henderson. They were to reinforce Worth if needed, and could counter any movement by the enemy in that sector. The infantry and artillery companies of Twiggs's First Division, together with Butler's Field Division of Volunteers, initially marched to the entrenched howitzer batteries and mortar, situated left of the Walnut Springs road, which had been guarded all night by the Fourth Infantry regulars and the First Kentucky volunteers. Twiggs was not with his division that morning, being ill. Taylor, who appears to have issued his orders thereafter from the area of the howitzer batteries, then brought on the eastern front's devastating battle of September 21 by sending the First and Third Infantry regiments, the Baltimore volunteers, and Bragg's mobile battery, all under the command of Lieutenant Colonel John Garland, to "make a strong demonstration" against Monterrey. They were to "carry one of the enemy's advanced works if it could be done without too heavy [a] loss." At the same time Major (by brevet) Joseph Mansfield was charged with designating the direction and point of attack of Garland's column, assisted by Captain William Williams and Lieutenant John Pope (Corps of Topographical Engineers). As it turned out, those seemingly reasonable decisions would result in a horrifying loss of life. Meanwhile "the Mortar, served by Capt. Ramsay of the Ordnance, and the howitzer battery under Capt. Webster, 1st Artillery, had opened their fire upon the Citadel."[39]

Garland had evidently known that a portion of his brigade would be directed to lead the initial assault on the eastern front. He stated that, pursuant to orders he received "on the field," he "moved to a safe position with the 3rd Infantry, 240 strong, and whilst awaiting a summons from the Chief Engineer Major Mansfield, to advance, Lieut. Col. Wilson, 1st Infantry, joined me with that Regiment and the Baltimore Battalion, the former 162 strong and the latter 239, making in all 640 bayonets."[40] While Garland was waiting for the chief engineer's signal, Joseph Mansfield received by a messenger General Taylor's verbal orders, which as he recalled directed him to show Garland the best way for his brigade to approach and capture "the redoubt." Evidently, as Mansfield believed, the general hoped Garland could capture La Tenería, the Mexican battery nearest the American forces. (Taylor, for his part, said Garland was directed "towards the lower part of the town" to demonstrate and "to carry one of the enemy's advanced works" if he could without "too heavy [a] loss," as mentioned above.) Mansfield, at once complying with the order as he understood it, sent John Pope to ask Garland, whose men were "assembled under cover in a corn field about one mile from the battery," to send one company "to advance in light Infantry order to drive back some few mounted men of the enemy in our front."[41] In response, Garland explained, "The leading Company of the 3rd Infantry, under Lieut. Hazlitt, was immediately ordered forward." Thus it so happened that Ulysses Grant's friend and classmate Bob Hazlitt was one of the first American infantry officers to enter Monterrey. Garland added that shortly thereafter "another Company was applied for, and Capt. [George P.] Field of the 3rd Infantry detached." Neither Field nor Hazlitt would survive the day's action.[42]

La Tenería, the redoubt called "No. 1" by Taylor, Garland, and others, was located, in Old Zach's words, "at the northeastern angle of the city," on the near side of the stream which divided Monterrey in that quadrant into two sectors. On the plaza side of the little river and slightly westward stood El Diablo ("redoubt No. 2"). Almost all of the fighting by the forces directly under General Taylor occurred in the vicinity of those two major works and the Purisima Bridge, slightly west of El Diablo.[43]

Both Mansfield and Garland thought that General Taylor's verbal orders, issued on the battlefield and relayed to each of them by aides, required that Mansfield should personally lead Garland's detachment into the city. Surely that understanding was erroneous. Perhaps Taylor did not make his intentions clear. He must have expected that Mansfield, an engineer staff officer, would merely point out to Garland, an experienced infantry colonel, the best route to take to reach the nearest enemy redoubt. Lives might have been saved if Garland had not proceeded without question to follow Mansfield's signals, and if they both had moved more circumspectly. At any rate Mansfield, dismounted and equipped only with his sword and a "spyglass," accompanied Hazlitt's and Fields's skirmishers into the suburbs surrounding Monterrey's eastern forts. When they were able to penetrate past a breastwork thrown across a narrow street without difficulty, Mansfield sent word to Garland to "come on," believing, as he would later assert, that Garland's men would, by taking cover "among the stone buildings," be able to protect themselves while seeking to "attain the gorge of the redoubt." Garland then advanced "in line of battle," the Third Infantry leading, followed by the First Infantry companies, and lastly the Baltimore Battalion, all of whom "soon encountered a direct fire of artillery from redoubt No. 1, and an enfilading fire from the citadel." Unfortunately, Garland thereupon directed his men to "quicken their pace" rather than to take cover, apparently judging that their supporting role required them to reach Mansfield's position as soon as possible. In so doing, they encountered not only artillery barrages from Tenería and the Citadel but musket fire from the houses and streets. Mansfield next signalled a movement to the right, Garland alleged, turning the column into a congested area where they "received a most destructive fire from three directions." Around that time "Bragg came up with his battery and asked for orders," but when his gunners tried and failed to dislodge nearby barricades Garland told him to move "to a place of greater security." Two of Bragg's lieutenants, John Reynolds and Sam French, were hampered as they withdrew by the fatal wounding of four of their horses.[44]

As Garland's men continued fighting in the streets, at some point a gun commanded by Reynolds was helped out of a tight spot by men in the battalion of Maryland and District of Columbia volunteers. Captain John Kenly of that unit recalled: "[T]he dead and dying were lying very thick, when there came tearing up . . . a section of Bragg's Battery, under Lieutenant John F. Reynolds. It looked as if . . . not much would have been left of it in a few minutes if not ordered out, which was done. To turn the leading piece was difficult in the narrow street; this was effected by lifting the gun-carriage jam up to the wall of the house, in front of which it had halted, by officers and men of the Baltimore Battalion."[45] Reynolds would write his sister Kate that during the greater part of the day, his twenty-sixth birthday, he was constantly under fire but was uninjured; and that although no officer in Bragg's company was wounded during the battle, their first sergeant and four men were killed, six or eight men were wounded, and more than a dozen horses were killed or wounded, his own horse having been hit twice.[46] The casualties he cited represented all of the battery's losses during the entire Monterrey campaign, but most occurred on September 21 (three privates killed and seven men wounded, five of them severely). Similarly, eighty percent of all of the American casualties in the eastern sector were sustained on the twenty-first.[47]

Mansfield, though suffering a severe leg wound, stoically remained on the field. He thought Garland's detachment was decimated because, "being unaccustomed" to fighting in city streets, they "exposed themselves, & advanced too rapidly into the City"; he also believed that "they should have inclined more to the left to the position taken by the first Regiment where the enemy was fast being driven out of the redoubt."[48] Taylor, lacking personal knowledge of the matter, indirectly echoed the claim of his injured engineer in reporting that his initial extreme losses on the twenty-first were attributable "in good measure to the order of the troops in pressing forward."[49] Garland acknowledged having instructed his men to hasten their approach into the city but noted, pointedly, that he had acted pursuant to orders. He asserted that the infantry "continued to press ahead" until Mansfield "advised us to retire to another position." He then "directed the command to retire in good order," in conformity with his understanding that he had been told "to support and consult with Major Mansfield." However, as he would report, the withdrawal was not ordered until they "had lost many men, and some of the most valuable and accomplished Officers of the Army."[50]

By that time Garland's detachment had splintered apart. The Baltimore Battalion became separated from the rest of his command, wrote a First Infantry captain, Electus Backus, when Garland moved to the right, away from the Tenería redoubt. Backus said that although he saw "many individuals of the [Baltimore] Battalion, both officers and men, in town during the day," thereafter the battalion was "without organization."[51] The Baltimore Battalion's Captain John Kenly told a slightly different story. He agreed that the Third and First infantry companies had preceded his battalion and had "caught the severity of the fire of the Mexicans," but insisted the battalion's troops had for the most part "followed as far as the mass of the brigade," which was "as far as brave men could go." With respect to Garland, Kenly thought the detachment's commander should have instinctively known better than to take a route that exposed his troops to an enfilading fire. At the same time, Kenly admitted: "As angry as I was, I could not but admire the courage of Colonel Garland, for even in that storm of missiles he seemed unwilling to withdraw." Of the order to retire, Kenly wrote that he himself "had got some men in a house and was firing from its rear windows upon the Mexicans at the bridge head" when he was "ordered out."[52]

Before the end of the day the Baltimore Battalion lost its commanding officer, Lieutenant Colonel William Watson. Kenly had spoken with him that morning, having been consulted about which of the battalion's companies should be assigned "as camp guard," and it was Kenly who later identified Watson's remains by the boots the colonel was wearing that day. Otherwise, the battalion's casualties on the twenty-first consisted of two sergeants and three privates killed, and fourteen privates wounded, seven severely.[53]

As for the First Infantry troops, Captain Backus said they followed the Third Infantry companies into the city "by a street running south, & which led nearly in the direction of one of the Mexican batteries, on the south side of the creek," referring to El Diablo and the branch of the San Juan that ran under the Purisima Bridge. It was there, between Tenería and Diablo, on the shores of the small channel, that the Third Infantry, the leading unit of Garland's detachment, received "a discharge of grape from the batteries, and of small arms from the trenches, which produced terrible havoc in its ranks." The First Infantry regiment, Backus explained, was thereupon halted and "faced to its front (left)." When he found he was the most senior officer in his vicinity, Backus led the men with him back toward the rear of Tenería to "a tannery, filled with the enemy." The Mexican troops in the building fired on the Americans but "were soon destroyed or dispersed." From the tannery's roof Backus was able to see Tenería in his forefront, and to fire on some of its defenders who were atop a nearby distillery. His own men were protected by the tannery roof's "stone battlement about 2 feet in height." After "a few shots" the distillery's defenders "retreated across the creek to Fort Diablo." Backus's First Infantry contingent continued to occupy the tannery despite being told by Mansfield and by Major William Lear (Third Infantry) that they would be compelled to "fall back." Backus heard an order to retire, but "not knowing from what authority it proceeded" he remained in his position, although he and his men descended into the tannery's yard at one point. The second time they mounted the tannery's roof, Backus discovered that the gorge of the Tenería redoubt "was open, offering . . . a fair shot into a crowded mass of men, & artillery, & mules," and the Americans "poured a deliberate fire into the open gorge." When the Mexican soldiers in the redoubt began to retreat toward El Diablo, the First Infantry troops pursued, capturing about twenty prisoners, most of whom escaped when Backus's attention was suddenly diverted by the storming of the Tenería redoubt by Quitman's brigade and the arrival at the tannery of Mississippi and Tennessee volunteers.[54]

General Taylor had sent reinforcements forward as soon as he realized, by the "discharges of Artillery, mingled finally with a rapid fire of small arms," that Garland's command "had become warmly engaged." He directed that General Butler and the First Ohio were to "enter the town to the right," while the First Kentucky was to "cover the mortar and howitzer" batteries entrenched facing the Citadel. The Fourth Infantry was ordered to precede Quitman's brigade of volunteers (the First Tennessee and First Mississippi) in an attack against Tenería. But the assault on Tenería ordered by Taylor was led by only three of the Fourth Infantry companies, the others having failed to learn of the general's instructions until somewhat later. The three Fourth Infantry companies that commenced the attack "had advanced within short range of the work when they were received by a fire that almost in one moment struck down one third of the officers and men and rendered it necessary to retire and effect a junction with the two other Companies then advancing."[55]

Charging the Tenería redoubt with the Fourth Infantry was Ulysses Grant. Due to his assignment as regimental quartermaster he was not obliged or expected to engage in the fighting, and in fact had been told to stay at the Walnut Springs camp. However, drawn by the firing from both sides at daylight, he had ridden to the "front," by which he doubtless meant the location of the American howitzer and mortar batteries, which his regiment had been guarding since the previous evening, and from which the Citadel and part of the city were visible. At any rate, he was with some element of the Fourth Infantry when the regiment received the "order to charge." Grant did not explain from whom he heard of the order, but he did describe the movement of the Fourth Infantry companies after they left the protection of the American batteries. As soon as they emerged onto the plain above their emplaced artillery, they were hit by enemy fire, first from the Citadel and then from the redoubt toward which they were marching. After "[a]bout one-third of the men engaged in the charge were killed or wounded in the space of a few minutes," they retreated considerably eastward from the Walnut Springs road, out of range of the Mexican cannon, to regroup. There Grant gave his horse to the Fourth Infantry's adjutant, Lieutenant Charles Hoskins, who was on foot, in poor health, and extremely tired from the regiment's exertions. As fate would have it, Hoskins was killed before the day ended, and Grant, who had obtained another horse from a soldier in the quartermaster's corps, "was designated to act in his place."[56]

Grant's appointment as the Fourth Infantry's acting assistant adjutant (officially dating from September 22) enabled him to participate actively in the regiment's subsequent attacks. He had at least one other harrowing experience. When Garland's brigade ran low on ammunition after being ordered once again into the city's streets, Grant volunteered to ride back to headquarters with this information. "Before starting I adjusted myself on the side of my horse furthest from the enemy, and with only one foot holding to the cantle of the saddle, and an arm over the neck of the horse exposed, I started at full run. It was only at street crossings that my horse was under fire, but these I crossed at such a flying rate that generally I was past and under cover of the next block of houses before the enemy fired." When he glimpsed an American sentry guarding a house, he pulled up and found it was "full of wounded American officers and soldiers," among them the fatally stricken Lieutenant John C. Terrett (First Infantry) and Captain William Williams (of the Topographical Engineers). Resuming his perilous ride, Grant reached the "east end" troops unharmed, intending to report the situation of the wounded men he had seen; but as he waited for ammunition to be collected, the regiments he was trying to assist withdrew. Terrett, Williams, and the soldiers with them "fell into the hands of the enemy during the night, and died." (The death of Williams, a cousin of Robert E. Lee's wife, was deeply regretted by the Lee family.)[57]

Grant lost a number of friends on September 21 in addition to his classmate Bob Hazlitt. In writing Julia, he merely included Hazlitt in listing, by name and unit, all of the regular army infantry officers who were killed or severely wounded on the northeastern front that first day of the fighting. Later he informed Hazlitt's brother James that no one other than a relative could have more deeply regretted Bob's death.[58]

As for the volunteers, when the Fourth Infantry companies that led the Tenería attack swerved eastward to regroup, the Tennesseans and Mississippians in Quitman's brigade marched in their wake toward that redoubt, while Major General Butler, with Hamer's First Ohio troops, attempted to enter the town at a more central location. General Butler, after meeting Mansfield and being advised that nothing could be accomplished by proceeding further in the direction he and Garland had taken, returned to consult with General Taylor, but Quitman's brigade, aided by the firing from Backus's men on the roof of the tannery, succeeded in capturing and holding the Tenería fort. Unfortunately, their seizure of that vitally important structure was marred by controversy: Colonel William Campbell (First Tennessee) and Colonel Jefferson Davis (Mississippi Rifles) each claimed—evidently in good faith—that his troops were the first to enter the fort.[59]

Campbell, in 1836 a captain of volunteers in the Florida Indian wars, was a Whig who had been voted commander of the First Tennessee regiment despite the fact that the vast majority of his officers and men were Democrats. A forty-year-old lawyer who had served two terms in Congress before deciding not to run for reelection, he was obviously well regarded in middle Tennessee. Campbell asserted that upon receiving orders from General Quitman's aide-de-camp, Captain William Nichols, his regiment marched to the left, "to support the body of troops who from the firing heard were engaged in an attack on the fortifications at the North East end of the town." His men were "subjected to a very frequent discharge of heavy artillery" from the Citadel, and a cannonball from Tenería "killed four men & wounded badly three others." By the time he ordered a charge, the enemy's fire had become "very destructive." He added, "In a few seconds I saw many of my men ascend the walls of the fort and discharge their arms at the retreating Mexicans, who were running in great numbers from the first fort & the fortified house in its rear toward the other fort. From the position I occupied (for I was on horseback) I could see that my Regiment were the first to enter the fort as a body of troops, although individuals of another Regt may have entered with the first of my Regt." The Mississippians, he said in his report, having marched behind his men, formed on his right and "came gallantly to the charge simultaneously with my own."[60]

On the other hand, Jefferson Davis, in claiming that his men were the first to enter the Tenería fort, scarcely mentioned the Tennesseans. Davis had not heard Quitman's order for the brigade to advance, having been directed earlier to move his regiment farther eastward to avoid being overexposed to enemy barrages; but when he saw the First Tennessee marching in the direction of Tenería, he and his men followed. Without any further references to Campbell's men, Davis wrote: "In a few minutes the fire of the enemy had so far diminished as to indicate the propriety of a charge, and being without instructions it was accordingly ordered." The person Davis credited with leading the assault was Lieutenant Colonel Alexander K. McClung, described by a Davis biographer as "a thirty-five-year-old former lawyer and newspaperman, intensely ambitious and equally contentious." Evidently McClung and Davis were each in immediate command of four companies of Mississippi Rifles, and each ordered a charge at about the same time. All of the Mississippians were facing the northwest front of Tenería, near the rear, open sally port, McClung's companies to the left of Davis's. They apparently did not see the Tennesseans, who were further left, "due north of the fort's northern wall." According to Davis, "Lieut. Col. McClung sprung before his old company and called on them to follow him. . . . The call was promptly answered. . . . The enemy fled from the rear sally-porte [*sic*] as we entered the front, leaving behind his Artillery, a considerable number of Muskets, his dead and wounded."[61]

General Quitman seems to have supported Campbell's claim that the Tennesseans led the attack, although he did not explicitly comment on the issue. He indicated that when his brigade was "directly opposite one front of the fort," he "concluded to storm the fort" and positioned the Mississippi companies in a "new alignment" which he thought "would render the Rifle [Regiment] still more effective in silencing the destructive fires of the Enemy from his batteries." Of the charge, he said: "While these movements were being executed I proceeded to the right of the Tennessee Regiment and ordered a charge upon the batteries. Col. Campbell with a portion of his command had anticipated this order and was advancing in a charge on the North front of the Fort. The charge was instantaneously general, and the Fort which but a few moments before had spread death in our ranks, was occupied by the brave men who had breasted its batteries."[62]

General Taylor diplomatically attributed the fort's capture to "Genl. Quitman's Brigade" rather than attempting to reconcile Davis's and Campbell's conflicting reports, but Old Zach singled out the Tennessee regiment as having suffered extremely heavy casualties, which was undeniable. The First Tennessee lost two officers and twenty-four men killed that day, while four officers and seventy-three noncommissioned officers and privates were wounded, most of them severely, several mortally. Davis lost seven killed and forty-seven wounded, three of them mortally. Three of his officers sustained comparatively slight wounds, including Lieutenant Colonel McClung. Since both regiments continued to fight in Monterrey's streets throughout September 21, as did Taylor's other troops in the northeasterly sector of the city, the casualties the Tennessee and Mississippi regiments suffered did not all occur necessarily during the attack on Tenería. However, the fact that the Tennesseans had about twice as many casualties that day as the Mississippians doubtless exacerbated the indignation of Campbell's troops when they learned that what they regarded as their noteworthy achievement had been challenged. Five months later, in a letter to his cousin David Campbell, a former governor of Virginia, Colonel Campbell wrote angrily: "In relation to the claim which Col Davis has set up for the Mississippi in taking the fort No. 1 at the battle of Monterey. It is most presumptuous, and as soon as I have time to devote to that subject I will expose his false statements."[63]

The question of whether Davis's or Campbell's regiment was chiefly responsible for the seizure of Tenería broadened into a more disruptive argument once the volunteers began alleging that no regular troops took part in that action. George Meade wrote his wife that this controversy arose due to Colonel Campbell's having reportedly stated in a letter that upon approaching the fort he saw none of the regulars he had been told to support but understood "they were behind stone walls and houses, protecting themselves." Meade, who admired Campbell, was convinced the Tennessee colonel was "the first to enter the enemy's batteries," but in his opinion Tenería's capture resulted chiefly from the charge of the "regulars; for had no attack been made by them, the volunteers could never have taken the battery from the front."[64]

Later on September 21, Jefferson Davis and a few of his Mississippi volunteers were instrumental in blocking a lancer attack on a section of the First Ohio column "near some fields at a distance from the edge of the town." The Ohio regiment, after having been turned back from the area in which Garland's detachment was decimated, had been directed to reenter the city by another route further to the east, and to advance toward El Diablo. General Butler led the Ohio troops within about "one hundred yards" of that fort and was on the verge of ordering an attack, despite being uncertain of its practicality, when he was seriously wounded, and his men began "falling fast under the converging fires of at least three distinct batteries." Forced to leave the field, Butler advised withdrawal of the Ohio troops "to a less exposed position." General Hamer, "on whom devolved the command," moved them back to the protection of the captured Tenería fort and the American field batteries.[65] In his report Butler not only praised his brigadier generals, Hamer and Quitman, but also extended his "special thanks" to Major Lorenzo Thomas, the assistant adjutant general on his staff, and to "Gen. A. Sidney Johnston of Texas, Actg. Inspector Genl.," both of whom remained "with the troops in the field" after Butler retired. Among those singled out for praise by General Hamer was his chief of staff, Lieutenant Joseph Hooker.[66]

The rest of the action in the northeast on the twenty-first consisted primarily of ineffectual efforts to penetrate further into the city. The First Ohio and Quitman's brigade were withdrawn from the town due to a conclusion that their troops could not carry the enemy's fort "Number 2" (Diablo) "without great loss." For a time most of General Taylor's regular army units were concentrated near Tenería and adjacent buildings—remnants of the First, Third, and Fourth infantry regiments, and the mobile light batteries of Bragg and Ridgely. They were all pinned down by "incessant fire" from the El Diablo fort (called "No. 2" by the Americans) and the other batteries on its right, and from the Citadel. At that juncture "General Twiggs, though quite unwell," joined Old Zach and "was instrumental in causing the Artillery captured from the enemy to be placed in battery and served by Capt. Ridgely against No. 2 [Diablo] until the arrival of Capt. Webster's howitzer battery, which took its place." With the arrival of the howitzer battery, General Taylor directed Colonel Garland to lead the infantry companies at hand to capture Diablo "if possible." But although Garland's regulars advanced beyond the Purisima Bridge and "sustained themselves for some time in that advanced position," with the assistance of "a section of Capt. Ridgely's battery," they were also finally recalled. Taylor informed the War Department that at dusk "all troops that had been engaged were ordered back to camp, except Capt. Ridgely's battery and the regular Infantry of the 1st Division, who were detailed as a guard for the works during the night, under Command of Lt. Col. Garland. One battalion of the 1st Kentucky Regiment was ordered to reinforce this Command."[67]

General Twiggs, reporting on the fighting, inserted a reference to the dragoons: "Owing to the position of the enemy and the nature of the ground the two Squadrons of 2d. Dragoons . . . were not brought into action. They were however actively and usefully employed in collecting and conveying the wounded to our camp." Twiggs also mentioned each of Bragg's and Ridgely's subalterns by name, including George Thomas, John Reynolds, and Sam French, saying that they deserved "the highest praise for their skill and good conduct under the heaviest fire of the enemy." In addition, among the men he praised were J. J. Abercrombie and Schuyler Hamilton (First Infantry); William T. H. Brooks (Third Infantry, acting adjutant general to Garland's brigade, who was "dismounted by the enemy's artillery"); and Don Carlos Buell (Third Infantry, the acting adjutant general on Twiggs's staff).[68]

The next day on the eastern front there were no "active operations" by the Americans, although those occupying Tenería and nearby redoubts were constantly exposed to enemy cannonades. The preceding night's guards, other than Ridgely's company, were "relieved at midday by General Quitman's Brigade." Bragg's battery was "thrown under cover in front of the town to repel any demonstration of cavalry in that quarter." Taylor did not explain why no attack on Diablo or other fortified Mexican works was ordered on September 22. Presumably, he decided on the basis of the previous day's limited progress that the troops under his immediate command would not be able to advance further into Monterrey until Worth's division managed to exert further pressure on the city's western sector. Also, Taylor was doubtless as dismayed as anyone at the unexpected cost, in terms of casualties, of his "diversion." Most of the regular army officers killed or mortally wounded on the twenty-first in the eastern sector of the city had served under him for more than two years, ever since his Corps of Observation had been stationed in Louisiana.[69]

With respect to Worth's movements on September 22, Taylor skimmed over them and their effect on the campaign in two sentences: "At dawn of day, the height above the Bishop's Palace was carried, and soon after meridian, the Palace itself was taken and its guns turned upon the fugitive garrison. The object for which the 2nd Division was detached had thus been completely accomplished, and I felt confident that with a strong force occupying the road and heights in his rear, and a good position below the city in our possession, the enemy could not possibly maintain the town." But to Worth and the men engaged on the southwestern front, the twenty-second was as full of glorious achievements as had been the previous day. Command of the troops selected to attack Independence Hill was assigned to Lieutenant Colonel Thomas Childs of the Artillery Battalion, a distinguished veteran of the Seminole Wars in Florida as well as the Palo Alto and Resaca de la Palma battles. His storming party consisted of three companies of the Eighth Infantry under Captain Richard Screven, one of which was A, led by James Longstreet; two companies of the Fourth Artillery, including Captain John B. Scott's I company to which John Pemberton and Mansfield Lovell belonged; Childs's own Company A, Third Artillery; and two hundred Texas riflemen under Colonel John Hays who acted "in cooperation" with the regular army units. They left Worth's camp at 3 a.m., conducted to the column's "point of ascent" by George Meade, John Sanders, and Dixon Miles. At dawn, Childs's men were within one hundred yards of the crest. The enemy troops that met them hastily retreated, firing ineffectually, and the Americans quickly took possession of the hill's highest fortifications.[70]

Yet breaching the "massive walls" of the heavily fortified Bishop's Palace was another matter. Despite being located below the crest of the hill's eastern face, that ancient stone edifice could not be taken without bringing up artillery "except at enormous sacrifice," it was decided. The artillery pieces that the Americans had captured the previous day on Federation Ridge were being fired from across the river at the Mexican defenders on Independence Hill; however, the Mexicans on Independence Hill had removed their artillery from the summit to the better-protected Bishop's Palace. To answer those guns, the Americans scrambled laboriously up the precipitous, rock-strewn hill with a dismantled twelve-pound howitzer under the supervision of a Second Artillery lieutenant, John Roland of Duncan's battery. Assisted by "fifty men from the line under Capt. Sanders," Worth reported of Roland, "that enterprising and gallant officer had his gun in position, having ascended an acclivity as rugged as steep, between seven and eight hundred feet in two hours." Meade said the howitzer was "taken to pieces and carried up by hand to the summit." Daniel Harvey Hill wrote that he attracted fire while in charge of a party escorting the ammunition for the howitzer. According to Dana, Childs's command was repulsed twice before the howitzer could begin firing on the Bishop's Palace. Moreover, direct hits on the two-story stone target and its redoubts did not immediately discourage its defenders.[71]

Worth had meanwhile summoned reinforcements from Federation Ridge—"the 5th, Major [Martin] Scott, and Blanchards Volunteers," who reached Independence Hill "in time to participate in the operations against the Palace." And Childs, anticipating an effort by the Mexicans to retake the heights, had "advanced, under cover, two companies of light troops under command of Capt. Vinton . . . and judiciously drawn up the main body of his command flanked on the right by [John] Hays, and left by [Samuel] Walker's Texans."[72]

The culminating clash was described by Dana, who no doubt witnessed much of it from his post on Federation Ridge: "When the [Mexican] cavalry had advanced halfway up the hill and [their] Infantry began to rattle their musketry, our twelve hundred fellows rose with a shout and rushed on to meet them. . . . They turned their horses' tails and struck off like quarter racers for the city, leaving some twenty or thirty of their fellows on the ground. Our men then took after the [Mexican] Infantry. . . . The Mexican tricolored flag was hauled down, and soon the Star-Spangled Banner waved over that dauntless band who had carried a fort and castle."[73]

The captured guns of the Bishop's Palace were then turned on Monterrey, as were the guns of Mackall's and Duncan's mobile batteries. All of the wounded were moved into the Bishop's Palace and the dead buried, including those of the enemy. "The investment was now complete," Worth reported with justifiable pride. "Except the force necessary to hold the position on *Independencia* and serve the guns (shifted to points whence the shot could be made to reach the great Plaza) the Division was now concentrated around the Palace, and preparations made to assault the city on the following day or sooner, should the general in chief either so direct, or, before communication be had, renew the assault from the opposite quarter."[74]

On September 23, the circumstances that obtained on the two fronts differed somewhat. In the first place Worth, waiting for orders that never materialized, did not send any of his men into the city until around 10 a.m., when "a heavy fire was heard in the opposite quarter." Convinced that "a main attack" by Taylor was in progress, he finally ordered two columns of light troops "to move along the two principal streets" leading from his position toward "the great Plaza." Worth did not specify which of his units were initially sent into the city but did say they were followed "at suitable intervals" by Mackall's and

Duncan's batteries. Earlier, however, Worth's forces "had opened fire on the town, with the enemy's guns at the Bishop's Palace," according to Meade, who had been ordered "forward on a reconnoissance [*sic*] to ascertain what batteries the enemy had" in the southwestern sector of Monterrey. Meade discovered "the enemy had abandoned all the portion of the town" near Worth's position and "retired to the central plaza of the town, where they were barricaded, and all the houses occupied by their infantry." General Worth's units, Meade wrote, "took possession, without resistance, of the plaza of La Pusrissima [*sic*], where we found a cemetery and church, which our infantry occupied, and where we placed an eight-inch mortar in excellent range to play into the plaza," now "the enemy's last stronghold."[75]

Another difference was that Worth's troops, once they reached barricaded streets and were within range of Ampudia's guns, immediately adopted the strategy of breaking through walls of buildings, using them as cover from the enemy's fire. This enabled them to move from house to house toward the main plaza with fewer casualties than might otherwise have been sustained. Some of the Americans also climbed up structures in order to shoot from the protection of sandbagged parapets, as did the Mexicans.[76]

Although Worth did not indicate which of his infantrymen he sent into the city that morning, an account was later provided by Captain William S. Henry (Third Infantry), who was engaged elsewhere but doubtless learned of developments in the southwestern sector from friends and official reports. Henry said the detachments that took possession of the cemetery "without a shot from the enemy" consisted of three companies each of the Seventh and Eighth infantries, advancing on separate streets parallel to the river and followed in each instance by a "piece of artillery." Colonel Thomas Childs and his Artillery Battalion came next, as did other elements of the Seventh and Eighth infantries. An Eighth Infantry company was ordered to protect "the mortar and ammunition train which had been sent round by General Taylor." Upon reaching the cemetery, the mortar was "placed in position by Major Monroe [John Munroe], assisted by Lieutenant [Mansfield] Lovell." Captain Henry also mentioned that Theophilus Holmes's Seventh Infantry command "was supported by Texans under [Samuel] Walker," then added: "When night arrived, the troops kept possession of the houses they had taken, excepting Captain Holmes, who being so far advanced, was without support, and having many of his men wounded, was forced to fall back. . . . During the night Lieutenant Lovell threw shells with great accuracy and execution, the enemy returning their fire with shells from their howitzers. . . . Lieutenant [Franklin] Gardner, of the 7th, greatly distinguished himself in leading the advance of the 7th with ladders and pickaxes."[77]

One member of the Artillery Battalion, Daniel Harvey Hill, was extremely disappointed to find himself in a column sent in the opposite direction from the city that morning with a mixed party of other artillerymen, a Fifth Infantry company, and Blanchard's Louisiana volunteers. Their commander, Major Harvey Brown (Fourth Artillery), had been ordered to occupy the stone buildings at the Molino de Jesus Maria pass, located some three miles west on the Saltillo road, with the assistance of Colonel John Hays's Texans. Enemy reinforcements were reported to be approaching it, and Major Brown was directed "to keep them in check at all hazards." Hill recorded his reluctance to turn his back on the pending battle for the city proper: "Of all things in the world I was most desirous to be engaged in a street fight on account of the novelty and excitement and 'twas with the bitterest of feelings imaginable I went with my company to the pass, although we there expected hot and heavy work." However, the American detachment sighted no opponents; and after strengthening defenses there they were "about to take dinner" when they were recalled to division headquarters. Not until "several hours" later did Hill enter the city, where his company, stationed in the cemetery (the Plaza de la Capella), came under fire throughout the night from the Citadel.[78]

The firing Worth heard early on September 23 emanated in large part from the men of Brigadier General Quitman's brigade. From their vantage point as occupiers overnight of the Tenería fort, Quitman's soldiers ascertained that the enemy, during the previous evening, had "evacuated nearly all his defenses in the lower part of the city," including El Diablo. Upon being informed of that good news, General Taylor authorized Quitman, at his discretion, to "enter the city, covering his men by the houses and walls, and advance carefully as far as he might deem prudent." Quitman assigned the task of reconnoitering to a detachment composed of two companies of the Mississippi Rifles, to be led by Colonel Jefferson Davis, and two of the First Tennessee under Lieutenant Colonel Samuel Anderson. Rendering them "valuable assistance and advice," Davis said, was Lieutenant Jeremiah Scarritt of the Corps of Engineers. As Quitman's men, ignoring musket fire from rooftops and barricaded streets, drove fleeing Mexican troops toward the central plaza, General Taylor examined the "abandoned works." Once he was convinced that Quitman's troops were "successfully forcing their way towards the principal plaza," Old Zach ordered up the Second Regiment of Texas Mounted Volunteers. They "entered the city, dismounted, and under the immediate orders of General Henderson cooperated with Genl. Quitman's brigade." Henderson in his report complimented Jefferson Davis and also Lieutenant George H. Thomas, Bragg's second in command, the latter for "the bold advance and efficient management of the gun under his charge."[79]

In summarizing that day's events on the eastern front, General Taylor said, "Our troops advanced from house to house, and from square to square, until they reached a street but one square in the rear of the principal Plaza, in and near which the enemy's force was mainly concentrated." But before nightfall, having decided that he should consult with Worth about a "combined attack upon the town," he ordered a withdrawal to the works abandoned by the Mexicans, and instructed Hamer's brigade to relieve Quitman's.[80]

That evening Ulysses Grant thought "the severest part" of the battle for Monterrey was over. He was right—Ampudia was on the verge of conceding defeat. The first message presaging surrender was delivered to General Hamer early on September 24. The troops in Hamer's brigade, which were occupying the Tenería and Diablo forts as well as "the Tannery between them," heard a bugle and saw a flag of truce "approaching the Forts." Accompanying the flag was "Col. Marino one of the Gen. Ampudia's Aids, bearing a letter to the General in Chief. He was conducted to me," Hamer wrote, "by Lieut. Col. [Jason] Rogers [First Kentucky], from the upper Fort, & I furnished him a horse and escort to Maj. Gen. Taylor's quarters in Camp."[81] Taylor, at "7 o'clock a.m.," rejected by letter Ampudia's initial proposal, which Old Rough and Ready characterized as including the evacuation of all of the Mexican army's "personnel and materiel of war." Instead, the American general informed Ampudia: "A complete surrender of the town and garrison, the latter as prisoners of war, is now demanded," although he promised his terms would be "as liberal as possible." When Colonel Marino left with Taylor's ultimatum it was understood that Old Zach would wait at Worth's headquarters "until 12 o'clock" for Ampudia to respond. Before noon, however, Ampudia contacted Worth with a request for a "personal interview" with Taylor. A meeting was scheduled for "one o'clock, and resulted in the naming of a Commission to draw up articles of agreement regulating the withdrawal of the Mexican forces and a temporary cessation of hostilities." Each side appointed three commissioners. Those chosen to represent the Americans were "General Worth, General Henderson, Governor of Texas, and Col. Davis, Mississippi Volunteers."[82]

That afternoon the "Terms of Capitulation" were formulated, versions in Spanish and English of the agreement's nine articles were prepared, and the document was signed by the commissioners and approval signified by Ampudia and Taylor. The next day Taylor gave a copy of the capitulation agreement to Captain Amos Eaton for delivery to Adjutant General Jones in Washington, together with a cover letter in which, after acknowledging that "the terms granted the Mexican garrison" were "less rigorous than those first imposed," he justified his concessions by explaining: "The gallant defense of the town, and the fact of a recent change of Government in Mexico, believed to be favorable to the interests of peace, induced me to concur with the Commission in these terms, which will I trust, receive the approval of the Government. The latter consideration also prompted the convention for a temporary cessation of hostilities. Though scarcely warranted by my instructions, yet the change of affairs since those instructions were issued seemed to warrant this course. I beg to be advised as early as practicable whether I have met the views of the Government in these particulars."[83]

President Polk commented in his diary on the main capitulation terms after Eaton, accompanied by secretary of war William Marcy and Adjutant General Jones, handed him Taylor's dispatches at dusk on Sunday, October 11: "The American army were left in possession of the City, and the Mexican army permitted to retire with their army, except the larger part of their ordinance [*sic*] & munitions of war which were delivered over to the American forces. An armistice was also agreed upon to continue for eight weeks." Without referring to other provisions in the agreement—such as the temporary truce's being subject to cancellation by either government—Polk recorded his condemnation of Taylor's actions at length: "In agreeing to this armistice Gen'l Taylor violated his express orders & I regret that I cannot approve his course. He had the enemy in his power & should have taken them prisoners, deprived them of their arms, discharged them on their parole of honour, and preserved the advantage which he had obtained by pushing on without delay further into the country, if the force at his command justified it. . . . It was a great mistake in Gen'l Taylor to agree to an armistice. It will only enable the Mexican army to reorganize and recruit so as to make another stand." During the following day's cabinet meeting it was agreed that Marcy should instruct Taylor to terminate the armistice, but that otherwise the secretary of war should express neither approbation nor condemnation of Taylor's actions until the general provided "further information or explanations."[84]

Later, when brevets for distinguished service during the Monterrey battle were announced, twenty-three regular army officers who would be leaders in the next war were among the recipients.[85] Those in Bragg's battery were particularly fortunate—all four were awarded brevet promotions. Bragg himself, a brevet captain after the Fort Brown siege, would now be a brevet major. Officers in the other light artillery units would be honored as well, yet it was Bragg who seems to have attracted the most attention. Many volunteer officers, while not eligible for brevet awards, were likewise commended in the reports of Taylor and others. In retrospect, of course, one of the battle's most significant aspects was the emergence to prominence of Jefferson Davis as a heroic Mexican War veteran.

Altogether, American casualties consisted of 120 killed, 368 wounded, 43 missing. At least two eminent twentieth-century historians, both generally critical of almost all of Taylor's tactics as commander of the Army of Occupation, fault particularly his management of forces on the eastern front during the Monterrey battle.[86] But their observations as to how his performance might have been improved are questionable at best. For instance, one suggests that if, on Sunday the nineteenth, Taylor had placed his mortar immediately in front of Tenería (rather than roughly east of the Citadel) he could have driven its garrison "out with a half a dozen well-aimed bombshells Monday morning," and then done the same the "following night and morning with El Diablo."[87] Yet any American troops supporting the mortar in such positions, even if shielded from Tenería's cannon by a "transverse ridge," as averred, could not have menaced nor have been protected from the Citadel's guns. The latter was a much more formidable and effective fortification, as proven by the constant, largely unimpeded firing of its defenders throughout the entire three-day battle. Another respected historian implies that Taylor should not have "committed units piecemeal."[88] While that may have been a valid point with respect to sending Fourth Infantry companies, initially unsupported, to attack Tenería, in all other cases a larger force than the ones employed could not have been concentrated sufficiently in the narrow streets of Monterrey to have made a difference. Indeed, unfortunate as were the casualties on the eastern front on September 21, it is difficult to envision ways in which General Taylor could have altered his orders to produce a decidedly better outcome unless he could have silenced the Citadel, and for that he obviously lacked sufficient firepower. Even general-in-chief Winfield Scott was complimentary, characterizing Taylor's Monterrey struggle as "Three glorious days."[89]

As for the "Terms of Capitulation" document, opinions have differed widely.[90] President Polk, predisposed to take exception to just about everything Old Zach did, never forgave him for approving the armistice. To the vast majority of his fellow Americans, Taylor's victory was all that mattered, and that was evidently true of most of the men who fought at Monterrey. "The fault finders in our army," Captain Luther Giddings stated, "were chiefly Texans,"[91] which appears to have been the case except for certain supporters of Worth and Polk. Old Zach saw no reason to sacrifice more people on both sides merely to impose harsher terms, and believed he was buying the goodwill of Mexican leaders in furtherance of an end to the conflict. At any rate, penetrating further into Mexico would have necessitated some regrouping of his forces, and he would have needed time to establish his control over Monterrey and to secure his line of communication. It was a judgment call, one that seems reasonable upon close examination of all the facts. He could not afford to wait a month or more for guidance from Washington.

9
Captain Robert E. Lee Joins General Wool's March into Mexico

Elements of a section of General Taylor's army called the "Centre Division," under the immediate supervision of Brigadier General John Ellis Wool, had been congregating in and around San Antonio de Bexar throughout August and September. As the battle of Monterrey was concluding, Wool's troops were commencing their march toward Chihuahua, the foremost Mexican town northwest of Monterrey and Monclova, located some two hundred miles below El Paso.[1]

General Wool and Secretary of War Marcy had met with President Polk on two successive days shortly after war was declared. At the time Wool was instructed to assist in raising volunteer regiments in Illinois and several other states. Though he was a sixty-two-year-old veteran of the War of 1812, he was perfect for the job of mustering in volunteers, for he had served as inspector general of the army from 1816 until his promotion to the rank of brigadier general in 1841. Within a month after conferring with Polk and Marcy, while Wool was obediently overseeing the formation of volunteer units, he received orders, dated June 11, directing him to lead a column to Chihuahua.[2]

President Polk was prejudiced against Wool before their first conference on May 27. Five days earlier, while venting his spleen against members of the Whig party as a whole, Polk wrote in his diary: "I learned yesterday and to-day that Gen'l Scott, Gen'l Wool, & Adjutant Gen'l Jones were using their influence with members of Congress to prevent the passage of the Bill now before the Senate authorizing the appointment of two additional Major Gen'ls and four Brigadier Generals. . . . These officers are all whigs [*sic*] & violent partisans, and not having the success of my administration at heart seem to throw every obstacle in the way of my prosecuting the Mexican War successfully." Nevertheless, Polk wrote no negative comments after his two sessions with Wool and Marcy, possibly having heard that Wool was in fact an inactive Democrat, or having found that Wool uncritically endorsed the president's plans. At any rate it was decided not only that Wool would lead a column of troops to Chihuahua but that the detachments assigned to him would concentrate at San Antonio, where Colonel William Selby Harney, now commanding the Second Regiment of Dragoons, and three companies of his regiment were stationed. Wool would report to General Taylor, of course, since Taylor was the commander of all of the government's forces in Texas and Mexico.[3]

Among the first troops to be assigned to Wool were the First and Second regiments of Illinois volunteers, who were transported down the Mississippi to New Orleans in mid-July. Wool, looking more like "a preacher than a soldier" according to one of his volunteer subordinates, joined some of the Second Illinois companies at Cairo, Illinois. On another steamer chugging toward New Orleans with six companies of the First Illinois was Brigadier General of Volunteers James Shields, one of President Polk's appointees. Both Wool and Shields would serve as general officers in the next war. On the roster of the First Illinois (commanded by Colonel John J. Hardin) were three future Civil War generals: Captain James D. Morgan, and Lieutenants Benjamin M. Prentiss and William H. L. Wallace. With the Second Illinois (Colonel William H. Bissell) were at least five men who would engage in that forthcoming struggle, though as colonels or majors. Those who would hold the rank of colonel consisted of Captain Julius Raith and Lieutenants Nathaniel Niles and Adolphus Engelmann.[4]

During his trip downriver Lieutenant William H. L. Wallace noted in his diary: "Yesterday some of the high-blooded lieutenants of the regiment saw fit to amuse themselves with the genteel game of poker. This morning General Shields called a meeting of the officers in the after cabin and read to them the army regulation respecting gaming. He also proposed to close the bar against all, both officers and men, which proposition met with general opposition." The twenty-five-year-old Wallace, "tall, with sandy hair and gray eyes," whose life would end from wounds received at Shiloh while he was serving as a Union brigadier general of volunteers, had emulated his law partner in enlisting in one of the first volunteer companies organized in La Salle County at the outbreak of the Mexican War.[5] The scenes Wallace observed while descending the Mississippi evidently reinforced his prejudices against abolitionists, judging from his comments about the "splendid plantations" visible along the banks of the river: "The Negro quarters generally appeared comfortable—even more, there is an appearance of neatness and order about them—their white-washed walls and thick green shade present an appearance of more comfort than the residence of nine-tenths of their fanatical friends at the North." Once in Mexico he remarked caustically on the system of peonage there: "A system of slavery exists here which is not an improvement on the slavery in our Southern States. Whenever a man is in debt, his creditor sues him, gets a judgment, and if the debtor has not the means to satisfy it, the creditor may take him as his servant and compel him to work out the debt at the rate of three dollars per month, finding his own clothes. . . . Before he can discharge the original debt, they [*sic*] have necessarily contracted others, and thus they continue for years in slavery until old age and hard labor have made them unfit for further service and then they are released to the wretched liberty of a penniless old age."[6]

On July 25, 1846, Wallace's company and two others sailed from New Orleans on the brig *Albertine*. That vessel and the steamer *Galveston*, aboard which were Wool and units of the Second Illinois, were anchored at Port Lavaca, about halfway between Galveston and Corpus Christi, by the first of August. Lieutenant Engelmann wrote his German-speaking parents after the steamer had paused two days at Galveston that about half of the town's settlers were German.[7]

General Wool, during the week he remained at Port Lavaca, arranged for the First and Second Illinois to camp together on the prairie close to a "clear stream" about twelve miles from the port until they were supplied with the wagons and provisions needed to follow him. He then rode on to San Antonio, a seven-day journey of about 160 miles, accompanied by an aide, Lieutenant Charles P. Kingsbury of the Ordnance Department. When they reached their destination Wool found the town "wholly without protection," although two companies of Texas Rangers were nearby. The only regular troops there were "a Major (sick); Lieut. [Washington I.] Newton, A.A.Q.M. & A.C.S. and eight or ten sick dragoons." Colonel Harney had, without authorization, started west on July 24 with his three companies of Second Dragoons, eight companies of Texas Rangers, and an irregular company of Indian scouts, and had crossed into Mexico near Presidio del Rio Grande (opposite Eagle Pass) on August 12. Thus most of the regular army troops who should have greeted Wool at San Antonio were not only absent but their current location was unknown.[8]

Taylor, before being notified by Wool of the situation at San Antonio, had learned via a letter from Harney that the dragoon colonel was commencing a foray into Mexico with a force of six hundred men. Old Zach had immediately instructed him to return, but evidently those orders did not reach Harney until August 15, when the little column had already retraced its westward intrusion and was camped on the right bank of the Rio Grande. From there Harney replied, defensively, that he had not received "official knowledge" of the government's plan to concentrate "a heavy force" at San Antonio until after his departure, and that he did not consider himself "guilty of the assumption of any authority except the crossing of the River." That initiative, he suggested, should be viewed as justified, inasmuch as he was under orders to protect settlers in the vicinity of San Antonio. Wool, however, without waiting to hear from Harney, wrote him on August 18 that he was under arrest, and gave command of the Second Dragoons to Major Benjamin Beall.[9]

Before Harney returned, Wool's anxiety was eased somewhat by the arrival of the bulk of the Illinois volunteers from the outskirts of Port Lavaca. After a march made difficult by the heat, the scarcity of water, considerable drunkenness among the troops, and the officers' inability to control their men, on the twenty-fourth they reached Camp Concepción, two miles east of San Antonio, where the sick dragoons were quartered. The next day they filed past the Alamo ruins to a nearby location thereafter called Camp Crockett, chosen by Wool for the assembling of his "Army of Chihuahua."[10]

Another of Harney's unauthorized initiatives was cancelled by Wool at the direction of Secretary of War Marcy—the proclamation Harney had issued upon hearing of the ambush that led to the American declaration of war. He had announced that anyone in Texas owing "allegiance to the government of Mexico" would be treated as an enemy.[11] The impulsive Harney had initially been commissioned as an infantry second lieutenant in 1818, six months before his eighteenth birthday. By age thirty-six he was a lieutenant colonel, fighting Seminoles in Florida with the newly formed Second Dragoons. Having recently succeeded Twiggs as the colonel of that regiment, he obviously believed his word was law in matters involving the San Antonio area, as indeed had been essentially true until General Wool arrived.[12]

For whatever reason, Harney suffered no serious career setback when he finally returned to Camp Concepción on August 27 with most of his complement of troops (sixty having been left to guard supplies gathered at Presidio). He was immediately reinstated as commander of the Second Dragoons. But shortly thereafter Wool disbanded the company of Delawares and Shawnees that Colonel Harney had mustered into service and broke up the regiment's Company G, thus reducing Harney's command considerably. In addition, Wool ordered Harney to move his regiment from Camp Concepción to Camp Crockett.[13]

On August 27, two companies of the First Regiment of Dragoons also swelled Wool's command. Both had marched in early July from Camp Gibson, on the northern bank of the Arkansas River, to Fort Smith, Arkansas, and then to Fort Towson, in Indian Territory, near the Red River border with Texas. Present with Company E (Captain Enoch Steen) were two future generals, Lieutenants Daniel H. Rucker and Abraham Buford. With Company A (Captain William Eustis) was another future general, Lieutenant James Henry Carleton. Three days later Carleton was given detached duty as an aide to Colonel (Inspector General) Sylvester Churchill, who had just arrived and was assigned as Wool's chief of staff.[14]

Wool and Churchill probably already knew Carleton, or at least knew of him. Born in Maine, Carleton had been on duty west of the Mississippi almost exclusively since entering the army as a second lieutenant in the First Dragoons in 1839, though he had spent a year at the Cavalry School at Carlisle Barracks, Pennsylvania. Stationed most of the time either at Fort Gibson, where he lost his bride of a year in 1841, or at Fort Leavenworth, he had been ordered on several important missions in Indian Territory. In his youth Carleton had dreamed of a career as a writer, and had even gone so far as to consult Charles Dickens about whether a move to London might be advantageous. (Dickens advised him to stay in America.) Before the Mexican War, Carleton had achieved some success as a journalist through the publication of articles describing meetings he attended in 1844 between the First Dragoons' officers and chieftains of the Pawnee and other Indian tribes. A "Second Log book," likewise published, covered his experiences while riding to Fort Laramie and South Pass with Colonel Stephen Kearny (as had also future generals Philip Kearny, Philip St. George Cooke, Richard Ewell, Andrew J. Smith, and William B. Franklin), holding councils with thousands of Sioux. That arduous expedition, which returned to Leavenworth via Fort Bent and the Santa Fe Trail, traveled a total of "2,200 miles in 99 days." In San Antonio in 1846, therefore, it was not surprising that Colonel Churchill should have depended on Carleton, now age thirty-two and a first lieutenant, to assemble the supplies, wagons, and animals for the Centre Division's march.[15]

For General Wool, August 27 was an eventful day. In addition to the arrival of Carleton and the squadron of First Dragoons, two companies of Sixth Infantry troops reached Camp Crockett. Company D (Captain William Hoffman) had left Fort Smith for San Antonio on July 13; Company H (Captain Albemarle Cady) had marched from Fort Gibson on July 7. In charge of this regular army infantry battalion, which would be increased with the arrival of a third company, C, from Port Lavaca on September 17, was Major Benjamin L. E. Bonneville, an already famous explorer of passages through the Rocky Mountains to the Pacific Coast, having led a wagon train of fur traders through the South Pass as early as 1832. One of the officers of Company D, Lieutenant Edward Johnson, would become a Confederate major general. Lieutenant Simon Bolivar Buckner of Kentucky, in the next war a Confederate lieutenant general, had been assigned to Company C effective May 9, upon promotion from the rank of brevet second lieutenant, but had not yet joined his regiment.[16] At some point an independent company of Kentucky volunteers (Captain John S. Williams, a future Confederate brigadier) was attached to Bonneville's battalion. A lieutenant of that company, Roger W. Hanson, would die in 1863 from wounds received at Murfreesboro, Tennessee, less than a month after being promoted to the rank of Confederate brigadier general.[17]

Wool's army continued to grow—on August 28 Colonel Archibald Yell's ten companies of Arkansas Mounted Volunteers camped on the outskirts of San Antonio, having traveled overland from Washington, Arkansas, via Shreveport, Louisiana. The officers serving with him who would be outstanding during the Civil War included Lieutenant Colonel John S. Roane, Captain Albert Pike, and Lieutenant James F. Fagan. Seven days later General Wool acquired a company of regular army artillery commanded by Captain John M. Washington. Belonging to Washington's Fourth Artillery battery was Brevet Second Lieutenant Darius Couch of New York, a member of the West Point class of 1846 who would become a Union major general of volunteers but who was on furlough until September 30, as was customary. Washington's six-gun field battery had begun its march to San Antonio from Carlisle Barracks, Pennsylvania, on June 25.[18] A month after their arrival on September 27, as sections of the Chihuahua-bound column were heading for the Rio Grande, Wool ordered two companies of Tennessee cavalry under Colonel Jonas E. Thomas, then at Port Lavaca, to be detached and sent to San Antonio. Those he designated for detachment were the companies of Captains Milton A. Haynes and William R. Caswell. The other eight companies of Colonel Thomas's regiment were directed to proceed to Camargo.[19]

Meanwhile, Wool's staff had been increased by the advent of four members of the U.S. Corps of Topographical Engineers, a branch of the army that was separate from the U.S. Corps of Engineers, as explained earlier. Wool's topographical engineer officers, in most instances the men the general selected to determine the best route for his army to follow, included Captain George Hughes, First Lieutenant Lorenzo Sitgreaves, Second Lieutenant William B. Franklin (later a Union major general of volunteers), and Brevet Second Lieutenant Francis T. Bryan. These "topogs," on whom Wool would depend more than on officers in his Engineers Corps, were aboard the "United States steamer transport John L. Day" when it reached Port Lavaca on August 30. Sitgreaves, Franklin, and Bryan were West Point graduates. While Hughes was not, he had attended the Academy prior to being appointed a captain in the Corps of Topographical Engineers.[20]

There being two roads from Port Lavaca to San Antonio, branching off from one another at Victoria, and the topographers being desirous of increasing what was known about that sector of Texas, they separated. Hughes and Sitgreaves took the shorter way, through Goliad, the one used by Wool for transporting supplies from Port Lavaca, while Franklin and Bryan took the longer one, which followed the "left bank of the Rio Guadalupe" and passed through Gonzales and Seguin. Hughes, in a report to the chief of the Topographical Corps, described San Antonio as containing "about two thousand inhabitants, mostly Mexicans; the greater part of the males are agriculturists and herdsmen. . . . The town . . . is built on both sides of the river of the same name . . . and its streets are washed by its waters running rapidly through them. . . . The Alamo, on the left bank of the river, if placed in a suitable state of repair, would accommodate a regiment."[21]

Lieutenant Engelmann, in the Second Illinois regiment, sent a more colorful description to his parents: "We came through a part of the city and stopped briefly to give the men the opportunity to see the spot where Crocket [*sic*] fell. These ruins are called 'Alamo' after the nearby poplar trees, so called by the Spaniards. The walls everywhere show bullet holes and the men dug out a good many." Somewhat later, after being permitted by Colonel Bissell to spend a Saturday in town, Engelmann wrote: "The little city has but few streets, most of the buildings are around the three squares, which with the stoutly built houses, the old church, the pretty stream, the many canals, the brown Mexicans (now citizens of the U.S.) and the drunken Texans altogether make up San Antonio with its peculiarities. . . . The town is full of saloons, faro games, bowling alleys and billiard halls and many other ways for a man to lose his money. During the course of the afternoon and evening I visited several and saw large sums lost at faro but no one won. Among others I saw the well known poet [Albert] Pike, now captain in an Arkansas Cavalry Regiment, lose $50.00 in five minutes."[22]

Aside from the men with the various regular army and volunteer units, individuals who would have notable responsibilities during the next war gradually joined Wool's staff: Lieutenant Irvin McDowell of the First Artillery, an aide-de-camp who from time to time served as Wool's chief of staff; Captain Robert H. Chilton of the Quartermaster Department; Major David Hunter, a paymaster; Lieutenant Marsena R. Patrick of the Second U.S. Infantry, serving as head of the division's Subsistence Department; and Captain Robert E. Lee, U.S. Army Corps of Engineers, assigned upon his arrival on September 25 as "Chief" of the members of his corps in Wool's division.[23]

Lee was strikingly handsome—brown eyes, black hair, a fulsome mustache, and nearly six feet tall. At thirty-nine years of age he—as was true before 1846 of so many regular army officers—had never been exposed to hostile gunfire. Of course, neither the officers in the Corps of Engineers or the Corps of Topographical Engineers were expected to fight as a rule, but nevertheless those attached to active field commands occasionally had an opportunity to win promotion by brevet, as had Joseph Mansfield (Corps of Engineers), for example. At any rate, Lee had been hoping that a war assignment would take the place of the duties in which he had been previously engaged for five years at Fort Hamilton, in the city of Brooklyn, New York—maintaining and improving Fort Hamilton and other nearby army fortifications. In fact, as early as 1845 he had indicated to Colonel Joseph Totten, chief of the Corps of Engineers, that if the United States should engage in "a war with any foreign government" he would want "active service in the field" even if that necessitated transferring to another branch of the regular army. Since graduating from West Point in 1829 (second in his class and with no demerits), Lee had acquired a wife, Mary Custis, and seven children (three boys, four girls). He had also completed engineering assignments as far south as Georgia, as far west as Missouri, and as far north as the Great Lakes, interspersed with tours in Washington. For a few months he had served under Joseph Mansfield at Fort Monroe, Virginia, in 1831. He had also met General Wool during an inspection of Fort Monroe in 1834, and while stationed in St. Louis he had become reacquainted with Ethan Allen Hitchcock, who was commandant of cadets when Lee graduated from the Academy.[24]

On August 19, when Lee received orders to report to General Wool, his wife, Mary (the only surviving child of Martha Washington's grandson George Washington Parke Custis and his wife), was evidently at Arlington House, her family's imposing residence across the Potomac from the capital, recovering from the birth of Mildred, the Lees' seventh child. By August 28 Lee was in Washington, filing his reports. In bidding a hasty farewell to his family at Arlington he seems to have skipped discussions with Mary about certain arrangements he had made as he prepared to depart, such as the storage of their Fort Hamilton household furnishings and the terms of the will he had executed, for he wrote her about these and other related matters while aboard a steamer bound from New Orleans to Port Lavaca. (In his will he freed, for some unknown reason, a female slave named Nancy and her children, but no others of the many he and his wife held in bondage.) With him when he disembarked on September 13 was an Irish servant, Jim Connolly, and a mare purchased in New Orleans which he called Creole. Eight days later he reported to General Wool at San Antonio.[25]

Although he was appointed chief of the officers in the Corps of Engineers who were with Wool's force, only one other representative of that corps was attached to the Centre Division, Captain William D. Fraser. Several years younger than Lee, Fraser likewise had been an outstanding student at West Point, graduating first in his class in 1834. Moreover, he had been promoted to the rank of captain only four years later, whereas Lee, appointed to that rank the same day as Fraser (July 7, 1838), had served nine years after graduating from the Academy before becoming a captain. However, the two men apparently worked peaceably and in tandem while with Wool. Fraser had arrived in San Antonio more than three weeks before Lee, and had reputedly started building a pontoon bridge to be used in crossing the Rio Grande. While Lee presumably spent most of his time at first helping Fraser obtain material for the pontoon bridge, Wool did not mention the Virginian again in written orders for several weeks after appointing him chief of the army's Corps of Engineers, whereas members of the separate Corps of Topographical Engineers received orders often. One of Lee's most startling first impressions upon reaching San Antonio was the sight of young Mexican women, wearing next to nothing, swimming in the river, a daily occurrence he thereafter attempted to avoid, evidently due to embarrassment or perhaps to discourage the erotic emotions to which he was prone. A visit to the Alamo shortly thereafter stirred him deeply, causing him to feel still more eager to see action, though he was ambivalent regarding the justice of the American cause. He was also sentimentally aroused to learn of the battlefield death at Monterrey of one of his wife's cousins, Captain William G. Williams.[26]

It was not Lee, however, but the topographical engineers whom General Wool selected to lead his column toward the Rio Grande. The topogs departed San Antonio on "the 23rd of September, at 5 o'clock p.m." Lieutenant Bryan having been temporarily detached as an aide to General Wool, the topographical party consisted of Hughes, Sitgreaves, Franklin, an interpreter, a hunter and guide, two wagoners, four laborers, "and two private servants."[27] The main body of Wool's troops, led by Colonel Harney, marched three days later. Wool, knowing he did not have enough wagons to transport supplies for all of his men, stipulated which units were to accompany Harney: the artillery; the Second Dragoons; Bonneville's Sixth Infantry brigade (including Captain Williams's independent company of Kentucky volunteers); six cavalry companies of the Arkansas regiment; and four companies of Illinois volunteers (those of Captains James D. Morgan and Benjamin M. Prentiss, First Illinois, and Captains Henry L. Webb and Julius Raith, Second Illinois). As for Wool himself, he announced that he would leave on the twenty-ninth, escorted by the First Dragoons. (Evidently Captains Lee and Fraser left San Antonio somewhat ahead of General Wool, since Captain Hughes reported that on October 2, "[t]he engineers came [into camp] with the pontoon train early; the general and staff and the advance of the army arrived in the afternoon . . .") Colonel Churchill was placed in charge of bringing up the rest of the troops as transportation and supplies became available.[28]

Having speedily caught up with his main column, General Wool left their camp on the Nueces River on October 4, taking with him the artillery and "two companies of cavalry" in an effort to reach the Rio Grande within another two days, having heard that the Mexicans were assembling a force near the river to block a crossing by the Americans. By the seventh Webb's and Raith's Second Illinois companies, and presumably most of the troops with Wool, were in sight of the Rio Grande, although on that day and the next their "route was parallel to the river." By the eighth Wool had established his "Camp on the Rio Grande" on the river's eastern bank, about 165 miles from San Antonio. No enemy force was visible, and they "had hardly arrived when a Mexican came across and said that all Mexican troops had left and that the mayor of the town [Presidio del Rio Grande, near the river's western bank] wanted to come across and turn the town over to Gen. Wool." Presidio's mayor, when he met with Wool, "reported that Gen. Taylor had won a bloody battle at Monterey."[29]

The first Americans to cross were the topographical engineers together with Colonel Harney, a squadron of Second Dragoons, and several staff officers. They were sent on the ninth to find a suitable place for Wool's column to "camp beyond the Presidio," after which they were to report back to headquarters that evening. Wool also issued orders praising his soldiers and informing them that they would cross into the enemy's territory the next day. He went on to say that any Mexicans who did not "take up arms" against the American troops would not be molested and would be paid "liberally" for supplies purchased from them. That evening, as Adolph Engelmann informed his parents, Wool gave a party for his officers: "The General treated to champagne, port wine and Mexican whiskey (miserable stuff, highly peppered and mixed with Muscat)."[30]

On the tenth Colonel Yell and the six companies of Arkansas cavalry with the main column were told to proceed "to the right bank of the Rio Grande" and report to Colonel Harney. The Arkansas men were to camp with the Second Dragoons at a location that offered "good grazing" and room for all of Wool's troops. Engelmann was under the impression that Harney and his dragoons had remained the previous evening west of the river, contrary to orders, occupying an area that was finally the one selected for the American camp.[31]

General Wool, upon fording the river on October 12, was confronted by a Mexican officer and two lancers. As Captain Hughes described the incident, after Wool was handed "a communication from the political chief of the State of Coahuila, enclosing a copy of the [Monterrey] articles of capitulation," the Mexican officer complained that the American advance "was in direct contravention" of the provisions of that document. Wool rejected the officer's protest and, as the meeting ended, declared he would "continue his forward movement."[32]

With respect to whether a pontoon "flying bridge" was utilized by the Americans, Captain Hughes's descriptive "Memoir" of the march is not consistent with Engelmann's account. Hughes stated: "Today [October 12] the whole army, wagons, etc., crossed the river, the infantry passing over the flying-bridge." Engelmann, who had on the ninth informed his parents that the army's pioneers were "busy building a floating bridge," wrote: "On the 11th the boats were done and we crossed, in loading one of the wagons it slipped and injured one of Capt. Webb's men whose death is expected. On the twelfth we got the boats which are drawn across by mules, we crossed in a heavy rain storm. The engineers had to abandon the plan of a floating bridge for lack of anchorage." At any rate most of Wool's column reached the river's western bank safely, marched five miles to the village of Presidio without opposition, and camped about three miles beyond the small town.[33] (Pontoon bridges would be relied on much more extensively in the Civil War, for instance during the Fredericksburg battle, and during William Tecumseh Sherman's march through Georgia.)

Catching up with the main column on the thirteenth were Colonel Hardin and the First Illinois volunteers who had belatedly left San Antonio, including the regiment's newly selected adjutant, Lieutenant William Wallace. The leadership in Wallace's company had changed in late September—his friend Captain T. Lyle Dickey had resigned due to illness. Elected in his place was Benjamin M. Prentiss, who would become a major general of Union volunteers in 1862, and Wallace had replaced Prentiss as the company's first lieutenant and the regiment's adjutant. As much as Wallace regretted seeing Dickey leave, he thought Prentiss was "the best officer in the two [Illinois] regiments."[34]

Lieutenant Engelmann, whose Second Illinois company (Raith's) had left San Antonio with the main body of the division, was as glad to greet Hardin's men as he would have the missing members of his own regiment, for the First Illinois contingent brought him the first letter he had received "since leaving Illinois." Responding immediately to an inquiry therein, he replied: "To answer Josephine's question, Gen. Wool as all officers of the Regular Army is an aristocrat, overbearing and withal very fond of flattery, these are his faults; his good qualities are, carefulness and determination as well as the way he put through our march through the wilderness to the good camp we now occupy.... We have little contact with the Captains and Lieutenants of the Regular service, who seem to think themselves above us Volunteer officers, being cold and distant. Consequently we act the same toward them."[35] Engelmann was nevertheless enjoying the novelty of being in Mexico: "Presidio is built much like San Antonio though one does not see any vacant houses, nor are they in as poor repair.... The camp is alive with Mexicans offering for sale bread, eggs, chickens, sugar cane, corn, sweet potatoes, figs, etc., all at ridiculous prices: 5 eggs 12 ½ c; a hen 25c; a young goat 75c; 15 dry figs 12 ½ c. Ten cents passes for a *real* (12 ½) and a 5c piece for a *medi-real* (6 ¼)."[36]

Both Engelmann and Wallace mentioned seeing Brigadier General Shields, who reached Presidio from Camargo on the thirteenth with an escort of a few Texas volunteers. Shields, though Irish by birth, was an influential, highly respected Illinois lawyer, which is presumably why Wool, upon learning that his command would consist primarily of volunteer regiments from that state, asked for Shields to be transferred to the Centre Division. And inasmuch as Shields was second in seniority now, rather than Colonel Harney, Wool had reason to be doubly glad the Illinois brigadier general had been assigned to his division. At once Wool reorganized the column, giving Shields command of all infantry present, regular and volunteer, and ordering Captain Robert Chilton of the Quartermaster Department to join Shields's staff. Reserving for himself the immediate command of the artillery and the squadron of First Dragoons,

Wool left Harney in charge merely of the Second Dragoons and the Arkansas cavalry.[37]

Since Shields served with Wool scarcely a month before being sent by Taylor to General Robert Patterson for duty, the extent of his influence on the Illinois volunteers is difficult to evaluate. Certainly they respected and admired him, which may have helped alleviate the tensions between the volunteers and the regular army officers; and no doubt he contributed to the notable improvement in discipline among the Illinois troops when compared with their behavior on the road from Port Lavaca to Camp Crockett.[38]

General Wool immediately dealt Colonel Harney another blow: when the column resumed its march, he announced that Shields would command the advance, to be composed of the Second Dragoons, the Arkansas cavalry, and all infantry units other than Captain Webb's battalion, which was to guard the provision train. Moreover, whether the cavalry or infantry troops should be in the lead was left up to Shields. Not surprisingly, Colonel Harney—finding himself, after twenty-eight years in the regular army, placed under the direction of a volunteer political appointee—promptly asked for a transfer to the contingent of Second Dragoons serving directly under General Taylor.[39]

General Wool had already told his men that they would be heading toward Monclova, located to the southwest, whereas Chihuahua lay about 450 miles directly west of San Antonio. As limited as his knowledge of Mexico was, Wool knew he would have to circle far to the south to avoid the mountains and wasteland blocking a westward movement from his camp on the Rio Grande. There being several roads to Monclova from Presidio, as there had been from San Antonio to the Rio Grande, the topographical engineers were assigned the task of searching for the most propitious route. Hughes wrote on October 14: "I received orders to proceed tomorrow morning, escorted by a squadron of dragoons, under the command of Lieutenant Colonel Roane, of the Arkansas mounted men, on the way to Santa Rosa, and on reaching the town, to wait for the advance of the army, or for further instructions. The object was to reconnoitre the country, especially in reference to supplies, water, and encampments, with directions to communicate the information thus obtained daily to the commanding general." Then under the date of October 15 he noted: "Left the Presidio camp at 7 ½ o'clock in the morning, accompanied by Lieutenant Franklin, with Pike's and [William G.] Preston's [Arkansas] companies of mounted men. There was no water to be found until we arrived within two miles of the town of San Juan de Nava."[40]

The main column, which left Presidio on the sixteenth, camped that evening near San Juan de Nava, and on the next night near "San Fernando, Coahuila." At the latter location Wool again issued a change in the order of march. This time the pioneers with their wagon and tools were to be under the direction of the "Chief Engineer," meaning Lee, and were to be preceded only by a guard three hundred yards in advance and two videttes. Toward the end of the column, following the wagon trains of various units, Wool placed the Second Dragoons and the Arkansas cavalry, followed by the rear guard. Lee was unimpressed and impatient with the duties assigned him by General Wool, then and subsequently. That is certainly understandable, in light of the multitude of his vital responsibilities while endeavoring to tame the Mississippi River at St. Louis, and recently while building four forts to span the Hudson Narrows, where the river provided access to the New York City harbor. Still, when we consider how, months later, he threw himself totally into supporting Winfield Scott's campaign at every step of the way from Veracruz to Mexico City, and his disappointment at failing thereby to gain advancement in the regular army, we are led to conclude that his irritability in the autumn and winter of 1846 indicated he was far more than merely eager—as were most of Taylor's subordinates—to experience active duty, and that he was perhaps already driven, more than any man in Taylor's army, to prove himself while under fire, in a cause with which he did not fully agree, though the impetus may have been only another manifestation of the drive to excel he had demonstrated as a cadet at West Point.[41]

On October 19, at his camp fifteen miles east of the Alamos River, Wool included in his orders a portion of a dispatch from Taylor's headquarters which provided a detailed summary of the Monterrey battle and its outcome. From the wording of Taylor's dispatch, Wool assumed the provisions for a cessation of hostilities did not encompass any limits on American movements north of Monterrey. Thus he continued on to Monclova, temporarily making camp about four miles above that town on October 29. Having decided, however, to occupy Monclova formally, on November 2 he directed Bonneville to take possession of it the next day, accompanied by Captain Albemarle Cady's Sixth Infantry company and Captain James Morgan's company of First Illinois volunteers. They were to occupy the barracks in the plaza, and the flag of the United States was to be raised and saluted at noon.[42] Lieutenant Engelmann wrote of marching through Monclova on the third and establishing a camp "just at the edge of town." He had not personally seen much of the settlement, but he did his best to give his parents some idea of its appearance: "I hear Monclova with its 5000 inhabitants is supposed to be one of the fine cities of Mexico. It has a theatre, churches, billiard halls, printing shop, schools and two saw mills. . . . Only a few of the streets are paved. . . . Only in the homes of the rich does one find knives and forks, even in the hotels one finds only spoons."[43]

By November 6, Colonel Churchill and the Second Illinois companies that initially had been left in San Antonio reached Monclova. That was also the date the troops were issued corn, along with hand mills to grind it, as a substitute for flour. They objected vociferously, and until the order was rescinded, "when Wool rode through camp the men brayed like mules" to protest being "fed mule feed." Dislike of their New York commander seems to have been increasingly evident in the volunteer ranks. After the "braying" episode, Engelmann wrote of Wool: "There is a tendency to criticize everything he does." Still later, Engelmann attributed the dissatisfaction among the troops to "lack of confidence in the General whose pettiness becomes daily more apparent." Continuing his analysis of the column's commander, he wrote: "Wool, 'the big Corporal' is so busy making mountains out of mole hills that he cannot see the things of real importance. . . . The 'Old One' likes compliments and is easily deceived and yet suspicious at the same time."[44]

Upon reaching Monclova, Wool had received a dispatch from Taylor telling him not to move further south until the armistice expired, at which time he would be sent new instructions. While waiting for further orders, Wool had his men build a depot. Inasmuch as no further supplies would be coming from San Antonio, his forces would have to subsist on whatever could be acquired locally unless Taylor responded positively to his request for provisions to be routed from Camargo. Fortunately, he was able to seize five tons of flour which had apparently been set aside for the use of Mexican troops. He had in the meantime decided that to reach Chihuahua he would be forced to march as far south as Parras, where a road to the northwest connected with one from Saltillo. Moreover, he had begun to question the advisability of continuing the expedition to Chihuahua, having concluded that the difficulties presented by such a march far outweighed any advantage that might be gained. Taylor, agreeing, informed the adjutant general to that effect but kept Wool at Monclova until he was sure the War Department shared their opinion.[45]

When no new instructions had reached Wool by the fourteenth, he sent Lieutenant William Franklin to Monterrey, escorted by Lieutenant Franklin W. Desha and six Arkansas volunteers, to ascertain what Taylor wanted him to do next. Doubtless Wool had not yet learned that President Polk had told Secretary of War Marcy to cancel the temporary armistice agreement, and that Taylor had done so, notifying Santa Anna that it would be terminated as of November 13. However, Wool knew the treaty was due to expire automatically within a few days, and he was impatiently preparing for the movement he favored toward Parras, a village about 125 miles southwest of Saltillo. On the eighteenth he specified which units were to be left to garrison Monclova, intending for his main column to march the following day. To his dismay, a dispatch from Taylor arrived that evening which stated that General Shields was to report to General Patterson for duty, and Colonel Harney was to proceed "with as little delay as practicable to Monterey," but contained no message authorizing Wool to leave Monclova. Chaffing at being stymied, as Shields and Harney were preparing to depart, Wool wrote a desperate plea to Bliss, and gave it to Lieutenant Irvin McDowell to deliver: "I hope the general will not permit me to remain in my present position one moment longer than it is absolutely necessary. Inaction is exceedingly injurious to volunteers. . . . I have to urge that you will submit this communication to the general; if he is not present send it forward, with my aid-de-camp [*sic*], to his headquarters, in order that he may receive from him such instructions as he intends to give me. . . . I trust we shall not remain here longer than to receive an answer from the general."[46]

On November 24, although he still had no authorization to do so, Wool began his march toward Parras. That evening at Castaños, ten miles south of Monclova, his column joined "Col. Yell, with the greater portion of the Ark. Regiment and Maj. Beall, with two companies of 2nd Dragoons," whom Wool had ordered there on the eighteenth. Neither McDowell nor Franklin had yet returned. Franklin, sent to Monterrey on the fourteenth, had ascertained upon arrival four days later that Taylor was in Saltillo, together with a force under General Worth. Following in their wake, Franklin met Taylor on the Saltillo road as the general was returning to Monterrey. Told to go on to Saltillo and await further orders, Franklin found there two lieutenants who were trying to reach the Sixth Infantry companies serving with Wool to which they had been assigned, Simon B. Buckner and Lewis A. Armistead. Accompanied by Buckner, Armistead, a guide, and the Arkansas escorting party, Franklin left Saltillo on November 25 with dispatches for Wool from Taylor. The next day Franklin, noting a large cloud of dust, questioned some volunteers who were repairing a wagon near an artificial reservoir and found that Wool's division was about fifteen miles to the southwest, on a road to Parras. Whether it was Franklin or McDowell who first conveyed Taylor's instructions to Wool is unclear, McDowell having also caught up with Wool on the twenty-sixth, but Lieutenant Engelmann wrote his parents that day: "It is now definitely settled we combine with Taylor and form his right wing."[47]

On December 5, Wool's column entered Parras. Those of his men who had commenced the march at Port Lavaca had, according to Captain Hughes, journeyed more than seven hundred miles, yet they seemed to be no nearer to a confrontation with Mexican troops than they had been at San Antonio. Lieutenant Engelmann, hopeful nevertheless that he and his comrades would eventually "get something to do," wrote his parents from Parras that the soldiers in Wool's army were "120 miles farther in Mexico than any other American troops." Less happy was Captain Robert E. Lee, who for some time had been fearing "that his ambition for battle would be permanently thwarted" if Wool's division failed to come into contact with enemy forces.[48]

10
Taylor's Changing Army and the Occupation of Saltillo

Taylor and Wool had undoubtedly been kept informed—by newspaper articles supplied by family members and friends as well as through official channels—about Brigadier General Stephen Watts Kearny's march during the summer of 1846 from Fort Leavenworth to Santa Fe, which Kearny peaceably occupied on August 18. Furthermore, four days later Kearny had written Wool, whom he assumed would soon reach Chihuahua, that he would send Wool any volunteers not needed in New Mexico. Thereafter, as Kearny was commencing his journey from Santa Fe to California that autumn, accompanied at first by about three hundred First Dragoons and a party of topographical engineers, he arranged for Colonel Alexander Doniphan and his First Regiment of Missouri Mounted Volunteers to join Wool at Chihuahua once Colonel Sterling Price reached Santa Fe with a second regiment of Missouri volunteers, and Doniphan had negotiated treaties with several Navajo groups scattered throughout the mountainous regions west of Santa Fe.[1]

Kearny and most of his "Army of the West" had started from Fort Leavenworth that June, a section at a time—a squadron of First Dragoons by the sixth and another by the twelfth; in a week or so, six companies of Colonel Doniphan's First Missouri Mounted Volunteers; topographers commanded by Lieutenant William Emory on the twenty-seventh; the next day, Doniphan and another two companies of his regiment; on June 30, Kearny with his staff and a battalion of Missouri light artillery; and shortly thereafter other companies of Missouri volunteers, to be commanded by Major Meriwether Lewis Clark when he later joined the line of march. Kearny's promotion from colonel of the First U.S. Dragoons to brigadier general was effective at the end of June, although his commission did not catch up with him until August 15, at Las Vegas. On August 30, he and his army entered Santa Fe.[2]

As at first envisioned by President Polk, the purpose of Kearny's column was "to protect a caravan of traders who, it was understood, had recently left

Missouri for Santa Fe." Orders to Kearny along those lines were drafted a few hours after Polk signed the bill containing Congress's declaration of war. But Polk was already anticipating the acquisition of California, for in his diary entry of May 13 he wrote: "I told [secretary of state James Buchanan] that though we had not gone to war for conquest, yet it was clear that in making peace we would if practicable obtain California and such other portion of the Mexican territory as would be sufficient to indemnify our claimants on Mexico, and to defray the expenses of the war which that power by her long continued wrongs and injuries had forced us to wage. I told him it was well known that the Mexican Government had no other means of indemnifying us." Furthermore, at Polk's direction his secretary of state, James Buchanan, had earlier informed Thomas O. Larkin, the American consul at Monterey, California, that Polk was interested in acquiring Alta (upper) California if it should become an independent entity. And by the end of May, Polk had decided that General Kearny should remain in New Mexico only long enough to take possession of the region and then, with a portion of his army, should continue on to California before winter if the general thought that course of action was practicable.[3]

Orders dated June 3 conveyed those instructions to Kearny, who toward the end of August issued a proclamation "claiming the whole of New Mexico, with its then boundaries, as a Territory of the United States of America." After drawing up a set of laws for the territory, appointing a governor and several other civil officials, and giving Lieutenant Jeremy Gilmer (Corps of Engineers) the task of "erecting a fort for the defense and protection of Santa Fe," Kearny turned toward California in late September, leaving most of his original column under the command of Colonel Doniphan. Thus two of Polk's initiatives—the expeditions of Wool and Kearny—were both being implemented that October. Moreover, the Second Regiment of Missouri Volunteers, led by Colonel Sterling Price, reached Santa Fe on October 2, and shortly thereafter a Mormon battalion under Colonel Philip St. George Cooke of the First Regiment of Dragoons followed Kearny to California by a different route.[4]

The conquest of New Mexico would prove of considerable assistance to the Army of Occupation in the long run. With American troops controlling New Mexico, there was no need for Wool's division to move northwestward against Chihuahua. As a consequence, Old Zach was able to allow Wool to proceed from Monclova to Parras, a town in a rich agricultural region southwest of Monterrey and Saltillo, close enough to Saltillo to reinforce any units Taylor might station there. Taylor intended, as he had for some time, to move a portion of his army to Saltillo, across the Sierra Madre range from Monterrey. Of course, he could not do so as long as an armistice with Mexico was in effect that prohibited such an advance. Thus, since Monterrey had fallen to his army on September 24, and he had agreed to a temporary truce, his forces had remained largely quiescent, with Worth's division occupying Monterrey while the men who had fought on the northeastern front continued to camp at Walnut Springs. There were personnel changes, however, one being the discharge in early October, at their request, of both regiments of Texas Mounted Volunteers. Old Zach likewise thanked and discharged Albert Sidney Johnston, who had been serving quasi-officially, without remuneration, as inspector general of the Volunteer Division. In addition, numerous leaves of absence were granted, for example one of sixty days to Colonel Jefferson Davis, who went home to Mississippi. In the same set of orders Captain Richard Gatlin, wounded by a musket ball through an arm during the Monterrey battle, received a leave of sixty days.[5]

Meanwhile Brevet Brigadier General Worth and most of the men who had served under him during the battle were quartered in Monterrey itself, often luxuriously. George Meade, for instance, after living a few days in a residence with Worth, moved into "one of the handsomest houses in town," a six-room abode furnished in a "magnificent" style which belonged to General Ortega. Sharing the beautifully appointed mansion were a fellow topographer, Lieutenant John Pope, and Lieutenant Jeremiah Scarritt of the Corps of Engineers. Meade, who was once again the senior topographical engineer on Taylor's staff due to the recent mortal wounding of Captain William G. Williams, had a mild attack of "chills and fever" around the middle of October, a mysterious malady from which, he told his wife, "[n]early one-third of the army" had been suffering, and which he attributed to the active life they had been leading "and to the injudicious use of the fruits of the country." Otherwise, Monterrey appeared to be "the garden spot of the earth, the air purity itself, and no source of malaria visible." He wished Margaretta could be there "to enjoy the delicious climate, to see the exquisite landscapes presented by the towering mountains, and the rich and fertile valley at their foot."[6]

Even better situated was Lieutenant Edmund Kirby Smith, a guest in the home of a prominent Mexican lawyer, "a member of Congress and once Governor of the Province." Writing to his mother after a brief illness probably similar to that described by George Meade, Smith extolled the Mexican family's kindness: "They were constantly giving me proofs of their regard, sending me sweetmeats and other nice things, and during my sickness, an old lady, who always called me her son, visited me and attended my bedside with all the interest and anxiety that a mother could manifest."[7]

Napoleon Dana was in less impressive quarters but was nevertheless pleased with them. By October 5, after moving from one house to another, he and Lewis Little had settled in "two very nice rooms" beneath the council chamber of the state of Nuevo León. "On the floor of the council chamber was the only carpet I have seen in Mexico," he informed Sue. "The men took it up, and I have had it put down in my room. I have now a nice little square room with three doors, two opening on two different streets and the third into Little's quarters. . . . I have a table with a drawer in it, three large mahogany armchairs, and a cot, besides a washstand. . . . General Worth, General Butler, General Smith, all have fine houses. Arista had just finished for himself here a perfect palace. . . . This we have made a hospital of."[8]

Daniel Harvey Hill boarded in the home of "Senora Lorencita Tato." He too had a spell of "chills and fevers" around the middle of October, and like Edmund Kirby Smith received extraordinary care while ill by the Mexican family with whom he lived. He was outraged that some of the volunteers, principally Texans who had not yet left the city, were committing "[m]urder, rape and robbery" in broad daylight, and burning "the thatched huts of the miserable peasants." To him, the person chiefly to blame for the atrocities was General Worth, the city's military governor. Hill thought the general made little effort to control the Texans, who cheered Worth as the hero of Monterrey whenever they caught sight of him. Later that month Hill went out to visit troops residing at the Walnut Springs camp. Although still feeling unwell, he rode with his Third Infantry classmate and good friend George Sykes over the ground where, on September 21, Sykes's regiment had fought. Hill thought any criticism of the performance of Sykes's regiment on the twenty-first was unfair: "So far from being astonished at the little they did, I wondered how they had achieved so much."[9]

Hill did not name in his diary any of the other officers whom he found "grouped around the camp-fires" at Walnut Springs, but a few days earlier a member of the West Point graduating class of 1846 had joined the Fourth Infantry there—Brevet Second Lieutenant Cadmus Wilcox, a North Carolinian reared in Tennessee who in 1863 would attain the rank of major general in the Confederate armed forces. Among Wilcox's shipmates from New Orleans to Brazos Santiago Island were two fellow southerners who would become Confederate brigadiers, Major Alfred Colquitt (a paymaster) and Brevet Second Lieutenant William M. Gardner (First Infantry, Wilcox's classmate). Gardner and Wilcox, after disembarking, had walked nine miles to the mouth of the Rio Grande, then traveled together upriver by steamer. Because Gardner succumbed to an attack of measles before they reached Camargo, they were delayed there for two weeks. On their march from Camargo to Monterrey, made perilous by the enemy's frequent attacks on small wagon trains, their party of regulars and volunteers was led by Ephraim Kirby Smith, whose leave of absence had resulted in his missing the Monterrey battle, much to his sorrow.

Wilcox and Gardner reported to their companies at Walnut Springs on October 23; Smith continued on to Monterrey to locate his brother Edmund—or "Ted" as the family called him—and their regiment.[10]

Wilcox seems to have been unperturbed by the inconveniences of life in the field at Walnut Springs. His principal memory was of being invited to join a mess to which belonged three of his regiment's officers who had thus far fought in all of General Taylor's battles. Two of them would die within two years—Lieutenants Sidney Smith of Virginia and Jenks Beaman of Vermont. The other was Lieutenant Ulysses S. Grant. Wilcox, in his history of the Mexican War, published in 1892, remarked that these were the men with whom he was "most intimately associated," and of Grant he said: "The subaltern, in manners quiet, plain and unobtrusive, with no pretension to genius, or, as believed at that time, to a high order of talent, but much esteemed among his immediate associates for kindly disposition and many excellent qualities, eclipsed all contemporaries. . . . [H]e died mourned and regretted by the whole country, and as sincerely and deeply by those he had confronted on bloody battle-fields as by those he had led to victory." If Wilcox was correct in describing Grant as "quiet, plain and unobtrusive" while they were stationed in Monterrey with the Fourth Infantry in the autumn of 1846, Julia's fiancé had changed considerably since his happy-go-lucky gambling days at Fort Jesup and Corpus Christi. Losing close friends and seeing the results of battles had evidently sobered him. He was beginning to take on the withdrawn though pleasant persona for which he would be known by 1861.[11]

Grant had been hoping for months that General Taylor's victories would persuade the Mexican government to settle its differences with the United States. Even before the Monterrey conflict he had informed Julia: "The Volunteers and other troops, who have arrived since the battles of the 8th and 9th of May are, of course, very anxious to have another fight, but those who were present those two days are not so particular about it. For my part I believe we are bound to beat the Mexicans whenever and where ever we meet them, no matter how large their numbers. But then wherever there are battles a great many must suffer, and for the sake of the little glory gained I do not care to see it." A few days after the Monterrey capitulation he wrote: "It is to be hoped that we are done fighting with Mexico . . . for we have shown them now that we can whip them under evry [*sic*] disadvantage. I dont believe that we will ever advance beyond this place, for it is generally believed that Mexico has rec'd our Minister and a few months more will restore us to amity. I hope it may be so for fighting is no longer a pleasure." But George Meade commented, when dispatches from Washington were received that ordered the eight-week truce to be cancelled: "So there is an end to all peace, and God knows now when we shall have it."[12]

Secretary of War Marcy's letter of October 13, instructing Taylor "to give the requisite notice that the armistice is to cease at once," was delivered to Old Zach by topographer Major James Graham, George Meade's brother-in-law, on the evening of November 2. In compliance with Marcy's order, Taylor wrote a letter addressed to the "Mexican General in Chief" at San Luis Potosí, where Santa Anna was reported to be assembling a vast army, advising that the truce would cease as of November 13. Taylor's dispatch was carried to Saltillo on the sixth by Major Graham (who was escorted by his brother, dragoon Captain Lawrence Pike Graham), and there turned over to Mexican officials.[13]

After receiving the War Department's "very cold" letter cancelling the armistice, in which Marcy had instructed the general to prosecute the war with "renewed vigor," Taylor quickly resolved to occupy Saltillo, the capital of the state of Coahuila, located seventy-five miles or so west of Monterrey, on the far side of mountains breached by the narrow Rinconada Pass.[14] However, before announcing his intention to penetrate further into the interior of Mexico, Taylor solved the problem that arose when the War Department promoted Thomas Sherman to the rank of captain in the battery that Brevet Captain Bragg had long led, the Third Artillery's Company E. Old Rough and Ready, it will be recalled, had prevented Sherman from superseding Bragg by assigning the former to quartermaster duty in Camargo. Sherman had eventually complained to General Winfield Scott, who had responded by ordering Sherman to take temporary command of the Third Artillery's Company D, to which Bragg had just been promoted and which was expected to land shortly at Point Isabel. As might have been anticipated, Sherman was not assuaged, for the arrangement took him even further from Taylor's headquarters and was also less prestigious, E being outfitted as horse artillery whereas D was not. But before Sherman reached Point Isabel, orders were issued changing the affiliations of both Sherman and Bragg. The solution to Taylor's quandary evolved from a fatal accident that had recently shocked the officers—the death on October 27 of Brevet Captain Randolph Ridgely following a fall from his horse on Monterrey's paved streets. By November 7 Bragg had been appointed to succeed Ridgely as commander of the Third Artillery's mobile Company C. Sherman was directed to "join his proper Company (E)."[15]

Since both C and E were camped on the outskirts of Monterrey, Bragg was able to assume his new duties immediately, and in fact he at once wrote Bliss that C was drastically under strength because nine men had been left ill at Matamoros and one at Camargo. Listing them by name and rank, he explained why he believed all of them should be returned to his company. Sherman, on the other hand, would not catch up with E until early February. In the meantime, the senior officer with E was Lieutenant George Thomas.[16]

After reassigning Bragg and Sherman, General Taylor issued orders informing his troops that the "temporary cessation of hostilities" would end November 13 and that Saltillo would then be occupied by General Worth and certain corps of the Second Division, namely James Duncan's battery, eight companies of the Artillery Battalion, the Fifth and Eighth infantry regiments, and Albert Blanchard's company of Louisiana volunteers. The movement toward Saltillo, scheduled to commence the day before the truce ended, was delayed when Taylor heard that the latest dispatches from Washington would arrive momentarily. The main thrust of the instructions from Secretary Marcy received on the twelfth was that Taylor should have four thousand of his men ready to engage in the expedition that the administration had earlier ordered General Patterson to lead southward to the port of Tampico. (In issuing its earlier orders, the Polk administration's unstated purpose had been to place General Patterson, a Democrat, in a position to lead an attack against Mexico City from Tampico if that appeared plausible geographically. Old Zach had cancelled those previous War Department orders because they contravened the Monterrey truce agreement; however, with the armistice no longer in effect the Polk administration expected the earlier orders to be implemented.) Marcy also indicated for the first time that those four thousand troops, as well as others of Taylor's army, might be employed in a move against Veracruz. Although the secretary of war suggested that meanwhile any intentions Taylor had of advancing beyond Monterrey should be reconsidered, he left that decision up to the general. Old Zach, taking the leeway offered, allowed Worth's detachment to proceed to Saltillo. He followed within a few hours, escorted by dragoons under Captain Charles May.

Taylor failed in his reports to reveal the reason he believed it was advisable, from a military standpoint, for a division of his army to advance beyond Monterrey, but he clearly thought it was imperative that his men should not merely hunker down in the city and await developments, as the Polk administration now apparently advocated, pending the possible development of a plan to move against Veracruz. Monterrey was porous in terms of access. The enemy's cavalry could lead a counterattack from any of four directions: Cadereyta, Marín, Monclova, or Saltillo. The Americans had demonstrated how vulnerable the city was; and Santa Anna would presumably have an advantage Taylor did not: active support from the city's remaining residents. By occupying Saltillo, Old Zach was at least making it more difficult for a Mexican army to freely reach Monterrey from that direction, the nearest to Santa Anna's headquarters at San Luis Potosí, while the Americans would benefit from fresh sources of provisions for their soldiers and animals.

Riding with the general's party to Saltillo was George Meade, replacing a recently joined captain of his corps, Thomas B. Linnard, who was ill. With the Eighth Infantry was James Longstreet, the acting commander of his company since June. With the Fifth Infantry was Charles Hamilton. John C. Robinson, also on the Fifth's roster but serving as an acting assistant quartermaster, probably rode with senior members of Worth's staff. Missing was Edmund Kirby Smith, transferred by promotion from the Fifth to the Seventh Infantry and previously ordered to join the latter, which was still garrisoning Monterrey. Taylor did not specify which artillery companies other than Duncan's were to participate in the movement, but among the artillery officers with Worth was Daniel Harvey Hill.[17]

Because Hill jotted down an almost daily record of his thoughts and observations while at Saltillo, we are indebted to him for considerable information concerning the village itself and events involving him and his fellow officers. Among his revelations: After encamping three afternoons along the route from Monterrey to Saltillo, on the sixteenth the American troops entered the capital of Coahuila "about half past two," where "persons having cakes and fruit for sale" lined the plaza's streets. The eight companies of the Artillery Battalion having been crowded into "Christ College," sixteen officers were assigned to share a small room so dirty that one lieutenant elected to sleep in front of their quarters "on the sidewalk." Hill, in his rambles around the town when not on guard duty or sitting as a member of a court-martial panel, spent most of his time noting the religious practices of the residents, visiting the town's principal cathedral, and examining its several shrines. He found much to admire, but of the cathedral he observed: "Rich as everything was the glaring colors used and the bad taste of the pictures detracts [*sic*] very much from the effect that otherwise would have been produced."[18]

George Meade also thought the cathedral impressive: "This building is very fine, having attached to it five chapels, all with magnificent altar-pieces." Yet, like Hill he criticized the manner in which it was decorated, particularly the wax figures of apostles and saints. As for the rest of the town, he explained to Margaretta after returning to Monterrey that he saw very little of it: "Besides the Cathedral, there are four other chapels, attached to monasteries. These I did not see, not having time, for the General sent me on a reconnoissance [*sic*] the day after our arrival, and I was absent on it three days, going about twenty-five miles in front of Saltillo, keeping up my reputation of always being among those who penetrate farthest into the country. . . . Upon my return from the reconnoissance, the General returned to [Monterrey], so that I had but little time to examine Saltillo."[19]

According to Meade, General Taylor, who had gone to Saltillo merely "to see the place," spent only four days there. As he was preparing to leave he replied to a letter from Santa Anna. The Mexican general had written General Taylor after learning that the American government was cancelling the armistice, implying that the action was not in accord with the Monterrey agreement. Taylor, in answering, first thanked Santa Anna for responding positively to his request for the release of several captured American troops. He then addressed Santa Anna's complaint courteously, reminding him of the provisions in the capitulation articles, and concluded by suggesting the advisability of accepting "the offer of the United States to enter upon an amicable negotiation of the difficulties and thus to establish permanent relations of good will and friendship between the Republics."[20] By November 23 Taylor and his party had returned to Monterrey, a day ahead of the general's sixty-second birthday, after encountering William Franklin along the way with dispatches from General Wool.

Reporting for duty at Taylor's headquarters two days later was Captain Francis Taylor of Virginia, commander of the First Artillery's K battery which had been led by Lieutenant William Mackall during the Monterrey campaign; and accompanying Captain Taylor was a brevet second lieutenant recently assigned to K, Thomas J. Jackson. Francis Taylor (not related to the general as far as is known) would die shortly before the Civil War erupted, but his handsome brown-haired and blue-eyed brevet second lieutenant would be known far and wide after 1861 as "Stonewall Jackson."[21] Like Cadmus Wilcox, Dabney Maury, and William Gardner, Jackson had just graduated that June from the United States Military Academy. As a student he seems to have been remarkable chiefly for the obviously laborious manner in which he attacked his courses. His early life had not prepared him for the Academy's stringent academic standards. By age six he had lost both of his parents and soon was separated from an older brother, Warren, and a younger sister, Laura. Raised mainly by a group of affectionate, prosperous bachelor uncles, principally Uncle Cummins Jackson, Tom grew to be a rugged, self-reliant youth despite an occasional digestive problem. He is said to have sold fish he caught, and to have worked for Uncle Cummins in various ways, such as by supervising slaves who cut wood for use at Jackson's Mill, near Weston, Virginia. His formal education was limited, but before entering West Point he taught school for two terms, held a summer job as an engineering assistant with a turnpike company building a road "toward far western Virginia," and by age seventeen was a constable in a Lewis County district.[22]

The circumstances that culminated in Jackson's admission to West Point were as unusual as his life to that point. Congressman Samuel Hays, a neighbor of the Jacksons, had the privilege of nominating someone from his district to attend the Academy. When the young man whom Hays chose as better qualified academically than Tom Jackson suddenly declined the honor, eighteen-year-old Tom rushed to Washington with saddlebags full of recommendations, saw Hays, and by June 20, 1842, was trudging up the rocky path from the

Academy's dock on the Hudson River to the eminence on which its buildings stood, having won his first campaign.[23]

His second campaign consisted of finding a way to pass the entrance examination and then four years of difficult courses. To teachers and classmates he was an oddity, with a farmer's shuffling walk and poor posture in the saddle despite his remarkable horsemanship, but with a natural reserve that forbade pity as he visibly struggled to improve his classroom performance, subject by subject. He was respected, even liked, yet was an anomaly—more determined, more serious, more intense, more honest, more forthright, more dutiful and obedient than most cadets. Never in danger of failing, his overall standing improved each year until, at graduation, he stood seventeen in a class of fifty-nine (the bottommost being George E. Pickett).[24]

That July, having been appointed a brevet second lieutenant in Company K, First U.S. Artillery, Jackson was ordered to report to Captain Francis Taylor at Fort Columbus, on Governor's Island adjacent to New York City. Captain Taylor had been instructed to pick up at Fort Hamilton, Brooklyn, forty horses and related equipment for duty with his battery in Mexico. On August 19 he and Jackson marched westward from Fort Hamilton with thirty recruits and the aforesaid equipment and horses. From Pittsburgh they traveled by riverboat to New Orleans. Although some of the recruits were a problem—five deserted, two were released due to illness, and two disappeared—the bulk of the little detachment reached Point Isabel by September 24 and were in Camargo by October 5. They were still there at the end of the month, Captain Taylor notified Adjutant General Jones, because they were waiting for some "heavy guns" the captain had been ordered to escort to Monterrey.[25]

Riding with Francis Taylor and Tom Jackson when they finally departed from Camargo on November 13 was one of Jackson's classmates, Brevet Second Lieutenant Dabney Maury, whose Company C of the new U.S. Regiment of Mounted Riflemen formed part of the column's escort. Maury and Jackson may have crossed paths earlier, since they were both camped in the vicinity of Camargo for nearly a month after Maury's arrival there on October 13, but in Maury's memoirs the veteran Confederate major general mentioned only one instance of having seen his friend Tom at that stage in their lives: "The Rifles moved on up the Rio Grande to Camargo, whence our colonel, Persifor Smith . . . had us ordered to Monterrey as escort to some siege pieces which, under the personal efforts of young Stonewall Jackson, were moving to that city. He worked at them in the muddy roads as he used to do at West Point, and ever did in his great career, and they had to move along."[26]

Maury, who rhapsodized about being from Fredericksburg, Virginia, and its environs, came from a much more privileged background than did Tom

Jackson. Though the fathers of both had died while Dabney and Tom were young children, the elder Maury had been a U.S. Navy captain, and his brother Matthew Fontaine Maury, who in effect became the guardian of Dabney and his brother William, was likewise a distinguished naval officer as well as a noted hydrographer. Dabney entered the University of Virginia at age seventeen, probably about the time his brother William died following a long illness. There for two years he "enjoyed the life of freedom from home surveillance, and the great pleasure of association with men well reared and educated." Upon leaving the university he studied law briefly in Fredericksburg, then in 1822 was admitted to West Point where, he declared, he spent "the only unhappy years of a very happy life." Although in the lower half of his class at graduation, from his record it is clear that he could perform superlatively once he resolved to master a subject.[27]

Upon being assigned after graduation to the Regiment of Mounted Riflemen (later the Third Cavalry), Maury found that only two of its companies had thus far been organized, C (Maury's) and F. Initially stationed at Fort McHenry, the two companies sailed from Baltimore on September 5, reaching Point Isabel after thirty-two days of floundering along the Atlantic coast in an "unseaworthy craft."[28] Inasmuch as the captain of C (Samuel Walker, the former Texas Ranger) was on special duty in Washington, command of the company devolved upon less senior officers, one being Lieutenant Benjamin S. Roberts, who joined C at Camargo in October. Roberts would rise to the rank of brigadier general of Union forces, as would the first lieutenant of Company F, Andrew Porter. Both Porter and Roberts were examples of President Polk's practice of selecting civilians to serve as officers of the Mounted Rifles, a tendency that Grant, Meade, and others thought unfair to men holding commissions in the regular army who could conceivably have gained higher rank through a transfer to the new regiment. Porter had entered West Point in 1836 but attended only half a year. Roberts was a graduate of West Point (1835) but had resigned his commission within three and a half years and was a lawyer when appointed as a first lieutenant of the Mounted Rifles in 1846.[29]

When Captain Francis Taylor's column reached Monterrey on November 14, Tom Jackson wrote his sister Laura that he was billeted in a house with "a beautiful orange orchard" in its backyard and a large pool for bathing; however, in less than a week his battery was ordered to reinforce Worth's division at Saltillo. Leaving on November 29, Captain Taylor's company reached Worth's headquarters by December 2, as Daniel Harvey Hill duly recorded in his diary. Hill was visited by Lieutenant James G. Martin of Taylor's battery, the North Carolinian who fought with Company K under Mackall's leadership during the Monterrey campaign. Martin gave Hill "a frightful account of the excesses of the Volunteers in Monterey."[30]

Dabney Maury, whose Mounted Rifles company remained in Monterrey until the middle of December, was grateful for the attention Ulysses Grant showed him during that period. In his memoirs Maury wrote: "Grant was then Quartermaster of the Fourth Infantry. I had been badly wounded while hunting at Camargo, so as to disable me from duty while in Monterey, and Grant being also, by the duties of his office, free to go when and where he pleased, we were much together and enjoyed the association. Grant was a thoroughly kind and manly young fellow, with no bad habits, and was respected and liked by his brother officers, especially by those of his own regiment."[31]

The men in Maury's Mounted Rifles Company C, as well as those in F, were among the troops forming the first echelon of the units selected to accompany General Taylor to Victoria, southeast of Monterrey. Victoria was located about halfway to Tampico, a leading port some 250 miles by land below Point Isabel and directly east of Santa Anna's headquarters at San Luis Potosí. Since October General Taylor had been corresponding with the War Department about a movement to seize and hold Tampico, the capital of the Mexican state of Tamaulipas. As mentioned previously, Old Zach could not sanction such a campaign until the Monterrey temporary armistice expired, but about November 1 the Mexican forces in Tampico withdrew, and on the fourteenth Commodore Conner, aboard the *Spitfire* and supported by other ships, sailed into the city's harbor at the mouth of the Pánuco River and occupied Tampico. At Conner's request it was soon garrisoned by several Second Artillery companies, sent by steamer from Brazos Santiago Island on the twenty-first, and reinforced on the thirtieth by a Louisiana field battery and fifty men from New Orleans. By December, two members of the Corps of Engineers, Lieutenant P. G. T. Beauregard of Louisiana and Captain John G. Barnard of Massachusetts, had been stationed there and were designing defensive works for approaches to the town.[32]

The Tampico garrison consisted of "eight strong companies of Artillery and the Alabama Regiment of Volunteers" by December 8, General Taylor informed the adjutant general. To reinforce those men he had instructed Major General Patterson to march to Tampico from Matamoros with three regiments of his volunteers, "one being the Tennessee horse." The troops accompanying Old Zach to Victoria, the first of whom left Monterrey on December 13, were to "effect a junction with Major General Patterson" at Victoria.[33]

Participating in Major General Patterson's march to Tampico were a few regular army officers, one being Brevet Second Lieutenant George Brinton McClellan. He was another of the Military Academy's 1846 graduates—the youngest in his class, with next to the highest record, assigned that July to the Engineer Corps. The son of a successful Philadelphia surgeon, and the third of five children, he had received, before entering West Point, "an excellent education," including two years at the University of Pennsylvania. Since others of his classmates were equally well prepared to enter the Academy, such as his friend Dabney Maury, it is clear that the youthful McClellan (who celebrated his twentieth birthday in Mexico that December) was an exceptional student. Said to have been "short and compact of build, with gray eyes and dark hair," he was particularly admired by southern cadets, his closest friends at the Academy. Maury wrote of him that he "bore every evidence of gentle nature and high culture, and his countenance was as charming as his demeanor was modest and winning," yet the tone of the youthful engineer's Mexican War diary points to his having already possessed, in 1846, a decided sense of the superiority and importance of his opinions. For instance, in commenting on his engineer company's "very pleasant passage, on the whole" from New York to Point Isabel, he recorded at length and in detail his views concerning the manner in which a ship transporting troops should be commanded.[34]

McClellan had been appointed to a component of the army called Company A of the Corps of Engineers, the only one of its kind, only recently authorized by Congress. Previously, officers of both army engineer departments, the Corps of Engineers and the Corps of Topographical Engineers, had been assigned individually to their duty stations, whereas when the unique Company A of the Engineers Corps left West Point on September 24 for Point Isabel after a few weeks of training it consisted of Captain Alexander J. Swift, Second Lieutenant Gustavus W. Smith, Brevet Second Lieutenant McClellan, and seventy-one rank and file, the latter "[a]ll Americans—all young—all intelligent—all anxious, very eager for the campaign—and above all, well drilled."[35]

After landing at Brazos Santiago on October 12, "probably the very worst port that could be found on the whole American coast," McClellan asserted, the company briefly camped nearby before marching to the mouth of the Rio Grande and boarding a steamer to Matamoros. There McClellan was "sick for nearly two weeks," as he also was after the company reached Camargo by water on November 2. But as soon as he was released from the army's hospital at Camargo he wrote his mother: "I would not have missed coming here for the world, now that I am well and recovering my strength, I commence to enjoy the novelty of the affair, and shall have enough to tell you when I return, to fill a dozen books." When he heard in mid-November that his unit was to "accompany General Patterson to Tampico," he regretted only that no fighting would be necessary since the town was already occupied by American troops. Aboard the steamer that took his company back downriver from Camargo, McClellan resented being subordinate to higher-ranked volunteer officers. "I was perfectly disgusted coming down the river. I found that every confounded Voluntario in the 'Continental Army' ranked me." He was also determined to climb further up the status ladder: "I have pretty much made up my mind that if I cannot increase my *rank* in this war, I shall resign shortly after the close of it. I cannot stand the thought of being a Second Lieutenant all my life." Then again, at the conclusion of this entry ("Dec. 5th, Mouth of the Rio Grande") his mood changed: "I have made up my mind to act the philosopher—to take things as they come and not to worry my head about the future—to try to get perfectly well—and above all things to see as much *fun* as I can 'scare up' in this country."[36]

General Taylor, in preparing "to effect a junction with Major General Patterson" at Victoria, had reorganized the First Division (Twiggs's), which was to accompany him to Victoria. Grant's regiment (Fourth Infantry) was detached from the division and, together with two companies of the First Artillery, ordered to serve as the garrison of the Citadel in Monterrey. The Seventh Infantry's men were deducted from Worth's division and added to a First Division brigade under Colonel Persifor Smith, as were the troops of the First Infantry, Mounted Riflemen, and Thomas Sherman's Company E, Third Artillery, currently led by Lieutenant George Thomas. In the First Division's other brigade, commanded by Colonel William Harney, were the Third Infantry, the Second Infantry (once it joined the main column at Montemorelos), two Second Dragoon squadrons, and Bragg's Third Artillery Company C. As for the volunteer units, the Maryland and District of Columbia Battalion was detached from the First Division, but those troops were transferred to Brigadier General Quitman's brigade, which along with the First Tennessee, Georgia, and Mississippi Rifles regiments were Victoria-bound with General Taylor. Major General Butler was to command Monterrey as well as all of the Army of Occupation's posts located below that city to the mouth of the Rio Grande.[37]

The regulars in Taylor's column marched on December 13, the volunteers on the following day, and General Taylor on the fifteenth. Among those riding with the general's party was Lieutenant George Meade, although he was no longer the senior topographical engineer with Taylor's army, Captain Thomas Linnard having replaced the late Captain Williams.[38] General Taylor was confident that while he was absent the forces at Parras (about 2,400 with six guns), at Saltillo (about 1,200 regular troops with eight guns, to be reinforced shortly with two regiments of volunteer foot and a portion of the Kentucky cavalry), and at Monterrey (those composing the city's regular army garrison together with Butler's volunteers), if combined as they could be on relatively short notice, would be able to block any movement in that direction by Santa Anna, who was still reported to be at San Luis Potosí with several thousand troops. Moreover, Saltillo was protected in part by the extreme aridity of the area between that city and San Luis Potosí. Any large army would have difficulty sustaining itself while crossing between the two towns, one of the chief reasons General Taylor had not attempted a major movement southward from Saltillo. Consequently he scarcely knew what to think when on the evening of December 17, at Montemorelos, an express rider delivered a message from General Worth advising that Santa Anna's army was believed to be moving northward toward Saltillo. Though Taylor doubted that an attack on Worth's position was imminent, he reversed direction the next day, taking with him all of the regulars in his column except George Meade and one artillery battery, the Third Artillery's Company E to which Lieutenants George Thomas, John Reynolds, and Sam French were attached. Meade and the officers and men of Company E were transferred to General Quitman's volunteer brigade, which was to proceed to Victoria where it was to combine with Major General Patterson's force as originally planned.[39]

After Taylor parted from Quitman's brigade, Meade wrote his wife: "I cannot tell you with how sad a heart I saw all of my old associates march away this morning, for I am left here with only five regular officers, and of the two thousand volunteers, I do not know a dozen. Then, to think that they are hurrying on with the expectation of having another battle, at which I shall not be present! Little as I like fighting, it is still a great disappointment." And although he had persuaded himself that the change of assignment would be on the whole advantageous, he added: "Still, I feel very much the separation from General Taylor and all the regulars. The old man was very kind to me on parting."[40]

Worth had also sent a plea to General Wool at Parras, asking him to put his troops "in rapid motion" for Saltillo, which Wool did within two or three hours after receiving Worth's dispatch on the afternoon of the seventeenth. Wool's army, scarcely pausing to eat or sleep, reached Agua Nueva, about 120 miles east of Parras and 18 miles below Saltillo, by the twenty-first. Two days earlier Major General Butler, together with the First Ohio and First Kentucky regiments and Captain Lucien Webster's First Artillery howitzer battery, had arrived at Saltillo from Monterrey. Old Zach, upon being informed while en route to Saltillo of Wool's and Butler's movements, and that Butler had called up additional volunteers from Camargo and stations lower on the river, ordered Butler on the twenty-second to remain in command of all the troops in and around Saltillo, including those of Wool's army, as well as those in Monterrey, Camargo, and the other Army of Occupation posts. Taylor also detached the Second Dragoons from Twiggs's First Division, and keeping with him only two of that regiment's companies he directed Colonel Harney to take the rest of his dragoons to Saltillo. Then on December 23 Taylor turned back toward Victoria with the remainder of Twiggs's division.[41]

On Christmas, at "New Leon," Old Zach received an unofficial letter from Scott, written from New York on November 25, advising that the general-in-chief expected to be at Point Isabel by December 17, "and at Camargo, say, 23rd, in order to be within easy corresponding distance" from Taylor. Scott went on to say: "I am not coming, my dear general, to supersede you in the immediate command on the line of operations. . . . My proposed theatre is different." He made no mention of a movement against Veracruz, though suggested that Taylor should be able to imagine his objective in light of letters from Secretary Marcy. He did say he would be obliged to take from Taylor "most of the gallant officers and men (regular and volunteer)" whom Old Zach had "so long and so nobly commanded," but termed that reduction in force a "temporary sacrifice." Taylor, criticized by several historians for thereafter continuing on to Victoria, was, as indicated above, in the process of completing the long-planned convergence with General Patterson's column from Matamoros. He had heard nothing from Washington concerning any new initiative involving Scott, nor anything further from Scott himself. In a reply sent via Camargo, which has repeatedly been condemned as spiteful but which contains no indication of spite or anger, he explained where he was and why, as well as what his current intentions were, concluding: "At all times and places I shall be happy to receive your orders, and to hold myself and troops at your disposition." Later, in a lengthy personal letter to secretary of state James Buchanan, he indicated that he did infer, from the contents of Scott's note from New York, why the general-in-chief was coming to the war zone. However, since he had received no communication from Scott saying that he expected or desired to meet with him, Old Zach had concluded there was no need for him to turn back before rendezvousing with General Patterson at Victoria unless he heard something further from Scott. There is no evidence that Taylor had previously felt any personal animosity toward Scott, as had for example Colonel Ethan Allen Hitchcock most notably. Taylor's subsequent expressions of anger stemmed chiefly from the fact that the War Department had failed to inform him of Scott's Veracruz expedition prior to its launching. He believed that at least he should have been told to expect extremely important orders. With sufficient forewarning he could have cancelled the long, hard trip to Victoria, with its resultant needless expense and loss of life. He thought the Polk administration's incredible lack of consideration for him was deliberate, but the truth seems to have been even worse—in the excitement over the Veracruz initiative, apparently little thought was given to Taylor's feelings or to the welfare of his soon-to-be-vastly-reduced Army of Occupation. (Months later Taylor would be told that Secretary of War Marcy had written him on November 25 "that Major General Scott had been ordered to the seat of war." The War Department should have realized that letter had never reached him, since he had not acknowledged its receipt, as was customary.)[42]

Santa Anna did not initiate a major campaign against the Americans in the Saltillo region in December or January, perhaps due to the concentration of Wool's and Worth's forces, but rumors of Mexican troops being seen in the vicinity of that town persisted throughout those months. As for General Taylor, he and the infantry and artillery units accompanying him reached Victoria without incident on January 4; but in late December a dragoon patrol led by Captain (Brevet Major) Charles May, which Taylor had detached to assist topographical engineer Captain Thomas Linnard in reconnoitering certain of the mountain passes between Montemorelos and Linares, was attacked as the dragoons moved single file through the extremely narrow Santa Rosa Pass, about twelve miles beyond San Pedro. The dragoons lost their baggage when the rear guard of May's command retreated after being separated from the rest of their party; otherwise, the only negative results of the encounter consisted of May's acrimonious charges against the subordinates responsible for his rear guard. In the same report May particularly praised "the prompt manner" in which his orders during the attack "were executed by Lts. [Reuben P.] Campbell and [Thomas J.] Wood."[43]

At Victoria, where Major General Patterson's column arrived the same day as Taylor's, the Americans had heard that General Winfield Scott was "in the country," planning "to organize an expedition against Vera Cruz," but General Taylor had still not been informed officially of either a Veracruz expedition or the arrival of General Scott. Taylor knew that President Polk and his advisors had long been considering whether to attack Veracruz. Indeed, Secretary of War Marcy had written Taylor as early as September 22 to inquire what would be needed in the way of manpower and supplies in that event, as well as whether other initiatives were advisable such as an overland advance from Saltillo or Tampico. Addressing Marcy's inquiries at length, Taylor had responded that if the government desired to strike a decisive blow at Mexico City he thought a landing at Veracruz or Alvarado might be the best course of action, but the War Department had not even acknowledged receipt of his comments. Thus Old Zach was not surprised when he was finally notified by Scott that a campaign to capture Veracruz had been approved, but was indignant that he had not been informed of the government's intentions much sooner, or that Scott would be in charge of the venture and the Army of Occupation's commander would have no part in it.[44]

Three months earlier President Polk had begun investigating the practicality of mounting an assault on Veracruz after being informed that the guns of the formidable fortress of San Juan de Ulúa, in the city's harbor, could be avoided by landing troops four miles or so below that castle. "It is believed," Polk recorded in his diary, "that if an army of a few thousand men can land at the point suggested that they could by besieging the City in the rear cut off all supplies from it, and that by keeping up a strict blockade by sea, the City and fortress of San Juan de Ulloa [*sic*] must in the course of a very few days surrender." By October 17 Polk had essentially adopted this suggested plan, although whether there should follow an advance against Mexico City remained under consideration. Another month elapsed before he reluctantly selected General Winfield Scott to implement the movement against Veracruz.[45] When on November 19 President Polk informed Scott that he was to command the expedition, the general was not slow, as he had been earlier, in acting on his instructions. A month later he was in New Orleans, having traveled there on the steamer *Union* from New York City. In another nine days he was at Brazos Santiago Island.[46]

President Polk was responsible for Scott's failure to inform Taylor immediately about the Veracruz initiative and what it would entail for the Army of Occupation. Before leaving Washington the general had shown Polk the letter he intended to send Taylor. The president noted in his diary that he directed Scott to "omit the part of it which related to the contemplated expedition to Vera Cruz," on the grounds that if it became "known to the young officers about Gen'l Taylor's person they might not see the necessity of keeping it secret, and that becoming public in the army the knowledge might reach the enemy." Polk also told Scott that Secretary of War Marcy had already given Taylor an "intimation" of the plan. Thus, although Scott's vague note from New York hinted at a change in strategy, it was not until December 20 at New Orleans that he wrote Taylor concerning the exact number of regulars and volunteers he intended to detach from the Army of Occupation for service with the Veracruz task force, together with his reason for doing so: to insure that sufficient army contingents would be on their way south by February, before the start of Veracruz's annual "black vomit" period. In the December 20 message, Scott also said: "Perhaps you may be able to meet me on the Rio Grande, say at Camargo, or lower down the river; and I shall send an officer to you, at an early date, who will be able to communicate my views to you in greater detail." However, Taylor had not received that letter when, on January 14, he at last learned of the general-in-chief's plans from letters written by Scott on January 3 at Camargo.[47]

Upon landing at Brazos Santiago Island shortly after Christmas, General Scott was unable to obtain definite information concerning Taylor's whereabouts. At Matamoros on December 30 he was told that Taylor was reportedly returning to Monterrey from Victoria "in order to support Brevet Brigadier General Worth, understood to be menaced at Saltillo by Santa Anna and a powerful army." Scott then wrote Marcy: "This information has determined me to proceed up the river to Camargo, in order to meet dispatches from Major General Taylor; and if his outposts should be seriously menaced, to join him rapidly." When Scott disembarked at Camargo four days later, Taylor's letter of December 26 awaited him; but as previously noted, in it Old Zach, after acknowledging receipt of Scott's inexplicit note from New York, had said little other than that he had started again for Victoria, having ascertained that "the cause of anxiety about the safety of [Saltillo] had been removed by the drawing in of Wool's column, and the arrival of reinforcements from below," although he added that he would be happy to receive and comply with Scott's orders at "all times." This caused Scott to write two letters from Camargo on January 3, one to Taylor and one to Butler, copies of which would finally enlighten Old Rough and Ready. In the letter to Taylor, Scott said he was sorry his letter of December 20, which he supposed would have brought Taylor back to Monterrey, had not been received. "As it is," Scott continued, "I am much embarrassed by your great distance from me. That circumstance, and extreme pressure of time, has thrown me upon the necessity of giving direct instructions, of a very important character, to your next in command." Scott's implied reprimand undoubtedly added to Taylor's sense of having been treated abominably, and apparently most of his subordinates also thought Scott had treated Old Zach very inconsiderately.[48] Indeed, from Scott's letter of December 20 from New Orleans it is evident that he had not conceived of any consultation as being called for except as a courtesy, for he had itemized at that time, as he did again from Camargo on January 3, the number and character of troops he required from Old Zach's army.

After hearing indirectly of Scott's arrival at Point Isabel, General Taylor had remained a week at Victoria, anticipating that the general-in-chief or the War Department would contact him there. When no such dispatch was received by January 12, Taylor issued orders preparatory to marching to Tampico with Twiggs's division and Patterson's volunteers for provisions and supplies. But only a portion of his forces had left Victoria for Tampico when, two days later, copies of Scott's two letters of January 3 arrived. The one addressed to Butler contained the worst news, Butler having been told by Scott to "put in movement, for the mouth of the Rio Grande, the following troops," each demand listed separately: "About five hundred regular cavalry, of the 1st and 2d regiments of dragoons, including Lieutenant [Philip] Kearny's troop; About five hundred volunteer cavalry . . . ; Two field batteries of regular light artillery, (say) Duncan's and Taylor's; and Four thousand regulars, on foot, including artillery, acting as infantry; the whole under Brevet Brigadier General Worth . . . ; In addition . . . 4000 volunteer infantry." Although included were provisions for certain deductions from the numbers specified, Scott also indicated that virtually all of the troops with Taylor's column at Victoria, other than those Taylor selected as an escort for his return to Monterrey, were to proceed to Tampico, where they would form a part of the Veracruz assault force.[49]

In response, Taylor wrote Scott two letters on January 15. The official one, addressed to Scott's chief of staff, was primarily a report on the units at Victoria, all of whom were being sent to Tampico by Taylor to await Scott's arrival with the exception of those retained as Old Zach's escort back to Monterrey. In his other letter, addressed to Scott personally, he protested being "expected, with less than a thousand regulars and a volunteer force, partly new levies, to hold a defensive line, while a large army of more than twenty thousand men" was in his front (referring to Santa Anna's forces at San Luis Potosí). He also remarked: "I feel that I have lost the confidence of the government, or it would not have suffered me to remain, up to this time, ignorant of its intentions." On the twenty-seventh he wrote similarly to the adjutant general, requesting that his letter be referred to the president. In one of his last orders from Victoria, Taylor thanked those of his forces who were leaving him at that juncture for Scott's command, a total of 4,733.[50]

Taylor's choice of escort contingents would prove remarkably auspicious later. In his official letter of January 15 to Winfield Scott's chief of staff (Lieutenant H. L. Scott), Old Zach explained: "I have retained Lieut. Colonel May's squadron as part of my escort to Monterey, and also the Mississippi regiment. . . . As I presume that General Butler, under his instructions, has ordered the batteries of General Worth's command [Duncan's and Francis Taylor's] to march with it to the mouth of the river, and as I infer from those same instructions, that not more than two batteries are required by Major General Scott, I have directed the return to Monterey of General Bragg's and Sherman's. If I have mistaken his wishes in this matter, I beg to be advised without delay, as the batteries may still join him in time."[51] Thus whatever General Scott's reasons were for having excluded Bragg's and Sherman's batteries from his orders pertaining to light artillery companies, obviously General Taylor hoped to keep these two with him. And his selection of Jefferson Davis's regiment to accompany him suggests that he had grown particularly attached to the Mississippian.

On the following day Taylor and his escort commenced their return to Monterrey. At Villa Gran, about fifty miles above Victoria, they stopped to investigate the murder, on January 13, of Lieutenant John A. Richey, who had been sent by General Butler, with an escort of ten dragoons, to deliver Scott's dispatches of January 3 addressed to Taylor. In reporting the lieutenant's death, Taylor wrote the adjutant general: "On reaching Villa Gran, he separated himself from his escort for the purpose of purchasing provisions and forage, and was set upon by a party of Mexican ruffians, who put him to death. . . . The despatches have undoubtedly been forwarded to the Mexican general-in-chief at San Luis. Among them were instructions of Major General Scott to me, of Jan'y 3rd, revealing the operations with which he is charged, and amount of force to be withdrawn from this frontier."[52] The delay in alerting Taylor to Polk's and Scott's plans had resulted, ironically, in seizure of the vital news by

Mexicans as it was being forwarded to Old Zach through enemy lines by a lone second lieutenant and a handful of dragoons.

More bad news after his arrival at Walnut Springs on January 24 caused Taylor to depart for Saltillo a week later with May's squadron, the batteries of Bragg and Sherman, and the Mississippi volunteers. Reconnoitering parties sent out by Butler and Wool had been surrounded and taken captive—on the twenty-second at Encarnación, a detachment of fifty Arkansas men under Major Solon Borland and a number of mounted Kentucky volunteers under Captain Cassius M. Clay, who were escorting Major John P. Gaines; and on the twenty-seventh, about thirty miles from Encarnación, another patrol of Kentucky cavalry.[53]

11
Battle of Buena Vista

By mid-January of 1847 the Army of Occupation had lost the vast majority of its regular army troops—indeed, all of its regular army infantry—and thousands of volunteers. At Victoria on January 14 General Taylor had released to General Scott not only the regiments of infantrymen in Twiggs's division (First, Second, Third, and Seventh) but the Mounted Rifles, the Corps of Engineers' Company A, most of the volunteers in General Quitman's brigade, and the volunteers who had marched with General Patterson from Matamoros to Victoria. In addition, lost to Taylor were the artillery units and volunteers already occupying Tampico or on their way there.[1] Meanwhile Major General Butler, in response to General Scott's instructions of January 3, had ordered General Worth to join the Veracruz expedition, taking with him the infantry regiments in his division, the Fifth and the Eighth, the latter now including twenty-one-year-old Brevet Second Lieutenant George E. Pickett, an 1846 West Point graduate (who had not joined his regiment until November, and who would become extremely close to James Longstreet); Blanchard's Louisiana volunteers; the Artillery Battalion; Duncan's and Taylor's light artillery batteries; the Sixth Infantry companies and one of Kentucky foot soldiers attached to the Sixth that had until then served under General Wool; seven companies of the Second Dragoons; Captain Philip Kearny's company of First Dragoons (which had reached Saltillo from Camargo on December 5, had been specifically requested by Scott, and currently included Lieutenant Richard S. Ewell); and the Fourth Infantry (which had been the chief component garrisoning the Citadel in Monterrey). Moreover, one of Wool's engineers, Robert E. Lee, had been instructed to report to Scott.[2]

Lee's duties after the Centre Division reached Parras on December 5 were largely routine, judging from General Wool's orders. On the ninth Lee was detailed to serve on a court-martial panel that tried Captain (Brevet Major) Benjamin L. Beall who, accused of "highly unofficial conduct and neglect of duty," was found not guilty. On the twelfth, Lee was instructed to conduct a reconnaissance, with the assistance of a company of Arkansas volunteers. From the seventeenth to the twenty-first the division was on a forced march from Parras to Agua Nueva, in response to Worth's plea for reinforcements, and Lee was presumably involved in the selection of Wool's campsites during that period as well as thereafter, at other locations near Saltillo to which the division was subsequently moved. In fact, Wool would write Taylor that Lee and topographical engineer George Hughes, after reconnoitering the area, selected Buena Vista as "the best position" the division could occupy to defend Saltillo. On the twenty-fifth, the first Christmas Lee and his wife of fifteen years had ever spent apart, he investigated a report of approaching enemy forces which proved erroneous. On the twenty-ninth, while Wool's command was at Buena Vista, five miles or so south of Saltillo, Lee, George Hughes, and Lorenzo Sitgreaves were told to go into quarters at Saltillo until they completed the work of making drawings and writing memoirs of the division's march from Parras. On January 10, below Buena Vista at La Encantada, Wool appointed Captain Lee to serve as acting inspector general of the Centre Division.[3]

Lee is said to have had one unusual adventure in late December. With Wool's approval, and guided by a young Mexican who lived nearby, he undertook a night reconnaissance to determine whether enemy forces were nearby. Upon finding fresh wagon tracks, and seeing campfires in the distance, he left his frightened guide and continued ahead until he saw white objects which, by the light of the moon, he concluded were tents. Pressing on, he discovered the white forms were sheep, and spoke to the surprised, peaceable drovers. His lengthy absence from camp caused Wool to arrest the guide's father, who was held until Lee finally returned.[4]

Apparently Lee never had any personal contact with General Taylor during the Mexican War. Years later, Lee reportedly said he had overheard certain humorous remarks made by Old Zach at Buena Vista, but evidently they were never at the same location at the same time. Although the exact date of Lee's departure from Wool's camp is not known, he must have left almost immediately after his promotion to the position of acting inspector general, for in writing to the adjutant general on January 16 Wool referred to Lee's having received transfer orders. Also unknown is who was responsible for directing Lee to join General Scott's expedition. But on his fortieth birthday, January 19, Captain Robert E. Lee must have been elated at the prospect of possibly engaging in a battle, his first, at Veracruz.[5]

Around the time of Lee's departure there occurred an "open rupture" in the relations between Brigadier General Wool and Major General Butler. It was payback time: Wool was in much the same irreconcilable position as that in which he had placed Harney—a veteran regular army officer forced to report to a political appointee plucked from civilian ranks, though in this instance one who had held an army commission decades earlier. Wool's reluctance to be commanded by Butler was no secret among the former's subordinates. Lieutenant William H. L. Wallace wrote his father two days before Christmas from Agua Nueva: "General Wool will not go to Saltillo because Major General Butler is there, and he is fearful of losing his command." Three days later Lieutenant Adolphus Engelmann informed his parents: "Wool wants to go back to Parras, where he would have no one in authority over him." Yet all Wool could do was to stay as far away from Butler as possible, in light of Taylor's having specifically given Butler command of Wool's division. For about a month their basic enmity manifested itself in arguments over which location below Saltillo would be the most advantageous, from a defensive standpoint, for Wool to occupy. At last the unhappy Wool wrote Taylor on January 20 from Buena Vista that he would prefer to be relieved of his command entirely rather than to continue serving under Butler. Taylor resolved this contretemps on January 28 by giving Wool command of all American troops stationed in the Saltillo area. Butler's sphere would be the forces still in Monterrey and in rearward posts and depots, other than those composing Taylor's escort from Victoria to Monterrey. Then Taylor moved his headquarters to Saltillo, arriving there on February 2 with the units under his personal command—Bragg's and Sherman's artillery batteries, Jefferson Davis's Mississippi regiment, and a squadron of Second Dragoons.[6]

By the end of January Ulysses Grant and his Fourth Infantry comrades had been relocated to a camp below Fort Brown, a few miles from the Palo Alto battlefield, where together with various contingents of Worth's command they were awaiting transport to a rendezvous with General Scott at Lobos Island. The Fourth Infantry had merged with the rest of Worth's column on January 11, the advance elements of which had started from Saltillo on the ninth. One memorable incident that occurred during the Fourth Infantry's march from Monterrey to Camargo was described by Cadmus Wilcox. Just before reaching Mier the regiment's officers pitched their tents near a "pretty and rapidly flowing stream" and could hardly wait to bathe in it. Lieutenant Sidney Smith, the first to approach the stream, startled from the undergrowth along its bank "a drove of Pecoros, resembling the hog very much in appearance." Since they could be "quite fierce at times," he "jumped upon the limb of a small sapling barely strong enough to bear his weight and about three feet from the ground." To his rescue went "Beaman, Grant, and others," and "the Pecoros fled."[7]

At Camargo, Wilcox recalled, "The Fourth Infantry, together with General Worth and staff, boarded the steamer *Colonel Cross* and descended the Rio Grande." They "remained at the mouth of the river two days" before returning "by steamer eighteen or twenty miles up the river" to Camp Palo Alto. From there on January 31 Ulysses Grant, in sending Quartermaster General Jesup his "monthly Summary Statement for the month of Jan. 1847 and Muster Rolls," confessed: "I had stolen from my Quarters in monteray [*sic*] a chest containing all my Quarter Master funds besides several hundred dollars more." Explaining that he was "not able at present" to replace the money, and that the loss was not attributable to his negligence, he pleaded that "it would be but justice that the Government should loose [*sic*] the amount and not me." Apparently in this instance he was not required to repay the missing quartermaster funds, but he would be held accountable for a similar loss in 1848.[8]

From Grant's point of view it was unfortunate that his regiment was now attached to the division led by Worth, for whom Grant had little respect. In his memoirs he would express much the same opinion of that officer as did Daniel Harvey Hill, Joseph Mansfield, and others at one time or another: "He was nervous, impatient and restless on the march, or when important or responsible duty confronted him." As for the Fourth Infantry's being sent to Veracruz, Grant had evidently resigned himself to that prospect, for on February 1 from the Palo Alto camp he told Julia: "Since we left Monteray I have been very far from well and now I could remain behind if I would but I think by the time our sea voyage is completed I will be well and while I am in the country I want to see as much of it as possible."[9]

The Fourth Infantry was already at Camp Palo Alto when the other infantry regiments in Worth's division landed there. Captain Ephraim Kirby Smith wrote in his journal that most of the companies of the Fifth Infantry reached that assembly point "at eight in the morning" of January 26, having left Camargo on the twenty-second aboard the *Rough and Ready,* and had erected their tents "on the left of the Fourth Infantry." On the Fifth Infantry's "extreme right" was the Artillery Battalion. The Sixth and Eighth infantry companies, upon their arrival, were to encamp on the left of the Fifth Infantry. As some were landing, others were departing—on February 2 five companies of the Artillery Battalion were transported to the mouth of the Rio Grande, among them Daniel Harvey Hill's. Commanded by Lieutenant John W. Phelps, Hill's company was one of two specifically included in the order directing that movement; the other was Captain Charles F. Smith's.[10]

Hill would have preferred to be back in Saltillo. He professed in his diary that he had fallen desperately in love with a beautiful daughter of the *alcalde,* though he had only caught glimpses of her occasionally and had never spoken to her. Also he was sorry to have left the environs of Monterrey and the family with whom he had boarded while stationed in that city. As his battalion had neared Monterrey on its march from Saltillo back to Camargo he had "spent a delightful evening" with Mrs. Tato, who welcomed him "warmly." Hill and one of his brothers, a Mississippi volunteer who had been ill and was on his way home, slept that evening at the Tato family's residence. At Punta Aguda on the sixteenth Hill heard a Mexican call the volunteers "Comanches of the North," which he thought was "the most appropriate name" for them he had heard. At Camargo, reached by his battalion at 6:30 a.m. on the nineteenth, Hill indicated that in his opinion their forced march had been unnecessary. "It seems folly for us to have made such hard marches at the rate of nearly twenty miles a day when there are no boats here when we arrive." Two companies of his battalion managed to embark that evening for the voyage downriver and three the next day, but not until the evening of the twenty-first did Hill's unit and two of the other artillery companies board ship, along with "Capt. Merrit's [Moses E. Merrill's] of the 5th Infantry and Capt. Blanchard's Louisiana Volunteers."[11]

The men of Hill's company, after leaving Camp Palo Alto for the mouth of the Rio Grande, were kept fifteen days at a sandy staging area near Brazos Island. There they were subjected to the bitter cold of "Northers," had no wood for campfires, and broke out again with chills and fevers, which prompted Hill to pen a reprise of his earlier protests: "It is wrong to bring troops to this sickly place when there are no transports ready. . . . 'Tis most unfortunate that we left Saltillo so early." Still, he was able to finish his fifth article for the *Charleston Mercury* on February 4. On the sixth he watched companies of the Eighth Infantry being taken aboard a transport, those of the Fourth Infantry on the thirteenth, and three companies of his battalion on the fifteenth, followed the next day by the Fifth and Sixth infantry regiments and seven companies of the Mounted Rifles. On the nineteenth it was finally the turn of another four Artillery Battalion companies, including Hill's, to leave Brazos Santiago. Crowded aboard the ship *Henry* along with a mixed detachment from several regiments and Blanchard's company of Louisiana volunteers, they got under way on the twentieth, with Hill and George Thomas bunking together. Five days earlier General Scott and his staff (including, surprisingly, Lieutenant Colonel Ethan Allen Hitchcock, who for decades had been openly critical of the general) had departed aboard the *Massachusetts.* At Tampico, where the Twiggs and Patterson columns had been camped since late January, Scott disembarked on February 19, was saluted by the firing of cannon, and was escorted to General Patterson's headquarters by four artillery companies. The next day the general-in-chief put to sea again, heading for his designated concentration point, Lobos Island; and sharing one of the cabins on his steamer were Captain Robert E. Lee and his seasick classmate and friend of many years, Captain Joseph E. Johnston (topographical engineer).[12]

As for General Taylor, he had moved his headquarters further south on February 5, to Agua Nueva, about eighteen miles below Saltillo. From there he wrote the adjutant general: "I am confirmed in my purpose of holding not only [Saltillo], but this position in its front," explaining that there were "powerful military reasons" for doing so. "The scarcity of water and supplies for a long distance in front compels the enemy either to risk an engagement in the field or to hold himself aloof from us, while if we fell back on Monterey, he could establish himself strongly at Saltillo and be in position to annoy more effectively our flanks and our communications." But at noon on the twenty-first he was reluctantly beginning the process of moving his 4,700 or so troops at Agua Nueva back toward the hacienda of Buena Vista, five miles south of Saltillo. The reconnoitering parties of Charles May and Ben McCulloch (the latter, with a few Rangers, and without orders, having fortunately reported to Taylor on February 4) had brought to headquarters convincing reports that a huge army under Santa Anna himself had already advanced from San Luis Potosí to La Encarnación, only thirty-five miles below Agua Nueva; and General Taylor had decided, as had General Wool previously, that the extremely narrow Angostura Pass, a mile and a half below the Buena Vista hacienda, would be the best place near Saltillo for his force to withstand an assault by a Mexican army believed to be three or four times larger than his. The Agua Nueva position was preferable from the standpoint of spaciousness and proximity to wood and water, but was located in a network of local roads that could be employed by a sufficiently large army to surround the Americans. In contrast, the valley between La Angostura Pass and the Buena Vista hacienda provided excellent cover for a defensive stand. The area was protected east and west by mountains from which deep gullies and corresponding ridges spread downward toward the Saltillo road. Moreover, if the road through the narrow pass were to be blocked by entrenched infantry and artillery units, as the Americans intended to do, the enemy would be forced onto the high sloping plateau east of it, since a small creek ran west of the road, and the terrain ascending from it was too eroded and precipitous for passage by artillery or sizeable numbers of troops. Although there were trails that circled completely around Saltillo, and one from Agua Nueva westward toward Parras which connected with a mule path to Saltillo, the distances involved in both instances would make an attack in concert with one from below La Angostura Pass improbable except for cavalry.[13]

Having given such matters "much consideration," General Taylor began withdrawing his field army from Agua Nueva to a position in front of the Hacienda San Juan de la Buena Vista at noon on February 21.[14] Left behind were Colonel Archibald Yell and his Arkansas Mounted Volunteers, to insure that wagons were loaded with the camp's remaining supplies and ammunition. As the main body of Taylor's column began erecting its tents in front of the hacienda, General Taylor and his staff continued on to Saltillo to oversee arrangements for the town's defense. Accompanying them was "a small force" (May's dragoons, Sherman's and Bragg's batteries, and Davis's Mississippi regiment). Taylor and his party bivouacked overnight in Saltillo, where some of his men were already stationed, but the general sent a detachment of First Dragoons and Kentucky Mounted Volunteers back to Agua Nueva to assist Colonel Yell. They were directed to "destroy the stores he might be unable to remove," and then to "fall back on the position occupied by the army."[15]

Taylor's field forces, in addition to the units that had escorted him from Victoria, consisted primarily of troops that had marched with General Wool from San Antonio (the First and Second Illinois regiments, a squadron of First Dragoons led by Captain Enoch Steen, Captain John Washington's Fourth Artillery mobile battery to which Brevet Second Lieutenant Darius Couch had now reported, and Colonel Yell's regiment of Arkansas Mounted Volunteers), together with contingents that were previously under Major General Butler: Captain Lucien Webster's First Artillery howitzer battery, a brigade of Second and Third Indiana regiments under Brigadier General Joseph Lane, Colonel Humphrey Marshall's regiment of First Kentucky Cavalry, Colonel William R. McKee's Second Kentucky regiment, a small Texas spy company led by Captain Ben McCulloch, and Captain Patrick Edward Connor's Texas Rifles company, which was attached to the Second Illinois.

In the Kentucky and Indiana regiments were several men who, like those mentioned earlier, would be appointed general officers in the Civil War: Captains Nathan Kimball and Lovell H. Rousseau (Second Indiana); Colonel James H. Lane and Major Willis A. Gorman (Third Indiana); Captain Speed S. Fry and Lieutenant Edward H. Hobson (Second Kentucky); and Colonel Humphrey Marshall and Lieutenant John Hunt Morgan (Kentucky Cavalry). Three men who were absent during the Buena Vista battle, due to their being held as Mexican prisoners of war, would likewise become general officers in the next war: Captain Cassius M. Clay, Lieutenant Thomas J. Churchill (Kentucky Cavalry), and Brevet Second Lieutenant Samuel Sturgis (Second Dragoons).[16]

On the evening of the twenty-first the American pickets at Agua Nueva were driven in by elements of Santa Anna's army. Hastily the men that had returned to assist Colonel Yell set fire to buildings the Americans had been utilizing as well as adjacent stacks of unthreshed wheat, and with their wagon train reached the Buena Vista camp early the following day. Later the Americans learned that Santa Anna had relentlessly forced his men to keep advancing as they crossed the arid wasteland between La Encarnación and Agua Nueva, believing he could surprise Taylor at the latter village and easily overwhelm the small force that had been camped there. Upon being told of Taylor's withdrawal earlier that day, Santa Anna assumed the Americans had panicked and were in full retreat. Anticipating that Taylor would attempt to escape through Saltillo, Santa Anna sent two detachments of cavalry on paths leading to the far side of that village in an effort to block the route to Rinconada Pass and Monterrey.[17]

The Americans guarding La Angostura Pass slept on their arms that night, most of them at their new camp "a little in front of the Hacienda Buena Vista,"[18] but with pickets "at Encantada, three and a half miles distant."[19] The First Illinois volunteers occupied "the high tongue of land commanding the road"[20] through the pass. The next morning, President George Washington's birthday—which coincidence elicited cheers when the Americans were reminded of the date's significance—bands played "Hail Columbia" as the men excitedly took stations assigned by General Wool, all to the east of the road except those serving Captain John Washington's eight guns, positioned across the narrow pass. The American right flank was protected, as pointed out above, by rugged promontories and gullies rising above the meandering stream on the western side of the valley.[21]

Around 9 a.m. Santa Anna's advance cavalry came into view and halted at a point facing Captain Washington's Fourth Artillery battery. As other Mexican divisions formed behind them and to their right, the center of the American line that reached eastward from the road (composed of First Illinois volunteers, and in their rear the Second Illinois and one company of Texans) seemed pitifully minute in comparison. "In a short time," Captain James Carleton would write later of the Mexican army, "their compact and serried masses, thus accumulated, with their flags and pennons flying, and their bright lances sparkling in the sun, extended from the stream nearly half way to the mountains on our left."[22] The whole panorama was visible to Brevet Lieutenant Colonel Joseph Mansfield and a fellow member of the Corps of Engineers, Lieutenant Henry Benham, as they arrived from the army's Saltillo headquarters, the first of Taylor's entourage to reach Buena Vista that morning. Taylor, not having completed his provisions for the defense of Saltillo, and not having as yet been informed that the Mexican advance was near La Angostura Pass, had sent Mansfield and Benham to locate a company of First Dragoons and with them to examine the various passes toward La Encarnación. The two engineers had ridden leisurely from Saltillo, "reconnoitering, taking the bearings, etc., and sketching the obstacles, cross-gullies, and hills" on their route until they met a dragoon with dispatches who called out that the enemy was in view. As Mansfield and Benham rode hurriedly to Wool's camp they observed that "some eighteen hundred of the Mexican cavalry" were "already up, and forming a line to their right, within a half a mile" of the American front line.[23]

Benham, a New Yorker who had graduated at the top of his West Point class in 1837, had arrived at Brazos Island in late January. At Camargo he had been given charge of a large wagon train bound for Monterrey. From there he and Captain Thomas W. Sherman, who was at last on the verge of joining the Third Artillery's Company E, had, in their haste to reach Taylor's headquarters, ridden to Saltillo without an armed escort. Benham would serve as a lookout during the forthcoming action, sending messages to Taylor and his staff members concerning "the numbers and kinds of troops of the enemy" on the field as best he could determine from the ridge on which he was posted. In his recollections of the battle he wrote: "I remained at that position till nightfall, with a small infantry picket, and counted the regiments as they came up as far as possible, and the pieces of artillery, etc., and sent the news in by dragoons from a mounted squad under cover of the spur in my rear. Some forty pieces of artillery were reported, with some eighteen to twenty bodies of infantry, mostly regiments, and sixteen regiments of brilliantly uniformed cavalry, drawn up in two lines on dress-parade that afternoon."[24]

But there was very little fighting on February 22. Taylor, upon reaching the battlefield about midmorning, received at 11 a.m. a letter from Santa Anna, under a flag of truce, saying that the Americans were surrounded by twenty thousand troops, and granting Old Zach an hour to "surrender at discretion." Taylor answered in one sentence: "In reply to your note of this date summoning me to surrender my force at discretion, I beg leave to say that I decline acceding to your request."[25] After that exchange the Mexican general still did not attack, although commencing at 3 p.m. Santa Anna's artillery threw occasional shells toward the American line, without effect. Taylor would report that a "demonstration" by the Mexicans on the right of the Americans resulted in his ordering detachments of artillery (Bragg's battery) and the Second Kentucky regiment to a position across the valley's small stream, west of Washington's battery, where they "bivouacked for the night." Taylor added that meanwhile "the Mexican light troops had engaged ours on the extreme left, (composed of parts of the Kentucky and Arkansas cavalry dismounted, and a rifle battalion from the Indiana Brigade under Major [Willis] Gorman, the whole commanded by Col. [Humphrey] Marshall) and kept up a sharp fire, climbing the mountain side and apparently endeavoring to gain our flank."[26] American soldiers followed suit, facing Ampudia's troops and firing as they climbed the adjacent ridge on the northeast, each of the two columns ascending steep mountainside slopes diagonal to the broad, slanting plain below. "From that time until dark," Carleton recalled, "these troops continued the conflict still higher up the mountain until, at last, there were two lines of combatants from near the plateau to its very summit."[27] At their highest points the two columns of men almost converged, but only four Americans were wounded. At dark, both sides ceased firing. General Taylor returned to Saltillo with the Mississippi regiment and the squadron of Second Dragoons. Most of the rest of Taylor's field army "bivouacked without fires and laid upon their arms"[28] near their Buena Vista camp.

Upon reaching Saltillo that evening, Taylor learned that "a body of [Mexican] cavalry, some 1500 strong, had been visible all day in rear of [Saltillo], having entered the valley through a narrow pass east of the city." To contend with that threat, he arranged for several units to guard his headquarters camp and its wagon train: four companies of volunteers under Major William B. Warren (First Illinois); Captain Lucien Webster's company (First Artillery), with two twenty-four-pound howitzers, in a redoubt on the southeast corner of Saltillo; and two companies of the Mississippi Rifles regiment under Captain William P. Rogers, together with a field piece borrowed from Bragg and commanded by Captain William H. Shover (currently serving as assistant quartermaster).[29]

There were a number of small clashes between opposing pickets during the night, and one Mexican picket was captured by men of the First Illinois. Lieutenant W. H. L. Wallace, adjutant of that regiment, alternated with his colonel, John J. Hardin, in standing watch at the breastwork adjacent to La Angostura Pass.[30] The First Dragoons worked half the night, having been "ordered by General Wool" to strike their camp at Buena Vista, "pack it in wagons, and then to park these carefully in one of the hollows between the hacienda and La Angostura."[31] The plateau on which the bulk of the army spent the night, Sam French would declare, was "6,140 feet above tide water." He almost perished from the cold before the night ended. "Yet there was nothing severely frozen," he recalled, "only the wind carried off all the heat from our bodies. . . . My servant was in camp in Saltillo, and I do not remember getting any breakfast; I know I had no dinner or supper." French slept on a blanket on the ground between Lieutenant John Reynolds and Major John Munroe. Reynolds, whose battery had been in reserve during the afternoon's action, wrote of the night: "It was a bitter cold night and I had a slight inclination to a chill and was fearful I should be sick the next day." However, fortified on the morning of the twenty-third with "a piece of ham and hard bread," he was ready for whatever lay ahead. "I never went into action in better spirits in my life, the excitement entirely dissipated any sign of a return of my chills—and tho' I know our Arty [artillery] was not as efficient as it should be, for we had only a few weeks ago received 30 recruits, so all our gunners, or cannoneers, were raw, and scarcely drilled men who had never been in a fight, our drivers were the old soldiers we had at Monterey."[32]

The battle of February 23 began where the previous day's fighting occurred, on the Americans' extreme eastern (left) flank. There, on the highest reaches of the battlefield, Kentucky and Arkansas dismounted cavalry, together with Indiana riflemen under Major Gorman, had clung to the mountainside all night. As Carleton would explain, this section of the American position was quickly augmented: "General Wool . . . detached Major [Xerxes] Trail of the 2nd Illinois Volunteers, with another small battalion of riflemen, including Captain

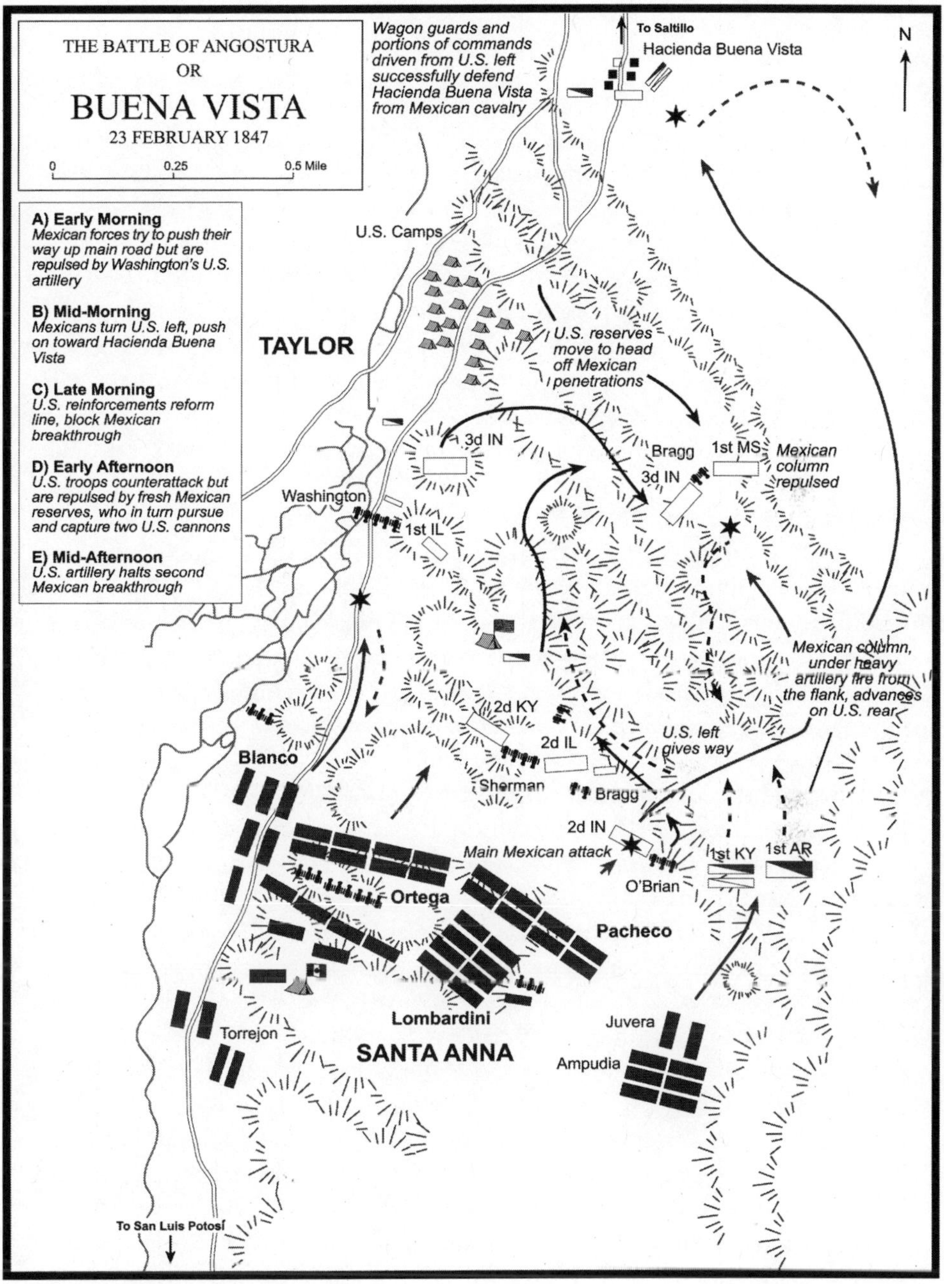

5. Buena Vista, February 22, 1847

Conner's [Patrick Edward Connor's] company of the Texas Volunteers, to reinforce the command which had there engaged the enemy with much spirit.... It was soon assisted, likewise, by Lieutenant [John P. J.] O'Brien [Fourth Artillery], who, along with the 2nd Indiana Volunteers, had remained at the upper edge of the plateau for the night. His pieces were one 12-pounder howitzer, one 6-pounder gun, and one 4-pounder."[33] To O'Brien's north, sheltered under the edge of an almost impassable gully, were several companies of Arkansas and Kentucky cavalry.

As for the other American units on the battlefield, there was a considerable gap between O'Brien's guns and the companies of Second Illinois volunteers directly below him. The Second Illinois men were at the head of a deep gorge between two others running down to the road south of La Angostura Pass. Flanking them were, on their left, Sam French with a howitzer and, on their right, a section of Captain Thomas Sherman's Third Artillery battery commanded by Lieutenant George Thomas. (Sherman himself and John Reynolds, with their guns, were initially held in reserve in the direction of the hacienda.) Next, below the Second Illinois in descending order were the positions occupied by the First Dragoons and by McCulloch's Texans. Then, considerably lower still, in the vicinity of the pass, was the rest of Captain John Washington's Fourth Artillery battery. It was sustained by eight companies of the First Illinois, located on a shelf above Washington's left and, in trenches dug during the night, on his right. Bragg's battery and the Second Kentucky, across the creek on the far right as they had been the previous evening, served as part of the army's reserve. In reserve also was the Third Indiana, on a promontory which divided the road in the rear of Washington's battery.[34]

The first setback for the vastly outnumbered Americans occurred at their highest, most eastern front, in the area of O'Brien's Fourth Artillery guns, where the battle opened. The Americans were pressed by the divisions of both General Ampudia and General Francisco Pacheco, the latter advancing up a ravine to the plateau. General Joseph Lane, who was the ranking American officer on the plateau, "ordered forward Lieutenant O'Brien, with his three pieces of artillery, and the Second Regiment of Indiana Volunteers to support him," Lane's intention being to move out of range of the Mexican eight-pounders at the top of a spur beyond the plateau, and perhaps to force General Pacheco's troops back into the ravine up which they were ascending.[35] O'Brien, assisted by Second Lieutenant Francis T. Bryan (topographical engineer), had been felling large numbers of the enemy, but as his battery commenced changing its position Colonel William A. Bowles (Second Indiana), erroneously concluding that the movement signalled a withdrawal, ordered his companies to cease firing and retreat. His Hoosiers, who had been under a heavy fire from the Mexican cannon, fled so rapidly and in such disorder that they could not again be organized as a regiment, though some eventually fought with other units. O'Brien, forced to withdraw when he was no longer supported by the Second Indiana troops, was unable to save one of his guns, the four-pounder, due to many of his horses having been killed or wounded; and at some point Company B, Second Illinois, part of Major Trail's detachment, lost all four of its officers and its first sergeant in a vain attempt to hold its position on the mountainside.[36]

In the meantime a Mexican division under General Mora y Villamil—composed of infantry, lancers, and three pieces of artillery—had marched straight ahead along the road toward La Angostura Pass. Of the skirmish that followed Carleton would write: "Captain Washington completely repulsed over 4000 of the flower of the Mexican army, and convinced them, beyond a doubt, of their inability to force him from his position. He was ably supported by his remaining three subalterns, Lieutenant [Thomas L.] Brent, [Henry M.] Whiting, and [Darius M.] Couch."[37]

Nevertheless, a second setback for the Americans occurred following the headlong retreat of General Lane's Second Indiana volunteers. General Pacheco's division, together with one that had ascended a ridge further south, General Manuel Lombardini's, now concentrated their fire on the forces at the center of the American line—the Second Illinois, the squadron of First Dragoons, and the guns of George Thomas and Sam French. In French's words, he and George Thomas "used canister as rapidly as men . . . could serve the guns." Suddenly French was so severely wounded by a musket ball which lodged in the upper part of his right thigh that, although he remained on the field all day, he had to be helped on and off his horse, and command of his battery was at last turned over to Lieutenant Robert S. Garnett. As for the other units supporting the Second Illinois, Captain Enoch Steen was ordered to move the hopelessly outnumbered dragoons back to the deep ravine north of the plateau, and McCulloch's mounted Texans likewise took cover. Soon the Mexican divisions succeeded in advancing a portion of their troops across the plateau, between the eastern mountains and Colonel Bissell's Second Illinois. As a result, the six Illinois companies and the batteries commanded by French and Thomas were being fired on "in front, on their left flank, and from their left and rear, at the same moment."[38] To prevent their being surrounded, Colonel Bissell was ordered to have his companies "fall back to a point near the ravine" in their rear.[39]

When General Taylor reached the battlefield from Saltillo early that morning, the Second Illinois and the batteries of Thomas and French had been "completely out flanked" and "compelled to fall back." A few of the reserve units had already been called up—the Second Kentucky and Bragg's battery from their position on the extreme right of the American line, and the guns under

Thomas Sherman and John Reynolds from an area behind the ravine that bordered Taylor's left and Santa Anna's right. Sent into the fray also were troops that had been in or near Saltillo—Davis's Mississippi regiment, May's squadron of Second Dragoons, Lieutenant Charles Kilburn with one piece from Bragg's battery, and an Arkansas squadron under Albert Pike that had been on detached duty between Saltillo and Monterrey, and which was placed under the immediate command of Charles May. To assist the Mississippians, Taylor dispatched as well the Third Indiana, until then stationed in reserve some distance behind Washington's battery on La Angostura Pass road. Old Zach also ordered up the First Dragoons under Captain Daniel Rucker from the ravine on the American left. At that point the Americans held only two of their earlier positions, one being the lower plateau nearest the road and the other Captain Washington's at La Angostura Pass.[40]

"The action was for a long time warmly sustained" on the sector of the plateau defended by the Mississippi and Third Indiana troops, General Taylor would report, "the enemy making several efforts both with Infantry and Cavalry" against the American left and "being always repulsed with heavy loss." Later that morning Old Zach, noting that "large masses of the enemy's cavalry" had forced their way along the base of the eastern mountains "further toward Saltillo" and "directly toward Buena Vista," and were opposed only by portions of Yell's and Marshall's mounted volunteers,[41] "ordered the handful of cavalry, then near him on the plateau, to move rapidly to the rear, in order to assist in repelling" those enemy forces.[42] Led by Brevet Lieutenant Colonel Charles May, the column "was composed of four companies of regular Dragoons, viz., one under Lieutenant [Daniel] Rucker, assisted by Lieutenant [Abraham] Buford, one under Lieutenant [James] Carleton, assisted by Lieutenant [Joseph] Whittlesey and Lieutenant [George] Evans, one under Lieutenant [Reuben] Campbell, and one under Lieutenant [Newton] Givens; besides Captain Pike's and Captain [William] Preston's companies of Arkansas Mounted Voklunteers."[43]

Just as a violent rainstorm began pelting the battlefield, a brigade of the enemy's cavalry under General Torrejón turned Taylor's left flank and penetrated as far to his rear as the Buena Vista hacienda. Sent after them were John Reynolds's battery and Charles May's command, but before Reynolds and May reached the hacienda the Mexican cavalry encountered resistance from Arkansas and Kentucky cavalry. Torrejón's lancers thereupon split apart, some escaping by wheeling eastward and a second group by circling the hacienda and galloping up a steep trail on Taylor's right flank. Among the numerous Americans killed during that action was Archibald Yell, colonel of the Arkansas Mounted Volunteers, who was fatally wounded as he urged those of his men who were near the hacienda to resist the Mexican charge. Succeeding him in command of the regiment was a future Confederate brigadier general, Lieutenant Colonel John Selden Roane.[44]

A pause occurred when two Mexican officers raised a white flag and were brought before Taylor. Old Zach ordered his troops to cease firing, assuming a parley was being proposed because the Mexicans claimed to bear a message from Santa Anna, an inquiry as to what Taylor wanted. Afterward the incident was thought to have been a ruse, since the Mexican batteries continued their bombardment as General Wool rode with the purported messengers toward Santa Anna's lines. Wool, once he realized the Mexican artillery was still shooting into the American ranks, immediately turned back to Taylor's position on the plateau.[45]

The incident that was the most widely praised at the time in American newspapers—and that was hailed even in the twentieth century as the one that "broke the back of the Mexican cavalry and won the battle" of Buena Vista[46]—apparently occurred during the afternoon of the twenty-third. Colonel Jefferson Davis, though his Mississippians had fought in the thick of the conflict for most of the day, acquired his nationwide acclaim as an innovative and brilliant officer principally for having aligned the forces then under his command (which included not only the Mississippi Rifles but members of the Indiana brigade as well as one of Captain Sherman's field pieces) in an open-topped, V-angle formation, meanwhile cautioning them to hold their fire until approaching Mexican cavalry surged heedlessly into his trap. But rather than being the product of inspiration, the formation's creation appears to have evolved chiefly as the result of the column's unplanned location between two ridges which merged downward, and Davis's celebrated success in slaughtering and dispersing the enemy on that occasion does not seem to have contributed any more significantly to the outcome of the battle than did other actions. In fact, Davis himself indicated in his official report that his regiment had rendered its most important service when it first attacked "greatly disproportionate numbers" of the enemy early that morning, without support,[47] and it was Braxton Bragg rather than Davis whom General Taylor would credit with having "saved the day." As General Lane remarked, "The fighting throughout consisted of different engagements in different parts of the field, the whole of them warm and well contested; many of them bloody and terrible."[48]

The fact that Davis was shot through the right foot that morning but continued to lead his regiment all day added poignancy to stories of his outstanding performance during the battle.[49] Sam French, who likewise was badly wounded that morning and stayed on the field without medical aid until darkness ended the struggle, would write that he and Davis were together "carried out" that night from the hacienda and "put in a common wagon" that took French to his tent in Saltillo where he was left unattended until morning.[50]

Davis was reportedly watched over by a friend who poured cold water on his wound throughout the night to prevent lockjaw.[51]

During Santa Anna's last advance of the day, which was against the center of the plateau, the American army lost Colonel John J. Hardin (First Illinois), Colonel William R. McKee (Second Kentucky), and Lieutenant Colonel Henry Clay Jr. (Second Kentucky). Santa Anna had moved his eight-pounder battery down nearer the plateau, and had ordered forward a large segment of his forces, including reserves, from a depression in which they had been concealed from the Americans. This column "of over 12,000 men" suddenly confronted and overwhelmed the Illinois and Kentucky troops who had been moving toward the head of the plateau in pursuit of retreating enemy units. Although O'Brien and Thomas fired on the attacking masses with canister, the Kentucky and Illinois men were "soon obliged to give ground" and to seek shelter in a nearby deep, slanting depression. All of the Americans forced into that declivity who were unable to scramble to the safety of Captain Washington's battery were killed by musket fire from the gorge's rim, or by the bayonets of their opponents.[52]

At the same time, a portion of that massive enemy column was advancing down the plateau toward the outpost where Taylor was directing the movements of his troops. No infantry or cavalry being immediately at hand, only "the artillery under Lieutenants O'Brien and Thomas" stood in the way of the attackers, but Taylor had summoned to the plateau Bragg's battery and the rest of Sherman's, as well as the Mississippi and Indiana regiments and the dragoons. Though he lost two more guns and was himself wounded, Lieutenant O'Brien with the assistance of George Thomas held off Santa Anna's horde long enough to permit Bragg's, Sherman's, Davis's, and Lane's men to reach Taylor's plateau position, although not before the general—who characteristically sat calmly on his horse, Old Whitey, in the midst of the fighting—had "his clothes torn and riddled with bullets."[53]

With the unlimbering and firing of Bragg's and Sherman's guns, the enemy's "whole column finally faltered a moment, then gave way." Thereafter the American forces were shifted about somewhat but by sunset the battle of February 23 was essentially over. At its conclusion the two armies were left "standing almost upon the same ground where they had respectively stood the night before."[54] That evening Taylor's troops were again compelled for the most part to "bivouack without fires," inasmuch as it was assumed the conflict would be renewed the next day.[55] Instead, they found that Santa Anna had withdrawn all of his forces overnight to Agua Nueva.[56]

General Taylor would inform the adjutant general that 267 American troops, including 28 officers, were killed on the twenty-third; 456 men were wounded, and 23 were missing. The enemy's casualties were estimated to number at least 1,500 and possibly 2,000; 500 of their dead "were left upon the field of battle."[57]

Brevet promotion would be awarded to nineteen of the officers who would have a prominent role in the Civil War.[58] Among them were artillerists Braxton Bragg (brevet lieutenant colonel); George Thomas, John Reynolds, and Thomas Sherman (brevet majors); and Samuel French (brevet captain). Bragg would also benefit particularly from the endlessly repeated but unlikely story, or various versions thereof, that his outstanding effectiveness at Buena Vista was associated with General Taylor's having instructed him to employ, in the firing of his cannon, "a little more grape" (one of several types of ammunition then in use that consisted of "a cluster of balls bound between wooden blocks" and that enabled the shot "to spray the area").[59]

Perhaps because the Americans came so very close to losing the Buena Vista battle, they tended to regard it as a monumental achievement. Lieutenant John Reynolds wrote his sister Jane that Buena Vista had been "the greatest battle yet," even tougher than Monterrey. Brevet Lieutenant Colonel Joseph Mansfield termed it the "greatest ever fought" by Americans. Captain James Carleton, in his 1848 account of the conflict, agreed: "When the disparity of number,—their condition, respectively, as they approached each other, and their comparative condition after they had separated,—are all carefully considered, the Battle of Buena Vista will probably be regarded as the greatest ever fought on this continent; and it may be doubted if there can be found one that surpasses it in the history of any nation or any age."[60]

General Taylor praised, specifically, each of the conflict's participants mentioned above as well as many others, including future generals Irvin McDowell (First Artillery aide to Wool); John Pope and William Franklin (Corps of Topographical Engineers); Speed Smith Fry (Second Kentucky); Amos B. Eaton (Subsistence Department); Henry H. Sibley (Quartermaster Department); and Thomas L. Crittenden of Kentucky (civilian aide to Old Zach).[61] Of course Taylor was himself widely praised at the time as well as thereafter by a number of his West Pointers. In his autobiography, Sam French wrote of Taylor: "Here we have the achievements of one plain, unpretending practical, common sense man, who was ever observant of duty, and whose declaration was, 'I will fight the enemy wherever I find him,' summed up in four victories—Palo Alto, Resaca, Monterey, and Buena Vista." Toward the end of the nineteenth century Henry Benham concluded his recollections of Buena Vista by stating: "Gen. Taylor, unambitious but to do right, an honest, reliable, well-judging soldier, holding these qualities in common with Grant and with Thomas more than any three prominent officers of the army I have ever known, became . . . president of the United States."[62] At least one of Taylor's critics has intimated that General Wool deserved the most credit for the victory, and that Old Zach was negligent in leaving the field of battle to go to Saltillo.[63] But Taylor trusted the judgment of Brigadier General Wool, whom he had known for many years, as shown by the fact that when controversy arose in January over who should be in command in the Saltillo area he chose Wool over Butler, and doubtless Taylor and Wool discussed in advance matters such as how the troops should be deployed in the former's absence.

General Wool thought the batteries commanded by Bragg, Sherman, and Washington were primarily responsible for the victory: "Without our artillery we could not have maintained our position a single hour." Yet there is certainly merit in Lieutenant W. H. L. Wallace's comments in a letter written a few days later: "Aside from the artillery, all the fighting was done by the citizen soldier. . . . An effort is now being made by regular officers to get up the impression that we [the volunteers] had greatly the advantage in position. . . . You will see by my description that at one time we were nearly surrounded. Where was the advantage of position then? No! nothing but the bull-dog courage and perseverance of the volunteers saved the day."[64]

Clearly the Buena Vista victory added greatly to the acclaim that catapulted Zachary Taylor into the White House, and it undoubtedly had a lot to do with Jefferson Davis's being chosen to lead the Confederacy. Ulysses Grant believed, as mentioned earlier, that it also significantly aided General Scott's victorious entry into Mexico City: "The battle of Buena Vista was probably very important to the success of General Scott at Cerro Gordo and in his entire campaign from Vera Cruz to the great plains, reaching to the City of Mexico. The only army Santa Anna had to protect his capital and mountain passes west of Vera Cruz was the one he had with him confronting General Taylor. . . . If he had been successful at Buena Vista his troops would no doubt have made a more stubborn resistance at Cerro Gordo."[65]

In Henry Benham's account of Taylor's last battle, published after the New Yorker's service as a Union brigadier general of volunteers, he revealed one particularly painful memory. During a pause in the action Benham made a bet with Lieutenant Robert Selden Garnett, a Virginian in the Fourth U.S. Artillery regiment, regarding the size of a shell "filled with musket balls" that "had earlier passed uncomfortably near" Benham. In ending his account of the battle, Benham wrote: "I could not but think sadly of the occurrence thirteen [fourteen] years after, when the winner of that bet [Garnett] lay before me at Corrick's [Carrick's] Ford, his last fight over, with a rebel star upon his shoulder."[66] Robert Selden Garnett, the first general officer on either side killed in the Civil War, died in the action at Carrick's Ford on July 13, 1861.

12
Last Days of Taylor's Army of Occupation

While General Taylor was winning the Buena Vista battle, his badly depleted forces of volunteers in his rear were losing control of the vital Camargo to Monterrey supply line. The route was anchored at its extreme eastern end, Mier and Camargo, by the First Indiana and Third Ohio regiments. At Camargo was the senior officer in that region, Colonel Samuel Ryan Curtis (Third Ohio), a West Pointer (class of 1831) who had resigned his initial Seventh Infantry assignment within a year but in 1862 would serve as a Union major general of volunteers. At the other end, Monterrey, were the First Ohio, garrisoning the city, and in the Citadel a contingent of the First Kentucky, both commanded at the time by Colonel Stephen Ormsby (First Kentucky). Strung along the road between those two locations were detachments of the Second Ohio "under its three field officers," Major William Wall at Punta Aguda, Colonel George Washington Morgan at Cerralvo, and Lieutenant Colonel William Irvin at Marín.[1]

None of them knew until February 24 of the attack on a train "near Ramos, killing about fifty of the wagoners and capturing the escort, which consisted of thirty soldiers of the 1st Kentucky regiment under Lieutenant [William T.] Barbour." In Monterrey, U.S. forces had been fearing that their line of communication had been cut, east and west, since no courier had recently arrived there. Also, Monterrey was unusually quiet—"like a city of the dead" Major Luther Giddings (First Ohio) would later state, leading him to believe residents had been warned that a counterattack might be pending. On February 23 an officer as well as a sentinel there heard firing in the direction of Saltillo, puzzling the city's American occupiers. They thought Taylor's field force was some miles further south, at Agua Nueva. Then on the twenty-fourth Colonel Ormsby received an unexpected appeal for help from a different direction, the eastern outskirts of Monterrey. A messenger from Colonel Irvin brought word "that the enemy had been for some time in force around Marin; that the little garrison was much harassed by the close siege and desultory attacks of the foe; that their ammunition was falling rapidly and that assistance would be acceptable."[2]

The enemy to the east, as was eventually ascertained, was a combination of General Urrea's lancers and General Canales's rancheros. (They were also responsible for the utter destruction that same day of the U.S. wagon train approaching Ramos, and the capture of Lieutenant Barbour's First Kentucky company, though the Americans at Monterrey would not learn of that incident until a weary Kentucky escapee reached them the following day.) Colonel Ormsby, upon learning that Irvin was under siege at Marín, "promptly dispatched Major [John B.] Shepherd of his regiment, with a mixed command of five companies [three First Kentucky, two First Ohio] and two [four-pounder] field pieces, to Irvin's relief." Shepherd, who marched at noon on the twenty-fourth, reached Marín at 9 p.m. without opposition and returned the next evening in advance of Irvin, saying the latter's column was following him and would arrive by nightfall. Fortunately, however, Irvin had camped below Marín, near San Francisco. There he was overtaken by Lieutenant Samuel D. Stuart (Second Ohio), who informed him that "Col. Morgan, with the remainder of the 2nd Ohio regiment, was surrounded by Urrea's troops a short distance from Agua Frio." Without Irvin's knowledge, Morgan's and Wall's detachments had been just behind him, having been ordered earlier to "move forward" to Monterrey, and having passed the terrible detritus of the Ramos massacre on the twenty-fifth where they found no wounded, only "horribly mutilated" bodies. Irvin not only turned his command back immediately on February 25 but also sent word to Monterrey of the situation, where Major Luther Giddings with two hundred men of the First Ohio "set out for the scene of action." Near San Francisco the troops of the First and Second Ohio regiments easily fought off the attackers, although in Morgan's command three men and one friendly Mexican were killed, one wagon driver was mortally wounded, and one soldier slightly. And with no Americans at the Punta Aguda, Cerralvo, and Marín posts, "the enemy obtained temporary possession of the country between Monterey and Camargo."[3]

General Taylor, still at his Saltillo headquarters in early March, evidently did not hear of those clashes for more than two weeks. After giving his brief accounts of the Buena Vista battle to his civilian aide (and future Union major general) Thomas L. Crittenden for delivery to Washington, he had arranged with Santa Anna's forces at Agua Nueva for an exchange of prisoners; had compiled a report on casualties; and upon being informed that Santa Anna's army was retreating further south, had followed it to Agua Nueva. From that village on March 6 his long report on the battle was written, or at least commenced.

Crittenden and his party reached Monterrey on March 3, and two days later started for Camargo, escorted by Major Giddings with a mixed force of some 250 soldiers (three companies of the First Ohio, two of the First Kentucky), two four-pounder cannon, "a dozen Arkansas horsemen," and 150 wagons.[4] The Americans at Monterrey had of course rejoiced and celebrated upon hearing of the Buena Vista victory, firing salutes and ringing the city's bells. They knew, however, that the route to Camargo remained perilous; and Giddings, aware that his column would doubtless encounter resistance, regretted being ordered to convoy wagons going to the rear for supplies, believing that without them a compact detachment, despite opposition, could reach Camargo in five days. As it was, Giddings wrote later, his train was the largest that had "ever passed over the road, . . . with perhaps seven hundred animals in harness," and extended while in motion nearly "two miles in length" along a passage "closely hedged by dense thickets, most suitable and convenient for ambuscading [*sic*]." Under those circumstances he divided the detachment, "three companies marching up in front and two in the rear of the train, each having a piece of artillery, which had the country been more open, would have afforded prompt and efficient protection to the flanks." With him, in addition to Crittenden's party, were "a number of clerks, camp-followers, and other Americans not connected with the army," including two or three children.[5]

Late that first day, Giddings parked the column at the deserted hamlet of Agua Frio, in the bend of a deep ravine, where they found articles "plundered from Lieutenant Barbour's train." The second day they passed through the abandoned villages of Marín and Ramos and "bivouacked at Papagallos." The absence of Mexican residents was perhaps due to the Ramos massacre ten days earlier, for at Ramos Giddings saw the cruelly mangled bodies of wagon drivers, "more than fifty of whom still lay festering there." The third day Giddings's train had almost reached Cerralvo, a distance of twenty-eight miles from Papagallos, when "a long array of Lancers" and other mounted attackers were seen pouring out of the town toward them. With difficulty the American artillery squads and infantrymen defended the train until dark, though they were completely surrounded and twice received proposals that they should surrender. They lost "two soldiers, fifteen drivers and about forty wagons," one filled with exploding ammunition. "Strong picket-guards were thrown out" that evening, "and the men were ordered to lie down in their places and sleep on their arms." But overnight "General Urrea evacuated the town," and on the morning of March 8 the Giddings detachment "took possession of Cerralvo," where they found two wounded Americans who had been "kindly treated by the citizens."[6]

Their troubles were not over, however. Inasmuch as "the teamsters positively and unanimously refused to drive," they could not resume their march to Camargo for four days. Luckily, a friendly Mexican smuggler, along with a disguised volunteer, managed to evade hovering enemy forces by approaching Camargo from the Texas side of the Rio Grande, and Colonel Curtis came to their rescue. With Curtis were "twelve hundred men," consisting of "his own, the 3d Ohio regiment, four companies of the new Virginia regiment under Lieutenant-Colonel [Thomas B.] Randolph,—a squadron of regular dragoons under Lieutenant-Colonel [Thomas T.] Fauntleroy,—four pieces of artillery; and a corps of Texas Horse, lately called into service." Giddings's train, having obtained from Curtis "some needful supplies" as well as "thirty Texas Rangers, to be employed as scouts and flankers," arrived at Camargo on the fifteenth "without further interruption." Five days later Giddings and the companies that left Monterrey with him, now commanded by Colonel Alexander M. Mitchell (First Ohio, recently recovered from his Monterrey wounds), headed back the way they had come with another large train, reinforced with companies of the Virginia regiment, one of dragoons, and one of Texas Rangers. By that time Urrea had retired toward Montemorelos and the Americans had reestablished their control over their line of communication. Yet at Ramos some of the Texans allegedly slaughtered twenty-four Mexicans, "the entire male population of a village." That, as Giddings pointed out, was "one of the darkest passages in the history of the campaign," one that could "not be justified" by "necessity of any kind." He added that "General Taylor made every effort to discover the offenders but without success."[7]

Old Zach had moved his headquarters to his camp near Monterrey on March 9, bringing with him from the Saltillo area "Lieutenant Colonel May's squadron of dragoons, Captain Bragg's battery, (of which the guns and carriages require renewal) the Kentucky horse and the Mississippi regiment." General Wool was left "in command of the troops in front." Not until March 22 did Taylor inform the adjutant general of the difficulty encountered by the Second Ohio detachments of Irvin, Morgan, and Wall in evacuating Punta Aguda, Cerralvo, and Marín. Evidently he had not heard of those skirmishes previously, perhaps because the Second Ohio had been "moved forward" to join General Wool, "leaving four companies under the major [William Wall] at the Rinconada." Furthermore, Taylor had obviously not had time to learn that Giddings's column had been stalled at Cerralvo until the twelfth, when the train was relieved by Colonel Curtis.[8] Nevertheless, apparently having assumed that his line of communication with Camargo had been interrupted, he dispatched a contingent of Kentucky cavalry to Marín under Colonel Humphrey Marshall on March 15 to investigate conditions there. As he later reported to the adjutant general, after Marshall's command departed Old Zach "was advised that the enemy's cavalry was in considerable force near Marin." That evening, "with a mixed command," Taylor rode northeastward, reaching Marín "early the next morning." From Colonel Marshall he learned that the enemy had been in the vicinity, watching a train from Camargo that had camped the previous night at Ramos. As it happened, the approaching wagons were escorted by Colonel Curtis. No doubt it was Curtis who told Old Zach of the Giddings rescue. At any rate, the general dispatched the train Curtis was leading toward Monterrey, "with a portion of the escort, and took up the march with the remainder, in the direction taken by the enemy." The direction indicated by Curtis must have been southward, below Monterrey, for when Taylor and his detachment reached Cadereyta the following morning the general was told that Urrea had retired still further southward, toward Montemorelos. From his "Camp near Monterey" on March 20 Taylor concluded his report of what proved to be his final effort to personally direct an encounter with "the enemy" by explaining: "Not having sufficient mounted force to pursue with any prospect of success, I returned to this place on the 18th instant."[9]

On March 28 Old Zach commenced a letter to the adjutant general by writing, "I have the honor to report that our communications with the rear are now measurably secure, no interruption having taking [*sic*] place since that reported on the 20th instant." By that time the war with Mexico was essentially over for him and for most of the men who fought with him at Buena Vista. While occasional brutal clashes occurred, initiated by first one side and then the other—attacks on American supply trains between Camargo and Monterrey by Mexican rancheros or guerrillas, interspersed with several by parties of American volunteers on noncombatant villagers thought to be harboring or cooperating with enemy brigands—such incidents were of little consequence except to those involved. Meanwhile, the severely wounded men like Sam French and Jefferson Davis were sent home once they were able to travel, and usually did not return. By summer, many volunteers who fought at Buena Vista would be discharged, their one-year enlistment terms having expired; and General Taylor, instructed by the War Department in July to forward yet more troops to Scott if they could be spared, had done so. Although a few replacements arrived, Taylor eventually realized he would not receive the support he would need to mount a new offensive. To Dr. Wood he insisted that Polk, Marcy, and Scott were consciously endeavoring to, in his words, "break me down." He thought that was because he was being promoted as a possible Whig candidate for the office of president in the 1848 elections. He never seems to have grasped how very little President Polk respected him, despite his victories, nor that he and his Army of Occupation had outlived their usefulness, as far as the Polk administration was concerned, except as a means of maintaining the status quo in northeastern Mexico. Nevertheless, he congratulated Scott on his Cerro Gordo victory, and kept him and the Polk administration informed concerning local developments. Moreover, not until Scott occupied Mexico City did Taylor turn over the Army of Occupation to General Wool and board ship for Louisiana on a six-month leave of absence.[10]

The Mexican War was almost over likewise for Colonel Alexander Doniphan's Missouri Mounted troops, among whom were two who would become Civil War brigadiers, Mosby M. Parsons (Confederacy) and John D. Stevenson (Union). Doniphan and his approximately nine hundred men had recently won two battles, the first on Christmas at Brazito, about twenty-five miles above El Paso. They had remained in El Paso, having occupied it without further opposition, until reinforced in early February by Major Meriwether Lewis Clark and one of his batteries. Although by then Doniphan knew he would not find General Wool at Chihuahua, he moved southward again on February 8, escorting a large wagon train. His last major engagement was a hard-fought victory at a Sacramento River crossing, some fifteen miles above Chihuahua, on February 28. Dispatches carried by a trader to and from General Wool followed, resulting in a five-hundred-mile hike for Doniphan's column, southwest through a desolate, rugged wasteland to Parras. When nearing that village the Missourians fought off an attack on a ranch by Lipan warriors, and in the process freed eighteen women and children being held captive by the Indians. After reaching Buena Vista on May 22, they immediately turned eastward, boarded ship at Reynosa on June 1, and were discharged that month, having traveled approximately 3,500 miles from Fort Leavenworth, in the twentieth century still judged to be "one of the most remarkable marches in military history."[11]

The war was winding down as well in New Mexico after the Buena Vista battle was fought, but certain hostile local leaders had earlier fostered an organized effort to rid the territory of Americans. Colonel Sterling Price, the senior American officer then in New Mexico (and a Confederate major general by 1862), having in mid-December arrested some of the conspirators, was not aware that a more widespread resistance to American rule was brewing until a series of murders occurred in the vicinity of Taos on January 19, 1847. Although Indians were believed to have been responsible for the massacre of Charles Bent, the territorial governor whom Kearny had appointed, Price learned that a massive New Mexico revolt was planned. Not wanting to leave Santa Fe undefended, he started north on January 23 with only 353 men and four howitzers. The next day his advance came across a body of about 1,500 insurgents but easily scattered them. At Embudo Pass two companies of Missouri volunteers together with a company of First U.S. Dragoons, to which Ulysses Grant's friend Lieutenant Rufus Ingalls was assigned, tangled with and dispersed a similar body of armed men. At Taos, which Price's detachment (now numbering 479) reached on February 3, the insurgents were barricaded within a compound containing a church and other buildings surrounded by thick adobe walls "pierced for rifles." Price's artillery, by then including a six-pounder gun, failed to create a break in the pueblo's walls that day, despite the best efforts of Lieutenant (future Union brigadier) Alexander B. Dyer. The following day Price's troops finally stormed the pueblo, chopped through the church's walls, and chased the fleeing defenders, killing fifty-one and capturing others. Seven Americans had been killed and forty-five wounded, some mortally, but the Taos victory virtually ended the insurrection in New Mexico.[12]

In January of 1847, one of the war's last major conflicts in California occurred. The previous September, as aforesaid, General Kearny had left Santa Fe with three hundred First Dragoons, a large wagon train, and a party of topographical engineers commanded by a West Point graduate, Lieutenant William H. Emory (class of 1831), a Union brigadier in 1862. Kearny's column, with still another West Pointer, Second Lieutenant John W. Davidson (class of 1845), a future Union brigadier, had followed the Rio Grande southward until they happened to meet Kit Carson on October 6. The celebrated frontiersman was headed eastward with dispatches entrusted to him by Commodore Robert F. Stockton whose naval forces, when Carson left California, had controlled several important ports. At Kearny's insistence, Carson reluctantly joined him, turning over his entrusted official papers to another courier. Then, relying on Carson's reassuring impression of the situation in California, Kearny sent most of his dragoons back to Santa Fe under the command of fifty-year-old Major Edwin V. Sumner who, though wounded later while serving with Scott at Cerro Gordo, would become a Union major general. Kearny next decided to carry his supplies on mules rather than in wagons. After the pack saddles he thereupon ordered from Santa Fe were delivered by Lieutenant Rufus Ingalls, his one-hundred-man expedition rode westward, primarily along the Gila River, ascending and descending steep Indian trails that taxed the strength of animals and men, particularly the mules pulling the column's two mountain howitzers. The troops met and traded with a number of Indian tribes and passed a few Mexican parties, but engaged in no combat until they were approaching San Diego. Upon intercepting mail from Mexican officials in California, they learned that Commodore Stockton had suffered extreme reverses. Kearny confirmed that dismaying revelation when he reached Warner's Ranch on December 2, some sixty miles east of San Diego. He immediately contacted Stockton, whom he had been told was currently headquartered in San Diego, requesting reinforcements. A few days later, on December 5, a mixed thirty-nine-man escort, led by Captain Archibald H. Gillespie, joined forces with Kearny. Unfortunately, as it turned out, Gillespie brought a fateful message from Stockton that a group of belligerent Californians was nearby. Kearny's scouts found them at San Pasqual, a band of about seventy-five lancers, and he decided to surprise them. The dawn attack of December 6 was disastrous from the standpoint of the American party's casualties—though accounts varied, at least eighteen were killed, and Kearny and twelve others severely wounded. The next day Kearny's reduced and battered force won a struggle with the lancers for control of Mule Hill, but their opponents, reinforced, blocked the road to San Diego. Finally, in response to Kearny's several frantic letters to the commodore, which were sneaked through the enemy's lines one at a time by an Indian guide, Carson, and a U.S. Navy lieutenant among others, a large detachment of sailors and marines showed up; and on December 12, with their assistance, Kearny's weary and decimated dragoon column entered San Diego.[13] A month later, in conjunction with Commodore Stockton's forces, Kearny's men engaged in one more major military action in California, the Battle of San Gabriel, which resulted in the successful recapture of Los Angeles and gave the United States indisputable control of Upper California.[14] Thus, after the first year of the war, the Americans in California, New Mexico, and northeastern Mexico were for the most part unchallenged.

The final engagements of the war with Mexico would be fought, over a period of some seven months, by Winfield Scott's forces, a combination of Army of Occupation veterans together with regular and volunteer troops that had not previously served in Mexico. Those of Taylor's officers who fought with him from Palo Alto until their transfer to Scott's command prior to the Buena Vista battle, and then with the general-in-chief throughout his Mexico City campaign—such as Ulysses Grant, James Longstreet, Charles F. Smith, and Edmund Kirby Smith—would have the most Mexican War combat experience, though the significance of that fact is unclear. As for the ones who remained in northern Mexico with the Army of Occupation after Old Zach's departure, morale was poor. In one instance, a pair of regular army topographical engineers enlivened their relatively peaceful duty, according to Braxton Bragg, by shamelessly riding in an "open carriage" along the streets of Monterrey with their youthful, allegedly kidnapped Mexican mistresses.[15]

For the men who would be prominent in the next war, their tours of duty with Taylor's or Scott's forces, or in Texas, New Mexico, or California, undoubtedly made an indelible impression on them, particularly those who had never before faced hostile fire. Apparently each one's Mexican War battle experiences affected his Civil War performance indirectly rather than directly, for the most part, for instance in the psychological realm, stemming from what they had learned of each other long before 1861, as Grant would say of himself. The fact that most were lieutenants or captains in the earlier war, whether in Scott's or Taylor's army or elsewhere, precluded their having had responsibilities at that time comparable to those they would assume in the next war; indeed, among those future generals were quite a few engineers, topographical engineers, and other staff officers who did not command so much as a company before leading Union or Confederate forces. Nevertheless they, as well as a surprising number of Taylor's company-grade officers who thereafter held no significant military command until the Civil War erupted, overnight became heads of regiments and even of vast armies in 1861. Factors other than their military records doubtless contributed to their advancement, of course, such as having influential friends; but clearly for many of its veterans the Mexican War was a springboard toward much higher rank in the next war than they had ever held previously. In the Civil War, therefore, both South and North relied extensively on men whose reputations for distinguished Mexican War service masked—even from themselves perhaps—how little prepared most were for the momentous tasks they were about to undertake. Having held a higher rank in the Mexican War would not necessarily have been helpful in the far more complex ethos of the Civil War; even some of the veterans of the earlier war who stayed in the "old army" until 1861 and had attained impressive ranks, such as Joe Johnston, would have difficulty handling enhanced duties. Yet the sudden advancement of Mexican War veterans with quite limited combat experience may have caused some of them to be overly impressed with their abilities and, as a consequence, overconfident, touchy, and inflexible.

Of the 173 or so future generals with Taylor's Army of Occupation, at least 81 (50 of them West Point graduates) would join Confederate forces, forsaking their earlier oaths to defend the United States. But judging from extant letters and diaries, few if any of Taylor's officers other than Ethan Allen Hitchcock were concerned about the possibility of a cataclysmic confrontation between southerners and northerners. Although some were Whigs and others Democrats, and some disapproved of the war with Mexico and some enthusiastically supported it, there appears to have been no overt political or sectional enmity between them. True, West Pointers tended to think President Polk did not value their expertise, but the only widely acknowledged animus in the Army of Occupation was that which existed between the regulars and volunteers, a particularly ironic situation in light of the dependence by both sides on the induction of civilians in the next war. However, the speed with which so many southern officers resigned their appointments with U.S. forces to join those of the Confederacy indicates there must have been lurking in their minds and hearts all along a sense of predominant loyalty, perhaps almost a tribal connection to the community they considered home, though no such indications appear to any extent in their Mexican War musings. Lacking also were expressions of pity for the slaves in the army's camps, or compassion for slaves who attempted to escape, or criticism of anyone for being a slaveholder. Undoubtedly the possession of slaves was considered an acceptable way of life by most of Taylor's officers, for others if not for themselves. There were, however, occasionally remarks by a few of Taylor's subordinates about the color of the

Mexican citizens they encountered and other matters that pointed to intrinsic racial, ethnic, and nationalistic prejudices or biases. Of course, the views of both northerners and southerners hardened once states began seceding.

Strangely enough, the American commander who won the Mexican War's first major battles continues to be unfairly maligned. In a biography written in the late twentieth century, a distinguished historian not only castigates Taylor time after time but throughout the work adopts a scathing portrayal which records of the period do not substantiate, averring that "Taylor's performance, especially when his activities were questioned by his superiors, illuminated his petulance," and alleging a "well-known ability to lose his temper over relatively petty incidents." And in one recently published biography of Winfield Scott, unwarranted old allegations concerning Taylor are approvingly repeated, for instance that he "held formal education in low esteem"; that he "often belittled his West Point subordinates" and they him; and that he avoided meeting Scott at Camargo out of "pure spite."[16]

The first two accusations in the Scott biography clearly are false. To quote a noted Taylor biographer, Holman Hamilton, "Like many men whose own cultural experience has been curtailed, the proper training of his children became one of the ruling passions of Zachary Taylor's life. He sent his son to Edinburgh, to Paris, to an exclusive Massachusetts preparatory school, and to Yale College."[17] And in letters written during the Mexican War to his son-in-law, Dr. Wood, Taylor incessantly cautioned that his grandchildren should be enrolled in good schools.[18] Equally absurd is the charge that Taylor was often not on good terms with his West Point subordinates. To the contrary, most of the West Pointers in his army seem to have admired him as much as did Grant, Mansfield, Sam French, Benham, and other Academy graduates whose adulatory comments are a matter of record. In fact, in 1848 Brevet Lieutenant Colonel Bragg would acknowledge, rightly, that his assignment to Taylor's command "made me all that I am." (Without Taylor's intervention on his behalf, Bragg would not have led a battery in the Monterrey and Buena Vista battles, and consequently might have exited the war with fewer brevets and less renown.) Lieutenant George Meade, after Old Zach had bidden farewell to thousands of his veterans at Victoria, wrote of Taylor in early February 1847: "Great anxiety is felt for our old and much-loved commander, and a feeling of indignation against the Government for stripping him of all his force is prevalent throughout the army." At about the same time, upon attending a dinner given at Tampico by the officers of the Second Infantry for those of the Second Artillery shortly after their regiments were transferred from Taylor's to Scott's command, a personal friend of Scott's, Captain Robert Anderson (Third Artillery, future defender of Fort Sumter), wrote his wife: "When Genl. Taylor and some others of the Mexican conquerors were toasted, the utmost enthusiasm prevailed. . . . No toast was given Worth—and none, except one not understood by one half at the table, was given to Genl. Scott, until towards the close of the dinner, and that one was very coldly received."[19] Without a doubt, even before his Buena Vista victory most of Old Zach's veterans, including his West Pointers, respected and admired the manner in which he had been conducting his campaign.

Critics of Taylor's failure to meet Scott at Camargo must have either dismissed or neglected to note several mitigating factors pointed out herein. Old Zach, with a division of regulars and one of volunteers, heading toward a rendezvous with General Patterson's column, which was marching from Matamoros, had started for Victoria on December 15, nine days before learning on Christmas Eve, upon receipt of Scott's letter of November 25 from New York, that the general-in-chief was on his way to the war zone. In that document, which was the only message Taylor received from Scott before reaching Victoria, there was no reference to the pending Veracruz expedition. Although Scott mentioned his intention of depriving Taylor of a large part of his army, he also indicated that any transfer of troops from the Army of Occupation would require only a "temporary sacrifice" by Taylor; and of Camargo he said merely: "By December 12th I may be in [New Orleans], at Point Isabel the 17th, and at Camargo, say, 23rd, in order to be within easy corresponding distance from you."[20] No meeting or consultation was suggested by Scott; and inasmuch as Taylor's response included an assurance that he would be "happy to receive" Scott's orders,[21] what basis is there for alleging that by proceeding to Victoria he was being spiteful or defiant? It is true that he was angry and hurt when he realized the government had failed to inform him of Scott's pending arrival in the war zone, and at having been excluded from what obviously portended to be a major new offensive campaign which threatened to leave him in a hazardous situation; but does that mean he should not have continued to Victoria? The War Department had been told of his plans (and presumably Scott had also); and an express sent from Brazos Santiago or Matamoros could have reached him just about as easily at Victoria as at Monterrey or Camargo. Moreover, how was Taylor to know Scott's location on Christmas Eve, assuming he should have endeavored to track down the general-in-chief? In his defense, Taylor was in the middle of a long-planned, complex, exploratory movement. Both Quitman's and Patterson's columns were scheduled to be waiting for him and for Twiggs's division at Victoria. And until further orders arrived, Taylor himself would not know what he should tell those units to do from that point on. Not until January 14, at Victoria, did he receive copies of Scott's fully explanatory communications of January 3 from Camargo, and he had still not received Scott's similarly detailed letter of December 20 from New Orleans. Surely no one cognizant of those circumstances would conclude that Taylor should be charged with having "studiously avoided a meeting" with Scott due to "anger over being stripped of his army," or of having acted out of "pure spite."[22]

Although Captain William Bliss may have smoothed out the language employed in Old Zach's orders and reports, as has often been suggested, the captain did not write the general's Mexican War letters to Surgeon Robert Crooke Wood, who had married the Taylor's eldest daughter, Ann, some seventeen years earlier. Despite an occasional misspelling and departure from standard English grammar (but scarcely more than invested the love letters of West Point graduate Ulysses Grant), those missives reveal an alert, knowledgeable, thoughtful, generous, amiable family man and absentee slave-holding farmer as well as a commander fully cognizant of the various units and subordinates in his large army. Usually several pages in length, they were written hastily before breakfast or at night, about every ten days, in response to communications from Dr. Wood, and were filled with family news and inquiries in addition to remarks on army matters. In almost all of them he evidenced anxiety about Ann and the education of the couple's children (two boys, ages sixteen and fourteen, and two younger girls); about Dr. Wood's tendency to become despondent over being separated from them; and over Medical Department developments. On at least three occasions Taylor, without prompting of any sort, sent Wood four or five hundred dollars. Repeatedly he emphasized some form of his credo that "what we can't remedy should be met & borne with resignation, fortitude & cheerfulness."[23] (Dr. Wood, a Rhode Islander, served the Union army as assistant surgeon general. His two sons fought with Confederate forces.)

Zachary's wife, Margaret, who was residing in Baton Rouge, was in a "feeble state of health" but usually at her side was "Betty" (Mary Elizabeth), the Taylors' youngest daughter, who in 1848 would marry the general's right-hand man, Brevet Lieutenant Colonel William W. S. ("Perfect") Bliss. The Taylors' only son, "Dick" (Richard), age twenty in 1846, suffered from rheumatism. He joined his father in Matamoros in the summer of 1846 but after a month returned to Louisiana for health reasons. In Old Zach's letters there is an undercurrent of concern about the seemingly aimless and footloose lifestyle of his son (who became a planter and a state senator in Louisiana, and by 1864 was a Confederate lieutenant general).

In his letters to Dr. Wood, General Taylor first mentioned on June 21, 1846, the possibility of his becoming a candidate for the presidency, saying he would decline the honor "if proffered," even if he could "reach it without opposition." In much the same words he continued to dismiss the subject until November, when he received the secretary of war's "very cold" letter cancelling the Monterrey temporary cease-fire. Then, commenting that he had heard "from high authority" (probably friends in Congress) of "an intrigue" against him, due to his being mentioned by "certain politicians" as a possible presidential candidate, he slightly changed the tenor of his references to political office: "Even admitting I aspired to that high office for which I have not the most distant intention of doing," he declared, "this is no time for agitating that question, it will be time enough to do so in 1848." A month later, on December 10, he remarked that he hoped the Whig party "would fix on some able politician to fill that high station without connecting my name with the same." He would not say that he would not serve "if the good people were to be imprudent enough as to elect me," though he would "much prefer," at the close of the war, "to retire from the bustle of public life." Thus Taylor had been considering the candidacy matter for some nine months when, in writing Dr. Wood shortly after the Buena Vista battle, he accused "Scott, Marcy & Co." of trying to "break me down," a conclusion that may have contributed to his receptivity to being promoted by influential Whigs as a superhero who deserved to be elected president. And contrary to the impressions of some modern historians, Taylor was not entirely mistaken about the absence of concern for him and his army by the general-in-chief and the secretary of war. While the Veracruz expedition was being assembled in early 1847, prior to the Buena Vista battle, no one in the Polk administration appears to have thought about the possibility that Taylor's hugely attenuated Army of Occupation might be in jeopardy. This lack of any apprehension that Taylor's army was perhaps being too greatly reduced in light of the defensive stand he was now expected to maintain in Mexico is evident in letters exchanged by Scott and Marcy; and when a number of Taylor's veterans attempted to speak with Scott at Tampico in mid-February, prior to Buena Vista, concerning Old Zach's vulnerable situation, George Meade's reaction to the general's response was: "He seemed to be quite insensible to everything but his own expedition, and although the strongest representations were made to him of the critical condition in which we believe General Taylor to be, he only answered, '*Men of straw, men of straw,*' and took no notice."[24]

Until January of 1847 Taylor had never criticized Scott in writing Dr. Wood, although he had occasionally expressed exasperation with, and even contempt for, a few other officers. To the contrary, in August of 1846 he had defended the general-in-chief, saying: "Genl Scott is a man of strong impulse, both writes & speaks with great flippancy & frequently without due reflection . . . but he means well on all occasions & is entirely mistaken if he supposes I am unfriendly to him, . . . the reverse being the case."[25] Furthermore, the shock, distress, and disillusionment Taylor felt when he was belatedly informed of Scott's Veracruz expedition did not immediately change the overall tone of his later letters to Wood, nor did it immediately change his position with respect to seeking the presidency. Yet in losing his respect for Scott, whom he had earlier said he hoped would be the Whig candidate in 1848, he had turned a corner. Though he only infrequently expressed outrage over the way he had been treated by the War Department, he sounded somewhat less modest overall than had formerly been the case. After Buena Vista, he occasionally stressed his accomplishments in writing to Wood and others, and he also began commenting on his political views. In June 1847 he mentioned that he was and always had been "a democrat of the Jeffersonian school, which embodies very many of the principles of the whigs of the present day." If elected, however, he would be "the president of a nation & not of a party."[26] By late September, perhaps around the time dissension began to percolate among Scott's officers following Mexico City's fall to the Americans, the thought of Scott being the Whig nominee had clearly become abhorrent to Taylor: "Between ourselves Genl Scott would stoop to any thing however low & contemptable [*sic*] as any man in the nation, to obtain power or place, & be as arbitrary in using it when in possession."[27] Though Old Zach took no position on the slavery issue before his inauguration, as president he would adamantly oppose the extension of slavery beyond the borders where it already existed, and would steadfastly uphold preservation of the Union as a first principle.

Ironically, Polk is credited with expanding the territory of the United States to nearly half again its previous size, but his achievements along those lines rested largely on the victories of Taylor and Scott, neither of whom he thought "fit for the command of the army." The president's failure to appreciate Taylor's effectiveness doubtless reflected to some extent the views of his fellow Tennesseean and close friend Gideon Pillow. As previously noted, upon dining with Old Zach in mid-August, Brigadier General Pillow had found him a "frank and manly old gentleman." Within three weeks, however, Pillow became resentful when Taylor took the First Tennessee regiment with him to Monterrey while leaving President Polk's favorite appointee in Camargo.[28] Yet it cannot be denied that in several instances Taylor played into the hands of men who tended to be biased against him. He had probably said to others, as he did to Dr. Wood several times, that he feared the Polk administration's obvious interest in depriving Mexico of its northwestern provinces, particularly California, would delay the peace negotiations for which Old Zach fervently longed. His terms for surrender following the Monterrey battle were indeed liberal, as he himself admitted (though he believed that stance would have a pacifying effect and thus would contribute toward ending the war). His approval of the temporary Monterrey cease-fire would lend credence to the accusations that he lacked "the instinct great commanders have for a final crushing blow." He protested bluntly when the War Department issued an order directly to General Patterson rather than through him, the field commander, as was customary, and again when Scott was permitted to divest him of nearly all of his regular army troops. He had already been many months out of favor when a personal letter to Old Zach's friend General Edmund P. Gaines was published which contained comments that infuriated President Polk. Though it was intended to be confidential, and was published without Taylor's consent, it of course caused a stir in Washington.

Yet whatever the shortcomings of "Old Rough and Ready" were, until late 1847 he continued to defend, to the best of his ability, the lines held by the United States in his area of command, though he could never forget having been elbowed aside by the Polk administration and Scott as the war progressed. He stayed with his army, fragile and seemingly neglected as it was, until Scott occupied Mexico City. Then Old Zach requested and was granted a leave of absence, and at Matamoros on October 4, 1847, he formally turned over the Army of Occupation to General Wool.

Certainly Taylor was not as brilliant as Scott, nor was he as astute politically; on the other hand, Old Zach was neither vainglorious nor power hungry. His inordinate courage may have verged on unwise brashness at times, and may have been somewhat responsible for an unfortunate tendency toward overconfidence among many of his veterans in their Civil War battles. Still, as was said of him in 1901 by one of Taylor's former West Point subordinates who became a Confederate major general, Samuel French: "Here we have the achievements of one plain, unpretending practical, common sense man who was ever observant of duty, and whose declaration was, 'I will fight the enemy wherever I find him,' summed up in four victories—Palo Alto, Resaca, Monterey, and Buena Vista."[29]

Zachary Taylor had hoped there would be no war with Mexico, although from past experience he knew that if war broke out he might well earn an additional brevet. The fact that he urged Mexican leaders to accept a peaceful settlement of the border dispute, as he did in writing General Ampudia before the outbreak of war, and General Santa Anna later, may have reflected merely a conservative Whiggish bias; but in retrospect, in light of his vow as a presidential nominee to represent *all* of the people, it is apparent he was convinced that a negotiated solution would be in the best interests of the United States. He was evidently not reluctant to move his army to the Rio Grande, believing a show of force would prevent Mexico from taking aggressive action. Once his dragoons were ambushed by General Torrejón's forces, however, it mattered as little to him as it did to Polk and Congress whether the war was justified due to American blood having been spilled on American soil. Yet there was clearly a difference in attitude between Old Zach, who longed for each battle to bring peace, and President Polk, whose thoughts dwelled more on what the United States would gain from Mexico at the war's conclusion.

President Polk clearly did not appreciate how well Taylor served the nation during the war's first ten months, nor did General Scott or Secretary of War Marcy. Modern historians, in emphasizing Scott's brilliance, have also tended to dismiss the significance of Taylor's campaign. Nevertheless, despite a lack of much-needed materiel and, at Buena Vista, the absence of regular army units siphoned off to fight with Scott in central Mexico, Taylor achieved a remarkable record as commander of the Army of Occupation. He deserves to be honored for that record, and for dedicating himself wholeheartedly to his duty as a wartime commander, to the welfare of the men in his army, and to the well-being of the United States.

Appendix
Future Civil War Leaders in Taylor's Army

Confederate	Union
Anderson, Richard H., USMA 1842, Lt. Gen. CSA	Abercrombie, John J., USMA 1822, Brig. Gen. USV
Anderson, Samuel R. Brig. Gen. CSA	Alvord, Benjamin, USMA 1833, Brig. Gen. USV
Armistead, Lewis A. Brig. Gen. CSA	Augur, Christopher C., USMA 1843, Maj. Gen. USV
Beauregard, Pierre G. T., USMA 1838, Gen. CSA	Baker, Edward D. Maj. Gen. USV
Bee, Barnard E., USMA 1845, Brig. Gen. CSA	Barnard, John G., USMA 1833, Brig. Gen. USV
Bee, Hamilton P. Brig. Gen. CSA	Beatty, Samuel Brig. Gen. USV
Blanchard, Albert G., USMA 1829, Brig. Gen. CSA	Benham, Henry W., USMA 1837, Brig. Gen. USV
Bragg, Braxton, USMA 1837, Gen. CSA	Brannan, John M., USMA 1841, Brig. Gen. USV
Bryan, Goode, USMA 1834, Brig. Gen. CSA	Brooks, William T. H., USMA 1841, Brig. Gen. USV (Maj. Gen. 6/1863, revoked 4/1864)

Buckner, Simon B., USMA 1844,
Lt. Gen. CSA

Buford, Abraham, USMA 1841,
Brig. Gen. CSA

Cheatham, Benjamin F.
Maj. Gen. CSA

Chilton, Robert H., USMA 1837,
Brig. Gen. CSA (not confirmed by Senate)

Churchill, Thomas J.
Maj. Gen. CSA

Clark, Charles
Brig. Gen. CSA

Colquitt, Alfred H.
Brig. Gen. CSA

Cooper, Douglas H.
Brig. Gen. CSA

Davis, Jefferson, USMA 1828,
President CSA

Early, Jubal, USMA 1837,
Lt. Gen. CSA

Elzey, Arnold, USMA 1837,
Maj. Gen. CSA

Ewell, Richard S., USMA 1840,
Lt. Gen. CSA

Fagan, James F.
Maj. Gen. CSA

Fauntleroy, Thomas T.
Brig. Gen. VA Vols. CSA

Forney, William H.
Brig. Gen. CSA

Buchanan, Robert C., USMA 1830,
Brig. Gen. USV (Bvt. Maj. Gen.)

Buell, Don Carlos, USMA 1841,
Maj. Gen. USV

Campbell, William B.
Brig. Gen. USV

Carleton, James H.
Brig. Gen. USV

Clay, Cassius M.
Maj. Gen. USV

Connor, Patrick E.
Brig. Gen. USV

Couch, Darius N., USMA 1846,
Maj. Gen. USV

Curtis, Samuel R., USMA 1831,
Maj. Gen. USV

Dana, Napoleon J. T., USMA 1842,
Maj. Gen. USV

Doubleday, Abner, USMA 1842,
Maj. Gen. USV

Eaton, Amos B., USMA 1826,
Brig. Gen. (Comsy. Gen. Sub.) USA

Franklin, William B., USMA 1843,
Maj. Gen. USV

French, William H., USMA 1837,
Maj. Gen. USV

Fry, Speed S.
Brig. Gen. USV

Gorman, Willis A.
Brig. Gen. USV

French, Samuel G., USMA 1843,
Maj. Gen. CSA

Frost, Daniel M., USMA 1844,
Brig. Gen. CSA

Gardner, Franklin, USMA 1843,
Maj. Gen. CSA

Gardner, William M., USMA 1846,
Brig. Gen. CSA

Garnett, Robert S., USMA 1841,
Brig. Gen. CSA

Gatlin, Richard C., USMA 1832,
Brig. Gen. CSA

Green, Thomas
Brig. Gen. CSA

Griffith, Richard
Brig. Gen. CSA

Hanson, Roger W.
Brig. Gen. CSA

Hardee, William J., USMA 1838,
Lt. Gen. CSA

Hill, Daniel Harvey, USMA 1842,
Lt. Gen. CSA

Hindman, Thomas C.
Maj. Gen. CSA

Holmes, Theophilus H., USMA 1829,
Lt. Gen. CSA

Huger, Benjamin, USMA 1825,
Maj. Gen. CSA

Jackson, Henry R.
Brig. Gen. CSA

Graham, Lawrence Pike
Brig. Gen. USV

Grant, Ulysses S., USMA 1843,
Lt. Gen. USA (Commander-in-Chief)

Hamilton, Charles S., USMA 1843,
Maj. Gen. USV

Hamilton, Schuyler, USMA 1841,
Maj. Gen. USV

Harney, William S.
Brig. Gen. USA

Haskin, Joseph A., USMA 1839,
Brig. Gen. USV

Hatch, John Porter, USMA 1845,
Brig. Gen. USV

Hays, Alexander, USMA 1844,
Brig. Gen. USV

Hays, William, USMA 1840,
Brig. Gen. USV

Hitchcock, Ethan Allen, USMA 1817,
Maj. Gen. USV

Hobson, Edward H.
Brig. Gen. USV

Hooker, Joseph, USMA 1837,
Brig. Gen. USA

Hunter, David, USMA 1822,
Maj. Gen. USV

Judah, Henry M., USMA 1843,
Brig. Gen. USV

Kearny, Philip
Maj. Gen. USV

Jackson, Thomas J., USMA 1846,
Lt. Gen. CSA

Johnson, Bushrod R., USMA 1840,
Maj. Gen. CSA

Johnson, Edward, USMA 1838,
Maj. Gen. CSA

Johnston, Albert S., USMA 1826,
Gen. CSA

Jordan, Thomas, USMA 1840,
Brig. Gen. CSA

Lane, Walter P.
Brig. Gen. CSA

Lee, Robert E., USMA 1829,
Gen.-in-Chief CSA

Little, Lewis H.
Brig. Gen. CSA

Longstreet, James, USMA 1842,
Lt. Gen. CSA

Lovell, Mansfield, USMA 1842,
Maj. Gen. CSA

McCown, John P., USMA 1840,
Maj. Gen. CSA

McCulloch, Benjamin
Brig. Gen. CSA

McCulloch, Henry E.
Brig. Gen. CSA

Mackall, William W., USMA 1837,
Brig. Gen. CSA

Kenly, John R.
Brig. Gen. USV

Kimball, Nathan
Brig. Gen. USV

King, John H.
Brig. Gen USV

Lane, James H.
Brig. Gen. USV (cancelled 1863)

Lawler, Michael K.
Brig. Gen. USV

McCall, George A., USMA 1822,
Brig. Gen. USV

McClellan, George B., USMA 1846,
Maj. Gen. USA (Commander-in-Chief)

McDowell, Irvin, USMA 1838,
Maj. Gen. USV

McGinnis, George F.
Brig. Gen. USV

Mansfield, Joseph K. F., USMA 1822,
Maj. Gen. USV

Marcy, Randolph B., USMA 1832,
Brig. Gen. USV

Meade, George G., USMA 1835,
Maj. Gen. USA

Milroy, Robert H.
Maj. Gen. USV

Montgomery, William R., USMA 1825,
Brig. Gen. USV

Morgan, George Washington
Brig. Gen. USV

McLaws, Lafayette, USMA 1842,
Maj. Gen. CSA

Magruder, John B., USMA 1830,
Maj. Gen. CSA

Maney, George E.
Brig. Gen. CSA

Marshall, Humphrey, USMA 1832,
Brig. Gen. CSA

Martin, James G., USMA 1840,
Brig. Gen. CSA

Maury, Dabney H., USMA 1846,
Maj. Gen. CSA

Morgan, John H.
Brig. Gen. CSA

Nelson, Allison
Brig. Gen. CSA

Parsons, Mosby M.
Brig. Gen. CSA

Pemberton, John C., USMA 1837,
Lt. Gen. CSA

Pickett, George E., USMA 1846,
Maj. Gen. CSA

Pike, Albert
Brig. Gen. CSA

Pillow, Gideon J.
Brig. Gen. CSA

Posey, Carnot
Brig. Gen. CSA

Rains, Gabriel J., USMA 1827,
Brig. Gen. CSA

Morgan, James D.
Brig. Gen. USV

Oglesby, Richard J.
Maj. Gen. USV

Patrick, Marsena R., USMA 1835,
Brig. Gen. USV

Patterson, Robert
Maj. Gen. Pa. Vols.

Paul, Gabriel R., USMA 1834,
Brig. Gen. USV

Peck, John J., USMA 1843,
Maj. Gen. USV

Phelps, John W., USMA 1836,
Brig. Gen. USV

Pitcher, Thomas G., USMA 1845,
Brig. Gen. USV

Pleasonton, Alfred, USMA 1844,
Maj. Gen. USV

Plummer, Joseph B., USMA 1841,
Brig. Gen. USV

Pope, John, USMA 1842,
Maj. Gen. USV

Porter, Andrew
Brig. Gen. USV

Porter, Fitz-John, USMA 1845,
Maj. Gen. USV

Potter, Joseph H., USMA 1843,
Brig. Gen. USV

Prentiss, Benjamin M.
Maj. Gen. USV

Ripley, Roswell S., USMA 1843,
Brig. Gen. CSA

Roane, John S.
Brig. Gen. CSA

Ruggles, Daniel, USMA 1833,
Brig. Gen. CSA

Scurry, William R.
Brig. Gen. CSA

Sibley, Henry H., USMA 1838,
Brig. Gen. CSA

Smith, Edmund Kirby, USMA 1845,
Gen. CSA

Smith, Gustavus W., USMA 1842,
Maj. Gen. CSA

Steele, William, USMA 1840,
Brig. Gen. CSA

Stevenson, Carter L., USMA 1838,
Maj. Gen. CSA

Twiggs, David E.
Maj. Gen. CSA

Van Dorn, Earl, USMA 1842,
Maj. Gen. CSA

Wilcox, Cadmus M., USMA 1846,
Maj. Gen. CSA

Williams, John S.
Brig. Gen. CSA

Ramsay, George D., USMA 1820,
Brig. Gen. Chief of Ord. USV

Reynolds, John F., USMA 1841,
Maj. Gen. USV

Reynolds, Joseph J., USMA 1843,
Maj. Gen. USV

Richardson, Israel B., USMA 1841,
Maj. Gen. USV

Ricketts, James B., USMA 1839,
Brig. Gen. USV

Roberts, Benjamin S., USMA 1835,
Brig. Gen. USV

Robinson, John C.
Brig. Gen. USV

Ross, Leonard F.
Brig. Gen. USV

Rousseau, Lovell H.
Maj. Gen. USV

Rucker, Daniel H.
Brig. Gen. USV

Sedgwick, John, USMA 1837,
Maj. Gen. USV

Sherman, Thomas W., USMA 1836,
Brig. Gen. USV

Shields, James
Brig. Gen. USV

Smith, Charles F., USMA 1825,
Maj. Gen. USV

Smith, Green C.
Brig. Gen. USV

Sturgis, Samuel D., USMA 1846,
Brig. Gen. USV

Sykes, George, USMA 1842,
Maj. Gen. USV

Thomas, George H., USMA 1840,
Maj. Gen. USA

Thomas, Lorenzo, USMA 1823,
Brig. Gen., A.G., USA

Van Derveer, Ferdinand
Brig. Gen. USV

Wallace, Lewis
Maj. Gen. USV

Wallace, William H. L.
Brig. Gen. USV

Williams, Seth, USMA 1842,
Brig. Gen. USV

Wood, Thomas J., USMA 1845,
Maj. Gen. USV

Wool, John E.
Maj. Gen. USA

Notes

ABBREVIATIONS

AAG	Assistant Adjutant General
AD	Autograph Document
ADS	Autograph Document Signed
AG	Adjutant General
AGO	Adjutant General's Office
ALS	Autograph Letter Signed
AOO	Army of Occupation
LC	Library of Congress
M	Microcopy, National Archives
NA	National Archives
UNC	University of North Carolina
USMA	United States Military Academy

PREFACE

1. Holman Hamilton, *Zachary Taylor, Soldier of the Republic* (Hamden, CT: Archon Books, 1966), 140; K. Jack Bauer, *Zachary Taylor: Soldier, Planter, Statesman of the Old Southwest* (Baton Rouge: Louisiana State University Press, 1985), 13–16, 82–83. For an example of a historian's usage of the nickname "Old Zach," see Edward J. Nichols, *Zach Taylor's Little Army* (Garden City, NY: Doubleday, 1963), 8. One author changed the spelling to "Old Zack": John S. D. Eisenhower, *So Far from God: The U.S. War with Mexico, 1846–1848* (New York: Random House, 1989), 29.

2. No complete list of regular and volunteer army officers who were engaged in both the Mexican War and Civil War has been located. The numbers of such officers estimated herein are a product of the author's search for the service records through 1865 of officers indicated by government documents as having served in the Mexican War. For Civil War service, sources chiefly relied on were biographies; Francis B. Heitman, *Historical Register and Dictionary of the United States Army, from Its Organiza-*

tion, September 29, 1789, to March 2, 1903 (2 vols., Washington, DC: Government Printing Office, 1903); *Appleton's Cyclopedia of American Biography* (6 vols., New York: D. Appleton and Company, 1888); Dumas Malone, ed., *Dictionary of American Biography* (20 vols., New York: Charles Scribner's Sons, 1927); and volumes 1 and 2 of George Washington Cullum, ed., *Biographical Register of the Officers and Graduates of the United States Military Academy* (3 vols., Boston: Houghton Mifflin, 1891).

3. Eisenhower, *So Far from God;* K. Jack Bauer, *The Mexican War, 1846–1848* (New York: Macmillan, 1974); Bauer, *Zachary Taylor,* 1985.

4. For the Mexican War as a training ground for the Civil War, see: Bauer, *Mexican War,* 395; Alfred Hoyt Bill, *Rehearsal for Conflict* (New York: Alfred A. Knopf, 1947), ix, x; Shelby Foote, *The Civil War, a Narrative* (3 vols., New York: Random House, 1958–74), 1:111; Edward J. Nichols, *Toward Gettysburg: A Biography of General John F. Reynolds* (State College: Pennsylvania State University Press, 1958), 47.

5. For presence in the war zone, see: Bvt. Capt. William Bliss to Adjutant General Roger Jones, August 3, 1846, List of the Commissioned Officers of the U.S. Army present in the actions of Palo Alto and Resaca de la Palma on the 8th and 9th days of May, 1846 (including those at Fort Brown), Letters Received by the AGO (Main Series), 1822–60, Record Group 94, M567, Roll 328, NA; Hal Bridges, *Lee's Maverick General, Daniel Harvey Hill* (New York: McGraw-Hill, 1961), 19, 20; John Sedgwick, *Correspondence of John Sedgwick, Major-General* (2 vols., n.p., 1902), 1:2; Charles P. Roland, *Albert Sidney Johnston, Soldier of Three Republics* (Austin: University of Texas Press, 1964), 125–27; Jefferson Davis, *Private Letters, 1823–1889,* ed. Hudson Strode (New York: Harcourt, Brace and World, 1966), 40; Stephen W. Sears, *George B. McClellan, The Young Napoleon* (New York: Ticknor and Fields, 1988), 14; Thomas Jackson Arnold, *Early Life and Letters of General Thomas J. Jackson, "Stonewall" Jackson* (New York: Fleming H. Revell, 1916), 78–82; Dabney Herndon Maury, *Recollections of a Virginian in the Mexican, Indian, and Civil Wars* (New York: Charles Scribner's Sons, 1894), 27–28; Douglas Southall Freeman, *R. E. Lee: A Biography* (4 vols., New York: Charles Scribner's Sons, 1934), 1:202–3; Winfield Scott, *Memoirs of Lieut.-General Scott, LL.D., Written by Himself* (2 vols., New York: Sheldon, 1864), 2:397–403.

6. Elizabeth Brown Pryor, *Reading the Man: A Portrait of Robert E. Lee through His Private Letters* (New York: Viking, 2007), 175.

7. For Lee and Longstreet at Appomattox, see Jeffry D. Wert, *General James Longstreet, the Confederacy's Most Controversial Soldier: A Biography* (New York: Simon and Schuster, 1993), 403.

8. Ulysses S. Grant, *Personal Memoirs* (2 vols., New York: Charles A. Webster, 1885–86), 1:193. See also Justin Harvey Smith, *The War with Mexico* (2 vols., Gloucester, MA: Peter Smith, 1963): "While vast concentrations of forces and complicated tactical operations on a grand scale were out of the question, the handling of even small armies at a long distance from home in a region that was not only foreign but strange, created problems of a peculiar interest and afforded lessons of a peculiar value, such as no earlier or later war of ours has provided" (1:vii).

9. George McClellan wrote Federica English on May 13, 1846, "Hip! Hip! Hurrah! War at last sure enough! Aint it glorious!" (as qtd. in Sears, *George B. McClellan,*

11); Grant to Julia Dent, October 3, 1846, in John Y. Simon, ed., *The Papers of Ulysses S. Grant* (15 vols., Carbondale: Southern Illinois University Press, 1967), 1:113.

10. For Roswell Ripley's "dim view of Taylor," see Nichols, *Zach Taylor's Little Army,* 266; Nathaniel Cheairs Hughes Jr. and Timothy D. Johnson, eds., *A Fighter from Way Back: The Mexican War Diary of Lt. Daniel Harvey Hill, 4th Artillery, USA* (Kent, OH: Kent State University Press, 2002), 8; Lew [Lewis] Wallace, *An Autobiography* (2 vols., New York: Harper and Bros., 1906), 1:121–92; Irving McKee, *"Ben-Hur" Wallace, The Life of General Lew Wallace* (Berkeley: University of California Press, 1947), 15–17.

11. Timothy D. Johnson, *Winfield Scott: The Quest for Military Glory* (Lawrence, KS: University Press of Kansas, 1998), 153, 162; Allan Peskin, *Winfield Scott and the Profession of Arms* (Kent, OH: Kent State University Press, 2003), 145–47, 203–4.

12. Grady McWhiney, *Braxton Bragg and Confederate Defeat,* Vol. 1 of 2 (1969; reprint, Tuscaloosa: University of Alabama Press, 1991), 106.

13. [Henry W. Benham], *Recollections of Mexico and the Battle of Buena Vista, Feb. 22 and 23, 1847, by an Engineer Officer, on Its Twenty-fourth Anniversary* (Boston: n.p., 1871), 26–27. For Maury's comparison of Stonewall Jackson and Zachary Taylor, see Maury, *Recollections of a Virginian,* 29.

14. Grant, *Personal Memoirs,* 1:134.

15. William H. Samson, ed., *Letters of Zachary Taylor from the Battle-Fields of the Mexican War* (Rochester, NY: Genesee Press, 1908), 28.

CHAPTER 1

1. AGO, Monthly Returns, Third and Fourth Infantry, NA, M665, Rolls 31 and 43, respectively; Second Dragoons, NA, M744, Roll 14; Post Returns, M617, Jefferson Barracks, Fort Jesup, and Camp Salubrity, Rolls 546, 555, and 1538 respectively. AGO, War Department General Orders 14 (April 11, 1844) and 18 (April 22, 1844), in *Army and Navy Chronicle, and Scientific Repository,* 3:653, 654; W. A. Croffut, ed., *Fifty Years in Camp and Field: Diary of Major-General Ethan Allen Hitchcock, U.S.A.* (New York: G. P. Putnam's Sons, 1909), 185; Hamilton, *Zachary Taylor,* 156–58; William Seaton Henry, *Campaign Sketches of the War with Mexico* (New York: Harper and Brothers, 1847), 7–9; Richard Bruce Winders, *Mr. Polk's Army: The American Military Experience in the Mexican War* (College Station: Texas A&M University Press, 1997), 18–19: "The Adjutant-General's Department linked the various components of the army together by acting as a clearinghouse for all official correspondence. . . . Official documents such as general and special orders, morning reports, and court-martial proceedings were deposited in the adjutant general's office at Washington, D.C."

2. Secretary of War William Wilkins to President John Tyler, May 13, 1844, *Army and Navy Chronicle,* 3:653; John Tyler, "Message from the President of the United States to the Senate," *Army and Navy Chronicle,* May 15, 1844, 3:652–53; Oliver Perry Chitwood, *John Tyler, Champion of the Old South* (Newtown, CT: American Political Biography Press, 1996), 351.

3. Bauer, *Mexican War,* 6–10; Chitwood, *John Tyler,* 6–40, 144–56; 342–66; Eisenhower, *So Far from God,* 17–20; Justin Smith, *War with Mexico,* 1:82–87.

4. AGO, Monthly Returns, Second Dragoons, NA, M744, Roll 14; AGO, Monthly

Returns, Mounted Riflemen, NA, M744, Roll 27; Albert Gallatin Brackett, *History of the United States Cavalry, from the Formation of the Federal Government to the 1st of June 1863* (New York: Harper, 1865), 37–39, 46–49; Joseph I. Lambert, *One Hundred Years with the Second Cavalry: By the Commanding Officer, Second Cavalry* (Fort Riley, KS: Capper, 1939), 8–9, 11–16, 24–25; Theophilus Francis Rodenbough, *From Everglade to Cañon with the Second Dragoons, 1836–1875* (Chicago: D. and C. H. Blakely, 1875), 19, 79–86; Hamilton, *Zachary Taylor,* 164; Justin Smith, *War with Mexico,* 2:48; Brainerd Dyer, *Zachary Taylor* (New York: Barnes and Noble, 1967, reprint), 118, 125.

5. AGO, Monthly Returns, Second Dragoons, NA, M744, Roll 14; Heitman, *Historical Register,* 1:499–919; Lambert, *One Hundred Years,* 24–25; Rodenbough, *From Everglade to Cañon,* 85.

6. AGO, Monthly Returns, Third and Fourth Infantry, NA, M665, Rolls 31 and 43 respectively; Wilkins to Tyler, May 13, 1844, *Army and Navy Chronicle,* 3:653; Croffut, ed., *Fifty Years in Camp and Field,* 190.

7. Bauer, *Mexican War,* 18; Croffut, ed., *Fifty Years in Camp and Field,* 1–185; Eisenhower, *So Far from God,* 33; Foote, *Civil War,* 1:266–67; Heitman, *Historical Register,* 1:532.

8. AGO, Monthly Returns, Third Infantry, NA, M665, Roll 31; Croffut, ed., *Fifty Years in Camp and Field,* 185; J. Fair Hardin, "Fort Jesup, Fort Selden, Camp Sabine, Camp Salubrity, Four Forgotten Frontier Army Posts of Western Louisiana," in *Louisiana Historical Quarterly* 16.1 (Jan. 1933): 5–26; 16.2 (Apr. 1933): 279–92; 16.3 (July 1933): 441–53; 16.4 (Oct. 1933): 670–80; 17.1 (Jan. 1934): 139–54; Hitchcock to Jones, May 1, 6, and 11, 1844, AGO, Letters Received, NA, M567, Roll 286.

9. Hardin, "Fort Jesup," 16.1 (Jan. 1933): 10–11, 20, 26; Henry, *Campaign Sketches,* 7–9; Croffut, ed., *Fifty Years in Camp and Field,* 189; Rodenbough, *From Everglade to Cañon,* 83.

10. AGO, Monthly Returns, Fourth Infantry, NA, M665, Roll 43; Vose to Jones, May 26, 1844, AGO, Letters Received, NA, M567, Roll 292; Henry, *Campaign Sketches,* 8.

11. Heitman, *Historical Register,* 1:990; Bvt. Brig. General William J. Worth to Maj. Gen. Winfield Scott, March 4, 1844, AGO, Letters Received, NA, M567, Roll 292; Vose to Jones, June 4, 1844, AGO, Letters Received, NA, M567, Roll 292; Ulysses S. Grant to Julia Dent, July 6, 1845, in Simon, ed., *Papers of Ulysses S. Grant,* 1:49.

12. Jones to Taylor, April 23 and 27, 1844, *Army and Navy Chronicle,* 3:654–55; Hamilton, *Zachary Taylor,* 119, 142–55, 157; Bauer, *Mexican War,* 6; Dyer, *Zachary Taylor,* 128–48.

13. Hamilton, *Zachary Taylor,* 21–33, 39–141; Heitman, *Historical Register,* 1:949; Dyer, *Zachary Taylor,* 3–127; Bauer, *Zachary Taylor,* 1–110.

14. John P. Hatch to Eliza, October 28, 1845, ALS, John P. Hatch Papers, LC, Washington, DC; Hamilton, *Zachary Taylor,* 153–54; Justin Smith, *War with Mexico,* 1:140–41; Wert, *General James Longstreet,* 36; Samson, ed., *Letters of Zachary Taylor,* vii–xxvi; Dyer, *Zachary Taylor,* 128–32.

15. Scott, *Memoirs,* 1:381–82; Wilkins to Tyler, May 13, *Army and Navy Chronicle,* 3:653–55; General Orders No. 14, April 11, and No. 18, April 22, *Army and Navy Chronicle,* 3:653–55; Jones to Taylor, April 23 and 27, 1844, *Army and Navy Chronicle,* 3:653–55.

16. Jones to Taylor, April 27, 1844, *Army and Navy Chronicle,* 3:654–55; Hamilton, *Zachary Taylor,* 157; Croffut, ed., *Fifty Years in Camp and Field,* 185; Dyer, *Zachary Taylor,* 147–48.

17. Taylor to Sam Houston, in Hamilton, *Zachary Taylor,* 157; Henry, *Campaign Sketches,* 7; Justin Smith, *War with Mexico,* 1:86; Heitman, *Historical Register,* 1:202; Dyer, *Zachary Taylor,* 148. Secretary of War Wilkins wrote that in the twenty-three companies of dragoons and infantry were "about eleven hundred and fifty men" (Wilkins to Tyler, May 13, 1844, *Army and Navy Chronicle,* 3:653).

18. Grant to Julia Dent, July 28, 1844, in Simon, ed., *Papers of Ulysses S. Grant,* 1:30.

19. Lloyd Lewis, *Captain Sam Grant* (Boston: Little, Brown, 1950), 3–113; Grant, *Personal Memoirs,* 1:17–51; William S. McFeely, *Grant: A Biography* (New York: W. W. Norton, 1981), 6–27; AGO, Post Returns, Jefferson Barracks, NA, M617, Roll 546. Grant was called "Uncle Sam" or "Sam" by friends at West Point. See Samuel G. French, *Two Wars: An Autobiography* (Nashville, TN: Confederate Veteran, 1901), 17; and Lewis, *Captain Sam Grant,* 62. However, Grant signed his extant letters to Julia Dent during the Mexican war as "Ulysses" or by an abbreviation thereof (Simon, ed., *Papers of Ulysses S. Grant,* 1:23–161).

20. James Longstreet, *From Manassas to Appomattox: Memoirs of the Civil War in America,* ed. James I. Robertson Jr. (Bloomington: Indiana University Press, 1960), 18; AGO, Monthly Returns, Sixth Infantry, NA, M665, Roll 65; Grant, *Personal Memoirs,* 1:46; Lewis, *Captain Sam Grant,* 102–110; James Longstreet, "Longstreet's Reminiscences," *New York Times,* July 24, 1885, p. 6. Grant, named "Hiram Ulysses" at birth, tried to enter West Point as "Ulysses Hiram Grant"; however, he was nominated by his congressman and admitted to the Academy as "U. S. Grant," and after graduation he signed his name in that manner on official army documents, and on personal correspondence typically as "Ulysses S. Grant" or some abbreviation thereof.

21. Grant, *Personal Memoirs,* 1:21–33, 45–46; AGO, Monthly Returns, Fourth Infantry, NA, M665, Roll 43; AGO, Post Returns, Jefferson Barracks, NA, M617, Roll 546; Lewis, *Captain Sam Grant,* 98–110; McFeely, *Grant,* 20–24; Jean Edward Smith, *Grant* (New York: Simon and Schuster, 2001), 30–32. Grant erred in indicating in his *Personal Memoirs* that "Colonel Steven Kearney [*sic*] . . . commanded the post" of Jefferson Barracks while Grant was there during 1843 and 1844 (1:45), and occasionally historians have repeated that mistaken assertion. As post and Fourth Infantry returns reveal, during that period Colonel Vose—or in his absence one of his subordinates—commanded both the post and the Fourth Infantry. Kearny, who was appointed commander of the Third Military Department in 1842, initially established his department's headquarters at Jefferson Barracks but moved them to St. Louis on November 1, 1843 (Dwight L. Clarke, *Stephen Watts Kearny, Soldier of the West* [Norman: University of Oklahoma Press, 1961], 83, 91). Note also that McFeely in his biography of Grant errs in stating that "after graduation, both Grant and Dent were assigned to the Fourth Infantry Regiment" (20). Frederick Dent, Julia's brother, was assigned directly after graduation from the Academy to the Sixth Infantry, which was headquartered at Fort Towson, in Indian Territory, and he reported to that regiment on October 6, 1843 (AGO, Monthly Returns, Sixth Infantry, NA, M665, Rolls 65 and 66; Heitman, *His-*

torical Register, 1:368; Cullum, ed., *Biographical Register*). Moreover, Grant mentioned in several letters to Julia that Fred was at Fort Towson (e.g., letter of July 28, 1844).

22. Lewis, *Captain Sam Grant,* 103–4, 105, 106–7; AGO, Monthly Returns, Third Infantry, NA, M665, Roll 31; Grant, *Personal Memoirs,* 1:45–48; McFeely, *Grant,* 23–24; Vose to Jones, April 28, 1844, AGO, Letters Received, NA, M567, Roll 292.

23. Grant, *Personal Memoirs,* 1:51; Lewis, *Captain Sam Grant,* 95, 96, 103; Winders, *Mr. Polk's Army,* 52; AGO, Monthly Returns, Fourth Infantry, NA, M665, Roll 43; Vose to Jones, May 7, 1844, AGO, Letters Received, NA, M567, Roll 292.

24. Grant, *Personal Memoirs,* 1:49; AGO, Post Returns, Jefferson Barracks, NA, M617, Roll 546.

25. Donald C. Pfanz, *Richard S. Ewell: A Soldier's Life* (Chapel Hill: University of North Carolina Press, 1998), 1–39; Percy Gatling Hamlin, ed., *The Making of a Soldier: Letters of General R. S. Ewell* (Richmond, VA: Whittet and Shepperson, 1935), 19–35, 37–59; Heitman, *Historical Register,* 1:410; AGO, Monthly Returns, First Dragoons, NA, M744, Roll 1; AGO, Post Returns, Jefferson Barracks, NA, M617, Roll 546.

26. Pfanz, *Richard S. Ewell,* 40; Ewell to Ben, August 1, 1844, in Hamlin, ed., *Making of a Soldier,* 52–53.

27. AGO, Post Returns, Jefferson Barracks, NA, M617, Roll 546; Lewis, *Captain Sam Grant,* 111–13; Grant, *Personal Memoirs,* 1:49; McFeely, *Grant,* 24–27; Donald Bridgman Sanger and Thomas Robson Hay, *James Longstreet* (Baton Rouge: Louisiana State University Press, 1952), 9; J. Longstreet, "Longstreet's Reminiscences"; J. Longstreet, *From Manassas to Appomattox,* 8.

28. Grant to Julia, June 4, 1844, in Simon, ed., *Papers of Ulysses S. Grant,* 1:24, 25; Grant, *Personal Memoirs,* 1:56; Hardin, "Fort Jesup", 17.1 (Jan. 1934): 143–46; Vose to Jones, May 26 and August 2, 1844, AGO, Letters Received, NA, M567, Roll 292.

29. Hamilton, *Zachary Taylor,* 70–71, 146–52; Taylor to Jones, August 9 and September 30, 1844, AGO, Letters Received, NA, M567, Roll 292; Bauer, *Mexican War,* 7; Chitwood, *John Tyler,* 348–55; Justin Smith, *War with Mexico,* 1:86.

30. Croffut, ed., *Fifty Years in Camp and Field,* 183–84; Lewis, *Captain Sam Grant,* 81.

31. Twiggs to Jones, August 9, 10, and 13, 1844; Twiggs to Wilkins, September 12, 1844; Twiggs to Jones, September 24, October 18, November 15, and December 23, 1844, AGO, Letters Received, NA, M567, Roll 292. In *Mr. Polk's Army,* Winders claims that "[a] government publication, *Cavalry Tactics,* served as the basis of instructions for the dragoons" (24). Samuel French, in *Two Wars,* stated that he prepared drawings to illustrate the publication's text (22, 24–25).

32. Grant, *Personal Memoirs,* 1:42; Grant to Jones, November 17, 1943, in Simon, ed., *Papers of Ulysses S. Grant,* 1:23; Brackett, *History of the United States Cavalry,* 51; Lambert, *One Hundred Years,* 24–25; Rodenbough, *From Everglade to Cañon,* 79–82, 85–89. Members of the USMA class of 1843 who were also assigned as brevet second lieutenants to Twiggs's regiment of riflemen were George Stevens, Lewis Neill, and Cave J. Couts (Heitman, *Historical Register,* 1:330, 742, 922).

33. Lewis, *Captain Sam Grant,* 70, 72, 75, 93, 96, 116; French, *Two Wars,* 16–17; McFeely, *Grant,* 20, 55; AGO, Monthly Returns, Second Dragoons, NA, M744, Roll 14; Heitman, *Historical Register,* 1:562.

34. Lewis, *Captain Sam Grant,* 108, 118; French, *Two Wars,* 17; AGO, Monthly Returns, Second Dragoons, NA, M744, Roll 14.

35. Grant to Julia, August 31, 1844, in Simon, ed., *Papers of Ulysses S. Grant,* 1:34; AGO, Monthly Returns, Fourth Infantry, NA, M665, Roll 43.

36. Taylor to Jones, Western Division, September 9, 1844, AGO, Letters Received, NA, M567, Roll 292; AGO, Monthly Returns, Fourth Infantry, NA, M665, Roll 43; AGO, Post Returns, Camp Salubrity, NA, M617, Roll 1538.

37. Bauer, *Zachary Taylor,* 37–38.

38. AGO, Regimental Monthly Returns, Fourth Infantry, NA, M665, Roll 43; Third Infantry, NA, M665, Roll 31; Second Dragoons, NA, M744, Roll 14; Second Lt. Richard H. Anderson to Lt. A. R. Johnston, September 20, 1844, ALS, USMA Library, West Point, NY. Alexander Hays was reported by his father to have received no orders and no directions concerning where to report following his graduation from West Point, in a letter to the AG dated September 3, 1844. In reply, Capt. William G. Freeman, AAG, wrote that he should report to Natchitoches, LA (AGO, Letters Received, NA, M567, Roll 286).

39. Bvt. Maj. Lorenzo Thomas to Taylor, September 17, 1844, in Hardin, "Fort Jesup" 17.1 (Jan. 1934): 140; Croffut, ed., *Fifty Years in Camp and Field,* 187; Taylor to Jones, October 15, 1844, AGO, Letters Received, NA, M567, Roll 292; Dyer, *Zachary Taylor,* 150; Bauer, *Zachary Taylor,* 113.

40. Croffut, ed., *Fifty Years in Camp and Field,* 185, 187; Bauer, *Zachary Taylor,* 113; Grant to Julia, January 12, 1845, in Simon, ed., *Papers of Ulysses S. Grant,* 1:41.

41. Grant to Hazlitt, December 1, 1844, in Simon, ed., *Papers of Ulysses S. Grant,* 1:39, and in Hardin, "Fort Jesup" 17.1 (Jan. 1934): 144–45; Croffut, ed., *Fifty Years in Camp and Field,* 189; Winders, *Mr. Polk's Army,* 53. One of the charges of which Col. William Whistler, Fourth Infantry, was found guilty when he was tried at Matamoros in July 1846 was "Drunkenness on Duty" (Record group 153, Records of the Office of the Judge Advocate General [Army], Court-Martial Case Files 1809–1894, EE 254, NA). He was sentenced to be cashiered, but President Polk disapproved the sentence and Whistler was returned to duty. The court's judge advocate was Capt. C. F. Smith, and Bvt. Maj. J. J. Abercrombie was one of the officers detailed to sit on the court.

42. Croffut, ed., *Fifty Years in Camp and Field,* 189; Taylor to Jones, December 26, 1844, AGO, Letters Received, NA, M567, Roll 292; Bauer, *Zachary Taylor,* 112.

43. Twiggs to Jones, January 13, 1845, AGO, Letters Received, NA, M567, Roll 305; Twiggs to Wilkins, January 16, 1845, AGO, Letters Received, NA, M567, Roll 305; Twiggs to Jones, April 19, 1845; AGO, Monthly Returns, Second Dragoons, NA, M744, Roll 14.

44. Bauer, *Mexican War,* 8; Chitwood, *John Tyler,* 342–59; Justin Smith, *War with Mexico,* 1:82–87; Eisenhower, *So Far from God,* 17–20.

45. Bauer, *Mexican War,* 9–10; Chitwood, *John Tyler,* 359–63; Eisenhower, *So Far from God,* 20, 24–26; Justin Smith, *War with Mexico,* 1:87; Vincent J. Esposito, chief ed., *The West Point Atlas of American Wars, Vol. I, 1689–1900* (New York: Frederick A. Praeger, 1959), map 13 material.

46. AGO, Monthly Returns, Fourth Infantry, NA, M665, Roll 43; AGO, Monthly

Returns, Second Dragoons, NA, M744, Roll 14; AGO, Monthly Returns, Eighth Infantry, NA, M665, Roll 90; AGO, Monthly Returns, First Dragoons, NA, M744, Roll 2.

47. AGO, Monthly Returns, Fourth Infantry, NA, M665, Roll 43; Grant, *Memoirs,* 1:50–51, 58; Grant to Julia, May 6, 1845, in Simon, ed., *Papers of Ulysses S. Grant,* 1:43. Grant stated in his *Memoirs* that during his visit to St. Louis in the spring of 1845 he obtained the consent of Julia's parents "for the union, which had not been asked for before" (1:53). However, in letters following his visit he indicated repeatedly that he remained unsure of her father's approval and believed Colonel Dent had promised to write him about the unofficial engagement. See, e.g., Simon, ed., *Papers of Ulysses S. Grant,* 1:46, 48, 49, 61, 65, 66, 68.

48. AGO Monthly Returns, Third and Fourth Infantry, NA, M665, Roll 31 and 43, respectively; Henry, *Campaign Sketches,* 9. Henry dates the arrival of the two companies from Fort Leavenworth as April 23, but a notation on the regiment's monthly return indicates they reached regimental headquarters on the twenty-fourth.

49. Twiggs to Jones, April 19 and 28, 1845; May 11 and 29, 1845; June 10, 12, and 14, 1845, AGO, Letters Received, NA, M567, Roll 305.

50. Bauer, *Zachary Taylor,* 114; Marcy to Taylor, May 28, 1845, in Henry, *Campaign Sketches,* 9; Hardin, "Fort Jesup" 17.1 (Jan. 1934): 146–47; Hamilton, *Zachary Taylor,* 159; Eisenhower, *So Far from God,* 30; Justin Smith, *War with Mexico,* 1:141; Taylor to Jones, June 8 and 18, 1845, AGO, Letters Received, NA, M567, Roll 305.

51. Grant to Julia, June 1845, in Simon, ed., *Papers of Ulysses S. Grant,* 1:46; AGO, Monthly Returns, Sixth Infantry, NA, M665, Roll 66; Grant to Julia, July 6, 1845, in Simon, ed., *Papers of Ulysses S. Grant,* 1:48–49.

52. Croffut, ed., *Fifty Years in Camp and Field,* 192; Henry, *Campaign Sketches,* 9–10; Hardin, "Fort Jesup" 17.1 (Jan. 1934): 146–48; AGO, Monthly Returns, Third and Fourth Infantry, NA, M665, Rolls 31 and 43, respectively; Taylor to Jones, June 30 and July 8, 1845, AGO, Letters Received, NA, M567, Roll 305; Dyer, *Zachary Taylor,* 153; Hamilton, *Zachary Taylor,* 159–60.

53. AGO, Monthly Returns, Third and Fourth Infantry, NA, M665, Rolls 31 and 43, respectively; Grant to Julia, July 11, 1845, and [July 17, 1845], in Simon, ed., *Papers of Ulysses S. Grant,* 1:50–53; Grant, *Personal Memoirs,* 1:58–59; Croffut, ed., *Fifty Years in Camp and Field,* 192–93; Henry, *Campaign Sketches,* 10; Hamilton, *Zachary Taylor,* 160; Bauer, *Mexican War,* 18; Justin Smith, *War with Mexico,* 1:141–42; Eisenhower, *So Far from God,* 32; Hardin, "Fort Jesup" 17.1 (Jan. 1934): 149–50.

54. Taylor to Jones, July 8, 1845, with copies of correspondence mentioned in Taylor's letter, AGO, Letters Received, NA, M567, Roll 305; Dyer, *Zachary Taylor,* 153; Bauer, *Zachary Taylor,* 115; AGO, Post Returns, Fort Jesup, NA, M617, Roll 555.

55. Grant to Julia, July 6, 1845, in Simon, ed., *Papers of Ulysses S. Grant,* 1:47; Grant, *Personal Memoirs,* 1:52–53. Winders writes: "On the eve of hostilities with Mexico, [the combat elements of] the army consisted of only eight infantry regiments, four artillery regiments, and two dragoon regiments" (*Mr. Polk's Army,* 21).

56. AGO, Post Returns, Camp Salubrity, NA, M617, Roll 1538; AGO, Monthly Returns, Fourth Infantry, NA, M665, Roll 43; Grant to Julia, July 6, 1845, in Simon, ed., *Papers of Ulysses S. Grant,* 1:48; Capt. Ephraim Kirby Smith to wife, September 9, 1845,

in Emma Jerome Blackwood, ed., *To Mexico with Scott: Letters of Captain E. Kirby Smith to His Wife* (Cambridge, MA: Harvard University Press, 1917), 16.

57. AGO, Monthly Returns, Fourth Infantry, NA, M665, Roll 43; Grant to Julia, [July 17, 1845], in Simon, ed., *Papers of Ulysses S. Grant,* 1:51–52; Grant, *Personal Memoirs,* 1:60; Henry, *Campaign Sketches,* 11–12.

58. Grant to Julia, [July 17, 1845], in Simon, ed., *Papers of Ulysses S. Grant,* 1:52.

59. Hamilton, *Zachary Taylor,* 161; AGO, Monthly Returns from Regular Army Regiments, June 1821–January 1901, NA, M727, 38 Rolls; Third Artillery, January 1841–December 1850, M727, Roll 19; Henry, *Campaign Sketches,* 12; McWhiney, *Braxton Bragg and Confederate Defeat,* 1:52; Heitman, *Historical Register,* 1:240 (Bragg), 529 (Hill), 825 (Reynolds), 953–94 (Thomas).

60. Nichols, *Toward Gettysburg,* 3–18; Freeman Cleaves, *Rock of Chickamauga: The Life of General George H. Thomas* (Norman: University of Oklahoma Press, 1948), 3–24; Wilbur D. Thomas, *General George H. Thomas, the Indomitable Warrior* (New York: Exposition Press, 1964), 45–79; McWhiney, *Braxton Bragg and Confederate Defeat,* 1:1–52; Henry, *Campaign Sketches,* 12; Bridges, *Lee's Maverick General,* 16–19. Much later, Hill and Bragg apparently became estranged (Bridges, *Lee's Maverick General,* 19). For Hill's comment on Sykes, see Bridges, *Lee's Maverick General,* 18.

61. AGO, Letters Sent, NA, M565, Roll 14.

62. Jones to Taylor, June 18, 1845, AOO, Letters Received, NA.

63. Jones to Taylor, December 9, 1845, AOO, Letters Received, NA. The adjutant general concluded: "The Company is one of foot artillery equipped with its proper armament, and no additional allowances can be authorized." No effort was made to reconcile that statement with Bragg's instructions of June 18, or the adjutant general's letter of that date to General Taylor.

64. Croffut, ed., *Fifty Years in Camp and Field,* 199; Henry, *Campaign Sketches,* 10–12. Among the several classmates of Thomas, Reynolds, and Hill in New Orleans at that time were Bushrod Johnson (USMA 1840); Don Carlos Buell and Israel Richardson (USMA 1841); and George Sykes (USMA 1842).

65. AGO, Monthly Returns, Third and Fourth Infantry, NA, M665, Rolls 31 and 43, respectively; Henry, *Campaign Sketches,* 12–13; Croffut, ed., *Fifty Years in Camp and Field,* 193; Eisenhower, *So Far from God,* 32–33; Dyer, *Zachary Taylor,* 154; Justin Smith, *War with Mexico,* 1:142; Bauer, *Mexican War,* 18. Bauer states that Taylor and the Third Infantry left New Orleans on the twenty-fourth, but Hitchcock, Henry, and the Third Infantry Monthly Returns all give the date of departure as the twenty-third. Grant, in his *Personal Memoirs,* mistakenly said the Fourth Infantry companies left New Orleans in early September (1:61).

CHAPTER 2

1. Taylor to Jones, July 28, 1845, AGO, Letters Received, NA, M567, Roll 305; Justin Smith, *War with Mexico,* 1:142; Croffut, ed., *Fifty Years in Camp and Field,* 193; Bauer, *Mexican War,* 18. (In *Campaign Sketches,* Henry mistakenly states that Taylor reached Aransas Bay on July 26 [14].)

2. Twiggs to Jones, September 14, 1845, AGO, Letters Received, NA, M567, Roll 305; Croffut, ed., *Fifty Years in Camp and Field,* 193–94; Lambert, *One Hundred Years,* 26; Rodenbough, *From Everglade to Cañon,* 93; (Lt.) George Stevens, "Sketch of the Line of March of the 2nd U.S. Dragoons, Commanded by Col. D. E. Twiggs, from Fort Jesup La. to Corpus Christi, Texas, between the 25th of July and 27th Aug. 1845," in Nathan Sturgis Jarvis, "An Army Surgeon's Notes of Frontier Service—Mexican War," *Journal of the Military Service Institute of the United States* 40 (May 1907): 436–37.

3. Taylor to Jones, July 28, 1845, AGO, Letters Received, NA, M567, Roll 305; AGO, Monthly Returns, Third and Fourth Infantry, NA, M665, Rolls 31 and 43, respectively; Croffut, ed., *Fifty Years in Camp and Field,* 194–95; Henry, *Campaign Sketches,* 14–15, 16.

4. Taylor to Jones, July 28 and August 15, 1845, AGO, Letters Received, NA, M567, Roll 305; Croffut, ed., *Fifty Years in Camp and Field,* 194; Henry, *Campaign Sketches,* 17; Jarvis, "An Army Surgeon's Notes," *Journal of the Military Service Institute of the United States* 40 (May 1907): 435; Dyer, *Zachary Taylor,* 155.

5. AGO, Monthly Returns, Third and Fourth Infantry, NA, M665, Rolls 31 and 43, respectively; Grant, *Personal Memoirs,* 1:63.

6. McLaws interview, July 24, 1885, *New York Times,* p. 6. Grant noted in his *Personal Memoirs* that the channel was deepened (1:64).

7. Justin Smith, *War with Mexico,* 1:142; Henry, *Campaign Sketches,* 19, 24; Croffut, ed., *Fifty Years in Camp and Field,* 196, 197, 198. By late September of 1845, two Ranger companies were in Federal service, one led by Capt. Richard A. Gillespie and one by Capt. John T. Price (Frederick Wilkins, *The Highly Irregular Irregulars: Texas Rangers in the Mexican War* [Austin, TX: Eakin Press, 1990], 24).

8. Meade to wife, October 16, 1845, in George Gordon Meade, *The Life and Letters of George Gordon Meade, Major-General United States Army* (2 vols., New York: Charles Scribner's Sons, 1913), 1:32; Grant, *Personal Memoirs,* 1:64–65; Jarvis, "An Army Surgeon's Notes," *Journal of the Military Service Institute of the United States* 40 (May 1907): 436; Croffut, ed., *Fifty Years in Camp and Field,* 196.

9. Jarvis, "An Army Surgeon's Notes," *Journal of the Military Service Institute of the United States* 40 (May 1907): 436; Henry, *Campaign Sketches,* 28, 29, 31; Croffut, ed., *Fifty Years in Camp and Field,* 195–96.

10. Twiggs to Scott, July 21, 1845, AGO, Letters Received, NA, M567, Roll 305; Twiggs to Jones, July 22, 1845, AGO, Letters Received, NA, M567, Roll 305.

11. Stevens, "Sketch of the Line of March of the 2nd U.S. Dragoons" in Jarvis, "An Army Surgeon's Notes," *Journal of the Military Service Institute of the United States* 40 (May 1907): 436–37.

12. Croffut, ed., *Fifty Years in Camp and Field,* 197; Henry, *Campaign Sketches,* 32; Jarvis, "An Army Surgeon's Notes," *Journal of the Military Service Institute of the United States* 40 (May 1907): 436. Bauer, in *Zachary Taylor,* mistakenly states that Taylor was "bound for San Patricio on an inspection trip" (120–21). Taylor had no troops stationed at San Patricio.

13. Croffut, ed., *Fifty Years in Camp and Field,* 196, 198; Henry, *Campaign Sketches,*

32, 35; Jarvis, "An Army Surgeon's Notes," *Journal of the Military Service Institute of the United States* 40 (May 1907): 435; Twiggs to Jones, September 4, 1845, AGO, Letters Received, NA, M567, Roll 305; Twiggs to Scott, December 6, 1845, AGO, Letters Received, NA, M567, Roll 305.

14. Croffut, ed., *Fifty Years in Camp and Field,* 195, 198, 199; John B. Porter, "Medical and Surgical Notes of Campaigns in the War with Mexico, 1845–1848," *American Journal of the Medical Sciences* 45 (January 1852): 14–15; Bauer, *Mexican War,* 121–22; Eisenhower, *So Far from God,* 108–110; George Winston Smith and Charles Judah, eds., *Chronicles of the Gringos: The U.S. Army in the Mexican War, 1846–1848, Accounts of Eyewitnesses and Combatants* (Albuquerque: University of New Mexico Press, 1968), 275–76, 318–25; Winders, *Mr. Polk's Army,* 139–56; Bauer, *Zachary Taylor,* 118.

15. Justin Smith, *War with Mexico,* 1:142; Henry, *Campaign Sketches,* 34; Croffut, ed., *Fifty Years in Camp and Field,* 198, 203; Bauer, *Mexican War,* 19–20.

16. AGO, Monthly Returns, Seventh Infantry, NA, M665, Roll 79; Fifth Infantry, NA, M665, Roll 55; Eighth Infantry, NA, M665, Roll 90.

17. J. Longstreet, *From Manassas to Appomattox,* 13–20; Lewis, *Captain Sam Grant,* 129; AGO, Monthly Returns, Eighth Infantry, NA, M665, Roll 90; Heitman, *Historical Register,* 640; Helen D. Longstreet, *Lee and Longstreet at High Tide: Gettysburg in the Light of the Official Records* (Gainesville, GA: published by author, 1904), 94–101, 144–47; Wert, *General James Longstreet,* 19–34; William Garrett Piston, *Lee's Tarnished Lieutenant: James Longstreet and His Place in Southern History* (Athens: University of Georgia Press, 1987), 1–7; J. Longstreet, "Longstreet's Reminiscences," 6. In his memoirs (*From Manassas to Appomattox*), Longstreet says his standing at graduation from West Point was sixty in a class of sixty-two (16). That statement is contrary to Heitman, *Historical Register,* 640, which shows his standing as fifty-four, and research indicates Longstreet stood fifty-four in a class of fifty-six. Also, apparently football was not introduced at the Academy until later, but of course the game may have been played by cadets before it was formally adopted as an organized sport.

18. Grant to Julia, September 14, 1845, in Simon, ed., *Papers of Ulysses S. Grant,* 1:54; Croffut, ed., *Fifty Years in Camp and Field,* 197, 200; Jarvis, "An Army Surgeon's Notes," *Journal of the Military Service Institute of the United States* 40 (May 1907): 436; Henry, *Campaign Sketches,* 35–37; McWhiney, *Braxton Bragg and Confederate Defeat,* 1:55; George Gordon Meade to wife, September 14, 1845, in Meade, *Life and Letters,* 1:25. Meade, writing on the fourteenth, mistakenly said the *Dayton* disaster occurred "yesterday," whereas the date of the explosion was September 12.

19. Meade, *Life and Letters,* 1:1–18. (Meade had a brother-in-law, Maj. James D. Graham, who was a member of the Bureau of Topographical Engineers.) Meade to wife, September 18, 1845, October 10, 1845, October 16, 1845, November 3, 1845, February 24, 1846, in Meade, *Life and Letters,* 1:26–27, 30, 32, 35, 49; Adrian G. Traas, *From the Golden Gate to Mexico City: The U.S. Army Topographical Engineers in the Mexican War, 1846–1848* (Washington, DC: Office of History, Corps of Engineers and Centers of Military History, United States Army, 1993), 4–6, 116–17.

20. Meade to wife, September 18, 1845, December 18, 1845, March 4, 1846, in Meade,

Life and Letters, 1:26, 40–41, 51. Meade's classmates who were at Corpus Christi in the fall of 1845 included Capt. George G. Waggaman and 1st Lts. Joseph H. Eaton, William S. Henry, Isaac V. D. Reeve, and Larkin Smith.

21. Meade to wife, September 14, 1845, October 9, 1845, in Meade, *Life and Letters,* 1:25, 27–29.

22. Henry, *Campaign Sketches,* 31, 34; Croffut, ed., *Fifty Years in Camp and Field,* 197–98; AGO, Monthly Returns, First, Second, Third, and Fourth Artillery, NA, M727, Rolls 3, 11, 19, and 27, respectively. The captain of Company E, Third Artillery, John A. Thomas, was assigned to duty at West Point.

23. John Porter Hatch to Eliza, October 14 and 28, 1845, ALS, John Porter Hatch Papers, Manuscript Division, LC; Heitman, *Historical Register,* 1:511.

24. Taylor, Order Books, Orders No. 10, September 9, 1845; Orders No. 17, September 30, 1845; Orders No. 22, October 14, 1845; Orders No. 25, October 22, 1845; Orders No. 36, November 5, 1845; Orders No. 42, November 16, 1845; After Orders, December 2, 1845; Orders No. 52, December 6, 1845; Special Orders No. 61, December 8, 1845; Orders No. 54, December 10, 1845; Orders No. 56, December 13, 1845; Orders No. 60, December 27, 1845, Record Group 94, Entry 134, Vol. 1, August 1845–April 1846, NA.

25. Taylor, Order Books, Special Orders No. 22, September 26, 1845; Special Orders No. 41, November 1, 1845; Orders No. 35, November 4, 1845; Orders No. 41, November 14, 1845; Special Orders No. 70, December 29, 1845, Record Group 94, Entry 134, Vol. 1, August 1845–April 1846, NA.

26. Meade to wife, November 3, 1845, in Meade, *Life and Letters,* 1:35; Hatch to Eliza, October 28, 1845, ALS, Hatch Papers, LC; Croffut, ed., *Fifty Years in Camp and Field,* 198–99; John F. Reynolds to his sisters, November 14, 1845, in Nichols, *Toward Gettysburg,* 18; Porter, "Medical and Surgical Notes," 14.

27. Samson, ed., *Letters of Zachary Taylor;* Bauer, *Zachary Taylor,* 243; Croffut, ed., *Fifty Years in Camp and Field,* 195, 198; Bliss to Jones, October 4, 1845, AGO, Letters Received, NA, M567, Roll 305; Taylor to Jones, October. 24, 1845, AGO, Letters Received, NA, M567, Roll 305; Napoleon Dana to his wife, October 17, 1845, ALS, Napoleon Dana Papers, USMA Library; Taylor, Order Books, Special Orders No. 46, November 7, 1845; Orders No. 14, September 26, 1845, NA. William Wallace Smith Bliss (USMA 1833), the son of a West Point graduate, was a Fourth Infantry line officer on special duty as an assistant adjutant general who had been assigned in December 1841 to serve with General Taylor, then commanding the Second Military Department (Fourth Infantry Returns, NA, M665, Roll 43). In December 1848 Bliss married the Taylors' daughter "Betty" (Mary Elizabeth). Napoleon Jackson Tecumseh Dana's letters to his wife, Sue, are in his papers (1826–1902) at the USMA Library, West Point, NY. Edited extracts of some of Dana's letters may be found in Robert H. Ferrell, ed., *Monterrey Is Ours! The Mexican War Letters of Lieutenant Dana, 1845–1847* (Lexington: University of Kentucky Press, 1990).

28. Taylor, Order Books, Special Order No. 55, November 28, 1845, NA; Special Order No. 56, November 29, 1845, NA.

29. Grant, *Personal Memoirs,* 1:78; Simon, ed., *Papers of Ulysses S. Grant,* 1:63, 64;

AGO, Monthly Returns, Fourth and Seventh Infantry, NA, M665, Rolls 43 and 79, respectively; Grant to Julia, January 2, 1846, in Simon, ed., *Papers of Ulysses S. Grant,* 1:67.

30. Grant to Julia, January 2, 1846, in Simon, ed., *Papers of Ulysses S. Grant,* 1:67.

31. Grant, *Personal Memoirs,* 1:74–78; AGO, Monthly Returns, Second and Fourth Infantry, NA, M665, Rolls 17 and 43, respectively; AGO, Monthly Returns, Fourth Artillery, NA, M727, Roll 27.

32. Grant, *Personal Memoirs,* 1:77–78; AGO, Monthly Returns, Fourth Infantry, NA, M665, Roll 43; George A. McCall, *Letters from the Frontiers* (Philadelphia: J. B. Lippincott, 1868), 1–485 passim; Foote, *Civil War,* 1:507; H. D. Longstreet, *Lee and Longstreet at High Tide,* 130; Wert, *General James Longstreet,* 143–44; J. Longstreet, *From Manassas to Appomattox,* 138. McCall may not have remembered Longstreet, since apparently they were never closely associated.

33. Croffut, ed., *Fifty Years in Camp and Field,* 43–44; Meade to wife, December 25, 1845, and January 10, 1846, in Meade, *Life and Letters,* 1:42, 44–45.

34. Meade to wife, December 25, 1845, January 10, 1846, January 21, 1846, in Meade, *Life and Letters,* 1:42, 44–45, 46.

35. James Knox Polk, *The Diary of James K. Polk during His Presidency, 1845–1849,* ed. Milo Milton Quaife (4 vols., Chicago: A. C. McClurg, 1910), 1:148; Smith and Judah, eds., *Chronicles of the Gringos,* 3; AGO, Monthly Returns, Fourth Artillery, NA, M727, Roll 27; Joseph Howard Parks, *General Edmund Kirby Smith, C.S.A.* (Baton Rouge: Louisiana State University, 1954), 44; Taylor, Order Books, Special Orders No. 4, 7, and 8, January 1846, NA; French, *Two Wars,* 36, 39.

36. Jarvis, "An Army Surgeon's Notes," *Journal of the Military Service Institute of the United States* 40 (May 1907): 438–40, 441; Smith and Judah, eds., *Chronicles of the Gringos,* 272, 285–86, 316–17; Henry, *Campaign Sketches,* 25–26.

37. Polk, *Diary,* 1:408–410; Bauer, *Mexican War,* 128.

38. Marcy to Taylor, January 13, 1846, ALS, Letters Sent to AOO, NA; Hamilton, *Zachary Taylor,* 170; Croffut, ed., *Fifty Years in Camp and Field,* 207; Dyer, *Zachary Taylor,* 162–63.

CHAPTER 3

1. Justin Smith, *War with Mexico,* 1:138–39, 144–45, Croffut, ed., *Fifty Years in Camp and Field,* 213; Polk, *Diary,* 1:34–35, 312.

2. Taylor, Order Books, Orders No. 13 and Special Orders No. 18, February 6, 1846, NA; Taylor to Jones, February 16, 1846, AGO, Letters Received, NA, M567, Roll 327; Jarvis, "An Army Surgeon's Notes," *Journal of the Military Service Institute of the United States* 40 (May 1907): 437; Meade to wife, December 1, 1845, in Meade, *Life and Letters,* 1:36–37; Bauer, *Zachary Taylor,* 121; Traas, *From the Golden Gate,* 121, 122; Nathaniel Cheairs Hughes Jr., "William Joseph Hardee, U.S.A., 1815–1861," (master's thesis, University of North Carolina, 1956), 84–85; Bauer, *Mexican War,* 37; Hamilton, *Zachary Taylor,* 171; Justin Smith, *War with Mexico,* 1:146.

3. Hughes, "William Joseph Hardee," 1–90; Nathaniel Cheairs Hughes Jr., *General*

William J. Hardee: Old Reliable (Baton Rouge: Louisiana State University Press, 1965), 3–27. Hardee was born October 12, 1815 (Hughes, *General William J. Hardee,* 6).

4. Jarvis, "An Army Surgeon's Notes," *Journal of the Military Service Institute of the United States* 40 (May 1907): 440; Hughes, "William Joseph Hardee," 85.

5. Traas, *From the Golden Gate,* 121–22.

6. Taylor, Order Books, Special Orders No. 29, February 27, 1846; Orders No. 26, March 4, 1846; Special Orders No. 33, March 5, 1846; Special Orders No. 35, March 7, 1846; After Orders, March 8, 1846, NA; Taylor to Jones, March 8, 1848, AGO, Letters Received, NA, M567, Roll 327; French, *Two Wars,* 41–42; AGO, Monthly Returns, Second Dragoons, NA, M744, Roll 15; AGO, Monthly Returns, Third Artillery, NA, M727, Roll 19; Bauer, *Zachary Taylor,* 124.

7. Taylor, Order Books, Orders No. 26, March 4, 1846, and Special Orders No. 34, March 6, 1846, NA; Mansfield to wife, March 9, 1846, ALS, USMA Library; Bauer, *Mexican War,* 37–38, 43n3; Justin Smith, *War with Mexico,* 1:146; Hamilton, *Zachary Taylor,* 171; Henry, *Campaign Sketches,* 52; AGO, Monthly Returns, Eighth Infantry, NA, M665, Roll 90; AGO, Monthly Returns, First, Second, and Fourth Artillery, NA, M727, Rolls 3, 11, and 19, respectively.

8. Ephraim Kirby Smith to wife, March 17, 1846, in Blackwood, ed., *To Mexico with Scott,* 22–23; Parks, *General Edmund Kirby Smith,* 45; Hamilton, *Zachary Taylor,* 171; AGO, Monthly Returns, Fifth and Seventh Infantry, NA, M665, Rolls 55 and 79, respectively.

9. McCall, *Letters from the Frontiers,* 439–40; Nichols, *Toward Gettysburg,* 22; Grant to Julia, March 29, 1846, in Simon, ed., *Papers of Ulysses S. Grant* 1:76–79; Croffut, ed., *Fifty Years in Camp and Field,* 210–11; Henry, *Campaign Sketches,* 52–53; Hamilton, *Zachary Taylor,* 171; Bauer, *Mexican War,* 38; AGO, Monthly Returns, Third Artillery, NA, M727, Roll 19; Third and Fourth Infantry, NA, M665, Rolls 31 and 43.

10. Taylor, Order Books, Special Orders No. 34, March 6, 1846, NA; Bauer, *Mexican War,* 37, 39; Justin Smith, *War with Mexico,* 146, 148; Hamilton, *Zachary Taylor,* 171, 174; Taylor to Jones, March 8 and 12, 1846, AGO, Letters Received, NA, M567, Roll 327; AGO, Monthly Returns, Fourth Artillery, NA, M727, Roll 27.

11. Taylor, Order Books, Orders No. 26, March 4, 1846, and Special Orders No. 37, March 10, 1846, NA; Robert Hazlitt to Mrs. Ingersoll, March 20, 1846, ALS, LC; AGO, Monthly Returns, Third Infantry, NA, M665, Roll 31; AGO, Monthly Returns, First Artillery, NA, M727, Roll 3; Grant to Julia, April 20, 1846, in Simon, ed., *Papers of Ulysses S. Grant,* 1:81; Hamilton, *Zachary Taylor,* 171.

12. Taylor to Jones, March 11, 1846, Letters Received, NA, M567, Roll 327; Grant, *Personal Memoirs,* 1:84–86.

13. Croffut, ed., *Fifty Years in Camp and Field,* 202–3, 210–11, 213–22; Grant, *Personal Memoirs,* 1:84; Taylor, Order Books, Orders No. 20, February 24, 1846, NA; Bauer, *Zachary Taylor,* 121. Historian K. Jack Bauer asserts in his biography of Taylor that Hitchcock thought the general "a self-centered petty schemer" (*Zachary Taylor,* xxi), but the very occasional criticisms of Taylor contained in Hitchcock's journal scarcely add up to such a harsh conclusion.

14. Taylor, Order Books, Orders No. 26, March 4, 1846, NA; McWhiney, *Braxton*

Bragg and Confederate Defeat, 1:58; Lewis, *Captain Sam Grant,* 134–35; Croffut, ed., *Fifty Years in Camp and Field,* 181–82.

15. Grant to Julia, January 12 and March 3, 1846, in Simon, ed., *Papers of Ulysses S. Grant,* 1:69, 74–75.

16. French, *Two Wars,* 1–19, 20–29; AGO, Monthly Returns, Third Artillery, NA, M727, Roll 19.

17. French, *Two Wars,* 43–44.

18. Taylor, Order Books, Orders No. 32, March 16, 1846, NA; Taylor to Jones, March 12, 1846, AGO, Letters Received, NA, M567, Roll 327.

19. Grant to Julia, February 7, 1846, in Simon, ed., *Papers of Ulysses S. Grant,* 1:74; Grant, *Personal Memoirs,* 1:86; McCall to brother, March 28, 1846, in McCall, *Letters from the Frontiers,* 440–41.

20. Ephraim Kirby Smith to wife, March 17–24, 1846, in Blackwood, ed., *To Mexico with Scott,* 22–27.

21. French, *Two Wars,* 42–43.

22. Taylor to Jones, March 18 and March 21, AGO, Letters Received, NA, M567, Roll 327; Ephraim Kirby Smith to wife, March 17–24, 1846, in Blackwood, ed., *To Mexico with Scott,* 29–31.

23. Taylor, Order Books, Orders No. 32, March 16, 1846, and Orders No. 33, March 19, 1846, NA; Taylor to Jones, March 21, 1846, AGO, Letters Received, NA, M567, Roll 327.

24. Taylor to Jones, March 21, 1846, AGO, Letters Received, NA, M567, Roll 327.

25. Ephraim Kirby Smith to wife, March 17–24, 1846, in Blackwood, ed., *To Mexico with Scott,* 30–31; French, *Two Wars,* 44; Grant, *Personal Memoirs,* 1:87–88; Croffut, ed., *Fifty Years in Camp and Field,* 210–11; Justin Smith, *War with Mexico,* 1:147; Bauer, *Mexican War,* 38–39; Eisenhower, *So Far from God,* 52–54; Dyer, *Zachary Taylor,* 165–66.

26. Grant, *Personal Memoirs,* 1:86–87, 191.

27. Grant, *Personal Memoirs,* 1:281; Freeman, *R. E. Lee,* 2:18; Foote, *Civil War,* 1:399; Blackwood, ed., *To Mexico with* Scott, 29–31; Henry, *Campaign Sketches,* 59–60; Stephen W. Sears, *To the Gates of Richmond: The Peninsula Campaign* (New York: Ticknor and Fields, 1992), 37–45; Cullum, ed., *Biographical Register,* 410; Heitman, *Historical Register,* 1:895.

28. Taylor to Jones, March 21, 1846, AGO, Letters Received, NA, M567, Roll 327; Taylor, Order Books, Orders No. 34, March 22, 1846, NA; Jones to Taylor, December 9, 1845, ALS, AGO, Letters Sent, NA; Henry, *Campaign Sketches,* 60; Ephraim Kirby Smith to wife, March 17–24, 1846, in Blackwood, ed., *To Mexico with Scott,* 31.

29. Taylor, Order Books, Orders No. 35, March 22, 1846, and Orders No. 36, March 23, 1846, NA; Croffut, ed., *Fifty Years in Camp and Field,* 211; Ephraim Kirby Smith to wife, March 17–24, 1846, in Blackwood, ed., *To Mexico with Scott,* 31–32; Henry, *Campaign Sketches,* 61; Justin Smith, *War with Mexico,* 1:147–48.

30. Taylor to Jones, March 25, 1846, AGO, Letters Received, NA, M567, Roll 327; Croffut, ed., *Fifty Years in Camp and Field,* 210; Ephraim Kirby Smith to wife, March 17–24, 1846, in Blackwood, ed., *To Mexico with Scott,* 31–33; French, *Two Wars,* 44–45; Henry, *Campaign Sketches,* 62–63; Hamilton, *Zachary Taylor,* 174; Dyer, *Zachary Taylor,* 166.

31. Taylor, Order Books, After Orders, February 24, 1846, and Orders No. 25, February 25, 1846, NA; Croffut, ed., *Fifty Years in Camp and Field,* 204–6; Justin Smith, *War with Mexico,* 1:144; Bauer, *Mexican War,* 35–36; Hamilton, *Zachary Taylor,* 167; Polk, *Diary,* 1:284–85, 308–9; Dyer, *Zachary Taylor,* 159–60.

32. Taylor to Jones, March 8 and 25, 1846, AGO, Letters Received, NA, M567, Roll 327; "Extra," *Corpus Christi Gazette,* March 8, 1846 (Beinecke Rare Book and Manuscript Library, Yale University, New Haven, CT); Croffut, ed., *Fifty Years in Camp and Field,* 213–15; French, *Two Wars,* 45; Henry, *Campaign Sketches,* 62–63; Ephraim Kirby Smith to wife, March 17–24, 1846, in Blackwood, ed., *To Mexico with Scott,* 32–33; Justin Smith, *War with Mexico,* 1:146; Bauer, *Mexican War,* 39; Eisenhower, *So Far from God,* 54.

33. Taylor to Jones, March 25, 1846, AGO, Letters Received, NA, M567, Roll 327; Taylor, Order Books, Special Orders No. 39, March 25, 1846, NA; Croffut, ed., *Fifty Years in Camp and Field,* 214, 215.

34. Taylor, Order Books, Special Orders No. 40, March 26, 1846, NA; Justin Smith, *War with Mexico,* 1:146–47.

35. Bauer, *Zachary Taylor,* 121. According to Justin Smith, both Taylor and Scott as well as President Polk, the members of his cabinet, and everyone in his circle of supporters thought "a bold military attitude" would help to avert a war with Mexico (*War with Mexico,* 1:152).

36. Polk, *Diary,* 1:305–8; Taylor to Jones, March 29, 1846, Letters Received, AGO, NA, M567, Roll 327; Croffut, ed., *Fifty Years in Camp and Field,* 215–17; Ephraim Kirby Smith to wife, March 29, 1846, in Blackwood, ed., *To Mexico with Scott,* 33; Henry, *Campaign Sketches,* 64–66; Lewis, *Captain Sam Grant,* 49; Bauer, *Mexican War,* 40; Dyer, *Zachary Taylor,* 166–68; Rhoda van Bibber Tanner Doubleday, ed., *Journals of the Late Brevet Major Philip Norbourne Barbour, Captain in the 3rd Regiment, United States Infantry, and His Wife Martha Isabella Hopkins Barbour, Written during the War with Mexico, 1846* (New York: G. P. Putnam's Sons, 1936), 17. Original Barbour journals are in the USMA Library.

CHAPTER 4

1. Taylor to Jones, March 29 and April 6, 1846, AGO, Letters Received, NA, M567, Roll 327; Doubleday, ed., *Journals of the Late Brevet Major Philip Norbourne Barbour,* 17–21; Ephraim Kirby Smith to wife, March 29, 1846, in Blackwood, ed., *To Mexico with Scott,* 33–34; Croffut, ed., *Fifty Years in Camp and Field,* 216–17; Henry, *Campaign Sketches,* 64–67; French, *Two Wars,* 45; Justin Smith, *War with Mexico,* 1:148.

2. Taylor to Jones, April 6, 1846, with enclosure: Minutes of meeting of March 28, 1846, between Worth and La Vega, AGO, Letters Received, NA, M567, Roll 327.

3. Taylor, Order Books, Special Orders No. 41, March 29, 1846; Special Orders No. 42, April 1, 1846; Orders No. 8, April 1, 1846; Special Orders No. 45, April 6, 1846, NA; Jarvis, "An Army Surgeon's Notes," *Journal of the Military Service Institute of the United States* 40 (May 1907): 448; Taylor to Jones, March 29 and April 6, 1846, AGO, Letters Received, NA, M567, Roll 327; Henry, *Campaign Sketches,* 70–71, 72; Croffut,

ed., *Fifty Years in Camp and Field,* 220–21; Meade to wife, April 2 and 7, in Meade, *Life and Letters,* 1:52, 53, 54; Doubleday, ed., *Journals of the Late Brevet Major Philip Norbourne Barbour,* 20–26.

4. Croffut, ed., *Fifty Years in Camp and Field,* 221; Simon, ed., *Papers of Ulysses S. Grant,* 1:76–99; Meade to wife, April 7, 1846, in Meade, *Life and Letters,* 1:53–56; Nichols, *Zach Taylor's Little Army,* 33–34; Winders, *Mr. Polk's Army,* 60–61; Ephraim Kirby Smith to wife, April 9, 1846, in Blackwood, ed., *To Mexico with Scott,* 37; Doubleday, ed., *Journals of the Late Brevet Major Philip Norbourne Barbour,* 23, 24–25, 28, 29, 30, 31; Henry, *Campaign Sketches,* 70, 72, 73; Napoleon J. T. Dana to Sue, April 11, 1846, ALS, Napoleon Jackson Tecumseh Dana Papers, USMA Library.

5. Taylor, Order Books, Orders No. 39, April 6, 1846, NA.

6. Mansfield to wife, July 10 and October 25, 1846, ALS, Joseph King Fenno Mansfield Papers, USMA Library. On October 4, 1846, Mansfield wrote his wife: "I am visited daily by Genl Taylor who has exhibited a great interest in me & been very friendly disposed from the time of the battles of the 8th & 9th May . . ." (ALS, USMA Library).

7. McCall to "M——," April 14, 1846, in McCall, *Letters from the Frontiers,* 442; Meade to wife, April 7, 13, and 21, 1846, in Meade, *Life and Letters,* 1:54, 55, 57, 58, 61, 63, and 65; Joseph J. Reynolds to William (his brother), April 19, 1846, ALS, Joseph Jones Reynolds Papers, USMA Library; Dana to Sue, April 15 and 17, 1846, ALS, Dana Papers, USMA Library; Grant to Julia, April 20, in Simon, ed., *Papers of Ulysses S. Grant* 1:80; Taylor to Jones, April 6, 1846, AGO, Letters Received, NA, M567, Roll 327; Ephraim Kirby Smith to wife, March 29, 1846, in Blackwood, ed., *To Mexico with Scott,* 34–35; Taylor, Order Books, Special Orders No. 52, April 14, 1846, NA.

8. Croffut, ed., *Fifty Years in Camp and Field,* 220–21; Taylor, Order Books, Orders No. 43, April 8, 1846, NA; Benjamin Alvord to Capt. Bradford R. Alden, April 11, 1846, ALS, Alden Family Papers, USMA Library.

9. Taylor, Order Books, Special Orders No. 47, April 8, 1846; Special Orders No. 49, April 10, 1846; Special Orders No. 53, April 15, 1846, NA (on resignations); Taylor, Order Books, Special Orders No. 49, April 10, 1846, NA (on Hitchcock's leave); Croffut, ed., *Fifty Years in Camp and Field,* 221, 222; Dana to Sue, April 1, 1846, ALS, USMA Library; AGO, Monthly Returns, Fourth and Seventh Infantry, NA, M665, Rolls 43 and 79, respectively.

10. Taylor, Order Books, Special Orders No. 51, April 13, 1846, NA; McCall to "M——," April 14, 1846, in McCall, *Letters from the Frontiers,* 441–42; Dana to Sue, April 15 and 17, 1846, ALS, Dana Papers, USMA Library (also in Ferrell, ed., *Monterrey Is Ours,* 43); Taylor to Jones, April 15, 1846, AGO, Letters Received, NA, M567, Roll 327; AGO, Monthly Returns, Fourth Infantry, NA, M665, Roll 43; AGO, Monthly Returns, Third Artillery, NA, M727, Roll 19; AGO, Monthly Returns, Second Dragoons, NA, M744, Roll 15.

11. Taylor, Order Books, Special Orders No. 55, April 21, 1846, NA; Taylor to Jones, April 15, 1846, AGO, Letters Received, NA, M567, Roll 327; Henry, *Campaign Sketches,* 74–75; Doubleday, ed., *Journals of the Late Brevet Major Philip Norbourne Barbour,* 36; Meade to wife, May 2, 1846, enclosing facsimile of his "Sketch showing the position

of the Army of Occupation on the left bank of the Rio Bravo opposite Matamoros, April 15, 1846," in Meade, *Life and Letters,* 1:74.

12. Taylor, Order Books, Orders No. 44, April 13, 1846; Special Orders No. 54, April 19, 1846; Orders No. 49, April 22, 1846, NA; Dana to Sue, April 17, 1846, ALS, USMA Library. Barbour's journal entry on April 13, 1846, says, "Colonel Whistler was placed in arrest this morning for neglect of duty and being 'tight.' Col. Garland now commands our Brigade" (Doubleday, ed., *Journals of the Late Brevet Major Philip Norbourne Barbour,* 36).

13. Taylor to Jones, April 15, 1846, AGO, Letters Received, NA, M567, Roll 327; Doubleday, ed., *Journals of the Late Brevet Major Philip Norbourne Barbour,* 32, 33, 34, 36, 38, 41; Ephraim Kirby Smith to wife, April 19, 1846, in Blackwood, ed., *To Mexico with Scott,* 38; Henry, *Campaign Sketches,* 73, 77, 79; Dana to Sue, April 11, 1846, ALS, USMA Library; Bauer, *Mexican War,* 46; Eisenhower, *So Far from God,* 63.

14. Taylor to Jones, April 15, 1846, AGO, Letters Received, NA, M567, Roll 327; Samuel Mercer, Commander, U.S. brig *Lawrence,* to Taylor, May 1, 1846, ALS, AOO, Letters Received, NA; Bauer, *Mexican War,* 47; Meade to wife, April 19 and 23, in Meade, *Life and Letters,* 1:69, 71; Dana to Sue, April 22, 1846, ALS, USMA Library.

15. Bauer, *Zachary Taylor,* 123; Doubleday, ed., *Journals of the Late Brevet Major Philip Norbourne Barbour,* 40; Polk, *Diary,* 2:317, 233; Henry, *Campaign Sketches,* 79–81; Hamilton, *Zachary Taylor,* 179.

16. Dana to Sue, April 17, 1846, ALS, Dana Papers, USMA Library (also in Ferrell, ed., *Monterrey Is Ours,* 44–45); Joseph J. Reynolds to William, April 19, 1846, ALS, Reynolds Papers, USMA Library; McCall to sister, April 23, 1846, in McCall, *Letters from the Frontiers,* 446. Barbour wrote in his journal on April 12, 1846: "Hatch is on picket tonight and I shall appropriate his blankets" (Doubleday, ed., *Journals of the Late Brevet Major Philip Norbourne Barbour,* 35).

17. Meade to wife, April 21, 1846, in Meade, *Life and Letters,* 1:66; Dana to Sue, April 21, 22, and 24, 1846, ALS, Dana Papers, USMA Library (also in Ferrell, ed., *Monterrey Is Ours,* 51–52); Doubleday, ed., *Journals of the Late Brevet Major Philip Norbourne Barbour,* 41, 42, 43; Henry, *Campaign Sketches,* 81–82; Ephraim Kirby Smith to wife, in Blackwood, ed., *To Mexico with Scott,* 39; Bauer, *Mexican War,* 46.

18. Dana to Sue, April 22, 1846, ALS, Dana Papers, USMA Library; Meade to wife, April 21 and 22, 1846, in Meade, *Life and Letters,* 1:67–68; Henry, *Campaign Sketches,* 77–78; Bauer, *Mexican War,* 46; Eisenhower, *So Far from God,* 64.

19. Meade to wife, April 22, 1846, in Meade, *Life and Letters,* 1:68; Grant to Julia, May 3, 1846, in Simon, ed., *Papers of Ulysses S. Grant,* 1:83.

20. Meade to wife, April 22 and 23, 1846, in Meade, *Life and Letters,* 1:69, 72; Dana to Sue, April 22, 1846, ALS, Dana Papers, USMA Library; Doubleday, ed., *Journals of the Late Brevet Major Philip Norbourne Barbour,* 40; Taylor, Order Books, Orders No. 47, April 18, 1846; Special Orders No. 55, April 21, 1846; Orders No. 49, April 22, 1846, NA. Volume 1 of the order books of General Taylor is entitled on its spine "Mexican War Army of Occupation Special Orders and Orders, Aug. 1845–Apr. 1846." On or about April 24, 1846, his general and special orders were entered in separate volumes. Volume 2 is designated "Mexican War Army of Occupation Orders Apr.–Dec., 1846." Vol-

ume 3 is devoted to special orders for that period. Volume 4 of Taylor's orders, covering those for 1847, includes once more both his general and special orders. The date and type of order indicates location better than volume number. Moreover, in the author's experience, when Taylor's order books are requested at the National Archives, they and other Mexican War order books are produced on a single trolley in the Reading Room.

21. Meade to wife, April 22, 23, and 26, 1846, in Meade, *Life and Letters,* 1:68, 70–72, 73–74; Doubleday, ed., *Journals of the Late Brevet Major Philip Norbourne Barbour,* 41, 42; Dana to Sue, April 23, 1846, ALS, USMA Library; Henry, *Campaign Sketches,* 79–81; Jarvis, "An Army Surgeon's Notes," *Journal of the Military Service Institute of the United States* 40 (May 1907): 451–52; McCall to sister, April 23, 1846, in McCall, *Letters from the Frontiers,* 445–46.

22. Meade to wife, April 23, in Meade, *Life and Letters,* 1:73.

23. Doubleday, ed., *Journals of the Late Brevet Major Philip Norbourne Barbour,* 45–48; Ephraim K. Smith to wife, April 28, 1846, in Blackwood, ed., *To Mexico with Scott,* 39–43; McCall to brother, May 6, 1846, in McCall, *Letters from the Frontiers,* 447; Jarvis, "An Army Surgeon's Notes," *Journal of the Military Service Institute of the United States* 40 (May 1907): 90–91; Henry, *Campaign Sketches,* 82–83; Rodenbough, *From Everglade to Cañon,* 99–101; Brackett, *History of the United States Cavalry,* 54–55; Bauer, *Mexican War,* 42, 48; Justin Smith, *War with Mexico,* 1:149–50; Hughes, "William Joseph Hardee," 88–90; Hughes, *General William J. Hardee,* 25–27; Proceedings of Court of Inquiry in the Case of Captain W. J. Hardee, Record Group 153, Records of the Office of the Judge Advocate General (Army), Court-Martial Case Files 1809–1894, No. EE 248, NA.

24. Proceedings of Court of Inquiry in the Case of Captain W. J. Hardee, NA.

25. Taylor to Jones, April 26, 1846, AGO, Letters Received, NA, M567, Roll 327; Hamilton, *Zachary Taylor,* 176; Polk, *Diary,* 1:386–95; Justin Smith, *War with Mexico,* 1:181–83; Bauer, *Mexican War,* 66–70; Eisenhower, *So Far from God,* 86–89.

26. Polk, *Diary,* 1:386–95; Justin Smith, *War with Mexico,* 1:181–83; Bauer, *Mexican War,* 66–70; Eisenhower, *So Far from God,* 86–89.

27. Taylor, Order Books, Orders No. 52 and 53, April 29, 1846, NA; Dana to Sue, April 29, 1846, ALS, Dana Papers, USMA Library (also in Ferrell, ed., *Monterrey Is Ours,* 55); Jarvis, "An Army Surgeon's Notes," *Journal of the Military Service Institute of the United States* 41 (1907): 91; Henry, *Campaign Sketches,* 83.

28. Hughes, "William Joseph Hardee," 90–96; Hughes, *General William J. Hardee,* 25–30; Proceedings of Court of Inquiry in the Case of Captain W. J. Hardee, NA; Paul D. Casdorph, *Prince John Magruder: His Life and Campaigns* (New York: John Wiley and Sons, 1996), 56.

29. Proceedings of Court of Inquiry in the Case of Captain W. J. Hardee, NA.

30. Proceedings of Court of Inquiry in the Case of Captain W. J. Hardee, NA. Captain Hardee would protest, in a three-page letter to Captain William Bliss on July 26, 1846, at being detached from his company by Twiggs's Orders No. 64 (enclosing the order), and being thereby sent to Point Isabel to train newly arrived troops for an indefinite period of time, just when his and the other Second Dragoon companies were

preparing to join Taylor at Camargo for his Monterrey campaign. He was convinced that the manifestly unfair and unusual order was related to the ambush controversy. (See Army of Occupation, Letters Received, NA.) The regiment's July roster shows that he did report to Point Isabel, sick but on duty with a detachment of recruits; however, he was reported as having been relieved on August 4, and by August 24 he was at Camargo (sick). Thus Twiggs's order was apparently contravened by General Taylor.

31. AGO, General Orders No. 35, August 10, 1846, Volume of General Orders, AGO, 1846–49, USMA Library; Hughes, *General William J. Hardee,* 28n17; McWhiney, *Braxton Bragg and Confederate Defeat,* 1:63; Doubleday, ed., *Journals of the Late Brevet Major Philip Norbourne Barbour,* 88.

32. Doubleday, ed., *Journals of the Late Brevet Major Philip Norbourne Barbour,* 48, 50; Jarvis, "An Army Surgeon's Notes," *Journal of the Military Service Institute of the United States* 41 (1907): 93; Henry, *Campaign Sketches,* 85.

33. McCall to Bliss, April 30, 1846, ALS, Letters Received, AOO, NA; Taylor, Order Books, Special Orders No. 58, April 29, 1846, NA; Doubleday, ed., *Journals of the Late Brevet Major Philip Norbourne Barbour,* 49.

34. Doubleday, ed., *Journals of the Late Brevet Major Philip Norbourne Barbour,* 50; Jarvis, "An Army Surgeon's Notes," *Journal of the Military Service Institute of the United States* 41 (1907): 93–94; Henry, *Campaign Sketches,* 85; Taylor to Jones, May 3, 1846, AGO, Letters Received, NA, M567, Roll 327. Captain Samuel Walker's company of Texas Mounted Rangers was mustered into U.S. service as of April 11, 1846, for three months (the usual enlistment term for these companies). Walker had reputedly fought in the regular army in the Seminole War; had served in two of Captain Hays's companies; and had been a prisoner for a year when the Texan expedition against Mier had failed. In the spring of 1846 he raised an unusually large company—ninety-one privates. It was a fifteen-man detachment of that unit that was surprised and nearly wiped out in Walker's absence on April 28 (presumably by the commands of Generals Canales and Torrejón). Accounts vary slightly with regard to the number killed and captured (Wilkins, *Highly Irregular Irregulars,* 25–28; Henry, *Campaign Sketches,* 85; Heitman, *Historical Register,* 1:997).

35. Doubleday, ed., *Journals of the Late Brevet Major Philip Norbourne Barbour,* 50–51; Jarvis, "An Army Surgeon's Notes," *Journal of the Military Service Institute of the United States* 41 (1907): 94; Henry, *Campaign Sketches,* 86; McCall to brother, May 6, 1846, in McCall, *Letters from the Frontiers,* 447; Taylor to Jones, May 3, 1846, AGO, Letters Received, NA, M567, Roll 327; AGO, Monthly Returns, Seventh Infantry, NA, M665, Roll 79; AGO, Monthly Returns, Second and Third Artillery, NA, M727, Rolls 11 and 19, respectively.

36. Dana to Sue, May 1, 1846, ALS, Dana Papers, USA Library (also in Ferrell, ed., *Monterrey Is Ours,* 57).

37. Taylor, Order Books, Orders No. 55, May 1, 1846, NA; Jarvis, "An Army Surgeon's Notes," *Journal of the Military Service Institute of the United States* 41 (1907): 94; Doubleday, ed., *Journals of the Late Brevet Major Philip Norbourne Barbour,* 51; Henry, *Campaign Sketches,* 86; Meade to wife, in Meade, *Life and Letters,* 1:74.

38. Dana to Capt. G. W. Cullum, August 26, 1859, ALS, Dana Papers, USMA Li-

brary; Cullum, *Biographical Register,* 1139, USMA Library; Dana to Sue, May 1, 1846, ALS, Dana Papers, USMA Library (also in Ferrell, ed., *Monterrey Is Ours,* 58). Except on one document, there appears to be no evidence of the fort opposite Matamoros ever having been called Fort Texas, as a number of historians have referred to it. A report sent by Maj. Jacob Brown to Bliss for the attention of General Taylor, dated May 4 (during the siege), referred to the fieldwork in its heading as "Fort Taylor." Some person (no indication of who, when, or where) struck out that designation and substituted "Fort Texas." General Taylor's report of April 26, in which he described what he knew of the ambush and indicated hostilities had commenced, was headed, as usual, "Camp near Matamoros, Texas." After the battles of May 8 and 9, of course, he issued an order naming it Fort Brown in honor of the late Maj. Jacob Brown.

CHAPTER 5

1. Dana to Sue, May 4, 1846, ALS, Dana Papers, USMA Library (also in Ferrell, ed., *Monterrey Is Ours,* 59).

2. Grant to Julia, May 3, 1846, in Simon, ed., *Papers of Ulysses S. Grant,* 1:83; Doubleday, ed., *Journals of the Late Brevet Major Philip Norbourne Barbour,* 52; Henry, *Campaign Sketches,* 88; Grant, *Personal Memoirs,* 1:92.

3. Ephraim Kirby Smith to wife, May 3, 1846, in Blackwood, ed., *To Mexico with Scott,* 44; Taylor to Jones, May 3, 1846, AGO, Letters Received, NA, M567, Roll 327; Henry, *Campaign Sketches,* 88.

4. Henry, *Campaign Sketches,* 88; Doubleday, ed., *Journals of the Late Brevet Major Philip Norbourne Barbour,* 52; Ephraim Kirby Smith to wife, May 7, 1846, in Blackwood, ed., *To Mexico with Scott,* 44–45; Jarvis, "An Army Surgeon's Notes," *Journal of the Military Service Institute of the United States* 41 (1907): 94–95; Meade to wife, May 5, 1846, in Meade, *Life and Letters,* 1:75.

5. Jarvis, "An Army Surgeon's Notes," *Journal of the Military Service Institute of the United States* 41 (1907): 94; Dana to Sue, May 4, 1846, ALS, Dana Papers, USMA Library (also in Ferrell, ed., *Monterrey Is Ours,* 58); Henry, *Campaign Sketches,* 88.

6. Henry, *Campaign Sketches,* 89; Doubleday, ed., *Journals of the Late Brevet Major Philip Norbourne Barbour,* 52–53; Ephraim Kirby Smith to wife, May 7, 1846, in Blackwood, ed., *To Mexico with Scott,* 44–45; Maj. Jacob Brown to Bliss, May 4, 1846, AGO, Letters Received, NA, M567, Roll 327; Meade to wife, May 5, 1846, in Meade, *Life and Letters,* 1:75–76. At the time, few regular army officers other than General Taylor appear to have appreciated the extreme importance of Sam Walker's infiltration through the Mexican lines surrounding the American fort opposite Matamoros. He was indeed the first American hero of the Mexican War (Wilkins, *Highly Irregular Irregulars,* 30–31). The Polk administration rewarded him with a regular army appointment as a captain in the Mounted Rifles Regiment, effective May 27, 1846, although he continued to serve with the Rangers through the Monterrey battle. He was killed October 9, 1847, during the Huamantla battle while serving under General Scott (Heitman, *Historical Register,* 1:997).

7. Taylor to Jones, May 3, 1846, AGO, Letters Received, NA, M567, Roll 327; Taylor,

Order Books, Orders No. 56, May 5, 1846; Orders No. 57, May 6, 1846; Special Orders No. 59, May 3, 1846, NA.

8. Dana to Cullum, August 26, 1846, ALS, Dana Papers, USMA Library; Dana to Sue, May 4, 11, 12, 1846, ALS, Dana Papers, USMA Library (also in Ferrell, ed., *Monterrey Is Ours,* 59–62).

9. Dana to Sue, May 11 and 12, 1846, ALS, Dana Papers, USMA Library (also in Ferrell, ed., *Monterrey Is Ours,* 60–62).

10. Taylor to Jones, May 7 and 9, 1846, AGO, Letters Received, NA, M567, Roll 327; Taylor, Order Books, Orders No. 58, May 7, 1846, NA; Henry, *Campaign Sketches,* 89; Doubleday, ed., *Journals of the Late Brevet Major Philip Norbourne Barbour,* 53; Ephraim Kirby Smith to wife, May 7, 1846, in Blackwood, ed., *To Mexico with Scott,* 45; Meade to wife, May 7 and 9, in Meade, *Life and Letters,* 1:77–79; Justin Smith, *War with Mexico,* 1:165–66; Bauer, *Zachary Taylor,* 154.

11. Meade to wife, May 7, 1846, in Meade, *Life and Letters,* 1:78.

12. Meade to wife, May 5, in Meade, *Life and Letters,* 1:76.

13. Justin Smith, *War With Mexico,* 1:164–65.

14. McCall to Peter, June 14, 1846, in McCall, *Letters from the Frontiers,* 450; Justin Smith, *War with Mexico,* 1:165; Taylor to Jones, May 9, 1846, AGO, Letters Received, NA, M567, Roll 327; French, *Two Wars,* 50.

15. Ephraim Kirby Smith to wife, May 10 and 13, 1846, in Blackwood, ed., *To Mexico with Scott,* 45–49; Doubleday, ed., *Journals of the Late Brevet Major Philip Norbourne Barbour,* 53–57; Meade to wife, May 9, 1846, in Meade, *Life and Letters,* 1:79–80; French, *Two Wars,* 49; Justin Smith, *War with Mexico,* 1:164–65; Henry, *Campaign Sketches,* 90–94; Jarvis, "An Army Surgeon's Notes," *Journal of the Military Service Institute of the United States* 41 (1907): 96; Grant to Julia, May 11, 1846, in Simon, ed., *Papers of Ulysses S. Grant,* 1:84–85; McCall to "M——," May 18, 1846, in McCall, *Letters from the Frontiers,* 448–49; McCall to Peter, June 14, 1846, in McCall, *Letters from the Frontiers,* 449, 450.

16. McCall to Peter, June 14, 1846, in McCall, *Letters from the Frontiers,* 450.

17. Henry, *Campaign Sketches,* 90; Justin Smith, *War with Mexico,* 1:158, 163–66; Bauer, *Mexican War,* 53; Bauer, *Zachary Taylor,* 154; Taylor to Jones, May 9 (No. 35 and No. 36), 1846, AGO, Letters Received, NA, M567, Roll 327.

18. Justin Smith, *War with Mexico,* 1:156–69; Grant to Julia, May 11, 1846, in Simon, ed., *Papers of Ulysses S. Grant,* 1:84–85; Grant, *Personal Memoirs,* 1:95; Lester R. Dillon Jr., *American Artillery in the Mexican War, 1846–1847* (Austin, TX: Presidial Press, 1975), 9–25.

19. French, *Two Wars,* 50; Doubleday, ed., *Journals of the Late Brevet Major Philip Norbourne Barbour,* 53–56; McIntosh to Bliss, December 2, 1846, ALS, UNC Library, McIntosh Papers; Justin Smith, *War with Mexico,* 1:166–67; McCall to Peter, June 14, 1846, in McCall, *Letters from the Frontiers,* 449; Jarvis, "An Army Surgeon's Notes," *Journal of the Military Service Institute of the United States* 41 (1907): 96; Taylor to Jones, May 9 and 17, 1846, AGO, Letters Received, NA, M567, Roll 327; Twiggs to Bliss, May 11, 1846, AGO, Letters Received, NA, M567, Roll 327.

20. McCall to Peter, June 14, 1846, in McCall, *Letters from the Frontiers,* 453.

21. McCall, June 14, 1846, in McCall, *Letters from the Frontiers,* 453; Grant to Julia,

May 11, 1846, in Simon, ed., *Papers of Ulysses S. Grant,* 1:85; Bauer, *Zachary Taylor,* 155–56; Henry, *Campaign Sketches,* 92–93; Doubleday, ed., *Journals of the Late Brevet Major Philip Norbourne Barbour,* 55, 56; Justin Smith, *War with Mexico,* 1:167–69.

22. Belknap to Bliss, May 15, 1846, AGO, Letters Received, NA, M567, Roll 327; Doubleday, ed., *Journals of the Late Brevet Major Philip Norbourne Barbour,* 56; Justin Smith, *War with Mexico,* 1:168–69; Henry, *Campaign Sketches,* 93; Bauer, *Zachary Taylor,* 155–56.

23. McCall to Peter, in McCall, *Letters from the Frontiers,* 454; Grant to Julia, May 11, 1846, in Simon, ed., *Papers of Ulysses S. Grant,* 1:85; Taylor to Jones, May 9, AGO Letters Received, NA, M567, Roll 327; Bauer, *Zachary Taylor,* 157 (on number of troops killed, wounded, and missing).

24. Taylor to Jones, May 9 and 17, 1846, AGO, Letters Received, NA M567, Roll 327; Meade to wife, May 9 and 11, 1846, in Meade, *Life and Letters,* 1:80; Doubleday, ed., *Journals of the Late Brevet Major Philip Norbourne Barbour,* 57–61; Ephraim Kirby Smith to wife, May 10 and 13, 1846, in Blackwood, ed., *To Mexico with Scott;* Jarvis, "An Army Surgeon's Notes," *Journal of the Military Service Institute of the United States* 41 (1907): 98–99; Henry, *Campaign Sketches,* 94–95; Porter, "Medical and Surgical Notes," 20.

25. Meade to wife, May 9, 1846, in Meade, *Life and Letters,* 1:80–81; Henry, *Campaign Sketches,* 94; Jarvis, "An Army Surgeon's Notes," *Journal of the Military Service Institute of the United States* 41 (1907): 98; Porter, "Medical and Surgical Notes," 20.

26. Taylor to Jones, May 9 and 12, 1846, AGO, Letters Received, NA, M567, Roll 327; McCall to Peter, June 14, 1846, in McCall, *Letters from the Frontiers,* 454; Taylor to Jones, May 17, 1846, with enclosures (C. F. Smith's report to McCall, May 13, 1846; McCall's report to Bliss, May 13, 1846), AGO, Letters Received, NA, M567, Roll 327.

27. Taylor to Jones, May 17, 1846, AGO, Letters Received, NA, M567, Roll 327; French, *Two Wars,* 51.

28. Taylor to Jones, May 17, 1846, Letters Received, NA, M567, Roll 327; French, *Two Wars,* 51–53; Longstreet, *From Manassas to Appomattox,* 27–28; Bauer, *Zachary Taylor,* 159–62.

29. Taylor to Jones, May 17, 1846, Letters Received, M567, Roll 327; Longstreet, *From Manassas to Appomattox,* 28; French, *Two Wars,* 54.

30. Longstreet, *From Manassas to Appomattox,* 26.

31. Taylor to Jones, May 17, 1846, AGO, Letters Received, NA, M567, Roll 327; Ephraim Kirby Smith to wife, May 10 and 13, 1846, in Blackwood, ed., *To Mexico with Scott,* 46–47, 49–53; Buchanan to Maj. G. W. Allen, May 10, 1846, AGO, Letters Received, NA, M567, Roll 327; Belknap to Bliss, May 14, 1846, ALS, Princeton University Library (evidently a rough draft of official report); Belknap to Bliss, May 15, 1846, AGO, Letters Received, NA, M567, Roll 327.

32. Belknap to Bliss, May 15, 1846, AGO, Letters Received, NA, M567, Roll 327; Taylor to Jones, May 17, 1846, AGO, Letters Received, NA, M567, Roll 327.

33. Taylor to Jones, May 9 and 17, 1846, AGO, Letters Received, NA, M567, Roll 327; Grant, *Personal Memoirs,* 1:97–98.

34. Taylor to Jones, May 9 and 17, 1846, AGO, Letters Received, NA, M567, Roll 327;

French, *Two Wars,* 54–56; Dana to Sue, May 12, 1846, ALS, Dana Papers, USMA Library (also in Ferrell, ed., *Monterrey Is Ours,* 63); Grant to Julia, May 11, 1846, in Simon, ed., *Papers of Ulysses S. Grant,* 1:84.

35. Taylor to Jones, May 9, 12, and 17, 1846, AGO, Letters Received, NA, M567, Roll 327; Taylor to Wood, May 9, 1846, in Samson, ed., *Letters of Zachary Taylor,* 1–2; Bauer, *Zachary Taylor,* 162.

36. Marcy to Taylor, January 13, 1846, ALS, AOO, Letters Received, NA; Taylor to Jones, May 19, 1846, AGO, Letters Received, NA, M567, Roll 327; Justin Smith, *War with Mexico,* 1:177; Bauer, *Mexican War,* 82; Bauer, *Zachary Taylor,* 162–64.

37. Barbour to wife, May 12, 1846, in Doubleday, ed., *Journals of the Late Brevet Major Philip Norbourne Barbour,* 174; Grant to Julia, May 11, 1846, in Simon, ed., *Papers of Ulysses S. Grant,* 1:86, 87; Meade to wife, May 11, 1846, in Meade, *Life and Letters,* 1:83; Edmund Kirby Smith to mother, May 13, 1846, in Parks, *General Edmund Kirby Smith,* 49.

38. Benjamin Alvord, Braxton Bragg, Robert Buchanan, Lawrence P. Graham, Alexander Hays, George McCall (two brevets, one for Palo Alto and one for Resaca), Joseph K. F. Mansfield, William R. Montgomery, Alfred Pleasonton, and Charles F. Smith (Heitman, *Historical Register,* 1:passim).

39. Taylor to Jones, May 12, 1846, AGO, Letters Received, NA, M567, Roll 327; Hughes, "William Joseph Hardee," 94n47; Hughes, *General William J. Hardee,* 27–28; Rodenbough, *From Everglade to Cañon,* 100; Thornton to Bliss, May 19, 1846, ALS, AOO, Letters Received, NA; Thornton to Jones, May 14, 1846, AGO, Letters Received, M567, Roll 327.

40. Taylor to Jones, May 12, 1846, AGO, Letters Received, NA, M567, Roll 327; Meade to wife, May 24, 1846, in Meade, *Life and Letters,* 1:89.

41. Taylor to Jones, May 12, 1846, AGO, Letters Received, NA, M567, Roll 327; Taylor, Order Books, Orders No. 59, May 11, 1846, NA; Taylor, Order Books, Orders No. 60, May 12, 1846, NA; Taylor, Order Books, Special Orders No. 62, May 12, 1846, NA.

42. Taylor, Order Books, Special Orders No. 64, May 14, 1846, NA; AGO, Monthly Returns, First Infantry, NA, M665, Roll 3; Taylor to Jones, May 18, 1846, AGO, Letters Received, NA, M567, Roll 327; Commodore D. Conner, U.S. Ship *Cumberland,* to Taylor, May 8, 1846, ADS, AOO, Letters Received, NA; Bvt. Maj. John Munroe, Point Isabel, to Bliss, May 9, 1846, ALS, Letters Received, NA; Capt. John Sanders, Corps of Engineers, Point Isabel, to Bliss, May 10, 1846, ALS; Lt. Col. Benjamin K. Pierce, First Artillery, Brazos Santiago, to Taylor, May 13, 1846, ALS; Col. James B. Walton, La. Volunteers, Point Isabel, to Bliss, May 15, 1846, ALS; Maj. Charles W. Thomas, Quartermaster Dept., Fort Polk, to Bliss, May 15, 1846, ALS; Lt. Col. Henry Wilson, Burrita, to Bliss, May 17, 1846, ALS; Capt. John Sanders to Bliss, May 16, ALS; Lt. Col. Wilson, Burrita, to Bliss, May 18, 1846, ALS; Maj. Charles W. Thomas, Fort Polk, to Bliss, May 18, 1846, ALS; Brig. Gen. Persifor Smith, La. Volunteers, Point Isabel, to Bliss, May 18, 1846, ALS.

43. Taylor to Wood, in Samson, ed., *Letters of Zachary Taylor,* 3; Taylor to Jones, May 18, 1846, AGO, Letters Received, NA, M567, Roll 327; Taylor, Order Books, Orders No. 61 and No. 62, May 17, 1846, NA.

44. Taylor, Order Books, Orders No. 61 and No. 62, May 17, 1846, NA; Taylor to Jones, May 18, 1846; Doubleday, ed., *Journals of the Late Brevet Major Philip Norbourne Barbour,* 61–64; Henry, *Campaign Sketches,* 104–8; Taylor to Wood, May 19, 1846, in Samson, ed., *Letters of Zachary Taylor,* 3–5; Meade to wife, May 25, 1846, in Meade, *Life and Letters,* 1:90.

CHAPTER 6

1. Taylor to Jones, May 18, 1846, AGO, Letters Received, NA, M567, Roll 327; Bauer, *Zachary Taylor,* 164.

2. Taylor to Jones, May 18, 1846, AGO, Letters Received, NA, M567, Roll 327.

3. Taylor to Jones, May 18, 1846, AGO, Letters Received, NA, M567, Roll 327; Meade to wife, May 19 and 27, 1846, in Meade, *Life and Letters,* 1:85–86, 90–91; Ephraim Kirby Smith to wife, May 19, 1846, in Blackwood, ed., *To Mexico with Scott,* 54–55; Doubleday, ed., *Journals of the Late Brevet Major Philip Norbourne Barbour,* 64–65; Jarvis, "An Army Surgeon's Notes," *Journal of the Military Service Institute of the United States* 41 (1907): 102; Henry, *Campaign Sketches,* 108–110; French, *Two Wars,* 57–58; Taylor to Wood, May 19, 1846, in Samson, ed., *Letters of Zachary Taylor,* 3–4.

4. Meade to wife, May 24 and 25, 1846, in Meade, *Life and Letters,* 1:89, 90; Doubleday, ed., *Journals of the Late Brevet Major Philip Norbourne Barbour,* May 21, 1846, 66–68; Jarvis, "An Army Surgeon's Notes," *Journal of the Military Service Institute of the United States* 41 (1907): 102; Henry, *Campaign Sketches,* 109–111, 114; Grant to Julia, July 2, 1846, in Simon, ed., *Papers of Ulysses S. Grant,* 1:99.

5. Meade to wife, May 25 and 27, 1846, AGO, Letters Received, NA, M567, Roll 327.

6. Taylor to Jones, May 21 and 24, 1846, AGO, Letters Received, NA M567, Roll 327.

7. Taylor to Jones, May 21 and 24, 1846, AGO, Letters Received, NA M567, Roll 327; Meade to wife, May 24, 1846, in Meade, *Life and Letters,* 1:88; Doubleday, ed., *Journals of the Late Brevet Major Philip Norbourne Barbour,* 66–68; Garland to Bliss, May 24, 1846, AOO, Letters Received, ALS, NA; Dana to Sue, May 23, 1846, ALS, Dana Papers, USMA Library; Jarvis, "An Army Surgeon's Notes," *Journal of the Military Service Institute of the United States* 41 (1907): 103; Henry, *Campaign Sketches,* 113.

8. Taylor, Order Books, Orders No. 63, May 21, 1846, NA.

9. Taylor, Order Books, Orders No. 64, May 22, 1846, NA; Doubleday, ed., *Journals of the Late Brevet Major Philip Norbourne Barbour,* 69.

10. Taylor, Order Books, After Orders, May 22, 1846, NA.

11. Taylor, Order Books, Orders No. 66, May 25, 1846, NA; Hardee, Court of Inquiry Proceedings, Judge Advocate General (Army), File EE248, NA; Doubleday, ed., *Journals of the Late Brevet Major Philip Norbourne Barbour,* 69, 70–73, 79, 82–84. Hugh McLeod, a West Pointer (1835), formerly in the Third Infantry and a friend of Capt. Philip Barbour, published an English-language paper in Matamoros named *Republic of the Rio Grande and the People's Friend* (Henry, *Campaign Sketches,* 117).

12. Meade to wife, May 19, 1846, in Meade, *Life and Letters,* 1:86; Henry, *Campaign Sketches,* 113–14; Doubleday, ed., *Journals of the Late Brevet Major Philip Norbourne Barbour,* 66; Grant to Julia, June 10, 1846, in Simon, ed., *Papers of Ulysses S. Grant,* 1:92–93;

Dana to Sue, May 21, 1846, ALS, Dana Papers, USMA Library (also in Ferrell, ed., *Monterrey Is Ours,* 81); Ephraim Kirby Smith to wife, May 19, 1846, in Blackwood, ed., *To Mexico with Scott,* 54; Doubleday, ed., *Journals of the Late Brevet Major Philip Norbourne Barbour,* 68; McCall to "M——," July 2, 1846, in McCall, *Letters from the Frontiers,* 456–57.

13. Taylor, Order Books, Special Orders No. 66, May 16, 1846; Special Orders No. 67, May 22, 1846; Special Orders No. 72, May 28, 1846; Special Orders No. 73, May 29, 1846, NA.

14. Taylor to Wood, May 19, 1846, in Samson, ed., *Letters of Zachary Taylor,* 4.

15. Taylor to Wood, June 24 and June 30, 1846, in Samson, ed., *Letters of Zachary Taylor,* 17 and 21, respectively. See also Polk, *Diary,* 1:450–51, 480–81.

16. Taylor to Jones, July 1, 1846, AGO, Letters Received, NA, M567, Roll 327.

17. Taylor to Wood, June 30, 1846, in Samson, ed., *Letters of Zachary Taylor,* 19–20; Meade to wife, July 16, 24, and 30, 1846, in Meade, *Life and Letters,* 1:114, 115–16; Bauer, *Mexican War,* 69–72, 83–84; Winders, *Mr. Polk's Army,* 69–70, 72; Hamilton, *Zachary Taylor,* 194.

18. Meade to wife, May 27, 1846, in Meade, *Life and Letters,* 1:91. See also his letters of June 28 (108–9) and July 9, 1846 (109–110).

19. Grant to Julia, July 25, 1846, in Simon, ed., *Papers of Ulysses S. Grant,* 1:102; Taylor to Wood, June 30 and July 7, 1846, in Samson, ed., *Letters of Zachary Taylor,* 22, 24. The reason Taylor had little control over the Texans was that he had asked their governor, J. Pinckney Henderson, for two cavalry regiments (and two of infantry); and Henderson, having appointed himself major general of volunteers for his state, was in Point Isabel awaiting the arrival of two volunteer cavalry units badly needed by Taylor, the companies of Henderson's First Mounted Rifles. In late June and early July those contingents were being sworn into federal service, but to keep them reenlisting after their customary three-month term of service required diplomacy. Taylor's remarks concerning their potential value demonstrate his shrewdness. Other than Sam Walker's company, the Rangers did not fight in the early battles at Palo Alto and Resaca de la Palma; but Capt. Ben McCulloch formed his own company, and by May 23 he and his men, as well as those in the companies of Captains Walker and Price, were stationed at Fort Brown. Thereafter they and other Ranger units performed invaluable service as scouts and escorts until they fought under Taylor and Worth at Monterrey. See Robarts, *Mexican War Veterans,* 74; Wilkins, *Highly Irregular Irregulars,* 35–45; Samuel C. Reid Jr., *The Scouting Expeditions of McCulloch's Texas Rangers; or the Summer and Fall Campaign of the Army of the United States in Mexico—1846. Including Skirmishes with the Mexicans, and an Accurate Detail of the Storming of Monterey; also, the Daring Scouts at Buena Vista* (Philadelphia: G. G. Evans, 1859), 38–42; Jack W. Gunn, "Ben McCulloch: A Big Captain," *Southwestern Historical Quarterly* 43.1 (July 1954): 7.

20. Taylor, Order Books, Orders No. 67, May 29, 1846, NA; AGO, Monthly Returns, Third, Fourth, Fifth, Seventh, and Eighth Infantry, NA, M665, Rolls 31, 43, 55, 79, and 90, respectively; AGO, Monthly Returns, Second Dragoons, NA, M744, Roll 15. See also Henry, *Campaign Sketches,* 117; Meade to wife, June 7, 1846, in Meade, *Life and Let-*

ters, 1:98; Doubleday, ed., *Journals of the Late Brevet Major Philip Norbourne Barbour,* 75, 80; Dana to Sue, June 5, 1846, ALS, USMA Library.

21. Jones to Taylor, May 12, 1846, ALS, AOO, Letters Received, NA.

22. Taylor to Jones, May 21 and June 3, 1846, AGO, Letters Received, NA, M567, Roll 327; Taylor to Wood, June 12, 1846, in Samson, ed., *Letters of Zachary Taylor,* 9.

23. Taylor, Order Books, Special Orders No. 78, June 4, 1846, NA. Mexican villagers had reason to fear occasional raids by Comanches. At Camargo, General Worth sent McCulloch's company after a party that had been raiding on both sides of the Rio Grande. The Rangers found carnage left behind by the Indians but were unable to catch up with them before they disappeared northward (Wilkins, *Highly Irregular Irregulars,* 2–67 passim).

24. Wilson to Bliss, June 10, 1846, ALS, AOO, Letters Received, NA; Meade to wife, July 7, 1846, in Meade, *Life and Letters,* 1:98; Doubleday, ed., *Journals of the Late Brevet Major Philip Norbourne Barbour,* 69–70, 84; Henry, *Campaign Sketches,* 117; AGO, Monthly Returns, First Infantry, NA, M665, Roll 3; AGO, Monthly Returns, Third Artillery, NA, M727, Roll 19. The Texas mounted Rangers accompanying Wilson to Reynosa were in Capt. John T. Price's company (Wilkins, *Highly Irregular Irregulars,* 45).

25. Wilson to Bliss, June 10, 1846, ALS, AOO, Letters Received, NA.

26. Meade to wife, June 28, 1846, in Meade, *Life and Letters,* 1:106–7.

27. Sedgwick to father, August 8, 1846, and Sedgwick to sister, August 15, 1846, in John Sedgwick, *Correspondence of John Sedgwick, Major-General* (2 vols., n.p., 1902), 1:8, 11–13.

28. Taylor to Wood, June 12, 21, and 30, 1846, in Samson, ed., *Letters of Zachary Taylor,* 9–10, 15, 20.

29. Polk, *Diary,* 1:395–96. See also Justin Smith, *War with Mexico,* 1:196–99.

30. Scott, *Memoirs,* 1:1–380 passim; Charles Winslow Elliott, *Winfield Scott: The Soldier and the Man* (New York: MacMillan, 1937), 1–416, passim; Grant, *Personal Memoirs,* 1:41–42.

31. Polk, *Diary,* 1:400–401.

32. Polk, *Diary,* 1:407–420; Justin Smith, *War with Mexico,* 1:198–200; Bauer, *Zachary Taylor,* 167.

33. Polk, *Diary,* 1:415–16, 417–18, 424–28, 438.

34. Taylor, Order Books, Orders No. 78, June 27, 1846, NA (quoting Polk's letter informing Taylor of his promotion).

35. Polk, *Diary,* 412–13, 424.

36. Grant to Julia, August 14, 1846, in Simon, ed., *Papers of Ulysses S. Grant,* 1:97–98; Meade to wife, June 12, 1846, in Meade, *Life and Letters,* 1:102–3. See also Henry, *Campaign Sketches,* 128; John F. Reynolds to sisters, June 12, 1846, ALS, Reynolds Family Papers, Franklin and Marshall College Library, Lancaster, PA (extract also in Nichols, *Toward Gettysburg,* 26).

37. Polk, *Diary,* 1:429, 434, 437–38.

38. Ibid., 2:50.

39. Ibid., 1:338, 470–71, 479.

40. Taylor to Wood, June 30, 1846, in Samson, ed., *Letters of Zachary Taylor,* 19–20.

41. Taylor to Wood, May 19, 1846, in Samson, ed., *Letters of Zachary Taylor,* 4; William Preston Johnston, *The Life of Gen. Albert Sidney Johnston* (New York: D. Appleton, 1878), 132–33. In one letter, Taylor calls Johnston "my friend" (Taylor to Wood, July 25, 1846, in Samson, ed., *Letters of Zachary Taylor,* 32).

42. Roland, *Albert Sidney Johnston,* 6–127 passim; Johnston, *Life of Albert Sidney Johnston,* 133, 134. For quote about Kendall, see Roland biography, page 127. Napoleon Dana, in a letter to Sue dated July 20, 1846, from Camargo, mentioned having just talked with Kendall for half an hour (ALS, Dana Papers, USMA Library). Johnston commanded the only regiment of Texas foot soldiers thus far raised (Wilkins, *Highly Irregular Irregulars,* 43).

43. Taylor, Order Books, Orders No. 83, July 7, 1846, NA. The companies disbanded were C, Second Artillery; I, Third Artillery; and E, Fourth Artillery.

44. Taylor, Order Books, Special Orders No. 99, July 8 and 13, 1846, NA.

45. Taylor, Order Books, Special Orders No. 104, July 15, 1846, NA.

46. AGO, Monthly Returns, Fourth Infantry, NA, M665, Roll 43.

47. Taylor, Order Books, Special Orders No. 113, July 28, 1846, NA.

48. Taylor, Order Books, Special Orders No. 106, July 18, 1846, NA.

49. AGO, Monthly Returns, Fourth Artillery, NA, M727, Roll 27; Hughes and Johnson, eds., *Fighter from Way Back,* 1, 2; Bridges, *Lee's Maverick General,* 20.

50. Judge Advocate General (Army), Court-Martial Case Files, 1809–1894, No. EE 254, NA.

51. Miles to Bliss, July 8, 1846, ALS, AOO, Letters Received, NA; Holmes to Bliss, July 8, 1846, ALS, AOO, Letters Received, NA.

52. Holmes to Bliss, July 8, 1846, ALS, AOO, Letters Received, NA; Miles to Bliss, July 14, 1846, ALS, AOO, Letters Received, NA; Holmes to Lt. F. N. Page (Adjutant, Seventh Infantry), July 15, 1846, ALS; Capt. R. H. Ross to Miles, July 16, 1846, ALS; Miles to Bliss, July 16, 1846, ALS; Taylor to Jones, July 22, 1846, AGO, Letters Received, NA, M567, Roll 328; Henry, *Campaign Sketches,* 120; AGO, Monthly Returns, Seventh Infantry, NA, M665, Roll 79.

53. Dana to Sue, July 13, 1846, ALS, Dana Papers, USMA Library; Holmes to Page, July 15, 1846, ALS, AOO, Letters Received, NA.

54. Miles to Bliss, July 14, 16, and 20, 1846, ALS, AOO, Letters Received, NA; Dana to Sue, July 13, 1846, ALS, Dana Papers, USMA Library (also in Ferrell, ed., *Monterrey Is Ours,* 101).

55. Miles to Bliss, July 20, 1846, ALS, AOO, Letters Received, NA; Capt. M. E. Merrill (Fifth Infantry) to Miles, July 20, 1846, ALS, AOO, Letters Received, NA; Dana to Sue, July 22, 24, 25, and 29, 1846, ALS, Dana Papers, USMA Library; Henry, *Campaign Sketches,* 123–25; Taylor to Jones, July 22 and August 10, 1846, AGO, Letters Received, NA, M567, Roll 328; Taylor to Wood, July 25, 1846, in Samson, ed., *Letters of Zachary Taylor,* 31; AGO, Monthly Returns, Fifth and Eighth Infantry, NA, M665, Rolls 55 and 90, respectively; Doubleday, ed., *Journals of the Late Brevet Major Philip Norbourne Barbour,* 95 (on Mier).

56. Doubleday, ed., *Journals of the Late Brevet Major Philip Norbourne Barbour,* 90–94, 99; Henry, *Campaign Sketches,* 94; Taylor to Jones, July 22, 1846, AGO, Letters Received, NA, M567, Roll 328; Dana to Sue, August 1, 1846, ALS, Dana Papers, USMA Library; AGO, Monthly Returns, Third and Fourth Infantry, NA, M665, Rolls 31 and 43, respectively; Grant to Julia, August 4, 1846, in Simon, ed., *Papers of Ulysses S. Grant,* 1:103.

57. Grant to Julia, Aug. 14, 1846, in Simon, ed., *Papers of Ulysses S. Grant,* 1:104–6; AGO, Monthly Returns, Fourth Infantry, NA, M665, Roll 43.

58. Miles to Bliss, July 14, 1846, ALS, AOO, Letters Received, NA; Holmes to Page, July 15, 1846, ALS, AOO, Letters Received, NA; Taylor, Order Books, Special Orders 112, July 25, 1846, NA (on two companies each of Third and Fourth Artillery); Orders 93, July 30, 1846, NA (on other artillery companies); AGO, Monthly Returns, First and Fourth Artillery, NA, M727, Rolls 3 and 27, respectively; Hughes and Johnson, eds., *Fighter from Way Back,* 1–9.

59. Taylor, Order Books, Orders No. 93, July 30, 1846, NA.

60. Taylor to Jones, August 10, 1846, AGO, Letters Received, NA, M567, Roll 328; Meade to wife, August 3, 1846, in Meade, *Life and Letters,* 1:117.

61. Grant to Julia, August 14, 1846, in Simon, ed., *Papers of Ulysses S. Grant,* 1:104–6; Taylor, Order Books, Orders No. 91, July 21, 1846, NA (on McCall); McCall to Bliss, July 21, 1846, ALS, AOO, Letters Received, NA; AGO, Monthly Returns, Fourth Infantry, NA, M665, Roll 43.

62. Grant to Julia, August 14, 1836, in Simon, ed., *Papers of Ulysses S. Grant,* 1:104; Meade to wife, August 10, 1846, in Meade, *Life and Letters,* 1:118.

63. John F. Reynolds to father, August 20, 1846, ALS, Reynolds Family Papers, Franklin and Marshall College Library; Doubleday, ed., *Journals of the Late Brevet Major Philip Norbourne Barbour,* 99; Henry, *Campaign Sketches,* 132–43, 151–52; AGO, Monthly Returns, Third Infantry, NA, M665, Roll 31; [Luther Giddings], *Sketches of the Campaign in Northern Mexico in Eighteen Hundred Forty-Six and Seven, by an Officer of the First Regiment of Ohio Volunteers* (New York: George P. Putnam, 1853), 76.

64. Mackall to wife, August 22, 1846, ALS, UNC Library; AGO, Monthly Returns, First Artillery, NA, M727, Roll 3; AGO, Monthly Returns, Second Dragoons, M744, Roll 15.

65. Taylor, Order Books, Orders No. 93, July 30, 1846, NA (on transportation of volunteer units); William Hugh Robarts, *Mexican War Veterans: A Complete Roster of the Regular and Volunteer Troops in the War between the United States and Mexico, from 1846 to 1848* (Washington DC: Brentano's, 1887), 39 (on Bryan and Forney), 42 (on Jackson and Nelson), 51 (on Fry and Hobson), 59 (on Davis, Cooper, Posey, and Griffith), 67 (on Morgan), 56 (on Kenly); John R. Kenly, *Memoirs of a Maryland Volunteer* (Philadelphia: J. B. Lippincott, 1873), 61–64; Roland, *Albert Sidney Johnston,* 129; Doubleday, ed., *Journals of the Late Brevet Major Philip Norbourne Barbour,* 100 (on the arrival of Johnston at Camargo); William C. Davis, *Jefferson Davis: The Man and His Hour, A Biography* (New York: HarperCollins, 1991), 127–38.

66. W. C. Davis, *Jefferson Davis,* 52–74; Clement Eaton, *Jefferson Davis* (New York: Free Press, 1977), 21–22; Steven E. Woodworth, *Jefferson Davis and His Generals: The*

Failure of Confederate Command in the West (Lawrence, KS: University Press of Kansas, 1990), 6–7; Hudson Strode, *Jefferson Davis, American Patriot, 1808–1861* (New York: Harcourt, Brace, 1955), 78–105; Dyer, *Zachary Taylor,* 96–99.

67. W. C. Davis, *Jefferson Davis,* 3–38; Eaton, *Jefferson Davis,* 1–20; Woodworth, *Jefferson Davis,* 1–7; Strode, *Jefferson Davis,* 3–49.

68. W. C. Davis, *Jefferson Davis,* 30–96, 128; Eaton, *Jefferson Davis,* 23, 35–36; Woodworth, *Jefferson Davis,* 7; Strode, *Jefferson Davis,* 106–157.

69. W. C. Davis, *Jefferson Davis,* 125–38; Eaton, *Jefferson Davis,* 23, 41, 47–51; Woodworth, *Jefferson Davis,* 7; Strode, *Jefferson Davis,* 157–63.

70. W. C. Davis, *Jefferson Davis,* 118, 134–37; Eaton, *Jefferson Davis,* 19–20.

71. Taylor, Order Books, Orders No. 99, August 17, and Orders No. 105, August 24, 1846, NA (on movements of First and Second brigades); Taylor to Jones, August 19 and 25, 1846, AGO, Letters Received, NA, M567, Roll 328; Taylor, Order Books, Special Orders No. 118, August 3, 1846, NA (on detachment under Colonel Hays); Taylor, Order Books, Special Orders No. 129, August 27, 1846, NA (on Colonel Hays at China); Taylor, Order Books, Special Orders No. 119, August 11, 1846, NA (on Mier reconnaissance); Robarts, *Mexican War Veterans,* 74–75 (on officers in regiment commanded by Colonel Hays). Taylor, in a letter to Jones of August 25, mentions that Colonel Hays occupied San Fernando on the way to China.

72. Taylor to Jones, August 10, AGO, Letters Received, NA, M567, Roll 328 (mentions taking six thousand troops with him, and McCulloch's reconnaissance to China); Taylor, Order Books, Orders No. 98, August 17, 1846, NA (formation of Fourth Brigade; other brigades as at Corpus Christi; initial plan of organization of marching troops); Taylor to Jones, September 3, 1846, AGO, Letters Received, NA, M567, Roll 328 (revised plan of organization).

73. Taylor to Jones, September 3, 1846, AGO, Letters Received, NA, M567, Roll 328; Taylor, Order Books, Orders No. 108 and 110, August 28 and 30, 1846, NA (on Butler and Field Division); Taylor, Order Books, Orders No. 93, July 30, 1846, NA (assigning Hamer the command of Ohio Brigade); Taylor, Order Books, Orders No. 112, September 2, 1846, NA (placing Mississippi Regiment under Quitman).

74. Winders, *Mr. Polk's Army,* 37–44; Bauer, *Mexican War,* 74–75.

75. Nathaniel Cheairs Hughes Jr. and Roy P. Stonesifer Jr., *The Life and Wars of Gideon J. Pillow,* Chapel Hill: University of North Carolina Press, 1993), 44, 46–50; Taylor to Wood, August 19, 1846, in Samson, ed., *Letters of Zachary Taylor,* 42.

76. Taylor to Wood, August 11 and 19, 1846, and September 3, 1846, in Samson, ed., *Letters of Zachary Taylor,* 39–40, 44, 50–51; Mansfield to wife, August 16, 1846, ALS, Mansfield Papers, USMA Library.

77. Taylor, Order Books, Special Orders No. 132, August 30, 1846, NA (Plummer); Taylor, Order Books, Special Orders No. 133, August 31, 1846 (King); Porter, "Medical and Surgical Notes," 23, 24; Taylor to Wood, August 23, 1846, in Samson, ed., *Letters of Zachary Taylor,* 50; Grant to Julia, August 14, 1846, in Simon, ed., *Papers of Ulysses S. Grant,* 1:106.

78. Robarts, *Mexican War Veterans,* 72 (on the First Tennessee Volunteers); William Bowen Campbell, "Mexican War Letters of Col. William Bowen Campbell, of Tennessee, Written to Governor David Campbell, of Virginia, 1846–1847," Intro. by St.

George Sioussat, *Tennessee Historical Magazine* 1 (June 1915): 140–41. See also [John B. Robertson], *Reminiscences of a Campaign in Mexico, by a Member of the "Bloody-First"* (Nashville, TN: John York, 1849), 109–110; and Christopher Losson, *Tennessee's Forgotten Warriors: Frank Cheatham and His Confederate Division* (Knoxville: University of Tennessee Press, 1989), 10.

79. Meade to wife, August 13, 1846, in Meade, *Life and Letters,* 1:121; Grant to Julia, September 6, 1846, in Simon, ed., *Papers of Ulysses S. Grant,* 1:109. See also Henry, *Campaign Sketches,* 159; Bauer, *Mexican War,* 83; Lew Wallace, *Lew Wallace, An Autobiography* (2 vols., New York: Harper and Brothers, 1906), 1:124–28; Taylor to Wood, August 19, 1846, in Samson, ed., *Letters of Zachary Taylor,* 42.

80. Taylor to Wood, July 25, 1846, and August 11, 19, and 23, 1846, and September 3, 1846, in Samson, ed., *Letters of Zachary Taylor,* 31–32, 39, 42, 45, 51.

81. Meade to wife, August 13, 1846, in Meade, *Life and Letters,* 1:121; Henry, *Campaign Sketches,* 159; Kenly, *Memoirs of a Maryland Volunteer,* 69–70; [Giddings], *Sketches of the Campaign in Northern Mexico in Eighteen Hundred Forty-Six and Seven* (New York: George P. Putnam, 1853), 30–31, 83–85; Winders, *Mr. Polk's Army,* 140–57. According to Winders, "[t]he list of former regular officers who led volunteers in the Mexican War was indeed long" (74).

82. Taylor to Wood, July 25, 1846, and August 11, 19, and 23, 1846, and September 3, 1846, in Samson, ed., *Letters of Zachary Taylor,* 31–34, 38–39, 41, 43, 45, 46, 50–51.

83. Taylor, Order Books, Orders No. 99, August 17, 1846, NA; Hughes and Johnson, eds., *Fighter from Way Back,* 6–9. Rev. Antony Rey, a Jesuit priest, accompanied Taylor's army at the request of President Polk but was not officially an army chaplain (Bauer, *Mexican War,* 85).

CHAPTER 7

1. Taylor, Order Books, Orders No. 99, August 17, 1846, NA.

2. Taylor to Wood, August 19, 1846, in Samson, ed., *Letters of Zachary Taylor,* 43–44; Meade to wife, August 18, 1846, in Meade, *Life and Letters,* 1:123.

3. AGO, Monthly Returns, Eighth Infantry, NA, M665, Roll 90; Meade to wife, August 28, 1846, in Meade, *Life and Letters,* 1:124; Hughes and Johnson, eds., *Fighter from Way Back,* 10–12.

4. Taylor to Jones, August 25, 1846, AGO, Letters Received, NA, M567, Roll 328; Taylor, Order Books, Orders No. 98, August 17, 1846; Orders No. 99, August 17, 1846; Orders No. 105, August 24, 1846, NA; AGO, Monthly Returns, Regiment of Mounted Riflemen, NA, M744, Roll 27; AGO, Monthly Returns, Fifth and Seventh Infantry, NA, M665, Rolls 55 and 79, respectively; Dana to Sue, August 24, 1846, ALS, Dana Papers, USMA Library. In his orders, Taylor spelled the name of the village near Cerralvo "Puntiaguda," and so did Dana in his letters, but Justin H. Smith, in *The War with Mexico,* spells it "Punta Aguda" (1:562, 2:603). Cerralvo was also variously spelled by Americans.

5. Dana to Sue, August 24 and 26, 1846, ALS, Dana Papers, USMA Library (also in Ferrell, ed., *Monterrey Is Ours,* 108–110).

6. Dana to Sue, August 27 and 28, 1846, ALS, Dana Papers, USMA Library (also in Ferrell, ed., *Monterrey Is Ours,* 110–11, 112–13).

7. Dana to Sue, September 1, 1846, ALS, Dana Papers, USMA Library (also in Ferrell, ed., *Monterrey Is Ours,* 110, 113).

8. Dana to Sue, August 27, 1846, ALS, Dana Papers, USMA Library. On August 17, General Taylor, in his Orders No. 99, placed Blanchard's company of Louisiana volunteers in the Second Brigade. Albert Gallatin Blanchard, a West Point graduate (1829) from Massachusetts who had resigned his Third Infantry appointment as a first lieutenant in 1840, would serve as a CSA brigadier general. His company of Louisiana volunteers appears to have been exceptionally well trained and effective.

9. Mackall to wife, September 4, 1846, ALS, UNC Library; Heitman, *Historical Register,* 1:670 (Mackall); 1:692 (Martin); AGO, Monthly Returns, First Artillery, NA, M727, Roll 3.

10. Doubleday, ed., *Journals of the Late Brevet Major Philip Norbourne Barbour,* 103; Henry, *Campaign Sketches,* 161–62; AGO, Monthly Returns, Third and Fourth Infantry, NA, M665, Rolls 31 and 43, respectively; Taylor, Order Books, Special Orders No. 126, August 22, 1846 (on Johnston's Texans mustered out of service); Special Orders No. 134, September 1, 1846, NA (on Johnston's new assignment); Taylor to Jones, August 25 and 31, 1846, AGO, Letters Received, NA, M567, Roll 328 (on Johnston); Roland, *Albert Sidney Johnston,* 131. Three hundred eighteen of Johnston's regiment voted to go home; 234 stayed and were assigned to other units (Wilkins, *Highly Irregular Irregulars,* 205).

11. AGO, Monthly Returns, Second Dragoons, NA, M744, Roll 15.

12. Taylor to Jones, September 3, 1846, AGO, Letters Received, NA, M567, Roll 328; AGO, Monthly Returns, Third Artillery, NA, M727, Roll 19.

13. Taylor, Order Books, Special Orders No. 130, August 28, 1846, NA; T. W. Sherman to Bliss, August 29, 1846, ALS, AOO, Letters Received, NA; AGO, Monthly Returns, Third Artillery, NA, M727, Roll 19; Heitman, *Historical Register,* 1:882.

14. Taylor, Order Books, Special Orders No. 130, August 28, 1846, NA; AGO, Monthly Returns, Third Artillery, NA, M727, Roll 19; Sherman to Bliss, August 29, 1846, October 3, 1846, and November 12, 1846, ALS, AOO, Letters Received, NA; Roger Jones, AG, to Sherman (extract), October 8, 1846, AOO, Letters Received, NA; Taylor, Order Books, NA, Special Orders No. 172, November 6, 1846 (directing Sherman to join Company E and assigning Bragg to Company C).

15. Reynolds to his sister Jane, March 19, 1848, ADS, Reynolds Family Papers, Franklin and Marshall College (qtd. in Nichols, *Toward Gettysburg,* 51).

16. Taylor, Order Books, NA, Special Orders No. 141, September 12, 1846, NA; French, *Two Wars,* 59; AGO, Monthly Returns, Third Artillery, NA, M727, Roll 19.

17. Taylor, Order Books, Orders No. 110, August 30, 1846, NA; Doubleday, ed., *Journals of the Late Brevet Major Philip Norbourne Barbour,* 103; Grant to Julia, September 6, 1846, in Simon, ed., *Papers of Ulysses S. Grant,* 1:108–9; Henry, *Campaign Sketches,* 161–62; AGO, Monthly Returns, Third and Fourth Infantry, NA, M665, Rolls 31 and 43, respectively.

18. Grant to Julia, August 14, 1846, in Simon, ed., *Papers of Ulysses S. Grant,* 1:104–6.

19. Grant to Garland [undated], in Simon, ed., *Papers of Ulysses S. Grant,* 1:106–7; Bliss to Garland, August 29, 1846, in Simon, ed., *Papers of Ulysses S. Grant,* 1:107 (footnote).

20. Kenly, *Memoirs of a Maryland Volunteer,* 80–83; Taylor to Jones, September 3, 1846, AGO, Letters Received, NA, M567, Roll 328; AGO, Monthly Returns, First Infantry, NA, M665, Roll 3; AGO, Monthly Returns, Third Artillery, NA, M727, Roll 19.

21. John F. Reynolds to sister Jane, September 3, 1846, ALS, Reynolds Family Papers, Franklin and Marshall College Library.

22. AGO, Monthly Returns, First Artillery, NA, 727, Roll 3.

23. Taylor to Wood, September 10, 1846, in Samson, ed., *Letters of Zachary Taylor,* 54; Taylor, Order Books, Orders No. 79, June 19, 1846, NA (on Garnett).

24. Taylor to Jones, September 3 and 4, 1846, AGO, Letters Received, NA, M567, Roll 328; Taylor to Wood, September 10, 1846, in Samson, ed., *Letters of Zachary Taylor,* 54; Taylor, Order Books, Orders No. 108, August 28, 1846, NA (on Patterson).

25. Taylor to Jones, August 19, 1846, AGO, Letters Received, NA, M567, Roll 328; Taylor, Order Books, Orders No. 93, July 30, 1846, NA; Heitman, *Historical Register,* 1:614; Robarts, *Mexican War Veterans,* 48; Bauer, *Mexican War,* 75. (Winders is evidently in error in stating that Lane was the colonel of the First Indiana regiment [*Mr. Polk's Army,* 40]. Other sources say he was colonel of the Second Indiana, and Lew Wallace, a member of First Indiana, says in his *Autobiography* that his colonel from the time the regiment was organized was James P. Drake [1:116], with which Robarts agrees [*Mexican War Veterans,* 47]).

26. [Giddings], *Sketches of the Campaign in Northern Mexico,* 106, 108; J. Davis *Papers of Jefferson Davis,* 1:21; J. F. H. Claiborne, *Life and Correspondence of John A. Quitman* (2 vols., New York: Harper and Brothers, 1860), 1:227, 236–42; Taylor to Jones, August 19, 1846, AGO, Letters Received, NA, M567, Roll 328; Robarts, *Mexican War Veterans,* 59 (on Mississippi Rifles), 66–67 (on First Ohio), 72 (on First Tennessee); Taylor, Order Books, Orders No. 107, August 25, 1846 (on Lorenzo Thomas); Orders No. 109, August 29, 1846 (on Nichols); Special Orders No. 115, July 30, 1846, NA (on Hooker).

27. Taylor, Order Books, Special Orders No. 126, August 22, 1846, NA (on Johnston's troops being mustered out); Taylor to Jones, August 25 and 31, 1846, AGO, Letters Received, NA, M567, Roll 328.

28. Roland, *Albert Sidney Johnston,* 126–27; Johnston, *Life of Albert Sidney Johnston,* 133; Robarts, *Mexican War Veterans,* 74; Taylor to Jones, August 25, 1846, AGO, Letters Received, NA, M567, Roll 328; Taylor, Order Books, Special Orders No. 129, August 27, 1846, NA; Taylor to Jones, September 3, 1846, AGO, Letters Received, NA, M567, Roll 328.

29. Taylor, Order Books, Orders No. 102, August 22, 1846, NA (on Kinney); Taylor to Jones, August 25, 1846, AGO, Letters Received, NA, M567, Roll 328; Robarts, *Mexican War Veterans,* 75.

30. Taylor to Jones, August 3, 1846, AGO, Letters Received, NA, M567, Roll 328 (on Gillespie's march); Taylor to Jones, August 31, 1846, AGO, Letters Received, NA, M567, Roll 328 (on spy companies); Taylor, Order Books, Special Orders No. 134, September 1,

1846, NA; Robarts, *Mexican War Veterans,* 74–75; Heitman, *Historical Register,* 1:661; Taylor to Jones, September 12, 1846, AGO, Letters Received, NA, M567, Roll 328.

31. Taylor to Jones, August 31 and September 3, 1846, AGO, Letters Received, NA, M567, Roll 328.

32. Taylor to Jones, August 10, 15 (with copy of Taylor to Wool), 25, 1846, and September 3 and 4, 1846, AGO, Letters Received, NA, M567, Roll 328; Taylor to Wood, September 10, 1846, in Samson, ed., *Letters of Zachary Taylor,* 54.

33. Dana to Sue, September 12, 1846, ALS, Dana Papers, USMA Library (also in Ferrell, ed., *Monterrey Is Ours,* 118).

34. Taylor to Wood, September 10, 1846, in Samson, ed., *Letters of Zachary Taylor,* 54, 55; Taylor to Jones, September 12, 1846, AGO, Letters Received, NA, M567, Roll 328; Dana to Sue, September 8, 1846, ALS, Dana Papers, USMA Library (also in Ferrell, ed., *Monterrey Is Ours,* 115); Meade to wife, August 28, 1846, in Meade, *Life and Letters,* 1:124.

35. Meade to wife, August 28, 1846, and September 3 and 17, 1846, in Meade, *Life and Letters,* 1:124, 125–26, 131; Bauer, *Mexican War,* 27–28, 76–77, 109; Eisenhower, *So Far from God,* 57–58, 114–16; Justin Smith, *War with Mexico,* 1:201–3, 218–19.

36. Meade to wife, September 11, 1846, in Meade, *Life and Letters,* 1:128–29. Among those who received brevet promotion for participation in the conflicts of May were Benjamin Alvord, Braxton Bragg, Robert Buchanan, John Garland, Lawrence Pike Graham, Alexander Hays, George McCall (two brevets), Joseph Mansfield, Alfred Pleasonton, and Charles F. Smith. General Taylor, referring to one of the several officers who received two brevets for the actions of May 8 and 9, one for each battle, said that in his opinion such men "had good friends at court" (Taylor to Wood, September 3, 1846, in Samson, ed., *Letters of Zachary Taylor,* 53).

37. Grant to Jesup, September 6, 1846, in Simon, ed., *Papers of Ulysses S. Grant,* 1:107; Grant, *Personal Memoirs,* 1:105–6. See also Henry, *Campaign Sketches,* 162–63.

38. Heitman, *Historical Register,* 1:368; AGO, Monthly Returns, Fifth Infantry, NA, M665, Roll 55. For letters from Grant to Julia regarding Fred, see the following pages in volume 1 of Simon, ed., *Papers of Ulysses S. Grant:* 81 (April 20, 1846); 88–89 (May 24, 1846); 90 (June 5, 1846); 93 (June 10, 1846); 100 (July 2, 1846); 104 (August 4, 1846); 105–6 (August 14, 1846); 108–9 (September 6, 1846); 113 (October 3, 1846); 115 (October 20, 1846); 118 (November 7, 1846); 120 (December 27, 1846); 124 (February 1, 1847); 127 (February 25, 1847). On April 2, 1847, Grant wrote Julia from Veracruz: "Fred is here and well. I see him evry [*sic*] day" (129)).

39. Grant to Julia, August 31, 1844, in Simon, ed., *Papers of Ulysses S. Grant,* 1:36 (on initial "S"); Heitman, *Historical Register,* 1:492; Grant, *Personal Memoirs,* 1:103; Simon, ed., *Papers of Ulysses S. Grant,* 1:121 (footnote) (for Hamer letter re Grant); Taylor to Jones, December 3, 1846, AGO, Letters Received, NA, M567, Roll 328 (in which Taylor said of Hamer's death in part: "The order of the Army announcing this sudden dispensation, expresses but feebly the high estimation in which the deceased was held by all who knew him. In council I found him clear and judicious, and in the administration of his command, though kind, yet always impartial and just"). See also Winders,

Mr. Polk's Army, 40, 47–48; Bauer, *Mexican War,* 75; Taylor to Wood, August 23, 1846, in Samson, ed., *Letters of Zachary Taylor,* 45n1.

40. Taylor to Wood, September 10, 1846, in Samson, ed., *Letters of Zachary Taylor,* 55 (on being detained at Cerralvo); Taylor, Order Books, Orders No. 115, September 11, 1846, NA (on garrison for Cerralvo); Taylor, Order Books, Orders No. 114, September 9, 1846, NA (on court-martial panel); Heitman, *Historical Register,* 1:783 (on Phelps); AGO, Monthly Returns, Fourth Artillery, M727, Roll 27.

41. Taylor, Order Books, Special Orders No. 138, September 9, 1846, NA (on Mackall and Webster); Taylor, Order Books, Orders No. 115, September 11, 1846, NA (on McCulloch, pioneer party, and Gillespie's company).

42. Taylor, Order Books, Orders No. 115, September 11, 1846, NA.

43. Meade to wife, September 3, 11, and 17, 1846, in Meade, *Life and Letters,* 1:126, 127, 129.

44. Taylor to Jones, September 12, 1846, AGO, Letters Received, NA, M567, Roll 328; Meade to wife, September 17, 1846, in Meade, *Life and Letters,* 1:129.

45. Taylor to Jones, September 17, 1846, AGO, Letters Received, NA, M567, Roll 328; Meade to wife, September 17, 1846, in Meade, *Life and Letters,* 1:129; Dana to Sue, September 15, 1846, ALS, Dana Papers, USMA Library (also in Ferrell, ed., *Monterrey Is Ours,* 119). From Marín, Taylor wrote of being "quite pleased to learn" that Col. Edward D. Baker (Fourth Illinois) was recovering from the "injury" he had received while endeavoring to halt a riot among First Georgia troops (Taylor to Wood, September 16, 1846, in Samson, ed., *Letters of Zachary Taylor,* 59). See also Bauer, *Mexican War,* 83; and Kenly, *Memoirs of a Maryland Volunteer,* 47–48.

46. Kenly, *Memoirs of a Maryland Volunteer,* 48–51, 91–92; Taylor to Jones, September 17, 1846, AGO, Letters Received, NA, M567, Roll 328; Dana to Sue, September 17, 1846, ALS, Dana Papers, USMA Library (also in Ferrell, ed., *Monterrey Is Ours,* 119).

47. Dana to Sue, September 17, 1846, ALS, Dana Papers, USMA Library (also in Ferrell, ed., *Monterrey Is Ours,* 120).

48. Meade to wife, September 17, 1846, in Meade, *Life and Letters,* 1:131; Dana to Sue, September 17, 1846, ALS, Dana Papers, USMA Library.

49. Taylor, Order Books, Orders No. 119, September 17, 1846, NA.

50. Taylor, Order Books, Orders No. 119, September 11 and Orders No. 120, September 18, 1846, NA; Meade to wife, September 27, in Meade, *Life and Letters,* 1:132; Henry, *Campaign Sketches,* 190; Bauer, *Mexican War,* 90; Eisenhower, *So Far from God,* 125; Justin Smith, *War with Mexico,* 1:237–39; Dyer, *Zachary Taylor,* 198. Captain Gillespie's company was in the lead on September 29, followed by the First and Second Texas regiments except for the rearguard companies (Wilkins, *Highly Irregular Irregulars,* 82).

CHAPTER 8

1. Meade to wife, September 27, 1846, in Meade, *Life and Letters,* 1:132; Bauer, *Mexican War,* 92; Taylor to Jones, October 9, 1846, AGO, Letters Received, NA, M567,

Roll 361; Henry, *Campaign Sketches,* 190–91; Justin Smith, *War with Mexico,* 1:239–41; Dyer, *Zachary Taylor,* 198–99.

2. Hughes and Johnson, eds., *Fighter from Way Back,* 21; AGO, Monthly Returns, Fourth Artillery, NA, M727, Roll 27; [Giddings], *Sketches of the Campaign in Northern Mexico,* 139–40; Henry, *Campaign Sketches,* 190.

3. Taylor to Jones, October 9, 1846, AGO, Letters Received, NA, M567, Roll 361; 1st Lt. Edmund Bradford of Pennsylvania, Fourth Artillery, Military Academy graduate (1837), (Confederate Major), to Carey (Miss Caroline Bradford, Philadelphia), September 27, 1846, ALS, Beinecke Rare Book and Manuscript Library, Yale University (qtd. in Smith and Judah, eds., *Chronicles of the Gringos,* 85–89); Meade to wife, September 27, 1846, in Meade, *Life and Letters,* 1:133; Henry, *Campaign Sketches,* 190–91; Hughes and Johnson, eds., *Fighter from Way Back,* 21. The Texans who first provoked enemy fire appear to have been members of Col. John Hays's regiment. Mansfield, escorted by twenty men under Lt. Walter Lane, initially rode out to examine the Citadel's defenses. On his later reconnaissance he was accompanied by Lt. R. A. Gillespie and some dragoons, while Captain Williams was escorted by contingents of the Second Texan regiment. That evening the Rangers also took some thirty prisoners (Wilkins, *Highly Irregular Irregulars,* 84).

4. Taylor to Jones, October 9, 1846, AGO, Letters Received, NA, M567, Roll 361.

5. Worth to Bliss, May 31, 1846, ALS, AOO, Letters Received, NA; Dana to Sue, September 8, 1846, ALS, Dana Papers, USMA Library (also in Ferrell, ed., *Monterrey Is Ours,* 116); Hughes and Johnson, eds., *Fighter from Way Back,* 20; Meade to wife, August 28, 1846, in Meade, *Life and Letters,* 1:125, in which he said he had been treated by Worth "with all possible courtesy and kindness" and hoped to remain with him "so long as he is in the advance."

6. Edward S. Wallace, *General William Jenkins Worth, Monterey's Forgotten Hero* (Dallas, TX: Southern Methodist University Press, 1953), 14–64.

7. Meade to wife, September 27, 1846, in Meade, *Life and Letters,* 1:133; Dana to Sue, September 27, 1846, ALS, Dana Papers, USMA Library (also in Ferrell, ed., *Monterrey Is Ours,* 128).

8. Worth to Bliss, September 28, 1846, AGO, Letters Received, NA, M567, Roll 361; Taylor to Jones, October 9, 1846, AGO, Letters Received, NA, M567, Roll 361.

9. Taylor to Jones, October 9, 1846, AGO, Letters Received, NA, M567, Roll 361; Worth to Bliss, September 28, 1846, AGO, Letters Received, NA, M567, Roll 361; Lt. Edmund Bradford to Carey, September 27, 1846, in Smith and Judah, eds., *Chronicles of the Gringos,* 86; Dana to Sue, September 27, 1846, ALS, Dana Papers, USMA Library (also in Ferrell, ed., *Monterrey Is Ours,* 129); Meade to wife, September 27, 1846, in Meade, *Life and Letters,* 1:133. Also with Worth was Col. Jack Hays's First Regiment of Mounted Texans, including among others, the companies of Gillespie, McCulloch, Walker, together with an "embedded" reporter, George Kendall of the *Picayune* (Wilkins, *Highly Irregular Irregulars,* 85–86).

10. Taylor to Jones, October 9, 1846, AGO, Letters Received, NA, M567, Roll 361; Dana to Sue, September 27, 1846, ALS, Dana Papers, USMA Library; Kenly, *Memoirs of a Maryland Volunteer,* 101–3; Henry, *Campaign Sketches,* 192; Justin Smith, *War with*

Mexico, 1:232–33, 239–41. The description of Monterrey and vicinity herein is based primarily on a letter from George Meade to his wife, which included "Sketch Showing the Position of the Army of Occupation at the Battle of Monterey" (Meade to wife, September 27, 1846, in Meade, *Life and Letters,* 1:133); Justin Smith, *War with Mexico,* 1:232, 240 (for maps); and Vincent J. Esposito, ed., *The West Point Atlas of American Wars,* vol. 1, *1689–1900* (New York: Frederick A. Praeger, 1959), map 14b.

11. Taylor to Jones, October 9, 1846, AGO, Letters Received, NA, M567, Roll 361; Kenly, *Memoirs of a Maryland Volunteer,* 99–100.

12. Worth to Bliss, September 28, 1846, AGO, Letters Received, NA, M567, Roll 361; Meade to wife, September 27, 1846, in Meade, *Life and Letters,* 1:133. Lt. Edmund Bradford, in his letter to Carey of September 27, said the column halted at about five in the evening; Worth, in his report to Bliss of September 28, said it halted at six. At sundown, after the Rangers led by Colonel Hays camped along the road, they were assaulted by "200 to 300" enemy cavalry. They succeeded in driving away their attackers but lost one killed and one wounded (Wilkins, *Highly Irregular Irregulars,* 85–88, citing Hays's official report on Monterrey).

13. Justin Smith, *War with Mexico,* 1:239–41.

14. Worth to Bliss, September 28, 1846, AGO, Letters Received, NA, M567, Roll 361; Meade to wife, September 27, 1846, in Meade, *Life and Letters,* 1:133.

15. Taylor to Jones, October 9, 1846, AGO, Letters Received, NA, M567, Roll 361; Dana to Sue, September 27, 1846, ALS, Dana Papers, USMA Library (also in Ferrell, ed., *Monterrey Is Ours,* 130); Robert G. Hartje, *Van Dorn, the Life and Times of a Confederate General* (Nashville, TN: Vanderbilt University Press, 1967), 3–35; Wilkins, *Highly Irregular Irregulars,* 88.

16. Worth to Bliss, September 28, 1846, AGO, Letters Received, NA, M567, Roll 361; Taylor to Jones, October 9, 1846, AGO, Letters Received, NA, M567, Roll 361.

17. Worth to Bliss, September 28, 1846, AGO, Letters Received, NA, M567, Roll 361.

18. Worth to Bliss, September 28, 1846, AGO, Letters Received, NA, M567, Roll 361. See also Wilkins, *Highly Irregular Irregulars,* 88–90.

19. Hughes and Johnson, eds., *Fighter from Way Back,* 22; Meade to wife, September 27, 1846, in Meade, *Life and Letters,* 1:133.

20. Dana to Sue, September 27, 1846, ALS, Dana Papers, USMA Library (also in Ferrell, ed., *Monterrey Is Ours,* 130–31).

21. Worth to Bliss, September 28, 1846, AGO, Letters Received, NA, M567, Roll 361.

22. Meade to wife, September 27, 1846, in Meade, *Life and Letters,* 1:133–34; Charles Hamilton to "Mrs. H——, Mary and Louise," October 16, 1846, in "The Letters of General Charles Hamilton, Written from the Seat of War in Mexico," *Metropolitan Magazine* 27 (1908): 318; Bradford to Carey, September 27, 1846, in Smith and Judah, eds., *Chronicles of the Gringos,* 86; Bauer, *Mexican War,* 93–94.

23. Meade to wife, September 27, 1846, in Meade, *Life and Letters,* 1:134; Mackall to wife, September 27, 1846, ALS, UNC Library; Bauer, *Mexican War,* 93–94.

24. Meade to wife, September 27, 1846, in Meade, *Life and Letters,* 1:134; Hughes and Johnson, eds., *Fighter from Way Back,* 23; Worth to Bliss, September 28, 1846, AGO, Letters Received, NA, M567, Roll 361.

25. Hughes and Johnson, eds., *Fighter from Way Back,* 23; Bradford to Carey, September 27, 1846, in Smith and Judah, eds., *Chronicles of the Gringos,* 87.

26. Dana to Sue, September 27, 1846, ALS, Dana Papers, USMA Library (also in Ferrell, ed., *Monterrey Is Ours,* 131).

27. Worth to Bliss, September 28, 1846, AGO, Letters Received, M567, Roll 361.

28. Ibid.

29. Dana to Sue, September 27, 1846, ALS, Dana Papers, USMA Library (also in Ferrell, ed., *Monterrey Is Ours,* 131–32); Bradford to Carey, September 27, 1846, Smith and Judah, eds., *Chronicles of the Gringos,* 87; Hughes and Johnson, *Fighter from Way Back,* 23; Worth to Bliss, September 28, 1846, AGO, Letters Received, NA, M567, Roll 361.

30. Dana to Sue, September 27, 1846, ALS, Dana Papers, USMA Library (also in Ferrell, ed., *Monterrey Is Ours,* 131–32); AGO, Monthly Returns, Seventh Infantry, NA, M665, Roll 79.

31. Hughes and Johnson, eds., *Fighter from Way Back,* 23; Dana to Sue, September 27, 1846, ALS, Dana Papers, USMA Library (also in Ferrell, ed., *Monterrey Is Ours,* 132); Worth to Bliss, September 28, 1846, AGO, Letters Received, NA, M567, Roll 361.

32. Worth to Bliss, September 28, 1846, AGO, Letters Received, NA, M567, Roll 361; Hughes and Johnson, eds., *Fighter from Way Back,* 23; AGO, Monthly Returns, Fifth Infantry, NA, M665, Roll 55.

33. Dana to Sue, September 27, 1846, ALS, Dana Papers, USMA Library (also in Ferrell, ed., *Monterrey Is Ours,* 132–33); Worth to Bliss, September 28, 1846, AGO, Letters Received, NA, M567, Roll 356. Reportedly, the Ranger captain R. A. Gillespie was first to enter Soldado, and Lt. Thomas G. Pitcher (Fifth Infantry) was one of the first (Wilkins, *Highly Irregular Irregulars,* 90–92).

34. Worth to Bliss, September 28, 1846, AGO, Letters Received, NA, M567, Roll 361; Dana to Sue, September 27, 1846, ALS, Dana Papers, USMA Library; Meade to wife, September 27, 1846, in Meade, *Life and Letters,* 1:135; Porter, "Medical and Surgical Notes," 24; AGO, Monthly Returns, Fifth, Seventh, and Eighth Infantry, NA, M665, Rolls 55, 79, and 90, respectively.

35. Taylor to Jones, October 9, 1846, AGO, Letters Received, NA, M567, Roll 361; Justin Smith, *War with Mexico,* 1:238, 250, 251, 256, 258, 261; Bauer, *Mexican War,* 96–97, 99, 100; Eisenhower, *So Far from God,* 138–39; [J. B. Robertson], *Reminiscences of a Campaign in Mexico,* 129.

36. Taylor to Wood, August 23, 1846, in Samson, ed., *Letters of Zachary Taylor,* 46.

37. Taylor to Wood, September 10, 1846, in Samson, ed., *Letters of Zachary Taylor,* 54.

38. Taylor to Jones, October 9, 1846, AGO, Letters Received, NA, M567, Roll 361; Taylor to Wood, September 28, 1846, in Samson, ed., *Letters of Zachary Taylor,* 60; Garland to Twiggs, September 29, 1846, AGO, Letters Received, NA, M567, Roll 361; Henry, *Campaign Sketches,* 194–95; French, *Two Wars,* 102–3; [Giddings], *Sketches of the Campaign in Northern Mexico,* 142, 144, 154–55; Kenly, *Memoirs of a Maryland Volunteer,* 102–3; Justin Smith, *War with Mexico,* 1:249.

39. Henry, *Campaign Sketches,* 193; Taylor to Jones, October 9, 1846, AGO, Letters Received, NA, M567, Roll 361.

40. Garland to Twiggs, September 29, 1846, AGO, Letters Received, NA, M567, Roll 361.

41. Mansfield to Taylor, October 9, 1846, AGO, Letters Received, NA, M567, Roll 361.

42. Garland to Twiggs, September 29, 1846, AGO, Letters Received, NA, M567, Roll 361.

43. Taylor to Jones, October 9, 1846, AGO, Letters Received, NA, M567, Roll 361; Henry, *Campaign Sketches,* 194; [Giddings], *Sketches of the Campaign in Northern Mexico,* 148 (map), 154; French, *Two Wars,* 61; Kenly, *Memoirs of a Maryland Volunteer,* 102; Justin Smith, *War with Mexico,* 1:240 (map), 249–58.

44. Garland to Twiggs, September 29, 1846, AGO, Letters Received, NA, M567, Roll 361; Mansfield to Taylor, October 9, 1846, AGO, Letters Received, NA, M567, Roll 361; Mansfield to wife, September 25 and October 4, 1846, ALS, Mansfield Papers, USMA Library. Garland would be promoted to the rank of brevet colonel for his service at Palo Alto and Resaca, but evidently the Army of Occupation had not yet been advised of the award, since Taylor's reports and others referred to him as a lieutenant colonel.

45. Kenly, *Memoirs of a Maryland Volunteer,* 111.

46. Reynolds to sister (Miss Kate Reynolds), September 25, 1846, in Nichols, *Toward Gettysburg,* 29. See also ALS, Reynolds Family Papers, Franklin and Marshall College.

47. AGO, Monthly Returns, Third Artillery, NA, M727, Roll 19; Taylor to Jones, October 9, 1846, AGO, Letters Received, NA, M567, Roll 361. Taylor stated that the number of casualties on the eastern front on September 21 was 394. His remarks concerning the total loss in killed and wounded during the campaign indicate that number as being 488. He did not mention the missing, but in an accompanying, inclusive tally signed by Bliss, 43 men were shown as missing. See also Bauer, *Mexican War,* 100. Taylor's October 10 report was amended several times thereafter but principally with respect to the names of those killed or wounded (see, e.g., Taylor to Jones, October 9, 1846 (correcting report of that date), February 14, 1847, and April 10, 1847).

48. Mansfield to Taylor, October 9, 1846, AGO, Letters Received, NA, M567, Roll 361; Mansfield to wife, October 4, 1846, ALS, Mansfield Papers, USMA Library.

49. Taylor to Jones, September 22, 1846, AGO, Letters Received, NA, M567, Roll 361.

50. Garland to Twiggs, September 29, 1846, AGO, Letters Received, NA, M567, Roll 361.

51. Capt. Electus Backus of New York (First Infantry, Military Academy graduate [1824], Union colonel), "Journal," qtd. in Smith and Judah, eds., *Chronicles of the Gringos,* 80–81; Henry, *Campaign Sketches,* 193–95. (Captain Backus said that Mansfield used "Mr. Kinney [Col. Henry L. Kinney from Corpus Christi]" as a guide, and that it was Kinney who signaled a right turn.)

52. Kenly, *Memoirs of a Maryland Volunteer,* 110, 112.

53. Ibid., 105–6, 115; Taylor to Jones, January 14, 1847, AGO, Letters Received, NA, M567, Roll 361, enclosing "Partial List of the Killed and Wounded and Missing of the Army of Occupation during the operations before Monterey Sept. 21, 22, and 23, 1846," signed by Bliss.

54. Backus, "Journal," qtd. in Smith and Judah, eds., *Chronicles of the Gringos,* 81.

55. Taylor to Jones, October 9, 1846, AGO, Letters Received, NA, M567, Roll 361.

56. Grant, *Personal Memoirs,* 1:110–11.

57. Grant, *Personal Memoirs,* 1:115–17. Grant implied that this ride occurred on September 23, but Captain Williams and Lieutenant Terrett were reported as having died on September 21 (Pryor, *Reading the Man,* 158, 169, 203–4, 230).

58. Grant to Julia, September 23, 1846, in Simon, ed., *Papers of Ulysses S. Grant,* 1:111.

59. Campbell to Quitman, September 27, 1846, AGO, Letters Received, NA, M567, Roll 361; Davis to Quitman, September 26, 1846, AGO, Letters Received, NA, M567, Roll 361; Hamer to Maj. L[orenzo] Thomas, September 25, 1846, AGO, Letters Received, NA, M567, Roll 361; Butler to Bliss, September 30, 1846, AGO, Letters Received, NA, M567, Roll 361; Quitman to Butler, September 29, 1846, AGO, Letters Received, NA, M567, Roll 361; Taylor to Jones, October 9, 1846, AGO, Letters Received, NA, M567, Roll 361; Kenly, *Memoirs of a Maryland Volunteer,* 114–15; Losson, *Tennessee's Forgotten Warriors,* 14.

60. W. B. Campbell, "Mexican War Letters," 129–67; Losson, *Tennessee's Forgotten Warriors,* 9, 11–12, 14; Campbell to Quitman, September 27, 1846, AGO, Letters Received, NA, M567, Roll 361.

61. Davis to Quitman, September 26, 1846, AGO, Letters Received, NA, M567, Roll 361; W. C. Davis, *Jefferson Davis,* 135, 141–44.

62. Quitman to Butler, September 29, 1846, AGO, Letters Received, NA, M567, Roll 361. See also [J. B. Robertson], *Reminiscences of a Campaign in Mexico,* 137–41, 167–74.

63. Taylor to Jones, October 9, 1846, AGO, Letters Received, NA, M567, Roll 361; Taylor to Jones, January 14, 1847 (with enclosure), AGO, Letters Received, NA, M567, Roll 361; W. B. Campbell to David Campbell, February 19, 1847, in W. B. Campbell, "Mexican War Letters," 154.

64. Meade to wife, September 27 and December 2, 1846, in Meade, *Life and Letters,* 1:140, 163–64.

65. Davis to Quitman, September 26, 1846, AGO, Letters Received, NA, M567, Roll 361; Ibid., Butler to Bliss, September 30, 1846, AGO, Letters Received, NA, M567, Roll 361.

66. Butler to Bliss, September 30, 1846, AGO, Letters Received, NA, M567, Roll 361; Hamer to Maj. L[orenzo] Thomas, September 25, 1846, AGO, Letters Received, NA, M567, Roll 361.

67. Taylor to Jones, October 9, 1846, AGO, Letters Received, NA, M567, Roll 361; Henry, *Campaign Sketches,* 197–200.

68. Twiggs to Bliss, September 29, 1846, AGO, Letters Received, NA, M567, Roll 361.

69. Taylor to Jones, October 9, 1846, AGO, Letters Received, NA, M567, Roll 361.

70. Taylor to Jones, October 9, 1846, AGO, Letters Received, NA, M567, Roll 361; Worth to Bliss, September 28, 1846, AGO, Letters Received, NA, M567, Roll 361; AGO, Monthly Returns, Eighth Infantry, NA, M665, Roll 90, and Second and Third Artillery, NA, M727, Rolls 11 and 19, respectively.

71. Worth to Bliss, September 28, 1846, AGO, Letters Received, NA, M567, Roll 361; Meade to wife, September 27, 1846, in Meade, *Life and Letters,* 1:136; Hughes and

Johnson, eds., *Fighter from Way Back*; Dana to Sue, September 27, 1846, ALS, Dana Papers, USMA Library.

72. Worth to Bliss, September 28, 1846, AGO, Letters Received, NA, M567, Roll 361.

73. Dana to Sue, October 4, 1846, ALS, Dana Papers, USMA Library (also in Ferrell, ed., *Monterrey Is Ours*, 135–36).

74. Worth to Bliss, September 28, 1846, AGO, Letters Received, NA, M567, Roll 361; Porter, "Medical and Surgical Notes," 24. The greatly admired and respected Ranger captain, Robert Gillespie, was mortally wounded in the assault on Independence Hill (Wilkins, *Highly Irregular Irregulars*, 94; Robarts, *Mexican War Veterans*, 75).

75. Worth to Bliss, September 28, 1846, AGO, Letters Received, NA, M567, Roll 361; Meade to wife, September 27, 1846, in Meade, *Life and Letters*, 1:136. See also Henry, *Campaign Sketches*, 206, 209–210.

76. Worth to Bliss, September 28, 1846, AGO, Letters Received, NA, M567, Roll 361; Dana to Sue, October 4, 1846, ALS, Dana Papers, USMA Library; Meade to wife, September 27, 1846, in Meade, *Life and Letters*, 1:136–37; Bradford to Carey, September 27, 1846, ALS, Beinecke Rare Book and Manuscript Library.

77. Henry, *Campaign Sketches*, 210–12.

78. Hughes and Johnson, eds., *Fighter from Way Back*, 25–26; Bauer, *Mexican War*, 99.

79. Taylor to Jones, October 9, 1846, AGO, Letters Received, NA, M567, Roll 361; Quitman to Hamer, September 28, 1846, AGO, Letters Received, NA, M567, Roll 361; Davis to Quitman, entitled "Additional Report," n.d., AGO, Letters Received, NA, M567, Roll 361; Henderson to Taylor, October 1, 1846, AGO, Letters Received, NA, M567, Roll 361. Quitman also wrote a report to Butler dated September 29.

80. Taylor to Jones, October 9, 1846, AGO, Letters Received, NA, M567, Roll 361. See also Bauer, *Mexican War*, 97–99.

81. Grant to Julia, September 23, 1846, in Simon, ed., *Papers of Ulysses S. Grant*, 1:110–11; Hamer to Bliss, September 28, 1846, AGO, Letters Received, NA, M567, Roll 361. Hamer sent an earlier report, dated September 25, to Maj. Lorenzo Thomas for the attention of Maj. General Butler.

82. Taylor to Jones, September 25, 1846, enclosing "Terms of Capitulation," AGO, Letters Received, NA, M567, Roll 328; Taylor to General Ampudia, September 24, 1846 (copy), AGO, Letters Received, NA, M567, Roll 328.

83. Taylor to Jones, September 25, 1846, AGO, Letters Received, NA, M567, Roll 328. Polk noted in his diary that Eaton had left Monterrey on September 25 with Taylor's dispatches (Polk, *Diary*, 2:181). Lt. John Sedgwick, in a letter to his sister from Reynosa dated September 28, wrote: "General Taylor's aid passed through here yesterday, on his way to Washington, bearer of dispatches. . . . As he left immediately after the battle, he only knew the general result" (*Correspondence of John Sedgwick*, 1:24).

84. Polk, *Diary*, 1:181, 184–85.

85. Abercrombie, John J.; Bragg, Braxton; Brooks, William T. H.; French, Samuel; Gardner, Franklin; Garnett, Robert S.; Gatlin, Richard C.; Hamilton, Schuyler; Holmes, Theophilus; Hooker, Joseph; Little, Lewis; Mackall, William W.; Mansfield, Joseph K. F.; Meade, George G.; Pemberton, John; Pope, John; Potter, Joseph H.; Ram-

say, George D.; Reynolds, John F.; Smith, Charles F.; Thomas, George H.; Thomas, Lorenzo; Twiggs, David E. (Heitman, *Historical Register*).

86. J. Smith, *War with Mexico,* 1:239–61; Bauer, *Mexican War,* 90–102; Bauer, *Zachary Taylor,* 177–85.

87. J. Smith, *War with Mexico,* 1:250.

88. Bauer, *Mexican War,* 96. See also Bauer, *Zachary Taylor,* 181; and J. Smith, *War with Mexico,* 1:260.

89. Qtd. in J. Smith, *War with Mexico,* 1:261; and Eisenhower, *So Far from God,* 149.

90. Taylor to Jones, September 25, 1846, enclosing copy of "Terms of Capitulation," signed by American and Mexican commissioners and General Taylor, AGO, Letters Received, NA, M567, Roll 328. For opinions of the treaty, see Bauer, *War with Mexico,* 100; Bauer, *Zachary Taylor,* 183–84; Eisenhower, *So Far from God,* 146–51; [Giddings], *Campaign in Northern Mexico,* 212; Henry, *Campaign Sketches,* 213–14. Taylor commented to Dr. Wood in a letter: "These terms were liberal but not considered too much so by all reflecting men belonging to the army here especially considering our situation; besides it was thought it would be judicious to act with magniminity [*sic*] towards a prostrate foe, particularly as the president of the U. States had offered to settle all differences between the two countries by negotiation, & the Mexican commander stating that said propositions he had no doubt would be favorably met by his go't as their [*sic*] was a gen'l wish for peace on the part of the nation" (Taylor to Dr. Wood, September 28, 1846, in Samson, ed., *Letters of Zachary Taylor,* 61).

91. [Giddings], *Campaign in Northern Mexico,* 212; Taylor to Wood, September 28, 1846, in Samson, ed., *Letters of Zachary Taylor,* 61.

CHAPTER 9

1. Wool to Jones, July 26 and August 4 and 5, 1846, AGO, Letters Received, NA, M567, Roll 330; Francis Baylies, "The March of the United States Troops, under the Command of General John E. Wool, from San Antonio, Texas, to Saltillo, Mexico, in the Year 1846," *Stryker's American Register and Magazine* 4 (1850): 297–98; Justin Smith, *War with Mexico,* 1:270; Bauer, *Mexican War,* 145–46.

2. Polk, *Diary,* 1:435–36; Bauer, *Mexican War,* 145; Eisenhower, *So Far from God,* 156; Heitman, *Historical Register,* 1:1059–60.

3. Polk, *Diary,* 1:417–18; Bauer, *Mexican War,* 145; Winders, *Mr. Polk's Army,* 34.

4. Engelmann to parents, July 22, 1846, in Adolph Engelmann, "The Second Illinois in the Mexican War, Letters of Adolph Engelmann, 1846–1847," trans. and ed. Otto B. Engelmann, *Journal of the Illinois State Historical Society* 26 (January 1934): 362; Isabel Wallace, *Life and Letters of General W. H. L. Wallace* (Chicago: R. R. Donnelley & Sons, 1909), 1–15; Robarts, *Mexican War Veterans,* 43–44.

5. I. Wallace, *Life and Letters of General W. H. L. Wallace,* 1, 2, 17; Heitman, *Historical Register,* 1:99.

6. I. Wallace, *Life and Letters of General W. H. L. Wallace,* 16–17; Wallace to father, November 6, 1846, in I. Wallace, *Life and Letters of General W. H. L. Wallace,* 23–24.

7. Wool to Jones, August 4 and 5, 1846, AGO, Letters Received, NA, M567, Roll 330; I. Wallace, *Life and Letters of General W. H. L. Wallace,* 18; Engelmann to parents, August 1, 1846, in Engelmann, "Second Illinois in the Mexican War," 364.

8. Wool to Taylor, August 15, 1846, ALS, AOO, Letters Received, NA; Kingsbury to Wool, August 14, 1846, AGO, Letters Received, NA, M567, Roll 330; Harney to Bliss, July 24, 1846, ALS, AOO, Letters Received, NA; Engelmann to parents, August 1 and 3, 1846, in Engelmann, "Second Illinois in the Mexican War," 363–65.

9. Harney to Bliss, July 24, 1846, ALS, AOO, Letters Received, NA; Harney to "Sir," August 15, 1846, ALS, AOO, Letters Received, NA; Wool to Taylor, August 18 and 23, 1846, ALS, AOO, Letters Received, NA; Wool to Beall, August 18, 1846, ALS, AOO, Letters Received, NA. See also George Rollie Adams, *General William S. Harney, Prince of Dragoons* (Lincoln: University of Nebraska Press, 2001), 85–95.

10. Engelmann to parents, "Camp 30 Miles from Victoria," n.d., and Engelmann to parents, Aug. 21, 22, and 26, 1846, in Engelmann, "Second Illinois in the Mexican War," 367–70, 370–78; Wool to Beall, August 18, 1846, ALS, AOO, Letters Received, NA.

11. Wool, Order Books, Orders No. 12, August 25, 1846, NA; Harney to "Sir," May 4, 1846, with proclamation dated May 2 attached, ALS, AOO, Letters Received, NA.

12. L. U. Reavis, *The Life and Military Services of Gen. William Selby Harney* (St. Louis: Bryan, Brand, 1878), 29–148, 154–55; Rodenbough, *From Everglade to Cañon,* 19–20, 24, 29–30, 34, 36–39, 45–46, 116; Brackett, *History of the United States Cavalry,* 38–41, 47, 60; Lambert, *One Hundred Years,* 9, 12, 17.

13. AGO, Monthly Returns, Second Dragoons, NA, M744, Roll 15; Wool, Order Books, Orders No. 22, August 29, and Orders No. 25, August 30, 1846, NA; Wool to Taylor, September 15, 1846, ALS, AOO, Letters Received, NA. See also Maurice Garland Fulton, ed., *Diary and Letters of Josiah Gregg, Southwestern Enterprises, 1840–1847,* (Norman: University of Oklahoma Press, 1941), 1:220–23, and Rodenbough, *From Everglade to Cañon,* 116.

14. AGO, Monthly Returns, First Dragoons, NA, M744, Roll 2; Wool, Order Books, Orders No. 24, August 29, 1846, NA; Aurora Hunt, *Major General James Henry Carleton, 1814–1873, Western Frontier Dragoon* (Glendale, CA: Arthur H. Clark, 1958), 97.

15. Hunt, *Major General James Henry Carleton,* 26–97.

16. AGO, Monthly Returns, Sixth Infantry, NA, M665, Roll 66; Wayne Andrews, ed., *Concise Dictionary of American History* (New York: Charles Scribner's Sons, 1962), 105–6; Heitman, *Historical Register,* 1:230 (Bonneville), 259 (Buckner); Fulton, ed., *Diary and Letters of Josiah Gregg,* 1:208, 217 (on Bonneville).

17. Robarts, *Mexican War Veterans,* 53 (on Independent Company Kentucky Volunteers); Stewart Sifakis, *Who Was Who in the Civil War* (New York: Facts on File, 1988), 281 (Hanson), 718 (Williams).

18. Walter Lee Brown, "The Mexican War Experiences of Albert Pike and the 'Mounted Devils' of Arkansas," *Arkansas Historical Quarterly* 12.4 (Winter 1953): 301–6; Robert Lipscomb Duncan, *Reluctant General: The Life and Times of Albert Pike* (New York: E. P. Dutton, 1961), 113–15; Fulton, ed., *Diary and Letters of Josiah Gregg,* 202–214, 217–20, 224, 227; Bauer, *Mexican War,* 146; Wool, Order Books, Orders No. 25, Au-

gust 30, 1846, NA; AGO, Monthly Returns, Fourth Artillery, NA, M727, Roll 27; Capt. J. M. Washington to AAG, AOO [Bliss], August 4, 1846, AGO, Letters Received, NA, M567, Roll 330.

19. Wool, Order Books, Orders No. 82, September 27, 1846, NA.

20. Hughes to Capt. J. H. Prentiss (First Artillery, General Wool's Centre Division), AAG, September 20, 1846, ALS, AOO, Letters Received, NA. See also Traas, *From the Golden Gate,* 149–51.

21. Hughes to Captain Prentiss, September 20, 1846, ALS, AOO, Letters Received, NA. See also W. B. Franklin to Maj. George W. Hughes, "Memoir," in Traas, *From the Golden Gate,* 282–84.

22. Engelmann to parents, August 26 and September 19, 1846, in Engelmann, "Second Illinois in the Mexican War," 376, 383.

23. Wool, Order Books, Orders No. 1, August 2, and Orders No. 9, August 24, 1846, NA (on Chilton); Orders No. 48, September 12, 1846 (on Hunter); Orders No. 60, September 16, 1846 (on Marsena Patrick); Orders No. 71, September 21, 1846 (on Lee).

24. Freeman, *R. E. Lee,* 1:1–202; Emory M. Thomas, *Robert E. Lee: A Biography* (New York: W. W. Norton, 1995), 23–132. Lee's 1845 letter to Col. Joseph G. Totten (Corps of Engineers) regarding his desire for "active service in the field" may be found in Pryor, *Reading the Man,* 178–79.

25. Freeman, *R. E. Lee,* 1:203; E. Thomas, *Robert E. Lee,* 113–15; Pryor, *Reading the Man,* 158–60. For Lee's will, see Pryor, *Reading the Man,* 148.

26. Baylies credits Fraser with building the pontoon bridge but misspells his name ("March of the United States Troops," 298). See also Captain Hughes's report in Traas, *From the Golden Gate,* 244. Freeman likewise states that Fraser constructed the bridge, though Freeman adds that "Lee doubtless had a hand in this" (*R. E. Lee,* 1:208) (Incidentally, note that Freeman is incorrect in remarking that Wool "associated Lee with Fraser, more or less as a supplementary officer, not assigned to definite duty." (See Wool's Orders, No. 71, September 21, 1846, noted above.) Justin Smith does not indicate who devised the bridge (*War with Mexico,* 1:270). Bauer says that Lee fashioned it (*Mexican War,* 147). At least it is clear from Wool's Orders No. 24 that Fraser reported to him by August 29, about three weeks before Lee arrived. Traas evidently concludes that Wool caused the bridge to be built: "The Corps of Engineers contingent supervised the assembly of a 'flying bridge,' prefabricated in San Antonio for the [Rio Grande] crossing. Wool, unlike Taylor, had the foresight not to wait for the pontoon bridging to arrive from the East" (*From the Golden Gate,* 152). Pryor, *Reading the Man* adds a variety of quotes from Lee's letters which for the most part deal with his experiences after joining General Wool in San Antonio (158–59, 203).

27. Traas, *From the Golden Gate,* 151; Hughes to Col. J. J. Abert, chief of Topographical Engineers, January 20, 1849, in Traas, *From the Golden Gate,* 237–38; Justin Smith, *War with Mexico,* 1:270; Bauer, *Mexican War,* 146.

28. Wool, Order Books, Orders No. 74, September 22, 1846; No. 77, September 23, 1846; No. 78, September 24, 1846; No. 81, September 27, 1846, NA; Baylies, "March of the United States Troops," 297–98; Bauer, *Mexican War,* 146; Traas, *From the Golden Gate,* 241. There has been some disagreement concerning the date that Wool's main

body, commanded by Harney, left San Antonio. Justin Smith, in *The Mexican War,* indicates the date was two days after the advance departed on September 23, thus September 25 (1:270), and Eisenhower, in *So Far from God,* states it was September 25 (156). However, Josiah Gregg, an eyewitness, recorded in his journal that it was September 26 (Fulton, ed., *Diary and Letters of Josiah Gregg,* 251), which comports with Wool's orders, and both Bauer and Baylies give the date as September 26.

29. Wool, Order Books, NA, Orders No. 86, October 8, 1846; Baylies, "March of the United States Troops," 298–99; Engelmann to parents, October 4 and 9, 1846, in Engelmann, "Second Illinois in the Mexican War," 388–89, 391–92; Fulton, ed., *Diary and Letters of Josiah Gregg,* 252–57.

30. Wool, Order Books, NA, Orders No. 88 and 89, October 9, 1846; Bauer, *Mexican War,* 147; Fulton, ed., *Diary and Letters of Josiah Gregg,* 256; Engelmann to parents, October 13, 1846, in Engelmann, "Second Illinois in the Mexican War," 393. Hughes to Abert, January 20, 1849, in Traas, *From the Golden Gate,* 244, dated the crossing of the topographical engineers with Harney, etc., as occurring on October 10.

31. Wool, Order Books, NA, Orders No. 90, October 10, 1846, NA; Fulton ed., *Diary and Letters of Josiah Gregg,* 258; Engelmann to parents, October 13, 1846, in Engelmann, "Second Illinois in the Mexican War," 393.

32. Hughes to Abert, January 20, 1849, in Traas, *From the Golden Gate,* 245. See also Engelmann to parents, October 13, 1846, in Engelmann, "Second Illinois in the Mexican War," 394; and Fulton, ed., *Diary and Letters of Josiah Gregg,* 258.

33. Hughes to Colonel Abert, January 20, 1849, in Traas, *From the Golden Gate,* 245; Engelmann to parents, October 13, 1846, in Engelmann, "Second Illinois in the Mexican War," 393; Bauer, *Mexican War,* 147; Fulton, ed., *Diary and Letters of Josiah Gregg,* 258; Cadmus Marcellus Wilcox, *History of the Mexican War,* ed. Mary Rachel Wilcox (Washington, DC: Church News, 1892), 147–48.

34. I. Wallace, *Life and Letters of General W. H. L. Wallace,* 20–21.

35. Engelmann to parents, October 14, 1846, in Engelmann, "Second Illinois in the Mexican War," 395.

36. Engelmann to parents, October 13, 1846, in Engelmann, "Second Illinois in the Mexican War," 394; Pryor, *Reading the Man,* 158–59, 203 (on Lee's reactions to volunteers, and conditions in Mexico at the time).

37. Engelmann to parents, October 13, 1846, in Engelmann, "Second Illinois in the Mexican War," 393; I. Wallace, *Life and Letters of General W. H. L. Wallace,* 21. See also Fulton, ed., *Diary and Letters of Josiah Gregg,* 259, 262; Hughes to Abert, January 20, 1849, in Traas, *From the Golden Gate,* 245; Bauer, *Mexican War,* 75, 147–48; William H. Condon, *Life of Major-General James Shields, Hero of Three Wars and Senator from Three States* (Chicago: Blakely, 1900), 9–55; Winders, *Mr. Polk's Army,* 41; Wool, Order Books, Orders No. 99, October 15, 1846, NA; and Justin Smith, *War with Mexico,* 1:270, 272.

38. Taylor, Order Books, Special Orders No. 174, November 10, 1846, NA; Engelmann to parents, October 15 and 23, 1846, in Engelmann, "Second Illinois in the Mexican War," 396, 400.

39. Wool, Order Books, Orders No. 101, October 15, 1846, NA; Bauer, *Mexican War,* 148.

40. Hughes to Colonel Abert, January 20, 1849, in Traas, *From the Golden Gate,* 245.

41. Wool, Order Books, Orders No. 104, October 17, 1846, NA; Freeman, *R. E. Lee,* 1:208–9; Pryor, *Reading the Man,* 55–69, 159, 186–89.

42. Wool, Order Books, Orders No. 106, October 19, 1846; Orders No. 119, November 2, 1846, NA; Bauer, *Mexican War,* 148–50; Fulton, ed., *Diary and Letters of Josiah Gregg,* 271–73; Hughes to Abert, January 20, 1849, in Traas, *From the Golden Gate,* 246–52, 254; Hunt, *Major General James Henry Carleton,* 98–99; Justin Smith, *War with Mexico,* 1:273.

43. Engelmann to parents, November 7, 1846, in Engelmann, "Second Illinois in the Mexican War," 407.

44. Engelmann to parents, November 7, 19, and December 16, 1846, in Engelmann, "Second Illinois in the Mexican War," 407–8, 409, 414–15. See also Lt. W. H. L. Wallace to father, November 6, 1846, in I. Wallace, *Life and Letters of General W. H. L. Wallace,* 25; Hughes to Abert, January 20, 1849, in Traas, *From the Golden Gate,* 254; and Bauer, *Mexican War,* 149.

45. Baylies, "March of the United States Troops," 304–5; Justin Smith, *War with Mexico,* 1:274–75; Bauer, *Mexican War,* 149; Fulton, ed., *Diary and Letters of Josiah Gregg,* 273; Hughes to Abert, January 20, 1849, in Traas, *From the Golden Gate,* 254; Taylor to Jones, October 15, 1846, AGO, Letters Received, NA, M567, Roll 328.

46. Baylies, "March of the United States Troops," 304–6; Bauer, *Mexican War,* 149–50; Fulton, ed., *Diary and Letters of Josiah Gregg,* 278, 285–86.

47. Fulton, ed., *Diary and Letters of Josiah Gregg,* 286, 290; Hughes to Abert, January 20, 1849, in Traas, *From the Golden Gate,* 256, 263; Franklin to Hughes, n.d., in Traas, *From the Golden Gate,* 291–96; Wallace to father, in I. Wallace, *Life and Letters of General W. H. L. Wallace,* 26; Engelmann to parents, November 26, 1846, in "Second Illinois in the Mexican War," 411. Bauer states: "McDowell returned on Nov. 26 with Taylor's instructions to proceed to Parras" (*Mexican War,* 150), but neglects to mention that Franklin returned on November 26 with dispatches for Wool. Josiah Gregg wrote of Franklin's return, not McDowell's (Fulton, ed., *Diary and Letters of Josiah Gregg,* 290).

48. Engelmann to parents, December 8 and 16, 1846, in Engelmann, "Second Illinois in the Mexican War," 413, 414; Justin Smith, *War with Mexico,* 1:275; Bauer, *Mexican War,* 150; Traas, *From the Golden Gate,* 155; Pryor, *Reading the Man,* 159.

CHAPTER 10

1. Kearny to Jones, August 24, 1846, in House Executive Document No. 60, Thirtieth Congress, First Session, 21; Kearny to Wool, August 22, 1846, in House Executive Document No. 60, Thirtieth Congress, First Session, 23; Kearny to Jones, September 16, 1846, in House Executive Document No. 60, Thirtieth Congress, First Session, 25–26; Lt. W. H. Emory to Col. J. J. Abert, September 1, 1847, in House Executive Document No. 41, Thirtieth Congress, First Session, 7–50; Lt. J. W. Abert to Lt. W. H. Emory, October 8, 1847, in House Executive Document No. 41, Thirtieth Congress, First Session, 386–405; J. Smith, *War with Mexico,* 1:288; Clarke, *Stephen Watts Kearny,*

148, 156, 161; John T. Hughes, *Doniphan's Expedition* (Cincinnati: J. A. and U. P. James, 1848), 143–44, 163, 204; Bauer, *Mexican War,* 127–39.

2. Lt. J. W. Abert to Lt. W. H. Emory, October 8, 1847, in House Executive Document No. 41, Thirtieth Congress, First Session, 386; Lt. W. H. Emory to Col. J. J. Abert, September 1, 1847, in House Executive Document No. 41, Thirtieth Congress, First Session, 14; Kearny to Jones, August 24, 1846, in House Executive Document No. 60, Thirtieth Congress, First Session, 21; Dwight L. Clarke, ed., *The Original Journals of Henry Smith Turner* (Norman: University of Oklahoma Press, 1966), 58–60; J. Smith, *War with Mexico,* 288; Brackett, *History of the United States Cavalry,* 69–71; Clarke, *Stephen Watts Kearny,* 113; Hughes, *Doniphan's Expedition,* 143–44; Frank S. Edwards, *A Campaign in New Mexico with Colonel Doniphan* (Philadelphia, Carey and Hart, 1847), 22–23; Isaac George, *Heroes and Incidents of the Mexican War, Containing Doniphan's Expedition* (Hollywood, CA: Sun Dance Press, 1971), 14–15, 23–25, 31–43; Bauer, *Mexican War,* 130–31, 151, 153.

3. Polk, *Diary,* 1:396, 397, 403–4, 436–39; Walter R. Borneman, *Polk: The Man Who Transformed the Presidency and America* (New York: Random House, 2008), 180–81.

4. Marcy to Kearny, June 3, 1846, in House Executive Document No. 60, Thirtieth Congress, First Session, 6–9; Kearny to Jones, September 16 and 22, 1846, in House Executive Document No. 60, Thirtieth Congress, First Session, 26, 27–76; Emory to Col. J. J. Abert, September 1, 1847, in House Executive Document No. 41, Thirtieth Congress, First Session, 45–46; Abraham R. Johnston, "Journal of Captain A. R. Johnston, First Dragoons," House Executive Document No. 41, Thirtieth Congress, First Session, 565; Capt. P. St. George Cooke to Col. J. J. Abert, December 6, 1847, in House Executive Document No. 41, Thirtieth Congress, First Session, 415–16; Justin Smith, *War with Mexico,* 284–97; Bauer, *Mexican War,* 138.

5. Taylor to Jones, November 9, 1846, AGO, Letters Received, NA, M567, Roll 328; Taylor, Order Books, Orders No. 124, October 1, 1846, NA; Taylor, Order Books, Special Orders 159, October 18, 1846, NA.

6. Meade to wife, September 27, and October 6 and 20, 1846, in Meade, *Life and Letters,* 1:135, 140, 144, 146–47.

7. Edmund Kirby Smith to mother, January 5, 1847, in Parks, *General Edmund Kirby Smith,* 55–56.

8. Dana to Sue, October 5, 1846, ALS, Dana Papers, USMA Library (also in Ferrell, ed., *Monterrey Is Ours,* 140–42).

9. Hughes and Johnson, eds., *Fighter from Way Back,* 27–32.

10. Cadmus M. Wilcox, *History of the Mexican War* (Washington, DC: Church News, 1892), 110–15; Ephraim Kirby Smith to wife, September 30 and October 26, 1846, in Blackwood, ed., *To Mexico with Scott,* 62–63, 65–67.

11. Wilcox, *History of the Mexican War,* 115–19; Lewis, *Captain Sam Grant,* 182–83.

12. Grant to Julia, August 4 and October 3, 1846, in Simon, ed., *Papers of Ulysses S. Grant,* 1:105, 112–13; Meade to wife, November 4, 1846, in Meade, *Life and Letters,* 1:150.

13. Taylor, Order Books, Orders No. 139, November 8, 1846, NA; Taylor, Order Books, Special Orders No. 172, November 6, 1846, NA; Wilcox, *History of the Mexican War,*

170–71; Justin Smith, *War with Mexico,* 1:263; Henry, *Campaign Sketches,* 239, 240, 243; Freeman Cleaves, *Meade of Gettysburg* (Norman: University of Oklahoma Press, 1960), 9; Taylor to Jones, November 9, 1846, AGO, Letters Received, NA, M567, Roll 328.

14. Taylor to Wood, November 18, 1846, in Samson, ed., *Letters of Zachary Taylor,* 66–67, 69.

15. Jones to Taylor, October 8, 1846, ALS, Letters Received, AOO, NA; Sherman to Bliss, November 12, 1846, ALS, Letters Received, AOO, NA; Taylor to Jones, October 28, 1846, AGO, Letters Received, NA, M567, Roll 328; Taylor, Order Books, Special Orders No. 172, November 6, 1846, NA; Bragg to Bliss, November 8, 1846, ALS, Letters Received, AOO, NA; Monthly Returns, Third Artillery, NA, M727, Roll 19. (Bragg was shown in Taylor's Special Orders No. 172 as promoted to Company D, but instead was given command of C, as his letter to Bliss of November 8 and the Third Artillery returns indicate.)

16. Bragg to Bliss, November 8, 1846, ALS, Letters Received, AOO, NA; Monthly Returns, Third Artillery, NA, M727, Roll 19.

17. Taylor, Order Books, Orders No. 139, November 8, 1846, NA; Bliss to Jones, November 8, 1846, Duplicate of Orders No. 139, AGO, Letters Received, NA, M567, Roll 328; Marcy to Taylor, October 22, 1846, in Wilcox, *History of the Mexican War,* 171–72; Meade to wife, November 13, 1846, in Meade, *Life and Letters,* 1:155; Henry, *Campaign Sketches,* 243–44; Ephraim Kirby Smith to wife, November 10, 1846, in Blackwood, ed., *To Mexico with Scott,* 76; Monthly Returns, Eighth Infantry, AGO, NA, M665, Roll 90; Charles S. Hamilton, "Letters of General Charles S. Hamilton," *Metropolitan Magazine* (1908): 439–40; Taylor, Order Books, Special Orders No. 174, November 10, 1846, NA; Taylor to Jones, November 16, 1846, AGO, Letters Received, NA, M567, Roll 328; Hughes and Johnson, eds., *Fighter from Way Back,* 35.

18. Hughes and Johnson, eds., *Fighter from Way Back,* 36–39.

19. Meade to wife, November 24, 1846, in Meade, *Life and Letters,* 1:157–58.

20. Meade to wife, November 13, 1846, in Meade, *Life and Letters,* 156; Taylor to Wood, November 26, 1846, in Samson, ed., *Letters of Zachary Taylor,* 71; Taylor to Jones, November 23, 1846, with enclosure of Taylor to Antonio López de Santa Anna (November 20, 1846), AGO, Letters Received, NA, M567, Roll 328.

21. Taylor to Wood, November 26, 1846, in Samson, ed., *Letters of Zachary Taylor,* 71; W. B. Franklin to Maj. G. W. Hughes, "From Monterey to Saltillo," in Traas, *From the Golden Gate,* 294; Monthly Returns, First Artillery, AGO, NA, M727, Roll 3; Lenoir Chambers, *Stonewall Jackson* (2 vols., New York: William Morrow, 1959), 1:82.

22. Chambers, *Stonewall Jackson,* 1:12, 19–48; Frank E. Vandiver, *Mighty Stonewall* (1957; repr., College Station: Texas A&M University Press, 1988), 2–12.

23. Chambers, *Stonewall Jackson,* 1:49–54; Vandiver, *Mighty Stonewall,* 12–13.

24. Chambers, *Stonewall Jackson,* 1:12, 54–76; Vandiver, *Mighty Stonewall,* 13–18.

25. Jones to Francis Taylor, July 21, 1846, ALS, Letters Received, AOO, NA; Vandiver, *Mighty Stonewall,* 20–21; Francis Taylor to Jones, October 31, 1846, AGO, Letters Received, NA, M567, Roll 328; Chambers, *Stonewall Jackson,* 79–80, 82–84; John C. Waugh, *The Class of 1846: From West Point to Appomattox: Stonewall Jackson, George McClellan, and Their Brothers* (New York: Warner Books, 1994), 76–77.

26. Maury, *Recollections of a Virginian,* 28–29.

27. Ibid., 1–26.

28. Ibid., 27–29.

29. Monthly Returns, Regiment of Mounted Rifles, AGO, NA, M744, Roll 27; Heitman, *Historical Register,* 1:798 (Porter), 1:835 (Roberts), 1:997 (Walker).

30. Chambers, *Stonewall Jackson,* 82–84; Hughes and Johnson, eds., *Fighter from Way Back,* 47.

31. Maury, *Recollections of a Virginian,* 29; Lewis, *Captain Sam Grant,* 183.

32. Lewis, *Captain Sam Grant,* 30; Monthly Returns, Mounted Rifles, NA, M744, Roll 27; Taylor, Order Books, Orders No. 156, December 10, 1846, NA; Taylor to Jones, AGO, Letters Received, October 12 and 15 and November 25, 1846, NA, M567, Roll 328; Taylor to Wood, November 26, 1846, in Samson, ed., *Letters of Zachary Taylor,* 72; Meade to wife, November 27, 1846, in Meade, *Life and Letters,* 1:159; Bauer, *Mexican War,* 119–20; Lt. P. G. T. Beauregard to Col. Joseph G. Totten, January 9, 14, and 30, and February 2 and 28, 1847, Beauregard Papers, Library of Congress; T. Harry Williams, *P. G. T. Beauregard: Napoleon in Gray* (Baton Rouge: Louisiana State University Press, 1955; paperback edition, 1995), 14.

33. Taylor to Jones, December 8, 1846, AGO, Letters Received, NA, M567, Roll 328.

34. Sears, *George B. McClellan,* 1–14; William Starr Myers, ed., *The Mexican War Diary of General George B. McClellan* (Princeton, NJ: Princeton University Press, 1917), 7–8.

35. Sears, *George B. McClellan,* 13–16; Gustavus W. Smith, "Company A Engineers in Mexico, 1846–1847," *Military Engineer* 56 (September–October 1964): 336–39, from article published by Smith in 1896 (see reprint edited by Leonne M. Hudson [Kent, OH: Kent State University Press, 2001]); Myers, ed., *Mexican War Diary of General George B. McClellan,* 7–8; McClellan to brother Tom, September 22, 1846, in Myers, ed., *Mexican War Diary of General George B. McClellan,* 7n1, qtd. from McClellan Papers, Vol. 1 (Manuscript Division, LC)).

36. Myers, ed., *Mexican War Diary of General George B. McClellan,* 7–18; Smith, "Company A Engineers," 336–39; Sears, *George B. McClellan,* 14–17.

37. Taylor, Order Books, Orders No. 156, December 10, 1846, NA.

38. Meade to wife, December 18, 1846, in Meade, *Life and Letters,* 1:170; Taylor, Order Books, Orders No. 157, December 11, 1846, NA (on Capt. T. B. Linnard of the Topographical Engineers); [J. B. Robertson], *Reminiscences of a Campaign in Mexico,* 186, 188.

39. Taylor to Jones, December 8 and 22, 1846, AGO, Letters Received, NA, M567, Roll 328; Monthly Returns, Third Artillery, NA, M727, Roll 19; Meade to wife, December 18, 1846, in Meade, *Life and Letters,* 1:170; Maury, *Recollections of a Virginian,* 29–30; French, *Two Wars,* 69; Henry, *Campaign Sketches,* 271–72.

40. Meade to wife, December 18, 1846, in Meade, *Life and Letters,* 1:170.

41. Wool to Taylor, January 20, 1847, ADS, Beinecke Rare Book and Manuscript Library; Bauer, *Mexican War,* 205; Taylor, Order Books, Orders No. 160, December 22, 1846, NA; Taylor to Jones, December 22 and 26, 1846, AGO, Letters Received, NA, M567, Roll 19; Hughes and Johnson, eds., *Fighter from Way Back,* 51; [Giddings], *Sketches of the Campaign in Northern Mexico,* 254–68.

42. Scott to Taylor, November 25, 1846, House Ex. Doc. No. 60, Thirtieth Congress, First Session, 373–74; Taylor to Buchanan, August 29, 1847, in Samson, ed., *Letters of Zachary Taylor,* 180; Wilcox, *History of the Mexican War,* 175–76. See also Dyer, *Zachary Taylor,* 220; Eisenhower, *So Far from God,* 170; Taylor to Scott, December 26, 1846, and Marcy to Taylor, May 6, 1847, House Executive Document No. 56, Thirtieth Congress, First Session, 38 and 313.

43. Hughes and Johnson, eds., *Fighter from Way Back,* 52–53; I. Wallace, *Life and Letters of General W. H. L. Wallace,* 30; Engelmann to parents, December 25, 1846, and January 2, 1847, in Engelmann, "Second Illinois in the Mexican War," 417–19, 423–24; Freeman, *R. E. Lee,* 1:213, 214, 216; Ephraim Kirby Smith to wife, December 16, 1846, in Blackwood, ed., *To Mexico with Scott,* 81–83; Taylor to Jones, January 14, 1847, AGO, Letters Received, NA, M567, Roll 361 (with enclosure of May to Bliss, January 2, 1847); Taylor to Scott, January 25, 1847, in House Executive Document No. 56, Thirtieth Congress, First Session, 51–52.

44. Meade to wife, January 7, 1847, in Meade, *Life and Letters,* 1:173; Taylor to Scott, January 15, 1847, House Executive Document No. 56, Thirtieth Congress, First Session, 51–52; Taylor to Jones, October 15, 1846, AGO, Letters Received, NA, M567, Roll 328; Taylor to Jones, January 27, 1847, House Executive Document No. 56, Thirtieth Congress, First Session, 290–92.

45. Polk, *Diary,* 2:180; 195–97; 244–46.

46. Polk, *Diary,* 2:244–46; Scott to Taylor, December 20, 1846, House Executive Document No. 56, Thirtieth Congress, First Session, 29; Croffut, ed., *Fifty Years in Camp and Field,* 231–32.

47. Polk, *Diary,* 2:246–47; Scott to Taylor, December 20, 1846, House Executive Document No. 56, Thirtieth Congress, First Session, 29–30; Scott to Taylor, January 3, 1847, House Executive Document No. 56, Thirtieth Congress, First Session, 38–40; Scott to Butler, January 3, 1847, House Executive Document No. 56, Thirtieth Congress, First Session, 41–43; Taylor to Scott, January 15, 1847, House Executive Document No. 56, Thirtieth Congress, First Session, 51–52; Taylor to Jones, January 27, 1847, House Executive Document No. 56, Thirtieth Congress, First Session, 290–92.

48. Scott to Marcy, December 30, 1846, House Executive Document No. 56, Thirtieth Congress, First Session, 34; Taylor to Scott, December 26, 1846, House Executive Document No. 56, Thirtieth Congress, First Session, 38; Scott to Taylor, January 3, 1847, House Executive Document No. 56, Thirtieth Congress, First Session, 38–40; Scott to Butler, January 3, 1847, House Executive Document No. 56, Thirtieth Congress, First Session, 41–43. For the reactions of Taylor's veterans to the treatment afforded him by Scott, see Robert Anderson, *An Artillery Officer in the Mexican War, 1846–1847, Letters of Robert Anderson, Captain 3rd Artillery, U.S.A.* (New York: G. P. Putnam's Sons, 1911), 23. Capt. Robert Anderson, a personal friend and admirer of Scott, believed the men who responded "very coldly" to a toast to the general-in-chief at Tampico in late January 1847 would change their negative opinions of Scott at their "first campaign under him." See also McCall, *Letters from the Frontiers,* 472–73 (from Victoria, January 5, 1847). Of General Taylor, Meade wrote his wife from Tampico on January 24, 1847, "He has been outrageously treated by the Administration"; and on February 17: "Great anxiety is felt

for our old and much-loved commander, and a feeling of indignation against the Government for stripping him of all his forces is prevalent throughout the army" (Meade, *Life and Letters,* 175, 182).

49. Scott to Butler, January 3, 1847, House Executive Document No. 56, Thirtieth Congress, First Session, 42; Taylor, Order Books, Orders No. 3, January 12, 1847, NA.

50. Taylor to Lt. H. L. Scott, A.D.C., General Winfield Scott's Headquarters, January 15, 1847, House Executive Document No. 56, Thirtieth Congress, First Session, 51–52; Taylor to General Scott, January 15, 1847, House Executive Document No. 56, Thirtieth Congress, First Session, 52–53.

51. Taylor to H. L. Scott, January 15, 1847, House Executive Document No. 56, Thirtieth Congress, First Session, 52.

52. Taylor to Jones, January 26, 1847, House Executive Document No. 56, Thirtieth Congress, First Session, 288–89.

53. Taylor to Jones, January 30, 1847, 296; Taylor to AG, February 4, 1847, 299–300; Taylor to Jones, January 27, 1847, 290–92.

CHAPTER 11

1. Scott to Taylor, December 20, 1846, House Executive Document No. 56, Thirtieth Congress, First Session, 29; Scott to Taylor, January 3, 1847, House Executive Document No. 56, Thirtieth Congress, First Session, 38–90; Taylor, Order Books, Orders No. 5, January 14, 1847, NA; Taylor to Jones, January 26, 1847, Letters Received, AGO, NA, M567, Roll 361; Dana to Sue, January 17, 1847, ALS, Dana Papers, USMA Library; Meade to wife, January 24, 1847, in Meade, *Life and Letters,* 1:174; Reynolds to sister Jane, January 27, 1847, ALS, Reynolds Family Papers, Franklin and Marshall College Library; Reynolds to brother, February 5, 1847, ALS, Reynolds Family Papers, Franklin and Marshall College Library; Monthly Returns, First, Second, Third, and Seventh Infantry, NA, M665, Rolls 3, 17, 31, and 79, respectively; Monthly Returns, Regiment of Mounted Rifles, NA, M744, Roll 27; Henry, *Campaign Sketches,* 298–99; French, *Two Wars,* 71–72; Jefferson Davis to brother Joseph, January 26, 1847, in J. Davis, *Papers of Jefferson Davis,* 3:114–16; Hamilton, *Zachary Taylor,* 221, 229; Justin Smith, *War with Mexico,* 1:356, 362, 365–66; Bauer, *Mexican War,* 238.

2. Scott to Butler, January 3, 1847, House Executive Document No. 56, Thirtieth Congress, First Session, 41–43; Worth to Scott, January 9, 1847, House Executive Document No. 56, Thirtieth Congress, First Session, 50; Ephraim Kirby Smith to wife, January 22, 1847, in Blackwood, ed., *To Mexico with Scott,* 91–92; Wool to Taylor, January 20, 1847, ALS, Beinecke Rare Book and Manuscript Library; Freeman, *R. E. Lee,* 1:218; Monthly Returns, Fifth, Sixth, and Fourth Infantry, NA, M665, Rolls 55, 66, and 43, respectively; Lewis, *Captain Sam Grant,* 189; Wilcox, *History of the Mexican War,* 189, 192–93; Monthly Returns, First Dragoons, NA, M744, Roll 2; Monthly Returns, Eighth Infantry, NA, M665, Roll 90; Bauer, *Mexican War,* 205. Richard Stoddert Ewell, upon promotion to 1st Lt. (on September 18, 1845), was assigned to Company G, First Dragoons, but had not joined it. Since October 6, 1846, he had been on temporary duty with Phil Kearny's Company F.

3. Wool, Order Books, Orders No. 152, December 9, 1846; Orders No. 158, December 12, 1846; Special Orders No. 150, December 12, 1846; Special Orders No. 266, December 29, 1846; Orders No. 189, January 10, 1847, NA; Wool to Taylor, January 20, 1847, ALS, Beinecke Rare Book and Manuscript Library; Freeman, *R. E. Lee,* 1:211–12; Engelmann to parents, December 25, 1846, in Engelmann, "Second Illinois in the Mexican War," 417–19; Baylies, "March of the United States Troops," 308–310; Wallace to father, December 23, 1846, in I. Wallace, *Life and Letters of General W. H. L. Wallace,* 28–29; Bauer, *Mexican War,* 205; Franklin to Hughes, in Traas, *From the Golden Gate,* 296–97, 155; Justin Smith, *War with Mexico,* 1:275–76.

4. Freeman, *R. E. Lee,* 1:214–16; E. Thomas, *Robert E. Lee,* 118; Fitzhugh Lee, *General Lee* (New York, Charles Scribner's Sons, 1904), 43.

5. Freeman, *R. E. Lee,* 1:217, 218. Lee habitually signed all letters, even those to his wife, as "RE Lee," with no periods after initials (see, e.g., Pryor, *Reading the Man,* 142). For years, Lee had been exchanging very amorous letters with Capt. William Williams's daughter "Cousin Markie" (Ibid., 204). Lee's wife was opposed to the war with Mexico; he, though questioning its righteousness, regretted not having been sent to the war zone earlier (Ibid., 156–60). He had little compassion for Mexicans, finding them "weak" and "primitive in their habits and tastes" (Ibid., 150).

6. Wallace to father, December 23, 1846, in I. Wallace, *Life and Letters of General W. H. L. Wallace,* 30; Engelmann to parents, December 26, 1846, and February 6, 1847, in Engelmann, "Second Illinois in the Mexican War," 420, 438; Taylor, Order Books, Orders No. 160, December 22, 1846; Orders No. 6, January 28, 1847, NA; Wool to Taylor, January 20, 1847, ALS, Beinecke Rare Book and Manuscript Library; Taylor to Jones, February 4, 1847, NA, M567, Roll 361; Reynolds to brother James, February 5, 1847, ALS, Reynolds Family Papers, Franklin and Marshall College Library; French, *Two Wars,* 73–74; Justin Smith, *War with Mexico,* 1:373; Bauer, *Mexican War,* 207–8.

7. Wilcox, *History of the Mexican War,* 192–94, 193 (footnote); Ephraim Kirby Smith, "Journal," January 22, 1847, in Blackwood, ed., *To Mexico with Scott,* 83–93; Grant, *Personal Memoirs,* 1:123–24; Grant to Julia, February 1, 1846 [1847], in Simon ed., *Papers of Ulysses S. Grant,* 1:123–25.

8. Wilcox, *History of the Mexican War,* 193–94, 198 (footnote); Grant to Jesup, January 31, 1847, in Simon, ed., *Papers of Ulysses S. Grant,* 1:122–23. On second theft, see Simon, ed., *Papers of Ulysses S. Grant,* 1:162–63, 240.

9. Grant, *Personal Memoirs,* 1:123–24; Grant to Julia, February 1, 1847, in Simon ed., *Papers of Ulysses S. Grant,* 1:123–25.

10. Ephraim Kirby Smith, "Journal," January 22 and 26, 1847, in Blackwood, ed., *To Mexico with Scott,* 91, 92; Hughes and Johnson, eds., *Fighter from Way Back,* 62.

11. Hughes and Johnson, eds., *Fighter from Way Back,* 48, 52–60.

12. Hughes and Johnson, eds., *Fighter from Way Back,* 61–66; Scott to Marcy, February 28, 1847, House Executive Document No. 56, Thirtieth Congress, First Session, 86; Anderson, *Artillery Officer in the Mexican War,* 50–51; Croffut, ed., *Fifty Years in Camp and Field,* 234–36; Meade to wife, January 24, 1847, in Meade, *Life and Letters,* 1:175; Dana to Sue, January 24, 1847, ALS, Dana Papers, USMA Library; Freeman, *R.E. Lee,* 1:219–21. Note that Joe Johnston did not serve under General Taylor during the

Mexican War, contrary to a statement in Joseph T. Glatthaar, *Partners in Command: The Relationships between Leaders in the Civil War* (New York: Free Press, 1994), 97.

13. Taylor to Jones, February 7, 1847, Letters Received, AGO, NA, M567, Roll 361; Taylor to Jones, March 6, 1847, NA, M567, Roll 362; James Henry Carleton, *The Battle of Buena Vista with the Operations of the "Army of Occupation" for One Month* (New York: Harper and Brothers, 1848), 1–20; [Henry W. Benham], *Recollections of Mexico and the Battle of Buena Vista* (Boston: n.p., 1871), 5–9; William B. Franklin, "The Battle of Buena Vista, February 22–23, 1847," in *Civil and Mexican Wars 1861, 1846, Papers of the Military Historical Society of Massachusetts* (Boston: Military Historical Society of Massachusetts, 1913), 13:549–52; French, *Two Wars,* 76; Henry, *Campaign Sketches,* 309–311; Bauer, *Mexican War,* 208, 209–210; Eisenhower, *So Far from God,* 180–81; Justin Smith, *War with Mexico,* 1:373, 382–83, 385–86. For Ben McCulloch's unexpected return and his vital contribution to intelligence, see Wilkins, *Highly Irregular Irregulars,* 125–30, 133–35.

14. Taylor to Jones, March 6, 1847, Letters Received, AGO, NA, M567, Roll 362; Carleton, *Battle of Buena Vista,* 19–20.

15. Carleton, *Battle of Buena Vista,* 24. See also W. H. L. Wallace to George Green, March 1, 1847, in I. Wallace, *Life and Letters of General W. H. L. Wallace,* 40; Reynolds to sister Jane, February 25, 1847, ALS, Reynolds Family Papers, Franklin and Marshall College Library; Mansfield to wife, February 24, 1847, ALS, Mansfield Papers, USMA Library; [Benham], *Recollections of Mexico,* 8–9; Franklin, "Battle of Buena Vista," 552; Henry, *Campaign Sketches,* 309, 311; Bauer, *Mexican War,* 208, 209; and Hamilton, *Zachary Taylor,* 231–32.

16. L. Wallace, *Lew Wallace,* 1:166–68, 192; Henry, *Campaign Sketches,* 309; Baylies, "March of the United States Troops," 310–12; Taylor to Jones, March 6, 1847, Letters Received, AGO, NA, M567, Roll 362; Carleton, *Battle of Buena Vista,* 236–38; Justin Smith, *War with Mexico,* 1:388, 555n5; Bauer, *Mexican War,* 208; Eisenhower, *So Far from God,* 183; Robarts, *Mexican War Veterans,* 10 (Second Dragoons), 48 (Second and Third Indiana), 50–51 (Kentucky Cavalry), 51–52 (Second Kentucky).

17. Taylor to Jones, March 6, 1847, Letters Received, AGO, NA, M567, Roll 362; Carleton, *Battle of Buena Vista,* 24–30; Franklin, "Battle of Buena Vista," 552; Henry, *Campaign Sketches,* 311; Bauer, *Mexican War,* 209–210; Justin Smith, *War with Mexico,* 1:384.

18. Taylor to Jones, March 6, 1847, Letters Received, AGO, NA, M567, Roll 362.

19. Wool to Bliss, March 4, 1847, Letters Received, AGO, NA, M567, Roll 362.

20. Carleton, *Battle of Buena Vista,* 20.

21. Carleton, *Battle of Buena Vista,* 8, 30–32; W. H. L. Wallace to George Green, March 1, 1847, in I. Wallace, *Life and Letters of General W. H. L. Wallace,* 40–41; Taylor to Jones, March 6, 1847, Letters Received, AGO, NA, M567, Roll 362; Wool to Bliss, March 4, 1847, Letters Received, AGO, NA, M567, Roll 362; Franklin, "Battle of Buena Vista," 552–53; French, *Two Wars,* 76–77; Reynolds to sister Jane, March 1, 1847, ALS, Reynolds Family Papers, Franklin and Marshall College Library; Bauer, *Mexican War,* 210; Justin Smith, *War with Mexico,* 1:384; Hamilton, *Zachary Taylor,* 232; Nichols, *Toward Gettysburg,* 38–39.

22. Carleton, *Battle of Buena Vista,* 33.

23. [Benham], *Recollections of Mexico,* 9–11; Wool to Bliss, March 4, 1847, Letters Received, AGO, NA, M567, Roll 362; Mansfield to wife, February 24, 1847, ALS, Mansfield Papers, USMA Library.

24. [Benham], *Recollections of Mexico,* 3–5, 11; Heitman, *Historical Register,* 1:210.

25. Taylor to Jones, February 24, 1847, with enclosures, Letters Received, AGO, NA, M567, Roll 362; See also Taylor to Jones, March 6, 1847, Letters Received, AGO, NA, M567, Roll 362; Wool to Bliss, March 4, 1847, Letters Received, AGO, NA, M567, Roll 362; Carleton, *Battle of Buena Vista,* 37; Hamilton, *Zachary Taylor,* 233–34; Eisenhower, *So Far from God,* 185–87.

26. Taylor to Jones, March 6, 1847, Letters Received, AGO, NA, M567, Roll 362; See also Wool to Bliss, March 4, 1847, Letters Received, AGO, NA, M567, Roll 362; Carleton, *Battle of Buena Vista,* 39–41; French, *Two Wars,* 77–78.

27. Carleton, *Battle of Buena Vista,* 41. See also Taylor to Jones, March 6, 1847, Letters Received, NA, M567, Roll 362; Wool to Bliss, March 4, 1847, Letters Received, NA, M567, Roll 362.

28. Taylor to Jones, March 6, 1847, Letters Received, AGO, NA, M567, Roll 362. See also Wool to Bliss, March 4, 1847, Letters Received, AGO, NA, M567, Roll 362.

29. Taylor to Jones, March 6, 1847, Letters Received, AGO, NA, M567, Roll 362.

30. W. H. L. Wallace to George Green, March 1, 1847, in I. Wallace, *Life and Letters of General W. H. L. Wallace,* 43.

31. Carleton, *Battle of Buena Vista,* 48.

32. French, *Two Wars,* 78; Reynolds to sister Jane, March 1, 1847, in Nichols, *Toward Gettysburg,* 39.

33. Carleton, *Battle of Buena Vista,* 50. See also Taylor to Jones, March 6, 1847, Letters Received, AGO, NA, M567, Roll 362; and Wool to Bliss, March 4, 1847, Letters Received, AGO, NA, M567, Roll 362.

34. A map drawn by Lieutenant Sitgreaves entitled "Plan of the Battle of Buena Vista," reproduced in Carleton, *Battle of Buena Vista* (following vii), indicates American positions on the morning of February 23. A portion of the same map may be found in French, *Two Wars,* 79. Similar maps are in Bauer, *Mexican War,* 213; Justin Smith, *War with Mexico,* 1:387; Henry, *Campaign Sketches,* 313; Smith and Judah, eds., *Chronicles of the Gringos,* 97 (drawn by engineer officer J. K. F. Mansfield); Hamilton, *Zachary Taylor,* 235 (based on that of Sitgreaves, and one by Captain Linnard "from surveys by Capt. Linnard and Lieuts. John Pope and William B. Franklin"). See also Esposito, chief ed., *West Point Atlas,* map 14©; and Eisenhower, *So Far from God,* 184. For written descriptions, see Taylor to Jones, March 6, 1847, Letters Received, AGO, NA, M567, Roll 362; Wool to Bliss, March 4, 1847, Letters Received, AGO, NA, M567, Roll 362; Carleton, *Battle of Buena Vista,* 50–53; [Benham], *Recollections of Mexico,* 14–15; Franklin, "Battle of Buena Vista," 554–55; McWhiney, *Braxton Bragg and Confederate Defeat,* 1:80; Henry, *Campaign Sketches,* 314–16; Justin Smith, *War with Mexico,* 1:389–90; and Bauer, *Mexican War,* 212.

35. Carleton, *Battle of Buena Vista,* 58. See also Taylor to Jones, March 6, 1847, Letters Received, AGO, NA, M567, Roll 362; Brig. Gen. Joseph Lane to Wool, February 25, 1847, Letters Received, AGO, NA, M567, Roll 362; Franklin, "Battle of Buena Vista,"

554; Henry, *Campaign Sketches,* 314; Bauer, *Mexican War,* 213–14; Justin Smith, *War with Mexico,* 1:390.

36. Taylor to Jones, March 6, 1847, Letters Received, AGO, NA, M567, Roll 362; Brig. Gen. Joseph Lane to Wool, February 25, 1847, Letters Received, AGO, NA, M567, Roll 362; Carleton, *Battle of Buena Vista,* 60–63; [Benham], *Recollections of Mexico,* 16; French, *Two Wars,* 80; Hamilton, *Zachary Taylor,* 236; Henry, *Campaign Sketches,* 314–15; Justin Smith, *War with Mexico,* 1:390; Bauer, *Mexican War,* 214; Eisenhower, *So Far from God,* 188; Robarts, *Mexican War Veterans,* 44 (footnote).

37. Carleton, *Battle of Buena Vista,* 68. See also Taylor to Jones, March 6, 1847, Letters Received, AGO, NA, M567, Roll 362; Wool to Bliss, March 4, 1847, Letters Received, AGO, NA, M567, Roll 362.

38. Carleton, *Battle of Buena Vista,* 64.

39. Ibid., 65.

40. Taylor to Jones, March 6, 1847, Letters Received, AGO, NA, M567, Roll 362; Wool to Bliss, March 4, 1847, Letters Received, AGO, NA, M567, Roll 362; Carleton, *Battle of Buena Vista,* 72–75; Franklin, "Battle of Buena Vista," 555; Hamilton, *Zachary Taylor,* 237; Brig. Gen. Joseph Lane to Wool, February 25, 1847, Letters Received, AGO, NA, M567, Roll 362; Col. James Lane to Brig. Gen. Joseph Lane, May 15, 1847, Letters Received, AGO, NA, M567, Roll 362; Henry, *Campaign Sketches,* 315; Bauer, *Mexican War,* 214; Justin Smith, *War with Mexico,* 1:391; Eisenhower, *So Far from God,* 188.

41. Taylor to Jones, March 6, 1847, Letters Received, AGO, NA, M567, Roll 362.

42. Carleton, *Battle of Buena Vista,* 79.

43. Carleton, *Battle of Buena Vista,* 80; Wool to Bliss, March 4, 1847, Letters Received, AGO, NA, M567, Roll 362.

44. Taylor to Jones, March 6, 1847, Letters Received, AGO, NA, M567, Roll 362; Wool to Bliss, March 4, 1847, Letters Received, AGO, NA, M567, Roll 362; French, *Two Wars,* 80; Reynolds to sister Jane, March 1, 1847, ALS, Reynolds Family Papers, Franklin and Marshall College Library; Carleton, *Battle of Buena Vista,* 91–106; Robarts, *Mexican War Veterans,* 40; Franklin, "Battle of Buena Vista," 555; Justin Smith, *War with Mexico,* 1:390; Bauer, *Mexican War,* 215.

45. Taylor to Jones, March 6, 1847, Letters Received, AGO, NA, M567, Roll 362; Wool to Bliss, March 4, 1847, Letters Received, AGO, NA, M567, Roll 362; Carleton, *Battle of Buena Vista,* 106–7; Franklin, "Battle of Buena Vista," 556, [Benham], *Recollections of Mexico,* 17; Justin Smith, *War with Mexico,* 1:393; Bauer, *Mexican War,* 215–16.

46. Foote, *Civil War,* 1:11.

47. Davis to Bliss, March 2, 1847, Letters Received, AGO, NA, M567, Roll 362. See also J. Davis, *Papers of Jefferson Davis,* 3:122–23; J. Davis, *Private Letters,* 46, 179–84; Eaton, *Jefferson Davis,* 63–64; Carleton, *Battle of Buena Vista,* 95–100; and W. H. L. Wallace to George Green, March 1, 1847, in I. Wallace, *Life and Letters of General W. H. L. Wallace,* 45. Col. Jefferson Davis, in his report to Bliss, commended among others three of his officers who would become Confederate brigadier generals: Douglas H. Cooper, Carnot Posey, and Richard Griffith. See also Douglas Cooper to Richard Griffith, March 1, 1847, in J. Davis, *Papers of Jefferson Davis,* 3:128–30.

48. Lane to Wool, February 25, 1847, Letters Received, AGO, NA, M567, Roll 362.

49. Davis to Varina, February 25, 1847, in J. Davis, *Papers of Jefferson Davis,* 3:122–23;

Davis to Bliss, March 23, 1847, Letters Received, AGO, NA, M567, Roll 362; Taylor to Jones, March 6, 1847, Letters Received, AGO, NA, M567, Roll 362.

50. French, *Two Wars,* 82.

51. Strode, *Jefferson Davis,* 182.

52. Carleton, *Battle of Buena Vista,* 109. See also Taylor to Jones, March 6, 1847, Letters Received, AGO, NA, M567, Roll 362; Wool to Bliss, March 4, 1847, Letters Received, AGO, NA, M567, Roll 362; W. H. L. Wallace to George Green, March 1, 1847, in I. Wallace, *Life and Letters of General W. H. L. Wallace,* 47–50; [Benham], *Recollections of Mexico,* 22; Henry, *Campaign Sketches,* 320; Justin Smith, *War with Mexico,* 394–95; Bauer, *Mexican War,* 216.

53. Carleton, *Battle of Buena Vista,* 112, 116. See also Taylor to Jones, March 6, 1847, Letters Received, AGO, NA, M567, Roll 362; Wool to Bliss, March 4, 1847, Letters Received, AGO, NA, M567, Roll 362; Franklin, "Battle of Buena Vista," 556.

54. Carleton, *Battle of Buena Vista,* 117, 124.

55. Taylor to Jones, March 6, 1847, Letters Received, AGO, NA, M567, Roll 362.

56. Taylor to Jones, March 6, 1847, Letters Received, AGO, NA, M567, Roll 362; Mansfield to wife, February 24, 1847, ALS, Mansfield Papers, USMA Library; Carleton, *Battle of Buena Vista,* 130–31; Henry, *Campaign Sketches,* 322; Justin Smith, *War with Mexico,* 1:397–98; Bauer, *Mexican War,* 217; Eisenhower, *So Far from God,* 191.

57. Taylor to Jones, March 6, 1847, Letters Received, AGO, NA, M567, Roll 362.

58. Benham, Henry W.; Bragg, Braxton; Buford, Abraham; Carleton, James H.; Chilton, Robert H.; Couch, Darius N.; Eaton, Amos B.; Franklin, William B.; French, Samuel G.; Garnett, Robert S.; McDowell, Irvin; Mansfield, Joseph K. F.; Pope, John; Reynolds, John F.; Rucker, Daniel H.; Sherman, Thomas W.; Thomas, George H.; Wood, Thomas J.; Wool, John E. (Heitman, *Historical Register,* passim).

59. McWhiney, *Braxton Bragg and Confederate Defeat,* 1:90–93; Dillon, *American Artillery in the Mexican War,* 14.

60. Reynolds (fragment of letter, no salutation, no date), ALS, Reynolds Family Papers, Franklin and Marshall College Library; Mansfield to wife, February 24, 1847, ALS, USMA Library; Carleton, *Battle of Buena Vista,* 158.

61. Taylor to Jones, March 6, 1847, Letters Received, AGO, NA, M567, Roll 362.

62. French, *Two Wars,* 84; [Benham], *Recollections of Mexico,* 26–27.

63. Bauer, *Zachary Taylor,* 196. See also Justin Smith, *War with Mexico,* 1:383, 395–96; and Bauer, *Mexican War,* 209, 217.

64. Wool to Bliss, March 4, 1847, Letters Received, AGO, NA, M567, Roll 362; W. H. L. Wallace to George Green, March 1, 1847, in I. Wallace, *Life and Letters of General W. H. L. Wallace,* 53.

65. Grant, *Personal Memoirs,* 1:134.

66. [Benham], *Recollections of Mexico,* 21.

CHAPTER 12

1. [Giddings], *Sketches of the Campaign in Northern Mexico,* 275, 287, 289–95; Bauer, *Mexican War,* 218–19; Bauer, *Zachary Taylor,* 207.

2. [Giddings], *Sketches of the Campaign in Northern Mexico,* 289–91.

3. Ibid.

4. Ibid., 297.

5. Ibid., 297–302.

6. Ibid, 302–320; Taylor to Jones, March 22, 1847, House Executive Document No. 56, Thirtieth Congress, First Session, 313.

7. [Giddings], *Sketches of the Campaign in Northern Mexico,* 321–25; The guilty Texans, if such they were, appear to have been members of a recently formed Ranger company led by Capt. Mabry B. Gray, who had been "arrested in Monterey for being drunk and acting in a disorderly manner." To his credit, Gray had been in Sam Walker's company "from the first"; and in his defense, allegedly his "entire family had been murdered in 1840, when outlaws under Canales raided Texas" (Wilkins, *Highly Irregular Irregulars,* 137–38).

8. Taylor to Jones, March 6 and 22, 1847, House Executive Document No. 56, Thirtieth Congress, First Session, 308, 313.

9. Bauer, *Mexican War,* 219; Bauer, *Zachary Taylor,* 207; Taylor to Jones, March 20 and 28, House Executive Document No. 56, Thirtieth Congress, First Session, 309–310, 315.

10. Taylor to Wood, March 20, 1847, April 4, 1847, May 9 and 30, 1847, June 23, 1847, July 13 and 20, 1847, August 5, 25, and 31, 1847, September 8, 14, and 27, 1847, October 5, 19, and 27, 1847, November 2 and 17, 1847, in Samson, ed., *Letters of Zachary Taylor,* 89–158; Hamilton, *Zachary Taylor,* 245–50; Dyer, *Zachary Taylor,* 244–46; Bauer, *Zachary Taylor,* 207–214; Bragg to French, October 13, 1847, ALS, USMA Library; McWhiney, *Braxton Bragg and Confederate Defeat,* 1:93–99; French, *Two Wars,* 86–87; W. Thomas, *General George H. Thomas,* 97–100; Cleaves, *Rock of Chickamauga,* 43–44; Richard W. Johnson, *Memoir of Major-General George H. Thomas* (Philadelphia: J. B. Lippincott, 1881), 24–25; Donn Piatt, *General George H. Thomas* (Cincinnati: Robert Clarke, 1893), 70; Reynolds to James, May 16 and July 25, 1847, ALS, Reynolds Family Papers, Franklin and Marshall College Library; Reynolds to Jane, May 26 and September 5, 1847, January 1 and March 19, 1848, ALS, Reynolds Family Papers, Franklin and Marshall College Library; Nichols, *Toward Gettysburg,* 44, 51; Carleton, *Buena Vista,* v; Hunt, *Major General James Henry Carleton,* 110; Mansfield to wife, April 14 and 25, 1847, May 2 and 23, 1847, June 5, 21, and 27, 1847, July 4, 6, 11, 12, and 25, 1847, August 10, 15, and 24, 1847, September 1, 7–8, and 21, 1847, October 11 and 27, 1847, November 28, 1847, ALS, Mansfield Papers, USMA Library (Mansfield's letter of November 28 states that Wool and staff marched with him and General Taylor from Monterrey to Camargo in November 1847); Davis to Varina, May 27, 1847, in J. Davis *Private Letters,* 47; Davis to Wool, March 25, 1847, in J. Davis, *Papers of Jefferson Davis,* 3:164; Davis to brother Joseph, April 10, 1847, in J. Davis, *Papers of Jefferson Davis,* 3:169–70; President Polk to Davis, May 19, 1847, in J. Davis, *Papers of Jefferson Davis,* 3:175–76; Davis to George H. Crosman, May 24, 1847, in J. Davis, *Papers of Jefferson Davis,* 3:177–78; Strode, *Jefferson Davis,* 185–88; Eaton, *Jefferson Davis,* 64–65; W. C. Davis, *Jefferson Davis,* 160–63; Robarts, *Mexican War Veterans,* 40, 43, 44, 48, 50, 51, and 59 (for discharge of volunteers); Bauer, *Mexican War,* 201–226 (for discharge of volunteers); Taylor to Scott, March 1 and 20,

1847; April 16, 1847; May 16, 1847 (on congratulation for Cerro Gordo); House Executive Document No. 56, Thirtieth Congress, First Session, 358–63. Among the Ohio troops who helped clear Taylor's line of communication were future generals Ferdinand Van Derveer (First Ohio); George W. Morgan and George F. McGinnis (Second Ohio); and Samuel R. Curtis and Samuel Beatty (Third Ohio). In almost all of General Taylor's letters to Adjutant General Jones dating from March 6 through July 27, 1847 (reproduced in House Executive Document No. 56, Thirtieth Congress, First Session, 308–339, 365–77), there are references to the discharge of volunteers, replacements of units discharged, and various other matters relating to troop strength in the Army of Occupation.

11. Hughes, *Doniphan's Expedition,* 120–203, 255–386; Frank S. Edwards, *A Campaign in New Mexico with Colonel Doniphan* (Philadelphia: Carey and Hart, 1847), 82–165, 172–78; William H. Richardson, *The Journal of William H. Richardson, a Private Soldier in the Campaign of New and Old Mexico, under the Command of Colonel Doniphan, of Missouri* (3rd ed., New York: William H. Richardson, 1849), 46–49; George Rutledge Gibson, *Journal of a Soldier under Kearny and Doniphan,* ed. Ralph P. Bieber (Glendale, CA: Arthur H. Clark, 1935), 279–363; John W. Reid (captain, First Missouri Volunteers) to General Wool, May 21, 1847, in House Executive Document No. 56, Thirtieth Congress, First Session, 334–35; Smith and Judah, eds., *Chronicles of the Gringos,* 134–43; Brackett, *History of the United States Cavalry,* 104–7; Wilcox, *History of the Mexican War,* 152–59; Justin Smith, *War with Mexico,* 1:298–314; Bauer, *Mexican War,* 151–58; Taylor to Jones, April 14, 1847, House Executive Document No. 56, Thirtieth Congress, First Session, 317; Doniphan to Wool, March 20, 1847, House Executive Document No. 56, Thirtieth Congress, First Session, 318–19; Taylor to Jones, May 26, 1847, House Executive Document No. 56, Thirtieth Congress, First Session, 333–34.

12. Price to Jones, February 15, 1847, in Smith and Judah, eds., *Chronicles of the Gringos,* 128–33; Hughes, *Doniphan's Expedition,* 386–96; Robert E. Shalhope, *Sterling Price: Portrait of a Southerner* (Columbia: University of Missouri Press, 1971), 56–66; Philip St. George Cooke, *The Conquest of New Mexico and California, An Historical and Personal Narrative* (1878; Albuquerque, NM: Horn and Wallace, 1964), 111–24; Brackett, *History of the United States Cavalry,* 107–111; Wilcox, *History of the Mexican War,* 159, 164; Bauer, *Mexican War,* 139–41; Eisenhower, *So Far from God,* 235–40.

13. William H. Emory, "Notes of a Military Reconnaissance from Fort Leavenworth in Missouri, to San Francisco, in California, Including Part of the Arkansas, Del Norte, and Gila Rivers," House Executive Document No. 41, Thirtieth Congress, First Session, 45–114; Johnston, "Journal of Captain A. R. Johnston," House Executive Document No. 41, Thirtieth Congress, First Session, 565–614; Clarke, ed., *Original Journals of Henry Smith Turner,* 76–124; Henry Smith Turner to wife, December 21, 1846, in Clarke, ed., *Original Journals of Henry Smith Turner,* 144–48; Clarke, *Stephen Watts Kearny,* 163–232; Christopher Carson, *Kit Carson's Own Story of His Life,* ed. Blanche Grant (Taos, NM: n.p., 1926), 77–83; Justin Smith, *War with Mexico,* 1:341–46; Bauer, *Mexican War,* 137–38, 186–89; Eisenhower, *So Far from God,* 219–26; Kearny to Jones, December 12, 1846, in Smith and Judah, eds., *Chronicles of the Gringos,* 156; Let-

ter of John M. Stanley (no salutation, no date), in Smith and Judah, eds., *Chronicles of the Gringos,* 157–59.

14. Emory, "Notes of a Military Reconnaissance," 115–23; Clarke, *Stephen Watts Kearny,* 233–53; Henry Smith Turner to wife, January 30, 1847, in Clarke, ed., *Original Journals of Henry Smith Turner,* 149–50; Carson, *Kit Carson's Own Story,* 83–84; Bauer, *Mexican War,* 189–92; Hampton Sides, *Blood and Thunder: An Epic of the American West* (New York: Doubleday, 2006), 130–65; Eisenhower, *So Far from God,* 226–29; Smith and Judah, eds., *Chronicles of the Gringos,* 156–65; Borneman, *Polk,* 275–76.

15. Bragg to French, October 13, 1847, ALS, Braxton Bragg Papers, USMA Library (qtd. in McWhiney, *Braxton Bragg and Confederate Defeat,* 1:96); Mansfield to wife, October 27, 1847, ALS, Mansfield Papers, USMA Library. Mansfield wrote concerning the two alleged offenders that Lt. John Pope was under arrest and that Capt. [Thomas B.] Linnard had been transferred to Saltillo.

16. Bauer, *Zachary Taylor,* 214, 322; Johnson, *Winfield Scott,* 153, 160, 162. See also Allan Peskin, *Winfield Scott and the Profession of Arms* (Kent, OH: Kent State University Press, 2003), 135–36, 145–47; Otis A. Singletary, *The Mexican War* (Chicago: University of Chicago Press, 1960), 46, 133; Smith, *War with Mexico,* 1:140–41; and Bauer, *Mexican War,* 237–38. There is one eyewitness account of Taylor's being "in a rage" in August 1847, but it pertained to an allegation that a Texas Ranger had murdered an innocent Mexican man at Medelina while on a scout the general had ordered. After a regular army officer who was with the Texans explained that the Mexican rider shot had "refused to obey the guards and would not stop when repeatedly warned," Old Zach apologized to the commanding Ranger (Wilkins, *Highly Irregular Irregulars,* 147).

17. Hamilton, *Zachary Taylor,* 29.

18. Taylor to Wood, in Samson, ed., *Letters of Zachary Taylor,* June 21 and 30, 1846, July 7, 1846, August 4, 11, 19, and 23, 1846, September 3, 1846, November 10 and 26, 1846, December 18, 1846; January 26, 1847, February 9, 1847, May 9 and 30, 1847, June 23, 1847, July 13 and 20, 1847, August 5 and 25, 1847, September 14 and 27, 1847, October 5 and 27, 1847, November 17, 1847.

19. McWhiney, *Braxton Bragg and Confederate Defeat,* 1:100; Meade to wife, February 8, 1847, in Meade, *Life and Letters,* 1:182; Anderson, *Artillery Officer in the Mexican War,* 23.

20. Scott to Taylor, November 25, 1846 (reproduced in Wilcox, *History of the Mexican War,* 175–76).

21. Taylor to Scott, December 26, 1846, House Executive Document No. 56, Thirtieth Congress, First Session, 38.

22. Johnson, *Winfield Scott,* 162 (citing Singletary, *The Mexican War,* 46); Bauer, *Mexican War,* 238; Bauer, *Zachary Taylor,* 190.

23. Taylor to Wood, June 21, 1846, in Samson, ed., *Letters of Zachary Taylor,* 12–13.

24. Taylor to Wood, June 30, 1846, July 25, 1846, August 4, 1846, November 10, 1846, December 10, 1846, March 20, 1847, June 23, 1847, 20–110; Meade to wife, February 24, 1847, in Meade, *Life and Letters,* 1:184.

25. Taylor to Wood, August 23, 1846, in Samson, ed., *Letters of Zachary Taylor,* 48.

26. Taylor to Wood, June 23, 1847, in Samson, ed., *Letters of Zachary Taylor,* 109. In December 1846, Abraham Lincoln was a charter member of a club of young Whig congressmen formed to support Taylor as their nominee in the next presidential election (Bauer, *Zachary Taylor,* 218).

27. Taylor to Wood, August 23, 1846, in Samson, ed., *Letters of Zachary Taylor,* 136.

28. Polk, *Diary,* 2:258, 328; Hughes and Stonesifer, *Life and Wars of Gideon J. Pillow,* 44–45.

29. French, *Two Wars,* 84.

Bibliography

OFFICIAL RECORDS IN THE NATIONAL ARCHIVES, WASHINGTON, DC

Office of the Adjutant General (Record Group 94)

Army of Occupation, Letters Received
Army of Occupation, Orders
Army of Occupation, Special Orders
General and Special Orders
Letters Received
Letters Sent
Returns from Posts
Returns from Regular Army Artillery Regiments
Returns from Regular Army Dragoon Regiments
Returns from Regular Army Infantry Regiments
Returns from Regular Army Mounted Rifles Regiment
General Zachary Taylor, Order Books
General John Ellis Wool, Order Books

Office of the Judge Advocate General (Record Group 153)

Courts of Inquiry Proceedings
Courts-Martial Proceedings

Office of the Secretary of War (Record Group 107)

Confidential and Unofficial Letters Sent
Letters Sent, Military Affairs
Records of the Headquarters of the Army (Record Group 108)
Letters Sent

CONGRESSIONAL DOCUMENTS

House of Representatives, Executive Document 41, Thirtieth Congress, First Session

"Notes of a Military Reconnoissance, from Fort Leavenworth, in Missouri, to San Diego, in California, Including Part of the Arkansas, Del Norte, and Gila Rivers, by Lieut. Col. W. H. Emory"

House of Representatives, Executive Document 56, Thirtieth Congress, First Session

"Correspondence between the Secretary of War and Generals Scott and Taylor, and between General Scott and Mr. Trist"

House of Representatives, Executive Document 60, Thirtieth Congress, First Session

"Occupation of Mexican Territory"

House of Representatives, Executive Document 62, Thirtieth Congress, First Session

"Regulars and Volunteers Engaged in the Mexican War"
Senate, Occupation of Mexican Territory, Sixty-Second Congress, Second Session

PERSONAL PAPERS

Beinecke Rare Book and Manuscript Library, Yale University, New Haven, CT

Edmund Bradford Papers
Samuel R. Curtis Papers
William W. H. Davis Papers
Jubal A. Early Papers
Amos B. Eaton Papers
John W. Geary Papers
Gideon J. Pillow Papers
Joseph R. Smith Papers
John D. Wilkins Papers
John E. Wool Papers

Historical Society of Pennsylvania, Philadelphia, PA

William W. S. Bliss Papers
John Garland Papers
George A. McCall Papers
George G. Meade Papers
Gideon J. Pillow Papers
John F. Reynolds Papers

Library of Congress, Washington, DC

John G. Barnard Papers
Pierre G. T. Beauregard Papers
Richard S. Ewell Papers
Ulysses S. Grant Papers
John P. Hatch Papers
Robert Hazlitt Papers
Ethan A. Hitchcock Papers
George B. McClellan Papers

Princeton University Library, Princeton, NJ

William G. Belknap Papers
Zachary Taylor Papers

Shadek-Fackenthal Library, Franklin and Marshall College, Lancaster, PA

John F. Reynolds Papers

Southern Historical Collection, University of North Carolina, Chapel Hill, NC

James P. Anderson Papers
Milledge L. Bonham Letter, John F. Hoke Papers
William R. Caswell Papers
Benjamin F. Cheatham Papers
Thomas Claiborne Papers
Robert C. Foster Jr. Papers
Julius P. Garesche Papers
Jeremy Gilmer Letters, Lenoir Family Papers
D. H. Hill Diaries
John F. Hoke Papers
Henry R. Jackson Papers
Robert E. Lee Papers
James S. McIntosh Papers
William W. Mackall Papers
George E. Maney Papers
John A. Quitman Papers
George W. Rains Papers
Edmund Kirby Smith Papers
Chatham R. Wheat Papers
Robert Crooke Wood Diary

United States Military Academy Library, West Point, NY

Edmund B. Alexander Papers
Bradford F. Alden Papers

Benjamin Alvord Letters
James W. Anderson Papers
Richard H. Anderson Papers
William P. Bainbridge Papers
Rufus L. Baker Papers
Philip N. Barbour Journals
Henry W. Benham Papers
Braxton Bragg Papers
John C. Casey Papers
William Chapman Papers
Thomas J. Cram Papers
Napoleon J. T. Dana Papers
James Duncan Papers
William M. Gardner Papers
Alfred Gibbs Papers
Charles C. Gilbert Papers
Ulysses S. Grant Papers
Robert Hazlitt Papers
Ethan A. Hitchcock Papers
Abraham R. Johnston Papers
Joseph K. F. Mansfield Papers
George W. Rains Papers
Joseph J. Reynolds Papers
Benjamin S. Roberts Diary
Winfield Scott Papers
Charles F. Smith Papers
Zachary Taylor Papers

NEWSPAPERS

Corpus Christi Gazette
Hartford Daily Courant
New York Herald
New York Times
New York Tribune

PUBLISHED ACCOUNTS OF PARTICIPANTS

Anderson, Robert, *An Artillery Officer in the Mexican War, 1846–1847, Letters of Robert Anderson, Captain 3rd Artillery, U.S.A.* New York: G. P. Putnam's Sons, 1911.

Archer, James J. "A Marylander in the Mexican War: Some Letters of J. J. Archer." *Maryland Historical Magazine* 54 (1959): 408–422.

Beauregard, Pierre Gustave Toutant. *With Beauregard in Mexico: The Mexican War Reminiscences of P. G. T. Beauregard.* Edited by T. Harry Williams. Baton Rouge: Louisiana State University Press, 1956.

[Benham, Henry W.]. *Recollections of Mexico and the Battle of Buena Vista, Feb. 22 and 23, 1847, by an Engineer Officer, on Its Twenty-fourth Anniversary.* Boston: n.p., 1871.

Blackwood, Emma Jerome, ed. *To Mexico with Scott: Letters of Captain E. Kirby Smith to His Wife.* Cambridge, MA: Harvard University Press, 1917.

Campbell, William Bowen, "Mexican War Letters of Col. William Bowen Campbell, of Tennessee, Written to Governor David Campbell, of Virginia, 1846–1847." *Tennessee Historical Magazine* 1 (1915): 129–67.

Carleton, James Henry. *The Battle of Buena Vista with the Operations of the "Army of Occupation" for One Month.* New York: Harper and Brothers, 1848.

Carson, Christopher (Kit). *Kit Carson's Own Story of His Life.* Edited by Blanche Grant. Taos, NM: n.p., 1926.

Chapman, William. "Letters from the Seat of War—Mexico [1846–1847]." *Green Bay Historical Bulletin* 4.4 (July–August 1928): 1–24.

Cooke, Philip St. George. *The Conquest of New Mexico and California, An Historical and Personal Narrative.* Albuquerque, NM: Horn and Wallace, 1964. First published 1878 by G. P. Putnam's Sons.

———. "Report of Lieut. Col. P. St. George Cooke of His March from Santa Fe, New Mexico, to San Diego, Upper California." House of Representatives Executive Document 41, Thirtieth Congress, First Session, 549–62.

Croffut, W. A., ed. *Fifty Years in Camp and Field: Diary of Major-General Ethan Allen Hitchcock, U.S.A.* New York: G. P. Putnam's Sons, 1909.

Davis, Jefferson. *Private Letters, 1823–1889.* Edited by Hudson Strode. New York: Harcourt, Brace and World, 1966.

———. *The Papers of Jefferson Davis.* Edited by James T. McIntosh. 3 vols. Baton Rouge: Louisiana State University Press, 1981.

Deas, George. "Reminiscences of the Campaign on the Rio Grande." *Historical Magazine* 7 (January–May 1870): 19–22, 99–103, 236–38, 311–16.

Doubleday, Rhoda van Bibber Tanner, ed. *Journals of the Late Brevet Major Philip Norbourne Barbour, Captain in the 3rd Regiment, United States Infantry, and His Wife Martha Isabella Hopkins Barbour, Written during the War with Mexico, 1846.* New York: G. P. Putnam's Sons, 1936.

Edwards, Frank S. *A Campaign in New Mexico with Colonel Doniphan.* Philadelphia: Carey and Hart, 1847.

Emory, William H. "Notes of a Military Reconnaissance from Fort Leavenworth in Missouri, to San Francisco, in California, Including Part of the Arkansas, Del Norte, and Gila Rivers." House of Representatives Executive Document 41, Thirtieth Congress, First Session, 7–126.

Engelmann, Adolph. "The Second Illinois in the Mexican War, Letters of Adolph Engelmann, 1846–1847." Translated and edited by Otto B. Engelmann. *Journal of the Illinois State Historical Society* 26 (January 1934): 357–452.

Ferrell, Robert H., ed. *Monterrey Is Ours! The Mexican War Letters of Lieutenant Dana, 1845–1847.* Lexington: University of Kentucky Press, 1990.

Franklin, William B. "The Battle of Buena Vista, February 22–23, 1847." *Papers of the*

Military Historical Society of Massachusetts Boston: Military Historical Society of Massachusetts, 1913. 1543–58.

French, Samuel G. *Two Wars: An Autobiography.* Nashville, TN: Confederate Veteran, 1901.

George, Isaac. *Heroes and Incidents of the Mexican War, Containing Doniphan's Expedition.* Hollywood, CA: Sun Dance Press, 1971. First published 1908 by Review.

Gibson, George Rutledge. *Journal of a Soldier under Kearny and Doniphan.* Edited by Ralph P. Bieber. Glendale, CA: Arthur H. Clark, 1935.

[Giddings, Luther]. *Sketches of the Campaign in Northern Mexico in Eighteen Hundred Forty-Six and Seven, by an Officer of the First Regiment of Ohio Volunteers.* New York: George P. Putnam, 1853.

Grant, Ulysses S. *Personal Memoirs.* 2 vols. New York: Charles A. Webster, 1885–86.

Hamilton, Charles. "Memoirs of the Mexican War." *Wisconsin Magazine of History* 14 (September 1930): 63–92.

Hamlin, Percy Gatling, ed. *The Making of a Soldier: Letters of General R. S. Ewell.* Richmond, VA: Whittet and Shepperson, 1935.

Henry, William Seaton. *Campaign Sketches of the War with Mexico.* New York: Harper and Brothers, 1847.

Herrick, W. B. "Surgery at Buena Vista." *Illinois and Indiana Medical and Surgical Journal* 2 (1846): 300–305, 414–18.

Heth, Henry. *The Memoirs of Henry Heth.* Edited by James L. Morrison Jr. Westport, CT: Greenwood Press, 1974.

Hill, Daniel Harvey. "The Real Stonewall Jackson." *Century Illustrated Magazine* 47 (November 1893–April 1894): 623–28.

Hughes, George W. "Memoir Descriptive of the March of a Division of the United States Army, under the Command of Brigadier General John E. Wool, from San Antonio de Bexar, in Texas, to Saltillo, in Mexico." In Adrian G. Traas, *From the Golden Gate to Mexico City: The U.S. Army Topographical Engineers in the Mexican War, 1846–1848.* Washington, DC: Office of History, Corps of Engineers and Center of Military History, United States Army, 1993. 229–303.

Hughes, John T. *Doniphan's Expedition, Containing an Account of the Conquest of New Mexico; General Kearny's Overland Expedition to California; Doniphan's Campaign against the Navajos; His Unparalleled March upon Chihuahua and Durango; and the Operations of General Price at Santa Fe.* Cincinnati: J. A. and U. P. James, 1848.

Hughes, Nathaniel Cheairs, Jr., and Timothy D. Johnson, eds. *A Fighter from Way Back: The Mexican War Diary of Lt. Daniel Harvey Hill, 4th Artillery, USA.* Kent, OH: The Kent State University Press, 2002.

Jarvis, Nathan Sturgis. "An Army Surgeon's Notes of Frontier Service—Mexican War, 1833–1848." *Journal of the Military Service Institute of the United States* 27 (July 1906): 1–41; 40 (1907): 435–52; 41 (1907): 90–105.

Johnston, Abraham R. "Journal of Captain A. R. Johnston, First Dragoons." House of Representatives, Executive Document 41, Thirtieth Congress, First Session, 565–624.

Kearny, Stephen W. "A Group of Kearny Letters." *New Mexico Historical Review* (January 1930): 17–37.

Kenly, John R. *Memoirs of a Maryland Volunteer.* Philadelphia: J. B. Lippincott, 1873.

Longstreet, James. *From Manassas to Appomattox: Memoirs of the Civil War in America.* Edited by James I. Robertson Jr. Bloomington: Indiana University Press, 1960. First published 1908 by J. B. Lippincott.

———. "Longstreet's Reminiscences." *New York Times,* July 24, 1885.

McCall, George A. *Letters from the Frontiers.* Philadelphia: J. B. Lippincott, 1868.

McClintock, William A. "Journal of a Trip through Texas and Northern Mexico in 1846–1847." *Southeastern Historical Quarterly* 34 (1930): 20–37.

McLaws, Lafayette. Interview. *New York Times,* July 24, 1885.

Maury, Dabney Herndon. *Recollections of a Virginian in the Mexican, Indian, and Civil Wars.* New York: Charles Scribner's Sons, 1894.

Meade, George Gordon. *The Life and Letters of George Gordon Meade, Major-General United States Army.* 2 vols. New York: Charles Scribner's Sons, 1913.

Myers, William Starr, ed. *The Mexican War Diary of General George B. McClellan.* Princeton, NJ: Princeton University Press, 1917.

Pike, Albert. "Albert Pike's Autobiography." *New Age Magazine* 38 (March 1930): 142–44.

Polk, James Knox. *The Diary of James K. Polk during His Presidency, 1845–1849.* Edited by Milo Milton Quaife. 4 vols. Chicago: A. C. McClurg, 1910.

Porter, John B. "Medical and Surgical Notes of Campaigns in the War with Mexico, 1845–1848." *American Journal of the Medical Sciences* 45 (January 1852): 13–37.

Richardson, William H. *The Journal of William H. Richardson, a Private Soldier in the Campaign of New and Old Mexico, under the Command of Colonel Doniphan, of Missouri.* 3rd ed. New York: William H. Richardson, 1849.

[Robertson, John B.]. *Reminiscences of a Campaign in Mexico, by a Member of the "Bloody-First."* Nashville, TN: John York, 1849.

Rogers, William P. "The Diary and Letters of William P. Rogers, 1846–1862." *Southwestern Historical Quarterly* 32.4 (April 1929): 259–85.

Samson, William H., ed. *Letters of Zachary Taylor from the Battle-Fields of the Mexican War.* Rochester, NY: Genesee Press, 1908.

Scott, Winfield. *Memoirs of Lieut.-General Scott, LL.D., Written by Himself.* 2 vols. New York: Sheldon, 1864.

Sedgwick, John, *Correspondence of John Sedgwick, Major-General.* 2 vols. n.p., 1902.

Sherman, William Tecumseh. *Home Letters of General Sherman.* Edited by M. A. DeWolfe Howe. New York: Charles Scribner's Sons, 1909.

———. *Memoirs of General W. T. Sherman.* 2 vols. New York: Library of America, 1990.

Simon, John Y., ed. *The Papers of Ulysses S. Grant.* 15 vols. Carbondale: Southern Illinois University Press, 1967.

Smith, Gustavus W. "Company A Engineers in Mexico, 1846–1847." *Military Engineer* 56 (September–October 1964): 336–40.

———. *Company "A" Corps of Engineers, U.S.A., 1846–1848, in the Mexican War,* Edited by Leonne M. Hudson. Kent, OH: Kent State University Press, 2001.

Stevens, George. "Sketch of the Line of March of the 2nd U.S. Dragoons, Commanded by Col. D. E. Twiggs, from Fort Jesup La. to Corpus Christi, Texas, between the 25th of July and 27th Aug. 1845, by Lieut. Stevens, 2nd Drgns." [Hand-drawn map.] In Nathan Sturgis Jarvis, "An Army Surgeon's Notes of Frontier Service—Mexican War," *Journal of the Military Service Institute of the United States* 40 (May 1907): 436.

Tennery, Thomas D. *The Mexican War Diary of Thomas D. Tennery.* Edited by D. E. Livingston-Little. Norman: University of Oklahoma Press, 1970.

Thorndike, Rachel Sherman, ed. *The Sherman Letters: Correspondence Between General and Senator Sherman from 1837 to 1891.* New York: Charles Scribner's Sons, 1894.

Turner, Henry Smith. *The Original Journals of Henry Smith Turner.* Edited by Dwight L. Clarke. Norman, OK: University of Oklahoma Press, 1966.

Wallace, Lew [Lewis]. *An Autobiography.* 2 vols. New York: Harper and Bros., 1906.

Wilcox, Cadmus Marcellus. *History of the Mexican War.* Edited by Mary Rachel Wilcox. 2 vols. Washington, DC: Church News, 1892.

SECONDARY SOURCES

Adams, George Rollie. *General William S. Harney, Prince of Dragoons.* Lincoln: University of Nebraska Press, 2001.

Ambrose, Stephen E. *Halleck: Lincoln's Chief of Staff.* Baton Rouge: Louisiana State University Press, 1962.

Andrews, Wayne, ed. *Concise Dictionary of American History.* New York: Charles Scribner's Sons, 1962. First published 1940 by Charles Scribner's Sons.

Arnold, James R. *Jeff Davis's Own: Cavalry, Comanches, and the Battle for the Texas Frontier.* New York: John Wiley and Sons, 2000.

Arnold, Thomas Jackson. *Early Life and Letters of General Thomas J. Jackson, "Stonewall Jackson."* New York: Fleming H. Revell, 1916.

Basso, Hamilton, *Beauregard, the Great Creole.* New York: Charles Scribner's Sons, 1933.

Bauer, K. Jack. *The Mexican War, 1846–1848.* New York: Macmillan, 1974.

———. *Surfboats and Horse Marines: U.S. Naval Operations in the Mexican War, 1846–48.* Annapolis: U.S. Naval Institute, 1969.

———. *Zachary Taylor: Soldier, Planter, Statesman of the Old Southwest.* Baton Rouge: Louisiana State University Press, 1985.

Baylies, Francis. "The March of the United States Troops, under the Command of General John E. Wool, from San Antonio, Texas, to Saltillo, Mexico, in the Year 1846." *Stryker's American Register and Magazine* 4 (July 1850): 297–312.

Bergeron, Paul H. *The Presidency of James K. Polk.* Lawrence, Kansas: University Press of Kansas, 1987.

Bill, Alfred Hoyt. *Rehearsal for Conflict.* New York: Alfred A. Knopf, 1947.

Birkhimer, William E. *Historical Sketch of the Organization, Administration, Materiel and Tactics of the Artillery, United States Army.* New York: Greenwood Press, 1968.

Bloom, John Porter. "Lieutenant J. F. Gilmer and the Construction of Old Fort Marcy." *El Palicio* 68.3 (Autumn 1961): 137–50.

Borneman, Walter R. *Polk: The Man Who Transformed the Presidency and America.* New York: Random House, 2008.

Brackett, Albert Gallatin. *History of the United States Cavalry, from the Formation of the Federal Government to the 1st of June 1863.* New York: Harper, 1865.

Bridges, Hal. *Lee's Maverick General, Daniel Harvey Hill.* New York: McGraw-Hill, 1961.

Brown, Walter Lee. "The Mexican War Experiences of Albert Pike and the 'Mounted Devils' of Arkansas."" *Arkansas Historical Quarterly* 12.4 (Winter 1953): 301–315.

Bushong, Millard Kessler. *Old Jube, a Biography of General Jubal A. Early.* Boyce, VA: Carr, 1955.

Carter, Arthur B. *The Tarnished Cavalier: Major General Earl Van Dorn, C.S.A.* Knoxville: University of Tennessee Press, 1999.

Casdorph, Paul D. *Prince John Magruder: His Life and Campaigns.* New York: John Wiley and Sons, 1996.

Chambers, Lenoir. *Stonewall Jackson.* 2 vols. New York: William Morrow, 1959.

Chitwood, Oliver Perry. *John Tyler, Champion of the Old South.* Newtown, CT: American Political Biography Press, 1996. First published 1939 by American Political Biography Press.

Claiborne, J. F. H. *Life and Correspondence of John A. Quitman.* 2 vols. New York: Harper and Brothers, 1860.

Clarke, Dwight L. *Stephen Watts Kearny, Soldier of the West.* Norman: University of Oklahoma Press, 1961.

Cleaves, Freeman. *Rock of Chickamauga: The Life of General George H. Thomas.* Norman: University of Oklahoma Press, 1948.

Condon, William H. *Life of Major-General James Shields, Hero of Three Wars and Senator from Three States.* Chicago: Blakely, 1900.

Coppée, Henry. *General Thomas.* New York: D. Appleton, 1893.

Cullum, George Washington, ed. *Biographical Register of the Officers and Graduates of the U.S. Military Academy from Its Establishment in 1802, to 1890.* 3 vols. New York: Houghton Mifflin, 1891.

Cummings, Charles M. *Yankee Quaker, Confederate General: The Curious Career of Bushrod Rust Johnson.* Cranbury, NJ: Associated University Presses, 1971.

Cyclopedia of American Biography. 7 vols. New York: Appleton, 1891.

Davis, William C. *Breckinridge: Statesman, Soldier, Symbol.* Baton Rouge: Louisiana State University Press, 1974.

———. *Jefferson Davis: The Man and His Hour, A Biography.* New York: HarperCollins, 1991.

DeVoto, Bernard. *The Year of Decision: 1846.* New York: Truman Talley Books, 2000.

Dillon, Lester R., Jr. *American Artillery in the Mexican War, 1846–1847.* Austin, TX: Presidial Press, 1975.

Donald, David Herbert. *Lincoln.* New York: Simon and Schuster, 1995.

Duncan, Robert Lipscomb. *Reluctant General, The Life and Times of Albert Pike.* New York: E. P. Dutton, 1961.

Dyer, Brainerd. *Zachary Taylor.* New York: Barnes and Noble, 1967. First published 1946 by Louisiana State University Press.

Eaton, Clement. *Jefferson Davis.* New York: Free Press, 1977.

Eckenrode, H. J., and Bryan Conrad. *James Longstreet, Lee's War Horse.* Chapel Hill: University of North Carolina Press, 1936.

Eisenhower, John S. D. *So Far from God: The U.S. War with Mexico, 1846–1848.* New York: Random House, 1989.

———. *Agent of Destiny: The Life and Times of General Winfield Scott.* New York: The Free Press, 1997.

Elliott, Charles Winslow. *Winfield Scott: The Soldier and the Man.* New York: Macmillan, 1937.

Esposito, Vincent J., ed. *The West Point Atlas of American Wars,* Vol. 1. *1689–1900.* New York: Frederick A. Praeger, 1959.

Fehrenbach, T. R. *Comanches: The Destruction of a People.* Bridgewater, NJ: Replica Books, 1999. First published 1974 by Knopf.

Foote, Shelby. *The Civil War, a Narrative.* 3 vols. New York: Random House, 1958–74.

Frazier, Donald S., ed. *The United States and Mexico at War: Nineteenth-Century Expansionism and Conflict.* New York: Macmillan Reference USA, 1998.

Freehling, William W. *The Road to Disunion, Secessionists at Bay, 1776–1854.* Vol. 1 of 2. New York: Oxford University Press, 1990.

Freeman, Douglas Southall. *Lee's Lieutenants: A Study in Command.* 3 vols. New York: Charles Scribner's Sons, 1941–46.

———. *R. E. Lee: A Biography.* 4 vols. New York: Charles Scribner's Sons, 1934.

Fulton, Maurice Garland, ed. *Diary and Letters of Josiah Gregg, Southwestern Enterprises, 1840–1847.* 2 vols. Norman: University of Oklahoma Press, 1941.

"General Harney." *Journal of the United States Cavalry Association* 3.8 (March 1890): 1–8.

Gordon, Lesley J. *General George E. Pickett in Life and Legend.* Chapel Hill: University of North Carolina Press, 1998.

Govan, Gilbert E., and James W. Livingood. *A Different Valor, The Story of General Joseph E. Johnston, C.S.A.* New York: Bobbs-Merrill, 1956.

Gunn, Jack W. "Ben McCulloch: A Big Captain." *Southwestern Historical Quarterly* 43.1 (July 1954): 1–21.

Hamilton, Holman. *Zachary Taylor, Soldier of the Republic.* Hamden, CT: Archon Books, 1966.

Hamlin, Percy Gatling. *"Old Bald Head" (General R. S. Ewell), The Portrait of a Soldier.* Strasburg, VA: Shenandoah Publishing House, 1940.

Hardin, J. Fair. "Fort Jesup, Fort Selden, Camp Sabine, Camp Salubrity, Four Forgotten Frontier Army Posts of Western Louisiana." *Louisiana Historical Quarterly.* 16.1 (January 1933): 5–26; 16.2 (April 1933): 278–92; 16.3 (July 1933): 441–53; 16.4 (October 1933): 670–80; 17.1 (January 1934): 139–54.

Hartje, Robert G. *Van Dorn, The Life and Times of a Confederate General.* Nashville, TN: Vanderbilt University Press, 1967.

Hassler, William Woods. *A. P. Hill, Lee's Forgotten General.* Richmond, VA: Garrett and Massie, 1957.

Hebert, Walter H. *Fighting Joe Hooker.* New York: Bobbs-Merrill, 1944.

Heitman, Francis B. *Historical Register and Dictionary of the United States Army, from Its Organization, September 29, 1789, to March 2, 1903.* 2 vols. Washington, DC: Government Printing Office, 1903.

Heyman, Max L., Jr. *Prudent Soldier: A Biography of Major General E. R. S. Canby, 1817–1873.* Glendale, CA: Arthur H. Clark, 1959.

Holzman, Robert S. *General "Baseball" Doubleday: The Story of Baseball and of Its Inventor.* New York: Longmans, Green, 1955.

Hughes, Nathaniel Cheairs, Jr. *General William J. Hardee: Old Reliable.* Baton Rouge: Louisiana State University Press, 1965.

———. "William Joseph Hardee, U.S.A., 1815–1861." Master's Thesis, University of North Carolina, 1956.

———, and Roy P. Stonesifor Jr. *The Life and Wars of Gideon J. Pillow.* Chapel Hill: University of North Carolina Press, 1993.

Hunt, Aurora. *Major General James Henry Carleton, 1814–1873, Western Frontier Dragoon.* Glendale, CA: Arthur H. Clark, 1958.

James, Marquis. *The Raven: A Biography of Sam Houston.* 1929. New York: Macmillan, 1990.

Johannsen, Robert W. *To the Halls of the Montezumas: The Mexican War in the American Imagination.* New York: Oxford University Press, 1985.

Johnson, Richard W. *Memoir of Major-General George H. Thomas.* Philadelphia: J. B. Lippincott, 1881.

Johnson, Timothy D., *Winfield Scott: The Quest for Military Glory.* Lawrence, KS: University Press of Kansas, 1998.

Johnston, William Preston. *The Life of Gen. Albert Sidney Johnston.* New York: D. Appleton, 1878.

Keleher, William A. *Turmoil in New Mexico, 1846–1868.* Santa Fe, NM: Rydal Press, 1952.

Krick, Robert K. *Lee's Colonels: A Biographical Register of the Field Officers of the Army of Northern Virginia.* 4th ed. Dayton, OH: Press of Morningside House, 1992.

Lacey, John F. "Major-General Frederick Steele." *Annals of Iowa.* 3rd series, 1897–1899. 424–38.

Lambert, Joseph I. *One Hundred Years with the Second Cavalry: By the Commanding Officer, Second Cavalry.* Fort Riley, KS: Capper, 1939.

Lee, Fitzhugh. *General Lee.* New York: n.p., 1894.

Lewis, Lloyd. *Captain Sam Grant.* Boston: Little, Brown, 1950.

———. *Sherman, Fighting Prophet.* Harcourt, Brace, 1932.

Liddell Hart, B. H. *Sherman: Soldier, Realist, American.* New York: Frederick A. Praeger, 1958.

Longacre, Edward G. *The Man behind the Guns: A Biography of General Henry Jackson Hunt, Chief of Artillery, Army of the Potomac.* New York: A. S. Barnes, 1977.

———. *General Ulysses S. Grant: The Soldier and the Man.* Cambridge, MA: DaCapo Press, 2006.

Longstreet, Helen D. *Lee and Longstreet at High Tide: Gettysburg in the Light of the Official Records.* Gainesville, GA: published by author, 1904.

Losson, Christopher. *Tennessee's Forgotten Warriors: Frank Cheatham and His Confederate Division.* Knoxville: University of Tennessee Press, 1989.

McCaffrey, James M. *Army of Manifest Destiny: The American Soldier in the Mexican War, 1846–1848.* New York: New York University Press, 1992.

McFeely, William S. *Grant: A Biography.* New York: W. W. Norton, 1981.

McKee, Irving. *"Ben-Hur" Wallace, the Life of General Lew Wallace.* Berkeley: University of California Press, 1947.

McWhiney, Grady. *Braxton Bragg and Confederate Defeat,* Vol. 1. Tuscaloosa: University of Alabama Press, 1991. First published 1969 by Columbia University Press.

———, and Perry D. Jamieson. *Attack and Die: Civil War Military Tactics and the Southern Heritage.* Tuscaloosa, Alabama: University of Alabama Press, 1982.

Malone, Dumas, ed. *Dictionary of American Biography.* 20 vols. New York: Charles Scribner's Sons, 1927.

Marshall, Park. *A Life of William B. Bate, Citizen, Soldier and Statesman.* Nashville, TN: Cumberland Press, 1908.

Marvel, William. *Burnside.* Chapel Hill: University of North Carolina Press, 1991.

Nichols, Edward J. *Zach Taylor's Little Army.* Garden City, NY: Doubleday, 1963.

———. *Toward Gettysburg: A Biography of General John F. Reynolds.* State College: Pennsylvania State University Press, 1958.

Nolan, Alan T. *Lee Considered: General Robert E. Lee and Civil War History.* Chapel Hill: University of North Carolina Press, 1991.

Parks, Joseph Howard. *General Edmund Kirby Smith, C.S.A.* Baton Rouge: Louisiana State University Press, 1954.

Payne, Darwin. "Camp Life in the Army of Occupation." *Southwestern Historical Quarterly* 73 (1969–70): 326–42.

Pemberton, John C. *Pemberton, Defender of Vicksburg.* Chapel Hill: University of North Carolina Press, 1942.

Perret, Geoffrey, *Ulysses S. Grant: Soldier and President.* New York: Random House, 1997.

Peskin, Allan. *Winfield Scott and the Profession of Arms.* Kent, OH: Kent State University Press, 2003.

Pfanz, Donald C. *Richard S. Ewell: A Soldier's Life.* Chapel Hill: University of North Carolina Press, 1998.

Piatt, Donn. *General George H. Thomas.* Cincinnati, OH: Robert Clarke, 1893.

Piston, William Garrett. *Lee's Tarnished Lieutenant: James Longstreet and His Place in Southern History.* Athens: University of Georgia Press, 1987.

Pryor, Elizabeth Brown. *Reading the Man: A Portrait of Robert E. Lee through His Private Letters.* New York: Viking, 2007.

Reavis, L. U. *The Life and Military Services of Gen. William Selby Harney.* St. Louis: Bryan, Brand, 1878.

Reid, Samuel C., Jr. *The Scouting Expeditions of McCulloch's Texas Rangers; or the Sum-*

mer and Fall Campaign of the Army of the United States in Mexico—1846. Including Skirmishes with the Mexicans, and an Accurate Detail of the Storming of Monterey; also, the Daring Scouts at Buena Vista Together with Anecdotes, Incidents, Descriptions of Country, and Sketches of the Lives of the Celebrated Partisan Chiefs, Hays, McCulloch, and Walker. 1847. Philadelphia: G. G. Evans, 1859.

Richards, G. W. *Lives of Gens. Halleck and Pope.* Philadelphia: J. Magee, 1862.

Robarts, William Hugh. *Mexican War Veterans: A Complete Roster of the Regular and Volunteer Troops in the War between the United States and Mexico, from 1846 to 1848.* Washington, DC: Brentano's, 1887.

Robertson, James I., Jr. *General A. P. Hill: The Story of a Confederate Warrior.* New York: Random House, 1987.

———. *Stonewall Jackson: The Man, the Soldier, the Legend.* New York: Macmillan Publishing USA, 1997.

Rodenbough, Theophilus Francis. *From Everglade to Cañon with the Second Dragoons, 1836–1875.* Chicago: D. and C. H. Blakely, 1875.

Roland, Charles P. *Albert Sidney Johnston, Soldier of Three Republics.* Austin: University of Texas Press, 1964.

Sanger, Donald Bridgman, and Thomas Robson Hay. *James Longstreet.* Baton Rouge: Louisiana State University Press, 1952.

Scheina, Robert L. *Santa Anna: A Curse upon Mexico.* Washington DC: Brassey's, 2002.

Sears, Stephen W. *George McClellan, The Young Napoleon.* New York: Ticknor and Fields, 1988.

———. *To the Gates of Richmond: The Peninsula Campaign.* New York: Ticknor and Fields, 1992.

Seigenthaler, John. *James K. Polk.* New York: Henry Holt, 2003.

Sides, Hampton. *Blood and Thunder: An Epic of the American West.* New York: Doubleday, 2006.

Shalhope, Robert E. *Sterling Price: Portrait of a Southerner.* Columbia: University of Missouri Press, 1971.

Sifakis, Stewart. *Who Was Who in the Civil War.* New York: Facts on File, 1988.

Simon, John Y. *The Personal Memoirs of Julia Dent Grant.* New York: G. P. Putnam's Sons, 1975.

Simpson, Brooks D. *Ulysses S. Grant: Triumph over Adversity, 1822–1865.* New York: Houghton Mifflin, 2000.

Smith, George Winston, and Charles Judah, eds. *Chronicles of the Gringos: The U.S. Army in the Mexican War, 1846–1848, Accounts of Eyewitnesses and Combatants.* Albuquerque: University of New Mexico Press, 1968.

Smith, Jean Edward. *Grant.* New York: Simon and Schuster, 2001.

Smith, Justin Harvey. *The War with Mexico.* 2 vols. Gloucester, MA: Peter Smith, 1963. First published 1919 by Macmillan Company.

Stickles, Arndt M. *Simon Bolivar Buckner: Borderland Knight.* Chapel Hill: University of North Carolina Press, 1940.

Stillwell, Lucille. *John Cabell Breckinridge.* Caldwell, ID: Caxton Printers, 1936.

Strode, Hudson: *Jefferson Davis, American Patriot, 1808–1861.* New York: Harcourt, Brace, 1955.

Thomas, Benjamin P. *Abraham Lincoln.* New York: Alfred A. Knopf, 1952.

Thomas Emory M. *Robert E. Lee: A Biography.* New York: W. W. Norton, 1995.

Thomas, Wilbur D. *General George H. Thomas, the Indomitable Warrior.* New York: Exposition Press, 1964.

Tinkcom, Harry Marlin. *John White Geary, Soldier-Statesman, 1819–1873.* Philadelphia: University of Pennsylvania Press, 1940.

Townsend, William H. *The Lion of Whitehall* [Cassius M. Clay]. Dunwoody, GA: Norman S. Berg, 1967.

Traas, Adrian G. *From the Golden Gate to Mexico City: The U.S. Army Topographical Engineers in the Mexican War, 1846–1848.* Washington, DC: Office of History, Corps of Engineers and Centers of Military History, United States Army, 1993.

Tyler, Ronnie C. *The Mexican War: A Lithographic Record.* Austin: Texas State Historical Association, 1973.

Vandiver, Frank E. *Mighty Stonewall.* College Station, TX: Texas A&M University Press, 1988. First published 1957 by McGraw-Hill.

———. *Ploughshares into Swords: Josiah Gorgas and Confederate Ordnance.* Austin: University of Texas Press, 1952.

Walker, C. Irvine. *The Life of Lieutenant General Richard Heron Anderson of the Confederate States Army.* Charleston, SC: Art Publishing Company, 1917.

Wallace, Edward S. *General William Jenkins Worth, Monterey's Forgotten Hero.* Dallas, TX: Southern Methodist University Press, 1953.

Wallace, Isabel. *Life and Letters of General W. H. L. Wallace.* Chicago: R. R. Donnelley & Sons, 1909.

Waugh, John C. *The Class of 1846: From West Point to Appomattox: Stonewall Jackson, George McClellan, and Their Brothers.* New York: Warner Books, 1994.

Webb, Henry W. "The Story of Jefferson Barracks." *New Mexico Historical Review* 21 (1946): 185–208.

Werstein, Irving. *Kearny, the Magnificent: The Story of General Philip Kearny, 1815–1862.* New York: John Day, 1962.

Wert, Jeffry D. *General James Longstreet, the Confederacy's Most Controversial Soldier: A Biography.* New York: Simon and Schuster, 1993.

Wessels, William L. *Born to Be a Soldier: The Military Career of William Wing Loring of St. Augustine, Florida.* Fort Worth: Texas Christian University Press, 1971.

Wilkins, Frederick. *The Highly Irregular Irregulars: Texas Rangers in the Mexican War.* Austin, TX: Eakin Press, 1990.

Winders, Richard Bruce. *Mr. Polk's Army: The American Military Experience in the Mexican War.* College Station: Texas A&M University Press, 1997.

Winslow, Richard Elliot. *General John Sedgwick, the Story of a Union Corps Commander.* Novato, CA: Presidio Press, 1982.

Woodward, Ashbel. *Life of General Nathaniel Lyon.* Hartford: Case, Lockwood, 1862.

Woodworth, Steven E. *Jefferson Davis and His Generals: The Failure of Confederate Command in the West.* Lawrence, KS: University Press of Kansas, 1990.

Index

Page numbers in italics refer to maps.